Comparative Disadvantages?

Comparative Disadvantages?

Social Regulations and the Global Economy

PIETRO S. NIVOLA

Editor

Brookings Institution Press
Washington, D.C.

Copyright © 1997 by

THE BROOKINGS INSTITUTION

1775 Massachusetts Avenue, N.W., Washington, D.C. 20036

Library of Congress Cataloging-in-Publication Data

Comparative disadvantages? : social regulations and the global
economy / Pietro S. Nivola, editor.
    p. cm.
Includes bibliographical references and index.
ISBN 0-8157-6086-8 (alk. paper). — ISBN 0-8157-6085-X
(pbk. : alk. paper)
    1. Law—Economic aspects—United States. 2. Trade regulation—
United States. I. Nivola, Pietro S.
KF385.C66 1997
337—dc21   97-21003
                                                                CIP

9 8 7 6 5 4 3 2 1

The paper used in this publication meets the minimum
requirements of the American National Standard for
Information Sciences—Permanence of Paper for Printed Library
Materials, ANSI Z39.48-1984.

Set in Palatino

Composition by Linda C. Humphrey
Arlington, Virginia

Printed by R. R. Donnelley and Sons Co.
Harrisonburg, Virginia

For my wife, Katherine Ann

Foreword

THE AMERICAN ECONOMY is expanding briskly because it is in many ways uniquely unencumbered. Entrepreneurs in the United States are freer to start new enterprises, import materials and products, reengineer productive facilities, and price their goods and services competitively. But the dynamism of extensive economic deregulation could be slowed by a steady accretion of social controls constraining businesses. From excessive shareholder litigation and strict product liability to zero-tolerance environmental standards and workplace rules, the legal risks as well as the responsibilities of doing business have multiplied. Much of the problem stems from what the authors of this volume call inordinate adversarial legalism, a punitive style of regulation that too often delivers insufficient social benefits in relation to its costs. How, if at all, does globalization complicate the situation? This book explores the question from a variety of vantage points.

U.S. policymakers frequently point to foreign laws and actions that are said to constrict international commerce and impair American prosperity. Yet some trade disputes have sprung from questionable rules made in the United States. At times U.S. legal strictures or environmental standards have formed barriers to imports and perhaps to foreign investors, as well as interfered with some U.S. exports. Even if these frictions have been of relatively minor consequence so far, inefficient legal and regulatory conventions could exact a larger toll on American living standards in the years ahead. The global economy of the twenty-first century will not only challenge national habits that retard productivity gains, but will offer more opportunities for companies to lessen their domestic burdens by outsourcing across borders.

Increasingly, in an economically integrated world anachronistic regulations of foreign countries protrude awkwardly and often require correction, but so do some of our own regulatory and legal practices. An international perspective, in short, can help inform the current debate about the merits of domestic regulatory reform. The discussions in this book take important steps in that direction.

The editor of this volume, Pietro S. Nivola, is a senior fellow in the Brookings Governmental Studies program. S. Lael Brainard, Robert W. Crandall, I. M. Destler, Sharyn O'Halloran, Anne O. Krueger, Robert E. Litan, Henry R. Nau, Walter Y. Oi, Walter K. Olson, and Barry G. Rabe provided constructive critiques of the manuscript. George A. Akerlof, Christopher H. Foreman Jr., Robert W. Hahn, Robert A. Katzmann, John W. Kingdon, Daniel Sichel, Wolfgang H. Reinicke, Clifford M. Winston, Daniel Yergin, and Michel Zaleski also offered useful insights. Thomas E. Mann and R. Kent Weaver wrote additional detailed comments.

Nancy D. Davidson, James R. Schneider, Deborah M. Styles, and Theresa B. Walker copyedited the book. Patricia E. Fowlkes, Laurel L. Imig, Kristen Lippert-Martin, Carole M. Plowfield, and Tara Adams Ragone verified its factual content, Ellen Garshick proofread it, and Robert Elwood compiled the index. John Guba provided research assistance and Ingeborg Lockwood administrative assistance.

Partial funding for this project was provided by the Alex C. Walker Educational and Charitable Foundation.

The views expressed here are those of the authors and should not be ascribed to the trustees, officers, or staff members of the Brookings Institution.

MICHAEL H. ARMACOST
President

May 1997
Washington, D.C.

Contents

x   Contents

Chapter 1

Introduction

Pietro S. Nivola

AS THIS BOOK was being edited during the summer of 1996, the United States was playing host to the centennial Olympic games in Atlanta. The coverage of the games by American television was being criticized. The foreign press complained that broadcasts focused disproportionately on the home team. Day after day, sports in which U.S. athletes were favored or touted seemed to dominate the airwaves. Toting up U.S. medals had become a media obsession.

If the disagreeable aspect of this spectacle had been its "shameful chauvinism," as one columnist described it, the criticism of the Atlanta Olympiad would not have been fair or interesting.[1] The world is full of consummate flag-wavers—and aspiring, or perceiving itself, to be Number One is almost every nation's impulse.

But the Olympics coverage illustrated something that was perhaps more notable about American popular culture in the 1990s. Call it insouciance. Here, after all, was a major media extravaganza of worldwide interest, transpiring in a big U.S. city, at the end of the twentieth century. Yet, occasionally oblivious to the ways American tastes and idioms hurtle into the global village, much of the event was aired as if it were just a local affair.

Something similar can be said about the way many Americans view their social regulations. This country has amassed voluminous rules to press consumer safety, energy saving, occupational health, disability rights, environmental deadlines, and, for selected groups, an extensive web of special protections, preferences, loans, contracts, and jobs. In no other society do citizens sue and punish each other as often to push these causes. The zealotry surpasses an understanding of how the consequences of our regulatory activities might spill beyond our shores and of how the activ-

1

ities might affect the way we do business in an increasingly borderless world.

The point of this book is to direct attention to the international context of these domestic policies and practices, some of which seem ill suited to today's global economic realities.

External Interface

It has become almost a truism to say that the American economy is singularly unfettered. Nowhere else in the industrial world is it easier to set up a discount store, start an airline, or shrink a payroll. But extensive economic deregulation has been matched by a burgeoning body of social law cracking down on business. From the surety of shareholder litigation, to the blistering penalties for negligence, to the latest proscriptions in personnel management, entrepreneurs run a gauntlet of legal hazards. How sustainable is this expanding agenda amid the forces of international economic integration?

Parts of the social regulatory regime have obstructed imports and exports. Parts may also be alienating foreign investors. And parts have stirred abrasive efforts to extend U.S. sanctions extraterritorially. So while U.S. policymakers perennially denounce the unfair tactics of trading partners, trade disputes have been ignited not only by the misdeeds of the European Union, Japan, or China, but sometimes by questionable rules made in the United States.

The fact that busy U.S. regulators and litigants sometimes impose unwarranted costs on outsiders creates diplomatic embarrassments. But even if those troubles are usually minor, a good deal of the activism also secures no appreciable net gain for American society. This failure to pass a reasonable cost-benefit test is worse than embarrassing. The price exacted in national productivity poses potentially serious implications for America's role on the international stage. Policies that retard economic growth can gradually drain even a superpower's influence, generosity, and resolve.

Amid the pressures of globalization, room for error has narrowed. Corporations in this country, as in others, are downsizing to remain competitive. To cut costs, companies contract with outside suppliers, frequently offshore. While most of this outsourcing has been driven by market forces, some has been more aggressive than necessary and may well be abetted by policymakers and plaintiffs piling on laws and lawsuits of dubious merit. A global economy opens opportunities to outsource. Increasingly, firms that need to lighten their regulatory overload seem poised to seize those opportunities. When they do, the consequences for the real compensation of American workers can be unsettling.

To be sure, most of the offloading of operations by U.S. corporations just transfers jobs to other companies within the United States. Even the expanding share of U.S. sourcing going abroad indirectly does much the same. The domestic jobs it may eliminate or the wages it may depress may be offset by more productive jobs and better paychecks in U.S. businesses whose exports improve. Modern international commerce in manufactures involves extensive intra-industry trade, which in turn brings reciprocal gains. U.S. firms are briskly exporting aircraft parts, semiconductor chips, and automotive components as well as importing them. Both sides of the two-way flow have been beneficial for the economy, and the relative shares of inputs imported and exported have changed little over recent years.[2] Still, if imperatives other than those of the marketplace are inducing firms to move work around the global factory, the "creative destruction" in the U.S. labor market may be causing more dislocation than it ought to.

Nor is it necessarily reassuring to be reminded that, in the aggregate, regulatory inefficiencies still subtract relatively little from national income. The losses exceed in magnitude the depredations we frequently impute to mischievous foreign competitors. Moreover, the same small subtractions that were once inconsequential may no longer be. Nanoseconds now separate sprinters in the 100-meter dash. Small things—a runner's shoes, or what he or she ate for breakfast—can make the difference between winning and losing. As major industrial economies converge and more industries compete head-to-head in contested markets, even a nation's marginally defective legal system may matter for many firms; they can and do take the system into account when deciding how to restructure or where to reposition capital and labor.

Perspectives

The next chapter in this volume provides a more detailed overview of most of these concerns, but each subsequent chapter also grapples with facets of them. The approaches vary. Some chapters draw broadly and eclectically from scattered accounts in secondary sources. Others have narrower gauges, using specific case studies. One chapter is based on impressions gleaned from interviews and fieldwork.

In chapter 3 David Vogel delves into the stories of two major programs regulating automobile manufacturers and oil refineries: the federal automotive fuel economy standards and the clean fuel requirements linked to the Clean Air Act of 1990. He finds that these initiatives have not been efficient tools for conserving energy or improving air quality in this country and have led to awkward commercial disputes with other countries.

In chapter 4 Robert A. Kagan and Lee Axelrad examine more comprehensively what they consider a distinguishing characteristic of U.S. legal and regulatory proceedings: "adversarial legalism." In many industrial countries, they contend, the ends or content of laws governing matters such as pollution or faulty consumer products are often comparable to U.S. laws, but the means of implementation differ significantly. In the United States the procedures tend to be more combative and legalistic. This feature, the authors conclude, exposes regulators and regulated firms to exceptional process, or "friction," costs. Such costs could be lowered without sacrificing cherished social aims if America assimilated more of the supposedly superior legal and administrative models of some other advanced democracies. The authors draw support for their conclusion from firsthand research they conducted on the experiences of several multinational corporations with U.S. and foreign-based operations.

In a similar vein, in chapter 5 Marc Landy and Loren Cass examine various U.S. environmental regulations. They begin by noting a problem well known among economists in the field: U.S. pollution abatement measures have contributed to lagging productivity in some prominent U.S. industries. Of course, this toll may be partly or even wholly counterbalanced by the social benefits of these measures. But serious shortcomings in environmental programs, including the excessive rigidity of many technology-forcing strictures, prevent them from maximizing net benefits. This situation, the authors imply, is less affordable in a world where regulated industries are feeling more competitive heat. Do other nations offer any valuable lessons in how to manage environmental policy cost effectively? Like Kagan and Axelrad, the authors see merit in some European methods, such as those of Germany and Great Britain.

In chapter 6 Thomas F. Burke deals with a single topic: a historic piece of legislation aimed at mainstreaming persons with handicaps. Congressional sponsors of this ambitious regulatory project, the Americans with Disabilities Act of 1990, promised that it would help, not hinder, the competitiveness of the U.S. economy by bringing large numbers of disabled people into the work force. Instead, Burke indicates, the act promises to impose substantial costs for public and private employers without greatly improving the employment prospects of the disabled. The most telling dimension of Burke's analysis, however, is not its assessment of economic impacts but its painstaking legislative history. His rich account helps explain an intriguing phenomenon: the adoption of unfunded federal mandates even under Republican administrations that professed to be probusiness, leery of intrusive government, and mindful of waste.

Appropriately, in the book's closing chapter Roger G. Noll takes a wider arc. He pulls together broad criteria to be considered in evaluating and correcting regulatory distortions such as those discussed in previous chapters.

At least three motifs emerge from these studies. One is the authors' unease with the status quo. Although the American economy remains among the most open and adaptable anywhere, smug certitude about its capacity to absorb an accretion of quirky legal bills and burdens is inappropriate. The regulatory institutions of all industrial countries face close inspection as they brush with the demands of global economics. The United States is riding into the next millennium with a considerable number of incongruous schemes of social control, some of which may become increasingly difficult to reconcile with Americans' desire for superlative living standards and smooth trade relations in a more competitive world.

The consensus among the authors is also that modes of social regulation in the United States are exceptionally beleaguered by litigation. The priorities of environmental policy are constantly shaped and reshaped in the courts. Civil jurisprudence, not just certification by public authorities, decides the worthiness of commercial products. In civil rights matters, emancipation from victimhood is primarily arranged by empowering each new category of claimants to sue.

What accounts for this polemicization? Kagan and Axelrad suspect that recourse to litigation is the natural habit of a society that distrusts government authority but nonetheless embraces an elaborate social wish list. Burke, as well as Landy and Cass, emphasizes the propensity of Americans to frame social needs or preferences as *rights*.[3] Courts of law are the traditional venue for the advocacy of rights. Whatever its roots, the incessant legal agitation with its mass mobilization of lawyers, often unreliable case outcomes, and collateral damage to civil trust is deemed by almost all the authors to be, on balance, a disadvantage.

Finally, two of the chapters (Vogel's and my own) observe some disharmony between the way the government designs domestic regulations and its avowed philosophy of free trade. In practice, rules with noble purposes—sanitizing the air, conserving energy, lending money to the poor—pass through the sausage maker of American politics. There, special interests and protectionists have an influence. Sometimes the end results are policies that improve neither this nation's welfare nor that of others.

Commentary

All the chapters were prepared by scholars who attended a conference at the Brookings Institution in 1996. The goal of that meeting and of this volume was to initiate an intellectual exploration and perhaps provoke further inquiry by a wider community of experts. The authors never intended to provide a systematic delineation of the many possible tensions between globalism and America's regulatory style, much less to draw a tidy road map for policymakers searching for quick remedies.

Inevitably, most of the essays came under critical scrutiny from discussants at the conference, many of whom discovered that the authors raised more questions than they answered. The comments of the discussants accompany each of the core chapters of the book and make enlightening reading. Some of their insights are as valuable as those of the papers themselves. Some will also help interested readers identify gaps the papers have left for future research to fill.

For example, in her discussion of my chapter, Anne O. Krueger stresses a pertinent consideration that I did not adequately contemplate. The fact that U.S. regulations place heavy costs, indeed often extraordinary costs by international standards, on various U.S. industries is not in itself a drawback, even if those industries lose market shares to foreign competition. Suppose Americans value environmental protection to the point of displacing with imports entire sectors of domestic production. The real standard of living in the United States might actually decline *less* than if they held onto the domestic polluters and relied on their products. Contrary to my thinking, in other words, the global economy may make it easier, not harder, for Americans to have things both ways: we can regulate ourselves more stringently *and*, by importing, consume more goods.

A second commentator, Henry R. Nau, sees the inner and outer orbits of regulatory policy intersecting less comfortably in the years ahead. The lowering of at-the-border restrictions among trading nations has exposed distortions wrought by behind-the-border policies. Many of these disputed policies now include conflicting rules on the microeconomy as industrial nations increasingly find their macroeconomic options constrained. Nau argues, however, that the United States is comparatively unencumbered by counterproductive regulations. Although American regulatory programs may be just as costly as Europe's, they are also more flexible. Bankruptcy laws are more accommodating here. New entrepreneurs face fewer entry barriers. Financial laws are more hospitable to venture capitalists and small-capitalization security markets. Where it counts, Nau concludes, Americans seem less intent than many Europeans on creating a risk-free and permanently secure society. Thus the United States seems uniquely well positioned to compete and profit in the world economy of the twenty-first century.

Authors who perceive considerable inflexibility in U.S. standards (as Landy and Cass do), or procedural complexity in U.S. law (as Kagan and Axelrad do), or risk-averse bias in too many U.S. rules (as I do) ought to have some of their worries allayed by Krueger and Nau. My only ready rejoinder, particularly to Nau, is that in a world where most people have their hands tied behind their backs, a man with one arm free holds an advantage. But he would still be better off with both hands free, and of course, best off if everyone's were untied.

I. M. Destler and Sharyn O'Halloran, the discussants of David Vogel's paper, raised a different kind of objection that might as easily be directed at nearly every other chapter in this volume. More proof is needed that the imperfect U.S. policies or practices in question do more damage than their alternatives, and even if they do, that those alternatives are politically feasible.

The U.S. method of saving oil by commanding automakers to meet corporate average fuel economy (CAFE) criteria is far from ideal and may have discriminatory effects on some foreign manufacturers. But realistically, CAFE's conservation effort may be better than no effort at all. The EPA's quest for cleaner fuels, which got off to a bad start by pushing the use of ethanol and advocating standards that discriminated against imported gasoline, suffered national and international setbacks. But, O'Halloran asks, would the nation ever have accomplished the Clean Air Act amendments of 1990 without some missteps along the way? Often, what appear to be blunders to an academic policy purist are in fact unavoidable political concessions needed to obtain a larger good.

One can quibble with these comments. O'Halloran may be overstating the political essentiality of ethanol mandates; the fact is, they (and the discriminatory gasoline rules) postdated passage of the 1990 Clean Air Act. Policy analysts may not know all there is to know about how to optimize energy policy, but they do know this: there is a proven alternative to CAFE standards. A simple gasoline tax would almost certainly achieve better results with fewer social costs, and would conform much more equitably to international norms.[4] That the U.S. political process seems incapable of adopting a straightforward substitute for CAFE is another story, but not one that deflates Vogel's main argument: these fuel regulations are, at once, inefficient and questionable from the standpoint of U.S. international obligations.

Nonetheless, more generally, Destler and O'Halloran have a point. The contributors to this book have not made an airtight case that the problems they cite are grave or extraordinary, much less correctable by aping the solutions preferred by many governments abroad.

Robert W. Crandall and Barry G. Rabe, for instance, urged Landy and Cass to look twice before leaping. Crandall, himself a frequent critic of U.S. pollution control strategies, argued that the original draft of their paper had attributed to environmental programs too much of the employment loss in regulated industries. This matter was resolved in a later version. But some others were not.

In Barry Rabe's view Landy and Cass's chapter does not adequately recognize the major strides U.S. policymakers have already made to improve the administration of programs. There has been, according to

Rabe, first-rate innovation at the federal and state levels. Collaborative, incentive-based regulatory approaches of some other regimes that Landy and Cass admire are finding their way here and often reflect the best elements of such models while shedding the worst.

If Landy and Cass find themselves underreporting the progress that has been made in refining U.S. environmental management, Kagan and Axelrad may be overstating the virtues of European or Japanese bureaucratic regulation and the vices of America's regulatory conventions: namely, unique procedural costliness, unpredictability, and burdensome delays (descriptions the authors use repeatedly). This characterization does not comport with my own impressions as a casual visitor to Japan or France or Italy. And it also seems hard to square with the bottom line. From 1979 to 1995 the American economy outperformed the European Union's in at least one crucial respect: whereas western Europe created 10.3 million jobs for 21.5 million new workers, the United States created 26 million jobs, absorbing 95 percent of the economy's new workers.[5]

There are at least two possibilities for explaining this disconnect. One, of course, is that the facts are the other way around: the workings of law and regulation are generally *less* burdensome to business in the United States than elsewhere. The other is that U.S. burdens are world-class but still do not matter enough to upend America's solid economic performance in current international comparisons. Kagan and Axelrad choose the latter interpretation.

But this resolution left their paper's discussants, S. Lael Brainard and Robert E. Litan, somewhat perplexed. Why be so wary of U.S. adversarial legalism if, at the end of the day, the phenomenon makes so little economic difference? Brainard urges the authors to dig deeper. In her words, "Obviously, the U.S. market has a number of features that attract companies even at the cost of paying a penalty to operate here. But what we really want to know is whether adversarial legalism on the margin shifts more production or innovative activity towards or away from the U.S. market or otherwise disadvantages U.S. companies, holding other market characteristics constant."

In his comments Litan also suggests a number of specific dependent variables upon which research like Kagan and Axelrad's could have focused. How, for example, might the costs of the U.S. legal system affect savings rates and thus the balance of trade? How do national variations in liability law affect the costs of industrial inputs (as opposed to product design)? What have been the effects on product innovation in particular industries?

Some parts of American social regulation are moving targets. It is by no means easy to determine how badly environmental rulemakers, for instance, are stuck in the ruts of adversarialism and punitive legalism. Perhaps an up-to-date analysis ought to celebrate the gentler techniques of policy implementation that, according to Rabe, are now being widely adopted in the United States. But in other areas the persistence of litigious enforcement, much of it minimally cost effective, is a lot less debatable. At first glance, for example, few of the nation's experiments in social engineering would seem more emblematic of the "take 'em to court" credo than the disabilities law Thomas Burke discusses.

Among the questions of central interest to readers of this book, however, are whether prominent domestic policies such as the Americans with Disabilities Act (ADA) were badly designed compared with the corresponding policies of America's economic competitors, and whether there might be any net increase in welfare from redesigning our policies to be more like their's. Burke's chapter drops hints, but ultimately provides few sure guidelines.

Burke's preference is clearly for taking implementation out of the hands of private litigants and placing it with public administrators. Other OECD countries have done so. Unhappily, their administrative fix has typically included arbitrary employment quotas on businesses. What would prevent a hypothetical U.S. disability agency from sidling toward similar mandates foisted formally or de facto? As Walter Y. Oi points out in his review of Burke's argument, the percentage of Americans claiming handicaps keeps growing even as objective surveys show a decreasing incidence of disabling conditions. Thus an administrative arrangement responsive to ever-expanding disability claims could quickly become extravagant.

To date, America's answer—in part a law that would secure jobs for the disabled through the courts—has been somewhat disappointing. (Another discussant, Walter Olson, was rather emphatic about this in his comments.) But the true costs, or even the extent, of ADA lawsuits remain uncertain. So conceivably the ADA could still prove a bargain in comparison with, for instance, the German solution.

Recommendations

All of which leads me to the prescriptive components of these papers. Although prescription was not meant to be a chief objective of such preliminary research, the contents of this book are not without policy implications. Indeed, some are explicit.

Reducing Trade Distortion

David Vogel urges consideration of the least trade-restrictive alternative when selecting among domestic regulatory strategies. Notice that Vogel is *not* saying legitimate public purposes should be compromised as a courtesy to trading partners. He is simply suggesting that some means to domestic ends are more efficient than others, and when the more efficient means also happen to further freer trade, a government is foolish or arrogant not to choose them.

Admittedly, choosing them is generally easier in theory than in practice. Often, as Sharyn O'Halloran insists, one has to settle for second best. But the prospects of sensible regulatory reform are bleak indeed if every wrongheaded government policy is regarded as a necessary act of political pragmatism and every adverse verdict at the World Trade Organization deemed an assault on sacred cows. For decades U.S. officials have berated countries such as Japan for harboring internal regulations that are at once self-destructive and detrimental beyond their borders. Now, in a globalizing economy the same U.S. officials will have to hear an occasional counterclaim. Vogel thinks they should listen. I agree, and so would Roger Noll.

In his chapter, Noll emphasizes that domestic regulations increasingly will require international coordination, but not because rules differ in style or severity among nations, nor just because the rules can affect trade flows. National regulatory differences reflect variations in circumstances and popular preferences. The mere existence of such differences is not legitimate grounds for international contestation any more than are the variations in national endowments, geography, or climate. Further, should a nation fret when some of its rules suck in imports by raising costs for domestic producers? And should it cheer when the producers who bear those costs are principally makers of nontradable goods, thereby shifting resources into the economy's export sectors? Not necessarily. Everything depends on whether the configuration of rules is correcting genuine market failures. If it is not, the resulting diversion of trade is inadmissible and is fair game for international negotiation.

In the realm of social regulation the concept of market failure runs the risk of becoming open-ended; for every desired social intervention there is, somehow, a perceived economic failing to be corrected. (Should the betterment of interstate commerce turn into a novel rationale for U.S. civil rights laws, for example? At least one federal judge recently thought so.)[6] There may not be much one can do about the tendency to invoke "market imperfection" as a justification for almost anything government wishes to do, but at least the internationalization of regulatory issues may encourage interventionists to select means that export fewer costs. In efforts to protect the environment, for instance, Noll observes that emissions trading and effluent fees are less likely to pose entry barriers for foreign traders and investors than are systems that rely on conventional permits.

Regulatory Assessment

Landy and Cass do not directly address the issue of how U.S. environmental rules might be better harmonized with the international trading system. Instead, they offer two general suggestions for making policy more cost sensitive. A "regulatory budget" might force lawmakers and rulemakers to spell out the costs of their projects so that fewer would be served up as a seemingly free lunch. In addition, the authors favor further devolution of responsibilities to states and localities: "Their taxpayers, not the nation's, ought to have greater responsibility in ranking environmental policies amid other priorities, in selecting alternative modes of intervention, and in footing a larger share of the bill."

A cost-conscious environmental mission could do some external as well as internal good for the country. If such a mission were to debilitate fewer domestic industries, for example, they might be less eager to seek compensatory protection from international trade.

Landy and Cass do not pretend that their ideas are original or detailed enough to spark much new debate. Some of what they envision (for example, decentralization) is already happening, though perhaps without the hoped-for savings. Nevertheless, their discussion alerts reformers to a general precaution: weighing economic costs will never become a steady pillar in regulatory decisions unless it rests on institutional bedrock.

The short-term prospects for such reinforcement may seem dim, at least judging from the sparse success of the 104th Congress in its various attempts to overhaul U.S. legal and regulatory anachronisms. But the longer-range forecast may be more eventful as misaligned national regulations become increasingly conspicuous sources of trade scuffles. In Noll's view, if these irritants become the focal points of future multisectoral trade agreements, domestic reform will receive an important international prod.

Foreign Lessons

Kagan and Axelrad, like Burke, intimate that elements of European statism offer viable alternatives to America's rampant legal strife. Vesting more control in professional civil servants and more resources in social insurance schemes presumably would mean fewer tort suits, fewer regulatory delays, greater clarity, and a more consensual relationship between business and government. When competing with imports or launching exports, U.S. producers would benefit from a domestic climate in which rules and rulings run up lower transaction costs.

The problems with this line of thought are obvious. First, as the authors themselves readily admit, the American political system resists the broad delegation of power to central bureaucracies. At least for the time being, American taxpayers are also questioning new outlays for the welfare state. So the European constructs seem implausible here.

Second, a vision of public administration is being invoked that is more utopian than empirically based, not only here but everywhere. The various authors acknowledge that bureaucratic regulation in the United States can seldom be successfully insulated from interest-group pressure, congressional micromanagement, and judicial encroachment. But are they sufficiently aware that the decrees of bureaucracies in western Europe, Canada, or Japan also pander to clients and are often no more dependable, coherent, or clever? A few years ago, experts were in awe of Japan's *dirigiste* industrial policy, for example. Today, most are having second thoughts. The vaunted "administrative guidance" of Japan turns out to be, well, a bum steer.

Add to the equation the steep tax rates needed to fund vast social safety nets, especially in Europe, and foreign models become even less alluring. If lavish public insurance programs and heavier taxes are the medicine that would have to be ingested to quell the feverish regulatory disputation and privatized legal squabbling in this country, the cure may be much worse than the disease. Before going Euro, so to speak, revisionists in the United States ought to try an honest dose of less conventional treatment, such as abolishing government programs that plainly yield no net benefits. That, at least, is the first phase of the therapy my chapter implicitly recommends.

Regardless of one's point of view, however, studies such as Kagan and Axelrad's perform an important service. Policymakers basking in the relatively good economic times of the mid-1990s are reminded, in effect, not to take for granted comparative advantages of the American regulatory state.

Five years ago, according to the Clinton-Gore campaign, the nation was suffering its "worst economic performance since the Great Depression," even inviting comparisons with "Sri Lanka."[7] More recently that rhetoric has been given a 180-degree spin. The U.S. economy, President Clinton proclaimed in his 1996 State of the Union address, "is the healthiest it has been in three decades." Surely, there must be some middle ground between Sri Lanka and this assertion that U.S. fitness is at a thirty-year high. Productivity growth is still trudging along at a third of its pre-1973 pace. In the past ten years the competitiveness of U.S. exports has had more to do with a relatively weak dollar than with improved productivity.[8] As a percentage of national output, the pool of net national savings is less than half as large as it was thirty years ago. Thus the cost of capital remains higher, net business investment continues to lag, and the corporate rush to downsize and outsource scarcely abates. Even the U.S. jobless rate looks a bit less exemplary when one factors in the millions of able-bodied persons incarcerated, discouraged, or otherwise dropped from the labor force.

A nagging question about this checkered side of an otherwise radiant economic picture is whether any of it reflects regulatory and legal muddles that, though hardly fatal, are inexpedient in a less forgiving world. And if changes are needed, is there anything worthwhile to be learned from institutions elsewhere? Kagan and Axelrad do not rule out the possibility. Neither do the other authors in this volume. Caution against complacency is always sound and timely advice.

NOTES

1. Charles Krauthammer, "Bad Sports," *Washington Post*, July 26, 1996, p. A27.

2. See David Richardson, "Productivity and International Trade: A Neglected Source of Improved U.S. Economic Performance," paper presented at the Conference on International Trade and the U.S. Economy, Aspen Institute, Washington, D.C., May 1996, p. 30.

3. For related arguments, see more generally, Lawrence M. Friedman, *Total Justice* (Russell Sage, 1985); and Stuart A. Scheingold, *The Politics of Rights: Lawyers, Public Policy, and Political Change* (Yale University Press, 1975).

4. This question was recently the subject of at least one thorough investigation. See Pietro S. Nivola and Robert W. Crandall, *The Extra Mile: Rethinking Energy Policy for Automotive Transportation* (Brookings and Twentieth Century Fund, 1995).

5. Robert J. Samuelson, "Why America Creates Jobs," *Washington Post*, July 24, 1996, p. A21.

6. See Cathy Young, "Rule of Law: Crime, the Constitution and the 'Weaker' Sex," *Wall Street Journal*, August 21, 1996, p. A15.

7. Quoted in Pietro S. Nivola, "Searching for Economic Answers," *Journal of Commerce*, March 21, 1996.

8. See Helene Cooper and Rebecca Blumstein, "As U.S. Firms Gain on Rivals, the Dollar Raises Pesky Question," *Wall Street Journal*, August 16, 1996, pp. A1, A4. By 1994, however, the dollar had strengthened.

Chapter 2

American Social Regulation Meets the Global Economy

Pietro S. Nivola

E ACH YEAR the U.S. government publishes a long report about the rest of the world's policies, practices, and acts that are said to impair American commerce and prosperity.[1] Less advertised is the possibility that some U.S. rules and acts create similar difficulties. To put matters in perspective, the projected annual costs in excess of benefits of the 1990 Clean Air Act alone exceed the estimated value of U.S. exports blocked by all of Japan's known import restrictions.[2] The burdensome regulations of foreign countries deserve attention. But so do the burdens we impose on ourselves and sometimes on others.

Talk of regulatory reform, to be sure, periodically fills the air. In the mid-1990s the need for fundamental changes in America's legal practices, public and private, was being intensely debated. The Republican party campaigned on the issue in 1994, sending to the top of the congressional agenda major legislative initiatives to revamp the nation's tort laws and rule-making procedures. Some state legislatures took what action they could. Popular sentiment seemed at least ostensibly receptive. Books such as Philip Howard's *The Death of Common Sense*, telling sorry tales of how "law is suffocating America," became national best-sellers.

But when the spirited deliberations ran their course, nothing like a revolution had transpired in Washington. Mostly opposed by the White House, reformers in Congress could count precious few legislative victories by the end of 1996. President Clinton signed sensible measures for regulating pesticides and drinking water.[3] A compromise bill that sought to discourage frivolous lawsuits by a company's shareholders was able to hurdle his veto, but a moderate bipartisan plan to restrain punitive damages in product liability cases was not.[4] Appropriations for the Environmental Protection Agency as well as for the Occupational Safety and Health Administration increased, although perhaps not enough to reassure administration officials who accused Congress of waging a "budgetary war on the environment."[5] Two Supreme Court decisions chipped away a little at affirmative action programs in federal contracts and at grossly excessive penalties in some civil suits.[6] In the sweep of the American regulatory state, these were modest revisions.

The nation's methods of social regulation remain in need of a thorough reassessment, not least because more and more of them now reverberate internationally.

Going Global

Forty years ago, a purely domestic focus for social regulatory policies would have been fine. In the immediate postwar period, the legal intricacies of environmental protection, consumer safety, workers' rights, and restitution for various underprivileged groups would not have rippled very far afield. Not only were there fewer such rules, but the U.S. economy was more or less self-contained. Trade amounted to a negligible fraction of the GDP, and inflows of capital from abroad were trivial. The economy's industrial might and technological supremacy were unchallenged, as were the rapidly rising wages of its work force. The performance of U.S. firms in offshore markets was also rarely at issue. And international competition had not yet put any squeeze on earnings at home. In this context, behind-the-border regulations or cultural idiosyncrasies that might form barriers to trade, investment, and productive growth warranted less scrutiny, here as well as elsewhere.

America's economic position near the end of the twentieth century is altogether different. The era of U.S. hegemony is long past. The average American household no longer experiences a rapid increase in real annual income. Other industrial powers have narrowed our technological lead, caught up with our rate of productivity improvement, and matched our standard of living. Imports and exports combined have grown to account for almost a quarter of GDP, with overseas sales and foreign investment in this country becoming vital engines of U.S. economic growth in recent years.[7] To finance trade deficits larger than the entire economic output of Switzerland and a multitrillion dollar overhang of debt, the United States is now the world's largest borrower, much exposed to the vagaries of an international financial market that transacts more than a trillion dollars of business each day.[8]

Amid this global economic integration, peculiarities in regulatory environments can amplify national variations in the fortunes of key industries or even in the margins of national living standards. Just as the strategic industrial policies of trading partners might contribute to their comparative commercial advantages (and disadvantages), so eccentricities in native legal cultures or regulatory styles may no longer be of little consequence in the global marketplace. In short, how we regulate ourselves now makes a bigger difference, for us and for the rest of the international community.

But what sort of difference?

Other parts of this book explore this question from a variety of specific perspectives. Using illustrative case studies, several probe both the consequences and causes of what Robert A. Kagan has aptly termed American "adversarial legalism."[9] The ensuing pages of this chapter, however, are meant to paint some preliminaries with a broader brush. I begin by outlining the problem of legalistic excess and by viewing that problem from a comparative perspective. Then I consider the interface with America's international economic performance, commercial relations, and developments in U.S. productivity, employment patterns, and incomes. Finally, I address how political forces intensified by those developments are altering U.S. economic leadership in the world.

The Long Arm of the Law

Imagine yourself a manager of a corporation doing business in America and perhaps elsewhere. Besides the growing rigors of finding qualified workers and of besting your competitors, a tangle of legalities complicates your task. If your company raises capital for investment through the U.S. stock market, you must submit a detailed, independent audit of the company's balance sheet to the Securities and Exchange Commission every year. The commission also expects quarterly updates and other interim reports of any events or changes affecting the value of the company's securities between regular filing periods. SEC requirements have helped make U.S. financial markets admirably transparent for investors. But the requirements, which include disclosures of a company's uncertain future liabilities, are also far more exacting than those conceived by financial regulators in any other country.[10] Inaccuracies in the documents can be felonies.

The same goes for environmental laws, the compliance costs of which can involve much more than paperwork. If your business happens to be a small cider mill, for instance, misreporting test results for apple juice runoff apparently can mean prosecution and years in prison under extant interpretations of the federal Clean Water Act. [11]

Regardless of what type of job your full-time employees do or how poorly they do it, you are not only required to remunerate them above a designated wage level, but also to pay various federally mandated supplements, some of which apply to workers that may have left the company and several of which add substantially to total compensation.[12] In administering any pension plan, the company will have to meet elaborate uniform standards pertaining to minimum participation, accrual and vesting, fiduciary responsibilities, and reporting requirements.

The company's employees are entitled to many other guarantees. A long list of health hazards in the workplace will have to be minimized. A worker who decides, for example, to have a larger family can take up to three months' leave with full reinstatement. If you need to recruit another person, even as a temporary replacement, you must verify (without using a polygraph) that he or she is not an ineligible alien. Special accommodations must be provided for workers with handicaps, which might include such conditions as obesity or even histories of alcoholism and drug abuse.

Whenever you have to hire or, for whatever reason, to dismiss anyone, people with these afflictions (or others, be they backaches, psychiatric disorders, or perhaps "poor judgment") cannot be screened without risking a federal suit.[13] The same goes for the selection of persons on the basis of age. Indeed, the composition of employees on the payroll with respect to age, race, sex, or ethnicity can be held against a company as prima facie evidence of racism, sexism, ageism, or other biases, in which case the burden will be on the company, not its accusers, to establish the truth. Innocent or not, a company cannot lay anybody off without at least sixty days written notice if it has one hundred or more employees. If the employees wish to be represented by a trade union, they are entitled by the National Labor Relations Act to bargain collectively over wage rates, benefits, and all other terms of their employment.

Whatever the products a firm manufactures, many will require federal or state certification and labeling. In the case of pharmaceuticals, the process is typically longer than it is in other industrial countries.

If a firm sells products abroad it may be subject to export licenses and to punishment for dealing in ways deemed corrupt by U.S. norms. If it depends on imports, whether of finished products or components, they could be subject to antidumping duties, a cost of business administered by the Commerce Department.

If the firm is a lending institution, it will come under close scrutiny from various federal agencies to ensure that it follows an array of financially sound procedures, but also that it allocates credit and services to underprivileged individuals or communities, sometimes at considerable risk.

If a firm seeks federal contracts or subcontracts, it must comply with additional labor standards (for hours, overtime compensation, benefits, and so on), it must take special measures to employ people with disabilities, it must guarantee a drug-free work environment, and its bids will have to compete with those of firms eligible for special programs aiding the "socially and economically" disadvantaged. Not long ago, the Equal Employment Opportunity Commission and the Office of Federal Contract Compliance Programs might have accused a company of employment discrimination if, for instance, its ranks were not filled in proportion to the racial makeup of the community's hiring pool.[14]

And such edicts are only a first layer. Even if the federal list were to stop growing, state mandates, covering many of the same areas, add other tiers of requirements.[15] So does the civil justice system. A great deal of regulation in this country is enforced through deputized private parties. Whether a firm produces cars or hot cups of coffee, sooner or later it is likely to run afoul of local tort litigants, often long after government agencies have ruled on the worthiness of its merchandise. If the company invents certain kinds of computer software, it can count on getting sued for patent infringement by a rival invoking long-term intellectual property rights.[16] Or if a company is practically any other high-technology manufacturer, whose securities are unavoidably volatile, it must steel itself for all-but-certain shareholder "strike" suits in the state of California.[17]

The Rise of Regulation

Maybe none of this is of any concern for you and for other entrepreneurs like you or for the American economy as a whole. Surely a prosperous, civilized country should be expected to combat harmful types of economic fraud and abuse, reduce socially corrosive inequities, bar morally repugnant forms of discrimination, and protect the health and safety of its citizens. The net worth of the policies summoned up by these exertions is often impossible to measure; society may gain from most of them more than it gives up. In any event, the efforts have long histories, and coping with their complexities has been an old story.

The principal laws protecting buyers of food and drugs date back to the Progressive Era. Basic rules governing labor relations were forged during the New Deal. The bulk of federal legislation in civil rights, environmental protection, occupational health, and consumer safety commenced almost three decades ago. Nor is the adversarialism and legal contestation associated with these cyclical assertions of rights and preferences entirely new. Roots can be traced to the earliest days of the republic. "There is hardly a political question in the United States which does not sooner or later turn into a judicial one," observed Alexis de Tocqueville in 1835.[18] In the year the Constitution was written, J. Hector St. John Crevecoeur lamented in his *Letters from an American Farmer* the way "our laws and the spirit of freedom . . . often tends to make us litigious." This litigiousness, he complained, enabled even "the most bungling" lawyer to "amass more wealth than the most opulent farmer with all his toil."[19]

Two centuries later, however, the impulse to litigate, if not to outlaw, life's every risk and misfortune finally reached the point of stirring more than distrust of lawyers. For a while, the congressional election of 1994 energized some genuine efforts to force fewer paternalistic rulings from government and perhaps even to moderate the long-standing habit epitomized in the words of the television show, *People's Court*: "Don't take matters into your own hands. Take'em to court."

What underlay this reaction?

Regulatory Overload

At the simplest level, the reaction had to do with the growth of rules and liabilities bearing down on private enterprise. Indeed, a paradox of the regulatory state has been its seemingly relentless expansion through the reigns of the past half-dozen administrations in Washington, all of whom spoke of a need to slow the trend. Presidents Clinton,

Bush, Reagan, Carter, Ford, and Nixon all professed in varying degrees a desire to shrink the bureaucracy, privatize or devolve various public services, deregulate, or cut the amount of red tape.

But at the end of the day, the staffs of federal regulatory agencies, their budgets, and the volume of pages they produced in the *Federal Register* were greater, not smaller.[20] In fact, more federal mandates on employers were legislated in the 1980s and early 1990s than in the 1970s. Among them were at least three new projects that carried extraordinary potential for legal strife and excessive costs: the Americans with Disabilities Act, amendments to the Civil Rights Act, and a fortified Clean Air Act.[21]

Tallies of federal legislation and rule-makings merely scratch the surface of what was going on. The coverage of some of the more recent enactments has been breathtaking. (The 1990 Clean Air Act has eight times as many pages as the 1970 version.) And there has been a qualitative change in the stringency of the laws. By the early 1990s, penalties were being meted out far more frequently and severely for transgressions of rules on government contracting, employment protocols, civil rights, proper corporate management, lending decisions, sanitary consumer goods, and almost every other target of American legal activism. Inspections of workplaces by the Occupational Safety and Health Administration were up significantly in 1994, as was the number of large fines.[22] Charges of employment discrimination based on race, sex, age, disability, or national origin rose by 50 percent between 1990 and 1994.[23] During the 1993 fiscal year alone, 135 perpetrators of environmental crimes were convicted and sentenced to 943 months of jail time.[24]

Instances of punitive overreach became common and sometimes legendary. After the Environmental Protection Agency had expanded, with little statutory basis, the scope of the Clean Water Act to include soil that was dry at the surface but moist within eighteen inches underneath, environmental criminals could include unwitting farmers planting crops, and even home gardeners planting flowers, on their own "wetlands."

What one uneasy observer has called the "criminalization of just about everything" seemed to grip all levels of government. During the past decade, against the grain of the Reagan administration's deregulatory initiatives, state legislatures and courts moved to invent new sanctions.[25] Nowhere was this more apparent than in employment regulation. Dozens of states rewrote the most basic legal doctrines on workers' rights, tilting the doctrines more in favor of employees. In pursuit of these protections, regulators and legal advocates in many states became so active that a 1994 survey by the General Accounting Office found employers often more concerned with state than with federal workplace rules.[26]

Lawsuits

The long shadow of civil litigation is not easy to delineate. Here, the big expansion began in the 1960s. Through the mid-1980s, malpractice and product liability claims exploded.[27] The rapid expansion has since moderated, thanks in part to legal reform measures adopted in a number of states.[28] However, an estimated 1 million tort actions were still being filed annually in state courts as of 1993.[29] The cost of America's penchant for tort litigation has continued to exceed the total economic output of Sweden.

That may be putting it mildly. No one can measure the complexity and expense of settling the vast majority of suits that never go to trial, the chilling threat of suits over a widening range of issues, the preparations needed to lessen the chances of being sued, or the fear instilled by the occasional outlandish jury award. Hot legal wars, so to speak, may not be much more frequent than they were fifteen years ago, but only owing to the added precaution of deploying larger armies of vigilant lawyers engaged in a kind of legal equivalent of defensive cold war. Witness the continual increase in the number of lawyers in relation to the total U.S. population and the rising share of GDP they consume.[30]

Whatever the extent of the litigation explosion, the variety of suits, not just the absolute sum, matters. Those who try to carry on their managerial duties in today's legal combat zone may have grown accustomed to the complaints about wrongful discharges of employees, harassments, health risks, or disappointing stock quotations. Less familiar are new possibilities of being hauled into court for providing former employees with insufficiently flattering references, failing to supply insurance coverage for infertility treatments, or not furnishing enough armed guards in the company parking lot.[31]

It is useful to think of these phenomena not merely as means of resolving personal disagreements, but as institutions of governance or social regulation. A civil jury that levies millions in punitive damages against a maladroit business is addressing more than a private matter. Much like an injunctive order from the Consumer Product Safety Commission or the Equal Employment Opportunity Commission, the civil verdict supposedly serves the public purpose of deterring some perceived threat to society.

Viewed this way, the overall regulatory picture in the United States is murkier than might be supposed. During the past couple of decades, federal "economic" controls—over rates, operating licenses, obligations to serve, and so on—have been lifted or greatly relaxed in transportation, energy, telecommunications, finance, and other important sectors. But two decades of decontrol have not yet come to terms with less direct regulatory foibles, including the full force of civil cases filed by the millions each year in the nation's courthouses.

Some International Contrasts

Skeptics doubting that American regulatory institutions create any relative disadvantages usually contend that conditions in other countries are immeasurably worse. As obstructionist as some of the machinery of law in the United States can be, it has coexisted with the world's largest, freest, and most productive economy, one that in the past decade created more jobs than did the other major industrial economies combined.[32] Germany's overtaxed and rule-bound economy, the critics emphasize, so thwarts labor mobility and raises unit labor costs that it is now common to find BMW or Mercedes plants locating in the United States. The present U.S. expansion, in stark contrast with Japan's sputtering bubble economy and with high unemployment in much of western Europe, suggests that if overregulation is doing damage, most of it is occurring somewhere else.[33]

Self-congratulation today, however, has followed too quickly yesterday's fits of self-flagellation. Although observations of Eurosclerosis and Japan's infirmity may be the latest conventional wisdom, the preferred paradigm was different five years ago. The talk then was all about German and Japanese ascendancy and American decline. In the 1992 presidential campaign the winning ticket described the country as suffering its "worst economic performance since the Great Depression," inviting comparisons with the economy of Sri Lanka.[34]

Such sloganeering aside, at least one trend did give genuine cause for concern. U.S. output per worker between 1979 and 1992 grew at less than half the average rate of the other G-7 countries.[35] As a result, measured in terms of real compensation per worker, no other major industrial nation experienced so great a change in expected living standards. Contrary to much recent journalistic speculation, there is little reliable evidence that a great rebound has been under way in the past five years. The situation continues to raise the fundamental question of whether institutional impediments are not just a Japanese or European problem, but partly an American one.

Different Strokes

Even if government is less overbearing in the United States than in other Western democracies, a tyranny of too much law can take many forms. In Japan, civil suits do not normally decide the safety of consumer products; the task is performed almost entirely through a ponderous process of bureaucratic certification. In much of Europe, national legislation covering all employees stipulates extremely generous rights to a minimum wage, paid holidays, disability payments, unemployment compensation, and health care.[36] Moreover, no-fault insurance programs settle a wide range of accident and injury claims.

Top-heavy or extravagant as these social compacts can be, they appear to offer one potential advantage: less litigation. Just because its public sector is comparatively modest does not necessarily mean American society is less encumbered by legal sanctions, only that more of them are ginned up by private plaintiffs. Bluntly stated, Americans may be trading lower levels of government interference and direct taxation for a greater frequency of costly civil actions finding faults and hearing grievances in every imaginable kind of purported injustice. One kind of social control is swapped for another because the perceived stakes and inducements for civil litigants and lawyers are larger (table 2-1 and figure 2-1). With tort rights being the functional equivalent of a privatized transfer program, the American political system has had difficulty setting limits on private standing to sue and on fantastic damage claims.[37] The hidden impost in this arrangement is, of course, not trivial. The costs of medical malpractice and product liability insurance in the United States—to glance at but

TABLE 2-1. *Product Liability Law in the United States, the European Union, and Japan*

Characteristic	United States	European Union	Japan
Types of claims	Bodily injury including mental suffering	Mostly property damage	. . .
Fault	Strict liability	Fault generally required, and several defenses available	Showing of fault required
Role of jury	Determines liability and amount of the damages defendant must pay	No jury in civil tort cases; judge determines liability and damages	No jury; judge determines liability and damages
Discovery	Extensive disclosures required in discovery	Very limited discovery	Parties have no discovery powers
Attorney fees	Contingency fee is primary method of compensation for tort lawyers; share ranges up to 50 percent of total recovery	Contingency fees not generally applicable; losing party often pays other side's attorney fees	No contingency fees; plaintiff must pay stamp fee to government based on the value of damages initially claimed
Pain and suffering	Available and determined by the jury	. . .	. . .
Punitive damages	Available, and limited in only some states	Generally not imposed in civil cases	. . .
Liability insurance	Ten times the average cost of insurance in other industrial nations; limited availability for certain products	. . .	. . .

Source: Adapted from Alfred W. Cortese Jr., and Kathleen L. Baner, "The Anti-Competitive Impact of U.S. Product Liability Laws," *Journal of Law and Commerce,* vol. 9 (1989), p. 183.

FIGURE 2-1. *Cross-National Comparison of Tort Costs as a Percentage of GDP, 1991*[a]

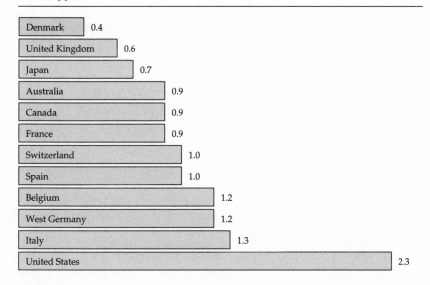

Denmark	0.4
United Kingdom	0.6
Japan	0.7
Australia	0.9
Canada	0.9
France	0.9
Switzerland	1.0
Spain	1.0
Belgium	1.2
West Germany	1.2
Italy	1.3
United States	2.3

Source: Tort Cost Trends: An International Perspective (Tillinghast, 1992), pp. 8, 14.
a. Tort costs include first-party benefits (the cost of legal defense and claims handling), benefits paid to third parties (claimants and plaintiffs), and an administrative, or overhead, component.

one part of the tithe—run five to ten times higher than insurance rates abroad (even though, after paying their lawyers, most U.S. victims of medical malpractice or product injuries ultimately recover nothing).[38]

In many areas the scope and stringency of American public law are second to none. U.S. food and drug regulation, with its long trial periods for proof of a drug's efficacy before it is put on the market, is an oft-cited example.[39] So is U.S. securities regulation.[40] Or consider pollution abatement, the component of social regulation with the highest direct compliance costs. U.S. regulators have been forcing larger investments by manufacturers in the United States than have those anywhere else, including such environmentally progressive societies as Germany, Holland, and Japan.[41] While the Office of the U.S. Trade Representative protests poor sales of American motor vehicles in Japan and Korea, U.S. environmental guardians sock producers and parts suppliers with a pollution-control bill several times steeper than the expense paid by Japan's automakers as a percentage of total investment in the manufacturing process.

Frequently the costs of environmental policies run high in the United States not because U.S. standards are better, but because the chosen mode of intervention is less efficient.[42] The principal U.S. energy conservation program, for example, consists of ungainly command-and-control regulations (the corporate average fuel economy, or CAFE, mandates) imposed on the automobile industry. Every other advanced country relies instead on a simpler technique: higher fuel taxes, which have helped keep consumption per capita far below that in the United States.[43] Similarly, some U.S. water quality regulations, however harshly enforced, may well be less cost effective than the Dutch and German experiments with effluent fees.[44]

Employment security provisions tend to be stronger in Japan and most of Europe than in the United States. So the American model of corporate restructuring, consisting of drastic (and sometimes mindless) downsizing, is less common in Japan, Germany, France, or Italy. However, the European and Japanese employment rules turn out to be less rigid than some casual observers might believe. Dismissal constraints (the supposed bane of European business) now differ less between key European countries and the United States.[45] How else could Daimler-Benz and Fiat have managed to discharge more than 90,000 workers since 1992?[46] And why else would once lifeless parts of British industry now enjoy an appreciable labor cost advantage over some U.S. manufacturing?[47] European and Japanese labor markets have their own ways of responding to business cycles. Employers in Japan and Germany, for instance, tend to reduce the work hours of employees before eliminating their jobs. Rates of labor turnover are thus lower than in the United States. But is less turnover always undesirable? Severing trained workers except as a last resort has a downside.[48]

Light Touch?

Meanwhile, in the United States, strictures in the workplace have proliferated. For example, American firms are enjoined from specifying a retirement age, but almost all Japanese employers retain the option of requiring retirement by age sixty. Thus the difference between the way labor markets adjust in the United States and Japan is partly semantic. During a downturn many U.S. workers are laid off, whereas many Japanese workers are asked to retire.[49]

In the realm of job discrimination policy, the severity of U.S. rules is sui generis. In most of the world, there is no recourse at all for the those who claim to be victims of employment bias. Western Europe, Canada, and Japan do give recourse. But the Civil Rights Act of 1991 moved U.S. law in new directions.[50] Its approach, which requires companies judged guilty to reinstate workers with full back pay, and provides punitive damages awarded by juries, has virtually no parallel in the legal systems of any other nation.[51] The European Union's "equal treatment directive" does not routinely remediate claims of indirect or unintentional bias (the statistically based "disparate impact" concept firmly embedded in American civil rights regulation). When European national courts award compensation, six months' back pay is typically the extent. Enforcement bodies like the U.S. Equal Employment Opportunity Commission are unusual; only the United Kingdom and Ireland have bureaucracies with faintly analogous functions. According to a 1990 report of the International Labour Organization, nowhere is alleged discrimination in employment policed as closely as in the United States.[52]

This country is also a remarkably rule-abiding society. Although its central government still dictates and taxes less than the Bourbonic bureaucracies and bloated welfare states in Europe, when the tax collectors and regulators come calling, most citizens here take them seriously. Not so in much of the rest of the world. In Italy, the G-7's polar opposite, for example, a time-honored aphorism says *"fatta la legge, trovato l'inganno"* (loosely translated, "enact a law; find ways to evade it"). If Italian firms complied assiduously with the mountains of antediluvian codes that theoretically govern business, Italy's economy would have been buried long ago. Instead it is the world's fifth largest. Evidently, many debilitating rules are respected about as much as the laughable national seat belt law. At a minimum, pervasive tax avoidance in Italy suggests that high official rates of unemployment cannot be imputed entirely to the onerous employer mandates that sustain public health plans, pensions, and other costs of the safety net.[53] The measure of regulatory impact on economic activity is not the nominal volume of law on the books but the amount of enforceable law. By this standard, regulatory pressure in the United States is comparatively uncompromising.

In fact, whether the target is unfair employers, environmental polluters, tobacco companies, or almost anyone else, a distinctive feature of the American regulatory regime is its querulous and censorious style. The objects of social regulation are never just businesses trying to meet a payroll; instead, the selective employers are racists or sexists, the polluters are criminals, the cigarette manufacturers are drug dealers. Firms are regarded as miscreants to be fiercely deterred and sternly coerced.[54] The distrustful mentality makes for considerable complexity.

A British environmental statute or a Japanese labor contract is more likely to be short and broadly worded, allowing decisionmakers on the spot considerable leeway to resolve problems by mutual consent.[55] By contrast, the American documents tend to resemble arms control treaties by mutually suspicious nations. The presumption is that the parties are antagonists to be closely monitored and controlled. Thus, long covenants attempt to micromanage every eventuality. Administrative discretion is narrowed; "invisible handshakes" are dreaded; each detail must be inspected and reinspected through formal proceedings, oversight, and judicial review.

The reality of regulatory politics in Japan or Britain is, of course, a lot less consensual and tidy than it appears to naifs on the outside. For sheer contentiousness, however, the process of social regulation in the United States seems hard to top. It is not unusual for decisions, buffeted by court challenges, to remain in limbo for years.[56] Regulated interests spend lavishly on lawyers and lobbyists. Their machinations are met by the countersuits and counterlobbying of organized advocacy groups, frequently armed with statutory private rights of action that few, if any, other governments would countenance.[57] Caught in the middle of the legal scuffles, not a few dazed entrepreneurs wait indefinitely for the next shoe to drop before making desirable investments.

In sum, despite extensive deregulation of prices and entry in various industries over the past twenty years, plenty of regulatory liabilities and uncertainties of doing business in America persist. Many are by no means moderate. Those who, in Lewis Lapham's felicitous phrase, "go around making things without permission" face a profusion of legal perils, often different from but not necessarily less exacting than the institutional restrictions in other places.

The Parasite Economy

Theoretically the blessings of vigorous regulation more than compensate for the burdens. The laws and the lawsuits, after all, are meant to correct flawed markets.

Desirable Results

Consumers cannot always make informed judgments about the characteristics of products. In the absence of standards, labels, and legal recourse against negligent producers, people might decline to purchase drugs, foods, and other consumer goods at prices that reflect their real economic value. By providing assurances of quality, standards and lawsuits may actually optimize the market for the goods and help price them correctly.[58]

Likewise, the aim of workplace standards is to prevent inefficient cost shifting in labor markets. In principle, the positive effects of reduced workmens' compensation payments, less wage inflation, and a more productive labor force make up for the onus of OSHA inspections.

Air and water are typically collective goods that cannot be rationed through normal market forces. Public intervention in some form may be necessary to approximate an efficient allocation of these resources. Clean air and water are in part intermediate goods whose benefits, such as improved health and amenity, may yield unambiguous economic gains. Environmental protection can cause a loss of jobs in industries that pollute but, imaginably, a larger increase of jobs in industries manufacturing pollution abatement equipment. Either way, environmental quality is also partly an object of final consumption, meaning that many people seek it as an end in itself, quite apart from any measurable contribution to employment or production. Even if regulatory controls exact a price in economic productivity, this does not prove they are bad for the national welfare. All it might show is that regulatory compliance diverts resources from uses measured in the national accounts to uses not measured in the accounts.[59]

Further, not all the undertakings that have been strangled by red tape and legal tangles ought to be mourned. Delays in commissioning extra nuclear power plants, developing synthetic fuels facilities, and subsidizing supersonic aircraft for commercial transport were once regarded as grave economic losses. In retrospect, such casualties of regulatory paralysis may have been serendipitous.[60]

Diminishing Returns

Nevertheless, it is also clear that the intended payoff of many regulatory initiatives is now costing more, sometimes enormously more, to obtain. A principal reason is that many of the low-cost opportunities for reducing health and safety risks were seized years ago; there are fewer low-hanging fruits left to pluck. Of more than fifty major health and safety regulations promulgated between 1967 and 1991, a third have been estimated to extend a human life for less than $1 million in regulatory costs; all but five predate 1986.[61] By contrast, most of the rules that cost more than $25 million to extend a life came afterwards.

For example, both a 1973 ban on flammable pajamas for children and a 1989 ban on asbestos prevent premature deaths. The first does so for less than $1 million per life saved, the second for $134.2 million. Wearing seat belts became de rigeur by 1984. Each premature death averted by this decision has cost society only $0.39 million. A 1987 rule limiting exposure to formaldehyde, however, has proved harder to justify; its probability of salvaging anyone is so small that each life saved would have to be worth nearly $93 *billion* for this standard to be cost effective.[62]

Some regulatory schemes—occupational safety and health enforcement, for example—operate on the false assumption that an unsafe environment is the primary cause of accidents, when the main problem is inept or careless behavior. Despite increased resort to criminal charges for workplace injuries, OSHA has been spinning its wheels; since the program's inception there has been very little, if any, discernible impact on workplace injury rates.[63] Similarly, the Consumer Product Safety Commission has scant measurable effect on fatalities among persons using the products it regulates, for the simple reason that only two-tenths of 1 percent of the deaths from these products can be attributed to correctable defects.[64]

Other laws have sought to go even farther, trying to rid the land of every hazard, no matter how minuscule, at any price: *no* carcinogenic additives in food, *zero* pollutants in waterways, and so on. These efforts have the defect of their virtue: their feasibility wanes as they near their goal. Purifying everything from rivers to groceries by 90 percent may be practicable, but the remaining 10 percent may not. Increasingly, today's regulators, more than yesterday's, find themselves toiling on these intractable tail ends.[65]

Public policies and civil jurisprudence in search of a risk-free existence inevitably run up big tabs, especially if dynamic effects on productivity and rates of technological innovation are factored in.[66] It takes a lot of putative benefits not to be badly stung by the costs, and increasingly those benefits have seemed elusive for regulatory ventures that indulge in extreme risk aversion. At least $100 billion and some 20,000 lawyers are projected to be involved in cleaning up toxic waste dumps.[67] The whole operation could be done with less if a third of the money were not used up in litigation and if "clean" did not mean removing the last few bits of contamination that scarcely affect health or safety.[68]

Certain types of benefits, moreover, are commonly double counted or undiscounted overtime, or are simply wishful thinking. All manner of facilities, from restaurants to rental cars, will have to be modified to comply with the handicapped access requirements of the Americans with Disabilities Act. The eventual cost for office spaces alone could top $45 billion, with no assurance that seriously disabled persons in much greater numbers will ever seek employment in these buildings.[69] What might look like a long-term employment gain associated with some pollution abatement programs may be mostly featherbedding. Environmental mandates may induce additional jobs in the pollution control industry, but these may still represent a net welfare loss if resources are being shifted from other, higher-valued uses. Society gains nothing in an economic sense if, say, compliance with a regulation causes firms to hire a lot of people, half of whom must dig ditches while the other half refills them.

Even accepting for the sake of argument the copious flow of benefits that government agencies tend to impute to their missions, corresponding costs frequently loom larger. The costs of federal water pollution regulations appear to outweigh discernible benefits by more than $20 billion annually.[70] The 1990 Clean Air Act is likely to impose additional compliance costs of $30 billion a year while generating estimated benefits only half that large.[71] Recently Robert W. Hahn of the American Enterprise Institute examined most of the major rules issued by the EPA, OSHA, the Consumer Product Safety Commission, the National Highway Traffic Safety Administration, and the Mine Safety and Health Administration between 1990 and 1995. Using the agencies' own figures, he found that more than half of their final rules would fail a net-benefit test.[72] Eliminating these inefficient rules would have saved more than $115 billion.

In part these remarkable outcomes are the inevitable result of statutory provisions that sometimes prohibit agencies from weighing the economic costs of their actions in the first place. The Clean Air Act, for instance, explicitly bars the EPA from considering costs in setting national emissions standards for hazardous air pollutants. The poor outcome also has to be the natural consequence of a regulatory agenda driven by citizen suits. In the words of EPA administrator Carol Browner, "litigation is essentially setting the priorities," diverting substantial agency resources to the pet projects of particular advocacy groups and away from administrative goals that might have a broader social payback.[73]

Torts

The cost of civil litigation is, in a very real sense, part of the economy's regulatory burden. In much of the past half century the visible costs of personal injury, product liability, and medical malpractice cases have multiplied faster than the GDP has grown, and now consume between 2 and 3 percent of it, an extraordinary amount compared to the percentages in other countries of the Organization for Economic Cooperation and Development.[74]

That figure might well be considered only a first installment. The vast majority of suits are settled without a trial and for undisclosed amounts. Besides the sums extorted from defendants that simply cannot dedicate months of managerial time and attention to open-ended pretrial discovery and to weeks in a courtroom, firms must devote substantial resources to warding off predators even when no complaint has been filed. Higher insurance premiums, along with big retainers to corporate attorneys and to a cottage industry of compliance consultants, are standard budget items. There are also less obvious costs: effects on morale, products abandoned or never developed, hours devoted to legally bulletproof record keeping, and so forth, all of which may be adding tens of billions to the true tariff of the litigation crisis.

Of course, this tax also buys some social good. Few would suppose that product liability complaints, malpractice cases, and other claims of mistreatment deter no wrongdoing and promise no deserved redress. Overall, however, is society getting its money's worth?[75] Increasingly, there is reason to suspect that much of what passes for the righting of wrongs is actually a massive transfer of rents. The U.S. tort system may be returning less than 50 cents on the dollar to the people it is designed to help.[76] Legal fees and other transaction costs chew up the rest.

Dedicating that much energy to transferring wealth instead of creating it feeds parasites, not producers adding value.[77] Economists in recent years have begun to provide some disturbing estimates of the parasitic effect. According to Stephen P. Magee of the University of Texas, "redistributive perversities" of the American legal system reduced GNP growth 10 percent below its potential in the 1980s.[78] Predatory litigation could be one of the factors reducing the U.S. pool of net national savings and the amount of gross private investment.[79]

Gnawing at Trade and Investment

If an infestation of lawsuits and fastidious rules in any way bleeds rates of saving and investment, the immediate implications for U.S. trade performance might seem obvious: external deficits worsen and the ability of firms to compete deteriorates.[80]

Actually, the relationship between regulation and relative competitiveness is not so simple. Every capitalist nation generates self-defeating regulatory policies, and in each case the devil lies in the details. Observers simply do not know enough about comparative regulation to be sure whose policy mix, other things equal, can claim more winners than losers. Keeping score is difficult even within narrow sectors. Compared to the prevailing procedures in Europe, FDA testing of certain pharmaceuticals has been a notoriously long and laborious process—arguably a distinct disadvantage for some U.S. drug manufacturers. But for bioengineered pharmaceuticals, U.S. tests and approval have tended to be comparatively swift.[81] Where, on net, does this combination of leads and lags leave U.S. firms? Or think of the Delaney clause. Those who regarded its costly zero-risk approach to carcinogens as unique should have looked again; the EU ban on the use of livestock growth hormones constitutes a zero-risk policy, too.[82] When both sides make similar or equivalent regulatory mistakes, the collective welfare is reduced, but not either side's comparative advantage.

Further, it is possible to think of situations in which stricter rules and liabilities in the United States might sharpen, rather than blunt, the competitive edge of U.S. producers. Imagine a world in which natural monopolies were only regulated here and were unregulated everywhere else. The result would be that monopolistic industries in this country would produce at higher levels of output and lower prices than their foreign counterparts. Or imagine that the United States were to eliminate all requirements for the performance, safety, and environmental impact of products while our competitors tightened their standards. The probable outcome would be even more foreign goods awash in global markets at the expense of U.S. goods that lack, so to speak, a Good Housekeeping seal of approval.[83] In certain instances the more stringent the quality control (either because of public licensing or private liability suits), the greater the pressure on firms to upgrade technology, innovate, and find new market niches. In some spheres of social regulation—environmental controls, for example—advanced nations seem to be, if anything, in a race to the top.[84] Thus industries anticipating the highest standards may be rewarded with "first-mover" advantages over the long haul.

It is also simplistic to assail regulations just because they may interfere with exports. When society improves water quality by imposing pollution controls, it is increasing the supply of a desired good that is produced and consumed almost entirely at home, thereby diverting resources from the production of goods for sale abroad. But there is no reason to accept less clean water—or for that matter to supply less lawn mowing, window washing, dry cleaning, or any other goods and services consumed domestically—just for the sake of maximizing exports. Limiting the domestic consumption of clean water or of clean windows to promote exports is like taxing one's own citizens to subsidize the citizens of other countries. America is not better off for it.

Harm to Exports

But alongside the regulatory practices that are irrelevant to the competitive position of American business, or that may even improve it, are a goodly number that are a nuisance to it while accomplishing little else. What useful policy purpose, foreign or domestic, is served by outmoded export controls on widely available products such as trucks?[85] Apart from enriching a maritime cartel, what is the point of merchant marine regulations that raise shipping costs for producers and consumers, while effectively pricing some major U.S. commodities (such as $7 billion to $15 billion worth of Alaskan crude oil) out of potential export markets?[86] Were motorists really much safer after the National Highway Traffic Safety Administration, having forced several massive recalls of Firestone radial tires, helped deliver that company's market into the waiting arms of the Japanese tire giant, Bridgestone?[87] And what social goal was attained by the free-wheeling litigation that inflated the prices of certain highly tradable products, from vaccines to general aviation airplanes?[88]

In the aircraft debacle, an entire U.S. industry was consumed by rapacious liability claims.[89] Insurance for the three principal companies, Piper, Beech, and Cessna, soared to between $70,000 and $100,000 for each airframe, surpassing each unit's total cost in material and labor. Before Congress finally got around to enacting some corrective legislation, domestic production of light aircraft, approximately a quarter of which used to be exported, had nearly collapsed.[90] The lawsuits laid out a red carpet for foreign producers to enter the breach; they subsequently snatched a rapidly growing share of the world market in general aviation, including commuter airliners. And with the costs of new American-made planes spinning out of control, U.S. buyers opted for used equipment. When the plaintiffs and trial lawyers were through, flying was not safer, just more expensive.[91]

The United States would like to keep building an export platform not just for logs and tuna, but for finished manufactures such as electronics, computers, laboratory instruments, medical devices, and environmentally benign chemical substitutes that have high value added. Yet, with an eye to legal risks, American companies sometimes have withdrawn technological breakthroughs from potential markets. Striking examples have included a replacement for asbestos, a nonchemical pesticide substitute, a chemical process that speeds up decomposition of hazardous wastes, and a portable kidney dialysis machine for home use.[92]

Some high-technology industries, known for their erratic stock prices, have also had to battle nonstop shareholder class action suits (or, more precisely, roving bands of professional plaintiffs).[93] Familiar names such as Apple Computer and Intel Corporation are among the companies that have had to fend off these attacks. The most inviting targets, however, have been smaller technology startups who, with less legal firepower, are more easily blackmailed into settling out of court.

Precisely how much havoc has been wrought in vital industries by these so-called strike suits is unknown and probably unknowable.[94] One doubts, however, that America's high-tech trade is much improved by a tort system that routinely distracts people from their work, compels multimillion dollar settlements in cases of doubtful merit, discourages risk taking just to minimize stock fluctuations, and rewards short-term thinking to deliver acceptable financial results every ninety days. Whether mild medicine like the recent Securities Litigation Reform Act promises much of a respite from these pathologies remains doubtful.[95]

Laws that stimulate exports as ends in themselves can waste resources. But when law suppresses the ability to export, and too often has nothing worthwhile to show for that outcome, the implications are worse. By 1991 the United States had regained its position as the world's largest exporter in absolute terms. Arguably, though, U.S. businesses were still underachieving in foreign markets. Most of the U.S. export boom reflected a weaker dollar after the mid-1980s. Booming or not, the export intensity of the U.S. economy as a share of GDP has remained far below that of many other industrial nations.[96]

Exports matter in the following sense. When a nation's capacity to sell domestically made products to external markets is artificially hindered, productive capacity moves offshore. A coerced exodus of production is surely detrimental; domestically domiciled export industries provide a more direct source of high-wage jobs at home than do the partially repatriated returns from the subsidiaries of multinationals operating overseas. With more U.S. companies deploying substantial assets abroad (foreign affiliates of U.S. parent corporations now account for more than a quarter of all their employment), unnecessary legal wrangles and regulations that might further tempt firms to exit rather than export from their home base inevitably give pause.[97]

Barriers to Foreign Investment in the United States?

No less counterproductive than these export disincentives are policies and practices that might repel foreign investment. Direct investment by foreign companies is beneficial for any modern economy. Foreign-owned businesses employed 4.7 million Americans in 1990.[98] Each year, numerous native firms are salvaged or bolstered through foreign mergers and acquisitions. In sectors spanning everything from manufacturing to financial services, direct investment has introduced new technologies, better managerial techniques, and other useful innovations. Tens of billions of dollars in U.S. exports flow from U.S.-based affiliates of foreign multinational corporations exporting goods to their parent companies. In fact, during the past twenty-five years, U.S. merchandise exports have been more closely tied to foreign investment patterns than to the growth of foreign demand.[99] Which company exports the most American-made automobiles? Honda.[100] Not surprisingly, issues of reciprocal market access for investors are likely to top the multilateral trade agenda for the foreseeable future.

Foreign direct investment in the United States crested in 1989, however, and accounts for barely over 4 percent of U.S. output.[101] Foreign investors experience their share of difficulties trying to operate profitable enterprises here. In fact, between 1983 and 1991 they were earning an average rate of return far below that of U.S. business in general, as well as that of U.S. investments abroad.[102]

Such results are somewhat baffling. The U.S. market is, in most ways, exceptionally hospitable.[103] Compared to other nations, the United States throws relatively few deliberate obstacles in the path of foreign-based firms making acquisitions or greenfield investments. U.S. law does not require such companies to take local firms as joint-venture partners. The U.S. dollar is a freely convertible currency, making the remittance of dividends to parent companies easy. Unlike labor unions in various European countries, American unions are typically too weak to dictate the order of work rules or codetermination in the restructuring that often follows acquisitions. Above all, the country's market is not only vast but stable politically and perceived as a safe haven. In light of all these attractions, what is the problem?

Perhaps many outsiders are just ill equipped to do business in a market as large as this one. Or perhaps they are simply unversed in the rough and tumble of American competition. But also plausible is a supplemental explanation: lurking under the surface of America's comparatively open economy are unfamiliar legal undertows, some of which may be less visible and more treacherous to foreign entrepreneurs than to our own.[104]

U.S. liability law, for example, can be daunting.[105] Many foreign companies prefer to get around it by exporting to the United States instead of establishing a major business presence. The companies immunize themselves by operating through independent export agents that take title to products before they are shipped. Although these middlemen are subject to American jurisdiction, they are often small operations with few assets; thus it is pointless to try to collect against them in liability judgments. Successful recovery against the parent company, safely across the border, is often impossible. This shell game might help explain why strict liability verdicts have managed to discourage, for example, U.S. sporting goods manufacturers from producing various kinds of athletic equipment but have virtually invited importation of the same equipment from factories in Sweden, Canada, and the Czech Republic.[106]

The giant multinational corporations of Canada, Europe, or Japan are more aggressive. While lesser prospectors limit themselves to exports, beg off entirely, or arrive and make many navigational errors, the big multinationals come ashore with the necessary legions of lawyers, accountants, and "culture auditors." But sometimes even the giants experience strange scrapes on the jagged reefs of the federated American legal structure.

In Alabama the buyer of a 1990 BMW sued the manufacturer for the dissatisfaction it caused him. His claim: BMW of North America had failed to disclose that his car's finish had been slightly damaged in shipping and touched up before sale. The jury in the case assessed the vehicle's defect at $4 thousand, but then went ahead and awarded punitive damages of $4 million, a verdict so reckless that the case was appealed to the state's highest court, where the settlement was reduced to $2 million, and then to the U.S. Supreme Court, where the unprecedented decision was made to throw out the $2 million settlement on the grounds that it was "grossly excessive" and thus unconstitutional.[107]

In another clash, a disgruntled American executive of the Toyota Motor Corporation filed suit in California state court on the grounds that he and other non-Japanese employees were held back from career advancements that were granted to Japanese nationals.[108] Never mind that the United States and Japan had signed a treaty of friendship, commerce, and navigation (FCN) explicitly granting foreign affiliates of the signatories the reciprocal discretion to prefer their own citizens for executive positions. The FCN Treaty, whose principles have been upheld repeatedly in U.S. federal courts, has scarcely deterred a string of discrimination charges against Japanese corporations operating in the United States.[109] The U.S. branches of Honda, Sumitomo, Sanyo, Matsushita Electric, Nissan, Toshiba, Mitsubishi's Quasar, Mitsubishi Motors, and Sweden's Astra AB have all been hit with sex, race, or age mistreatment suits.[110] The main question about some of these cases is not how the aggrieved parties found standing to sue, however; it is whether foreign firms unaccustomed to the fine points of U.S. civil rights statutes and affirmative action guidelines stumble into some unexpected legal pits in the United States.

Savvy foreign companies learn how to play the game. Huge corporations like Mitsui U.S.A. train their America-bound managers in U.S. employment law. The trainees are taught how to conduct job interviews, for instance, in which no questions can be asked about age, medical histories, marital status, and family background, inquiries that would be routine and deemed highly relevant in Japan.[111] Big German companies such as Daimler-Benz figure out how to attach minority advisory boards to their U.S. plants and how to accommodate demands for "inclusion, inclusion, inclusion."[112] Certainly major foreign banks have not fled despite a torrent of redlining accusations in some parts of the United States. Institutions such as Sumitomo or the Bank of Tokyo have figured out how to placate community groups (and an array of federal bank regulators) calling for more loans to minority and female-owned businesses.[113]

The larger issue is whether such exactions, like the side deals that have to be cut to operate in many countries, become, if hardly conclusive determinants of the investment climate, at least an added consideration in investment decisions already freighted with other uncertainties and complications. When foreign companies such as Sanyo and JVC sack several thousand U.S. workers and shift their North American production of television sets or microwave ovens to Tijuana, who knows whether the moves are only parrying low-ball imports from Korea or exploiting Mexico's low-wage labor?[114] "There's no question that the American legal system is a minefield for anybody doing business there," recounts the chairman of a Canadian company. "I am not aware of anything comparable to the American system in another democratic country."[115]

Trade Issues

One might dismiss such speculation out of hand if U.S. trading partners were indifferent to the legal and regulatory pitfalls in the U.S. market. But they are not. Just as the U.S. trade representative assembles an annual list of grievances about unfair foreign barriers to trade and investment, other countries also compile lengthy itemizations of U.S. practices they consider questionable.[116] Some of these complaints, too, seem legitimate. And many involve social regulatory oddities that Americans seldom think of as trade issues.

Thus the European Union notes that government set-aside programs for minority contractors are at odds with the principle of open procurement.[117] The Community Reinvestment Act, which cajoles banks into lending money to disadvantaged borrowers, raises national treatment questions.[118] Various state regulations, such as California's environmental rules for recycling glass and purifying drinking water, are criticized for their apparent conflicts with GATT codes. The bewildering patchwork of federal, state, and local product certification and labeling requirements is cited as a technical impediment to market access.[119] Not long ago, a GATT panel challenged aspects of the U.S. automotive fuel-conservation program.[120] One of the first appeals lodged with the World Trade Organization involved a dispute over trade inequities in the rules implementing the 1990 Clean Air Act's provisions for reformulated gasoline.[121]

What can be especially awkward about some of these internationally contested mandates is that their value or efficacy for the U.S. national interest is also suspect. For example, despite a welter of product labels, no amount of precaution seems to prevent businesses from being stalked by bizarre lawsuits over safety. McDonald's Corporation had begun placing warning labels on its coffee cups in 1991. Yet three years later a jury ordered it to pay $2.9 million to a woman who scalded herself by spilling coffee on her lap. An astonished world watched as the case, far from being a fluke, set off a rash of similar suits against other fast-food and coffee chains, some of whom have taken to supplementing the warnings on cups by training employees to tell customers how to drink the contents carefully.[122]

The merits of federal set-asides are now very much in doubt; in 1995 the Supreme Court finally decided that they often lacked a "compelling" rationale.[123] Affirmative action for lending institutions is not just an inconvenience for bankers; the Community Reinvestment Act's critics argue that low-income neighborhoods gain little from it.[124] The U.S. automotive-fuel economy standards are an inefficient means of saving oil.[125] For a while, the Clean Air Act offered a pretext for the promotion of ethanol as an oxygenate in reformulated gasoline. Besides providing another unwarranted subsidy to corn farmers, the expensive new fuel was likely to increase nitrogen oxide emissions while offering only small reductions in volatile organic compounds and leaving unchanged the worst health-impairing pollutant: airborne particulate matter.[126]

Protectionism

The growth of social regulation also may entrench more deliberate trade restraints. Chemicals, steel, autos, textiles, agriculture, and other major industries bruised by environmental litigation, consumer and worker safety complaints, or other legal brawls have often been especially aggressive in seeking import duties, market quotas, or price supports.[127] During the 1980s steel companies alone were responsible for fully a third of all the antidumping petitions submitted by U.S. firms.[128] As recently as 1992 a dozen American steel corporations again bombarded their rivals in more than twenty countries with a barrage of charges that foreign steel was being imported at less than fair value. When regulatory costs, on top of Japanese competition, began mounting sharply in the early 1980s, U.S. automobile manufacturers acquired a multibillion dollar protective shield against imports.[129] Later, a new round of domestic costs—more special contracting, more emission controls, more colossal liability suits—would be followed by intensified disputes over insufficient market shares in Japan and Korea.[130] As restrictions on pesticides and on chemical runoffs from farming stiffened, so did the farm lobby's claim on residual subsidies supposedly needed to remain competitive in international markets. No U.S. business has won more protection over the years than have textile producers. The competitive weakness of this industry is aggravated by delays in modernizing its equipment. Liability expenses have driven a number of textile machinery manufacturers out of business.[131]

A connection between self-inflicted regulatory hardships and the incidence of trade bars imposed on international competitors may be more than coincidental. When distressed businesses run to the government, they often knock first on the accessible doors of Washington's trade bureaucracy.[132] A beleaguered steel producer or automobile company is less likely to shake off the civil justice system's bounty hunters and gain regulatory relief from the Environmental Protection Agency than it is to find compensatory trade remedies in the Commerce Department. The department's mission, standard operating procedures, and congressional overseers serve the interests of its business clientele, whereas the EPA's watchdogs and "private attorneys general" have exactly the opposite bias, keeping U.S. business on the straight and narrow.[133]

Not infrequently, protectionist provisions are attached directly to social regulatory programs, either as an inevitable consequence of logrolling in the enactment of their authorizing statutes or in the subsequent promulgation of rules. The trade restrictions buy off domestic producers that would otherwise fight the rules or statutes. In the next chapter of this book, David Vogel traces two such cases of what might be termed protectionist "capture" of domestic regulations. Both provoked major disputes in GATT and the WTO. In one instance, discriminatory provisions were inserted in the CAFE legislation at the insistence of the United Automobile Workers. The second controversy arose from congressional efforts to mollify an odd coalition of domestic refineries and environmental groups by getting the EPA to adopt an import-restrictive standard for reformulated gasoline under the 1990 Clean Air Act.

No major trading nation has done more than the United States to strip off flagrantly protectionist policies since the end of the Second World War. But when it comes to less visible forms of trade obstruction—arcane sanctions against "unfairly" priced imports or backdoor barriers tucked into environmental programs—the record has been less exemplary. No sooner was the EPA gasoline rule found to violate WTO standards than U.S. trade officials raced to appeal the WTO decision.[134] During virtually every GATT round, including the final stages of the Uruguay Round, U.S. negotiators have declined to dismantle tendentious antidumping laws.[135] Knowing this was where their bread was buttered, various native industries celebrated. For them, the regulatory state partially counterbalances its weight on domestic businesses by also sitting on some of their foreign competition.

Fixing the Playing Field

Perhaps the most natural response to one's regulatory handicaps is the temptation to push them onto everyone else. If every heavily regulated U.S. industry could either secure trade relief or vote with its feet, there would be little advantage in trying to extend American-style legalism to other societies. However, since few industries are completely footloose or protected, their remaining option is to insist that their burdens be shared. The burden-sharing pleas of businesses, moreover, are often matched, indeed outdone, by the missionary activities of other interest groups—organized labor, environmentalists, consumer advocates, rights activists, and so on—with a stake in extending the transnational reach of social regulation.

True, the process of regulatory equalization can move in different directions. At times it may spur a defusion of deregulatory initiatives across borders. At least as often, however, it takes the form of demands to tighten standards. Although the idea at times is to improve global welfare by overcoming negative spillovers among nations, frequently less civic-minded motives can also be involved.[136] By pressing for greater symmetry in national regulatory systems, even when the process spreads costs instead of lowering them, domestic lobbies take comfort in seeing their foreign competitors or adversaries lose a putative free ride.

In Search of Astroturf

The range of foreign commercial conduct deemed pernicious has continued to widen with each major piece of U.S. trade legislation. [137] Long dissatisfied with the antitrust measures of other countries, for example, Congress has repeatedly broadened its conception of illegal pricing of goods imported into the United States. Whereas dumping was once defined strictly as predation (the intent of the part of the dumper being to "injure or destroy" an American industry), U.S. antidumping provisions have gradually come to encompass pricing patterns that are common business practice. Whereas subsidies that underprice imports were originally defined as direct "bounties or grants" bestowed by foreign governments, by the mid-1980s precedents existed for U.S. countervailing duties on everything from regional development programs to industrial adjustment payments. At one time, section 301 of the 1974 Trade Act was meant to take aim at countries that breached their international trade agreements with the United States. By 1988 Congress came close to insisting that the provision apply to such offenses as failure to meet standards of minimum wages, hours of work, and occupational health or safety, even though the United States had not signed the international agreement that specified those workers' rights.[138]

The drumbeat of legislative proposals extending U.S. trade sanctions to additional foreign regulatory practices considered objectionable or inadequate did not subside after 1988, even though that was the last year in which Congress enacted omnibus trade legislation. Of the forty-eight bills on environmental matters introduced between 1990 and 1991, thirty-one included provisions for such sanctions. During the debate over the revised Clean Air Act in 1990, the Senate narrowly defeated, 52 to 47, an amendment imposing tariffs on "any product imported into the United States that has been subject to processing, or manufactured from a process, which does not comply with the air quality standards of the Clean Air Act." According to the amendment's sponsor, Americans "should do everything we can to encourage policies which are similar to our own in the rest of the world, whether it has a direct impact on air quality in the United States or not." During the same debate, another Senate amendment proposed to expand the definition of foreign unfair trading to include any practice that "constitutes a failure to establish effective natural resource protection and effective pollution abatement and control standards to protect the air, water and land."[139]

The following year a proposed International Pollution Deterrence Act defined pollution as an impermissible subsidy and authorized the imposition of countervailing duties against countries whose pollution cleanup policies did not meet U.S. standards. This bill called for placing half of the revenues into a Pollution Control Export Fund to be used to assist developing countries in purchasing American-made pollution control equipment. (The other half of the duties would be handed to American companies to develop the control technologies.) As the author of this scheme explained to the Senate, "The bill recognizes that a country's failure to require and enforce meaningful pollution controls constitutes a subsidy no different, but more dangerous than, practices such as cash grants to money-losing State enterprises which have long been actionable under U.S. law. By making such absence countervailable, we allow U.S. companies to level the playing field by removing the cost advantage derived from freedom to pollute."

Not surprisingly, traces of this logic have found their way into major trade negotiations. Much as the question of "social dumping" came to dominate deliberations about regulatory harmonization in Europe, the North American Free Trade Agreement teetered for a time over stipulations about environmental and labor regulations for Mexico. No sooner was the ink dry on these NAFTA side agreements than the Clinton administration sought to drag the same contentious issues onto the WTO's agenda, as well as into bilateral dealings with Indonesia, Malaysia, Chile, and other developing countries.[140]

Momentum

In the end, there may be less to all this than meets the eye. Third world countries may successfully resist what they regard as the latest form of Western paternalism. Modern corporate interests with a stake in those economies may prevail over import-competing firms and unions pursuing their age-old campaign against foreign "pauper labor." Republican congressional leaders are less eager than were their Democratic predecessors to attach environmental and social provisos to more trade deals. In their zeal to promote U.S. exports, Clinton's trade diplomats may even quit trying to link commerce and rights altogether: to wit, the administration's about-face on conditioning most-favored-nation status for China.

Still, an expectation that the rest of the world should play the game of global economics by our preferred rules is likely to keep resurfacing in other ways. Private parties will press the cause independently. In 1990 a lawsuit by animal rights defenders invoking the U.S. Marine Mammal Protection Act forced the Bush administration to ban imports of Mexican tuna, although a GATT panel would soon rule against the U.S. law.[141] Three years later, a suit brought by Public Citizen, Friends of the Earth, and the Sierra Club temporarily placed a restraining order on the implementation of NAFTA.[142] The plaintiffs demanded an environmental impact statement for the entire treaty, and a federal district court concurred. Once legal avenues were in place to enforce NAFTA's side accords, public interest groups began filing more complaints, such as a reproach of Mexican authorities for their "persistent failure" to police working conditions in Sony Corporation plants.[143] Worried about finding themselves in the crosshairs of media exposés, U.S. multinational companies have begun adopting "socially correct" codes for the treatment of foreign contract workers.[144] For now, such codes are voluntary, but pressures to make them universally accepted are building.[145]

Increasingly, work forces beyond the border are being targeted by unions and their allied advocacy groups. Their understandable aim, of course, is largely to stop the transfer of jobs to less regulated sites abroad, but also partly to create a kind of two-level game on the domestic political front: extraterritorial application of fair employment precepts can refract attention onto any lax enforcement of labor standards in the United States.[146]

Misgivings

Besides becoming an irritant to other countries, who may see some of this exportation of morals and legal prescriptions as indirect economic imperialism, too much pleading and shoving to level the playing field poses several dangers.

Holding developing economies to standards that advanced societies seldom recognized during their own industrial revolutions may retard progress.[147] Pious contemporary preferences notwithstanding, how many nations in history developed a modern manufacturing sector without first passing through something like a sweatshop phase? Even minimal standards—a categorical, universal ban on child labor, for example—raise questions. Will moving underage workers out of factories and onto the streets really improve their prospects in Bangladesh or Brunei, or will it just impoverish their families longer? And how simple is it to champion the civil rights of young workers without doing the same for older ones? Unlike the United States, most nations have not outlawed mandatory retirement. So why not argue that, by permitting employers to discriminate against senior employees (who tend to draw higher salaries), these other nations reap an unfair cost advantage?[148]

Distributing legal baggage to other economies can also tighten the regulatory screws on U.S. industries.[149] Sometimes this is precisely what the advocates of international standardization have in mind.

But often we Americans seem surprised when trading partners cite inconsistencies between what we expect from them and what we are willing or able to ask of ourselves. Certain labor standards in various U.S. states trail those in other countries. Even prohibitions against child labor are underenforced in some states. Sooner or later, scolding places like Mexico for unfair employment practices could trigger counterclaims.

So could other attempts to straddle the separate rails of workers' rights and trade liberalization. U.S. trade policymakers fought long and hard to crack the Japanese apple and orange markets. But if the WTO is brought into the business of enforcing rights, the United States may face a new dispute with Japan about apples and oranges, this time concerning allegations that the migrant laborers who picked those fruits work under substandard conditions, at miserable pay, in antiunion states.[150]

Perhaps the greatest risk in the quest to ratchet up global standards is that of equating fairness with uniformity, as if healthy commerce depends on making other economic systems become identical to one's own. But stern regulations in one setting may not make any sense in another. And trade occurs precisely because national settings differ. Just as differences in factor endowments provide a basis for trade, so do variations in savings behavior, industrial organization, social conditions, or even legal traditions and regulatory methods. The reason the United States and Japan trade with one another (or with Saudi Arabia, for that matter) has nothing to do with whether the rules of their societies are sufficiently similar; it has everything to do with the simple fact that each side gains.

Losing Ground?

Homespun legal knots and punctilious rules without net benefits complicate more than the lives of businessmen. Immoderate regulation ultimately takes a toll on national well-being. Is the toll noteworthy? Buried in a $7 trillion economy, the item usually looks like small change. Yet a seemingly slight drag on the rate of productivity growth leads to large losses of wealth over time. A sizable body of empirical research has delved into parts of this question (see the appendix). And for the most part, it has detected signs of trouble.

FIGURE 2-2. *Labor Productivity, Bias Adjusted, 1959–95*[a]

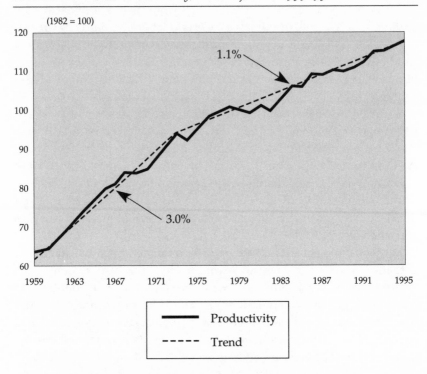

Source: Dan Sichel, Brookings, May 10, 1995. Nonfarm business productivity from Bureau of Labor Statistics. GDP figures from Bureau of Economic Analysis. Bias-adjusted productivity and trend based on author's calculation.

a. Trend drawn through 1960, 1973, and 1988. Nonfarm business output per hour for all persons multiplied by ratio of chain-weighted GDP divided by 1987 dollar GDP index.

Productivity Doldrums

Productivity growth in the United States fell off sharply beginning in the early 1970s. There have been upswings since then, but adjusted for cyclical effects and measurement error, the overall rate of growth continues to lag significantly the pre-1973 pace.[151] On a chain-weighted basis, labor productivity generally shows a long-term trend of only 1.1 percent annual growth, almost one-third the rate before 1973 (figure 2-2).[152]

FIGURE 2-3. *Real Family Income Growth, Income by Quintile, 1950–78, 1979–93*

Percent

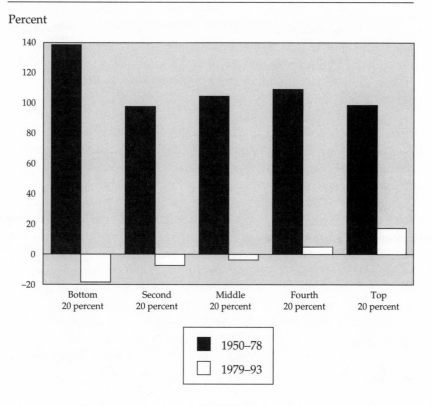

| | Bottom 20 percent | Second 20 percent | Middle 20 percent | Fourth 20 percent | Top 20 percent |

■ 1950–78
□ 1979–93

Source: Bureau of the Census in *Washington Post,* January 6, 1995, p. B2.

Anemic productivity growth has meant that real incomes have been rising less rapidly than they had during the quarter century after World War II. When output per person was growing at 2.5 percent a year or better, the income of an average American could be expected to double in less than thirty years.[153] Since 1973 Americans have had to wait twice as long to see their incomes double. Many may have to wait much longer. Whereas practically all U.S. families experienced real growth of incomes between 1950 and 1978, only the top two-fifths saw appreciable growth from 1979 to 1993 (figure 2-3).

Granted, these data are far from flawless. Consumption expenditures per capita have been climbing faster than income, suggesting that income data have been overadjusted for inflation, underreported, and conflated by demographic changes.[154] Prosperity cannot be measured just by salaries. Fringe benefits remunerate work as well, and from housing to autos to VCRs, contemporary consumers are often enjoying goods of higher quality for each dollar earned and expended.[155] Still, these caveats do not explain away enough of the troublesome trend in American living standards. Nor do other considerations.

Some of the wage stagnation might be imputed to a normal lead time before investments in labor-saving technology begin to yield higher earnings. Some is related to the decline of trade unions, some to the shift of employment from manufacturing to services, and some to the influx of women and immigrants into the labor force. Initially, procompetitive deregulation of important sectors—transportation, telecommunications, energy production, and financial services, for instance—also may have moved prices closer to marginal costs and thus wages closer to marginal product.[156] Massive energy shocks temporarily destabilized economies throughout the industrial world in the 1970s. In addition, lower tariffs have exposed more of the U.S. market to foreign competition, presumably depressing wages.

Puzzles persist, however. If technological reengineering has spurred an authentic, sustained upsurge of productivity over several years, a marked and sustained rise in the real median earnings of workers in full-time employment now seems overdue.[157] If the service sector, too, has been automating rapidly, the shift to a service economy probably explains less of the slower productivity growth than previously assumed.[158] If deregulation in some sectors has outpaced the widening reach of regulation in others, long-term efficiency gains should be lifting, not lowering, incomes.[159] If oil shortages pummeled industrial productivity during the 1970s, an abundance of cheap energy since then should have had an equal and opposite effect. If 88 percent of the goods and services consumed by Americans are still produced by Americans, import competition cannot account for very much of their deteriorating wages.[160] Either some of our purported productivity increase of recent years has been illusory, or additional intervening forces may be slowing its translation into higher incomes.

Whatever else has limited productivity growth or increases in Americans' take-home pay in the past couple of decades, a possible surfeit of social regulation could be at least partly implicated.

Regulation and Restructuring

There are signs that more than a few corporations in the United States may have restructured more than was called for by market forces alone. For their pains, some of these firms have registered little or no improvement in worker productivity in their U.S. operations and thus barely any improvement in domestic wages. In fact, much of the cost cutting by American industry over the past decade has not come from increasing output per worker hour. It has come from reducing labor costs by restraining salaries, shrinking staff, and shifting work outside the company or across borders.

Outsourcing is the name of the game. Overall value added produced within U.S. multinational parent companies has drifted downward. Of the 4 percent drop during the 1980s, roughly 1 percentage point reflected production offloaded to domestic contractors; the rest represented sourcing from abroad.[161] U.S. firms with foreign operations essentially ceased contributing to U.S. employment growth after 1977.[162] These multinationals tend to use the rapidly expanding markets of Asia, for instance, as a processing base for products that are ultimately returned for sale in the United States.[163] Competitive heat at home, skilled low-wage labor abroad, and advances in communications and transportation help explain the pattern. But impatience with the legal and regulatory freight that companies have to haul in the U.S. market may also play a part, sometimes inducing a retrenchment that borders on "corporate anorexia."[164]

It is not hard to see how this sequence might be a distinct possibility. As mandates and exposure to legal risks multiply in employment relations, for instance, the disinclination to maintain full-time employees can deepen.[165] Firms perceive an added reason to downsize, substitute contingent workers for permanent ones, farm out more functions, and perhaps move some basic production to greener pastures. Occasionally, even some supposedly innocuous social engineering such as the bureaucratic or judicial purveyance of diversity goals could contribute the final justification for situating productive facilities in less sentient cultures. Why, a pressured company might ask, must it put up with the encumbrance of investing millions in special recruitment programs, sensitivity training sessions, and the sometimes bizarre services of human-resource counselors or "facilitators" (as well as the usual dream teams of lawyers and insurance salesmen peddling protection against employment bias suits), when high-quality workers, available simply on the basis of merit and cost, beckon elsewhere?[166]

I am not inferring that legal and bureaucratic vexations in the United States typically expatriate whole enterprises.[167] Larger considerations—proximity to markets, quality of infrastructure, political stability, and so on—generally determine the locational decisions of companies. Comprising a vast federated polity, moreover, the American states offer considerable variation in regulatory policies. Inasmuch as "tort taxes" might make a difference in deciding where to invest, for example, a company uncomfortable with the outsized liability awards in Alabama need not set sail for Malaysia; it can move to Tennessee. At times businesses also exaggerate the ills of regulatory directives whose actual costs turn out to be mild. Dire predictions about the consequences of provisions for family leave and for advance notification of layoffs, to take two hotly disputed pieces of legislation, soon faded.[168]

By the same token, it is naive to assume that, in the complex calculus of direct overseas investment, the national regulatory and legal climate never exerts any influence on the sourcing or contracting patterns of firms.[169] There is no shortage of press accounts reporting the riposte of big firms like Bayer, Hoechst, Siemens, and BMW to the costs and rigidities of labor regulations in Germany: in the past five years German industry has invested three times more capital outside the country than foreigners invested inside.[170] The exit strategy of German business is only an extreme rendition of what is happening in most other globalizing economies, including our own.[171]

More than a few anecdotes have accumulated about American companies that instead of exporting have gone abroad to make and market products so as to extricate them from the U.S. liability maze and from regulatory delays.[172] A recent survey of 500 U.S. medical equipment manufacturers found that more than 60 percent planned to commercialize advanced devices overseas before introducing them in the United States. More than 90 percent of the companies cited the long FDA product review requirements.[173] Twenty-two percent of medical device companies in a 1994 survey by the American Electronics Association said they had already moved jobs offshore for the same reason.[174]

The General Accounting Office tracked a score of sizable furniture manufacturers in southern California that had relocated all or parts of their operations to Mexico between 1988 and 1990, eliminating perhaps as many as 2,500 U.S. jobs.[175] Seventy-eight percent of these companies gave as an explanation the EPA's "stringent air pollution emission controls standards for paint coating and solvents." What of the EPA itself? Reportedly it, too, had gone outside for some regulatory relief, if not by heading south of the border, at least by subcontracting the agency's data center "to gain flexibility in hiring and firing."[176]

Or witness the perverse incentives of CAFE regulations. At one point, this mechanism for coercing automobile manufacturers into producing energy saving cars drove at least one producer, Ford Motor Company, to start producing abroad and then importing more than a quarter of the parts for certain models of vehicles.[177] At the costs of hundreds of American autoworkers' jobs, the tactic helped Ford meet requisite fuel economy standards for its overall fleet. Ironically, while CAFE was inducing greater reliance on foreign-made products, trade officials bewailed the nation's growing trade imbalance in autos and autoparts.

Employment and Wages

Business executives have held the perilous legal environment, particularly in states such as California, partly responsible for plant closures, work force reductions, and some industrial emigration.[178] If there is anything to these perceptions, exactly how bad is the resulting "tax" on employment or wages? While the research on this specific point is thin, fragments suggest partial answers. When suits at the workplace began to soar in California in the mid-1980s, for instance, a study by the Rand Corporation estimated that the direct and indirect costs for companies translated into a 10 percent penalty on payrolls.[179]

At first glance, such findings only raise additional questions. If today's workplace regulations and litigation significantly raise the costs of labor services, the overall level of employment, not just wages, in the United States might be expected to suffer, much as it has in Europe. American managers might reason, no differently than those in Germany, France, Italy, or Spain, that employees are a liability, best avoided by hiring as few as possible. For a time, particularly during the so-called jobless recovery following the recession of 1990–91, there was considerable speculation that just such a Europeanization of the

U.S. labor market was under way.[180] Aggregate employment in this country, however, regained a robust rate of growth two years later. What seems to distinguish the American brand of industrial streamlining is not the substitution of capital equipment for labor but an expansion of lower-cost jobs that absorb workers cast off when large employers "rightsize." Thus persons shed by some companies are taken in by others, though often in lower-paying jobs of lesser quality. The trend in various sectors is toward lean, even "virtual," firms that limit their legal and regulatory overhead by tapping a growing body of external or contract labor for services formerly supplied in-house.[181] By 1996, approximately 86 percent of major corporations outsourced at least some services to independent contractors, up from 58 percent in 1992.[182] In some industries, more and more of this external contracting is global. (The McDonnell Douglas Corporation's MD-95 jetliner has homemade avionics but British engines, an Italian fuselage, an Austrian interior, a Japanese tail, Korean nose and wings, and Israeli landing gear.)[183] In most, the outsourcing is still stateside, hence causing no net loss of U.S. jobs. Either way, however, it forces workers to scramble and keeps their compensation in line.[184] In short, this is not an economic engine that wrecks employment, as in Europe. But it is one that has become exceptionally adept at compelling wage restraint.

Into the Age of "Low Politics"

Inasmuch as aspects of the American social regulatory regime may be among the factors stalling productivity gains or delaying their conversion into a rapid rise in the national standard of living, the political repercussions could be far-reaching.

Neoisolationism

The main political effect is likely to be further erosion of support for internationalism, a process well under way since the end of the cold war. Americans see less reason now to commit resources and incur risks, financial as well as military, in the name of global security interests. Fundamental changes in the economy—the globalization of production, the shakeout in job markets, the relentless wage squeeze—have contributed greatly to the introspective attitude.

Economic insecurity was a persistent undercurrent in all of the last three national elections. In 1992 almost two-thirds of the electorate endorsed presidential candidates who ignored international issues altogether and fixated on domestic economic woes (as Bill Clinton did) or who blamed foreign commercial entanglements for those woes (as Ross Perot did).[185] In 1994 the Republican midterm triumph was stoked by voter resentment of a wasteful government suspected of taxing and borrowing too freely from frozen incomes in order to fund a multitude of unaffordable federal handouts, from welfare payments to foreign aid.[186] Key components of the GOP's campaign Contract with America spoke directly to this distemper, promising deep tax and spending reductions that would "renew the American Dream." Even in today's good times, surveys show about half of all adult Americans gloomy about the economic horizons of their children, and two-thirds remain convinced the economy is either declining or not expanding at all.[187] Hardly gloating over the nation's full employment, the Clinton White House still figured that "whether wages will grow or stagnate" would be "what the 1996 election is all about."[188]

A public perceiving static living standards has grown more mistrustful of politics in Washington but also increasingly skeptical of international obligations vaguely suspected of impinging on national sovereignty or on economic self-interest. Thus for nearly four years a reprise of ethnic cleansing and national dismemberment in Europe's backyard was regarded as a peripheral perturbation of little relevance to the leadership responsibilities of the world's only superpower. Calls for stanching immigration have moved from the political fringe to the mainstream. A fierce congressional backlash early in 1995 nearly blocked all U.S. efforts to rescue Mexico from financial collapse. And deference to the very foundations of an orderly multilateral trading system, specifically the adjudicatory role of its governing body, the World Trade Organization, were rattled by exploits in both the legislative and executive branches.

The Clinton administration's tactics during a flare-up about automotive exports to Japan, for example, were unsettling.[189] American negotiators had complained for years about the lack of a binding international mechanism for resolving commercial disputes. Nevertheless, after precisely such a mechanism (the WTO) finally came into being at great U.S. insistence, Clinton's trade strategists appeared to finesse its procedures; a countdown to sanctions was begun without awaiting the international organization's review of the U.S. case. Despite Republican legislative majorities contemptuous of other facets of the president's foreign policy, congressional support for the administration's trade militancy was nearly unanimous. If anything, Republican lawmakers raised further questions about adherence to the World Trade Organization. Senator Robert J. Dole, for instance, introduced legislation that would have impaneled a special commission made up of U.S. federal judges to oversee and possibly challenge WTO proceedings perceived as contrary to U.S. interests.

An inward turn in American politics has already delayed several trade-expanding objectives. Appealing in part to the large populist swing constituency that boosted Perot's candidacy in 1992, both major parties during the 1996 election year assiduously avoided reauthorizing fast-track procedures to negotiate any ambitious new international trade treaties.[190] The accession of Chile and other Latin American countries to a hemispheric free trade zone was placed on hold. Prospective accords on financial services and maritime trade were shelved.[191] Progress toward some of these trade deals was likely to revive after the election, but in the meantime, according to Dole, Congress needed a "cooling off period"; America was "choking on free trade agreements."[192]

In 1992 House Majority Leader Richard Gephardt (Democrat of Missouri) had declaimed that for Americans the North American Free Trade Agreement "is rapidly becoming, substantively and symbolically, representative of everything that is wrong with their lives."[193] That assessment was melodramatic then and would still be so, but its small kernel of truth has been getting larger. Disappointment seems to be the main feeling about NAFTA these days. Even with the Democratic party's economic nationalists no longer in control of Congress, movement along the lines of a wider NAFTA or a new multilateral trade round that, however faintly, hints of further creep toward a borderless world seems likely to meet more resistance today than it did in 1993.[194] In sum, considerable confusion attends America's global stewardship these days, and greater clarity seems a dim prospect as long as the nation's penurious mood persists.

Commercializing Foreign Affairs

Actually, American foreign policy has pulled in two directions. Alongside the temptation to disengage on some levels has been an

impulse to intervene assertively on others, such as in bilateral arguments over market access.[195] So, for example, policymakers vacillated
for years before beginning to halt with force a genocidal war on the
doorstep of Europe. Yet when the vending of semiconductors or car
parts overseas was at issue, there was no prolonged rumination nor
abdication under the cover of multilateralism. To the contrary, unilat-
eral action was deemed fitting or at least expedient.

Interestingly, the emphasis and energy on the commercial side of
U.S. international relations are occasionally reminiscent of the aveng-
ing spirit in some domestic policy discourse, which, as Thomas Burke
observes in another chapter of this book, seeks to frame needs as
rights and to stack heavy legal remedies against any lingering unfair-
ness. Thus, much of the activist trade rhetoric has been animated by
a portrayal of American businesses as victims of discriminatory
foreign trading practices.[196] Victims presumably deserve reparations
with measurable results. How are the results to be obtained? Trade
managers have drawn explicitly on the civil rights metaphor: numerical quotas (formal or de facto) should be set and backed by stiff sanctions to ensure consignments in contested foreign markets.[197] Here
was the way a chief U.S. negotiator characterized his delegation's
demands for an allocation of the microchip market in Japan: "In
effect, like disadvantaged U.S. minorities, we wanted an affirmative
action program that would offset the effects of past discrimination by
actively working to increase imported chips."[198]

It can seem strange for envoys of the United States to go around
representing major business interests of the world's leading economy
in such terms. But there are at least two reasons why statecraft has
made a remedial sales pitch for corporations. At times the international marketing campaign for corporate clients has appeared to
reflect in part an abstract conviction that the post–cold war era's
strategic paradigm is primarily about geoeconomics (a kind of zero-
sum rivalry among vendors of merchandise), not about the old-fash-
ioned geopolitical themes of war and peace. More basically, the ma-
terialistic strain in foreign affairs has been compelled by domestic
economic realities. With most American consumers still suspecting
that their incomes were flat or falling throughout the first half of the
1990s, most were spending less than in any other recovery since
1960.[199] So U.S. growth seemed more dependent on consumption expenditures in other markets; they would give a lift to an economy

that needed more high-paying jobs, more favorable terms of trade, and greater gains in the standard of living.

Conclusion

The implications of overzealous social regulation, broadly construed, no longer stop at the water's edge. At times, practices with a strictly domestic intent have constricted the flow of various U.S. exports. Possibly some of the practices have affected foreign direct investment in the country (though I am unaware of any systematic investigation of this hypothesis). In addition, not all the institutionalized obstacles to international trade and the resulting tensions with other major trading nations are attributable to their legal and regulatory systems; some are associated with our own. These wider ramifications need to be better understood and taken seriously. They can compound the costs of rules and rulings that in many instances are already overtaking benefits.

A little relief might be on the way. At least a tendency to export blame for domestic troubles is not as pronounced today as it was a decade ago. Then, the preoccupation was almost monomaniacally with other countries' regulatory structures that inhibited U.S. commerce. (It is not too much to say that the economic program of the Democratically controlled 98th, 99th and 100th Congresses consisted entirely of gargantuan pieces of legislation purporting to correct unfair trade.) Six consecutive years of solid growth have since allayed, at least for the moment, most fears that U.S. industry was becoming uncompetitive. Moreover, despite continuing partisan conflict on the specifics, all sides now seem to share greater recognition that getting one's own house in order is the precondition for success with a globalizing economy. Up to a point, there is even consensus that the essential home repairs should include an overhaul or reinvention of defective regulatory fixtures.

How concrete and sustained these changes will be remains unclear. The expansionary mid-1990s have yet to deliver a conspicuous improvement where it really counts politically: in much higher incomes for the American middle class.[200] And until that happens, globalism is likely to be viewed with growing suspicion by a substantial bloc of voters. When analyzing the politics of paychecks in the United States, bear in mind that more than one faction (Gephardt Democrats, Perot independents, Buchanan Republicans) view world trade, which always looks neither free nor fair, as a central culprit. This restless constituency, ranged among a number of possibly pivotal points on the political spectrum, will remain hard to ignore. At a minimum, its stirrings could abet deceleration of trade-liberalizing initiatives, deeper skepticism about international institutions such as the World Trade Organization, new digressions into fruitless confrontations with "pernicious" trading partners, and a further tilt of foreign policy toward pocketbook issues.

Regenerative macroeconomic adjustments alone are unlikely to suffice as an antidote. Budgetary discipline can help narrow politically sensitive trade deficits. Lower rates of taxation on capital gains and savings would spur some additional investment and growth. Yet productivity gains and wages could still get ground down by other millstones that, so far, have proven excruciatingly hard to dislodge—most notably, a propensity to keep regulating and suing in pursuit of more and more social protections or rights.

Integration of the U.S. economy with the rest of the world, though not a direct cause of stagnant wages, may magnify the effects of injudicious regulation. The methods of social regulatory intervention in the United States, much reliant on legalistic commands and controls and on punitive civil litigation, are sometimes singularly inefficient. Their dead weight (even if seemingly modest in relation to overall national output or seemingly sustainable compared to the grand total of self-destructive political habits in other countries) is not inconsequential for key businesses that compete internationally. Market forces already create considerable incentives for firms to shift their work around the global factory. The liberal laying on of hands, so to speak, by social regulators and plaintiffs' lawyers can augment those incentives. And when it does, American payrolls may be on the line.

One does not sense that the significance of this potential trade-off has been grasped by a president that continued to frustrate, for instance, elementary correctives for a malfunctioning tort system. Though some national efforts to curb cost-oblivious regulation and inordinate litigiousness have borne fruit, many now seem to be wilting.[201] Even if a dispirited Congress manages to revive them, the labors of some Republican lawmakers are not always reassuring either. As this essay was being drafted, these engineers, too, were poised to perpetuate or erect a few more monumental edifices of social protectionism. How did leading industrialists regard "reforms" such as a recent bill that would have restricted sharply an influx of skilled immigrants? A "masterpiece," as Microsoft's Bill Gates put it, "if you want to prevent companies like ours from doing work in the United States."[202]

Much of what I have said in this chapter is unapologetically conjectural. Almost all invites much more rigorous research. The proximate net benefits of the American social regulatory agenda, let alone its international permutations, are unresolved empirical questions. Provocative perspectives, such as those opened in several parts of this book, will hardly tranquilize debate. They could, however, help broaden its scope.

Appendix: Studies of Regulatory Impact

A number of studies have attempted to assess the effects of some forms of social regulation on U.S. productivity and economic growth. Regrettably, this body of work has two deficiencies: it largely overlooks the past fifteen years, and it tells relatively little about the costs of social regulatory activity other than environmental and occasionally occupational health programs (where direct effects are relatively measurable). Despite its narrow gauge, however, the available research is suggestive.

Economywide Effects

Martin L. Weitzman finds that the total of direct expenditures for environmental improvement significantly underestimates the true social cost of this kind of regulation because indirect effects on growth are not being measured. While the bill for direct compliance totaled 2.1 percent of GNP in 1990, Weitzman contends that the actual "environmental drag" was 4 to 6 percent of GNP. See "On the 'Environmental' Discount Rate," *Journal of Environmental Economics and Management*, vol. 26 (1994), pp. 200–09.

Dale W. Jorgenson and Peter J. Wilcoxen find that pollution abatement lowered the annual growth rate of the economy by 0.191 of a percentage point from 1973 to 1985. See "Environmental Regulation and U.S. Economic Growth," *RAND Journal of Economics*, vol. 21 (Summer 1990), pp. 314–40.

Michael Hazilla and Raymond Kopp also maintain that the costs of environmental regulation are typically underestimated. They believe that the nominal environmental cleanup expenditures of $648 billion for 1981–90 understate the social cost by over $300 billion. Compared to their base case, they find that the level of real GNP was lowered by 2 percent as of 1981 and 6 percent as of 1990. These writers stress that the economic costs of environmental regulation are not confined to the regulated industries: "while pollution control investments were required in only 13 sectors, the cost of production increased, and output and labor productivity fell, in all production sectors." See "Social Cost of Environmental Quality Regulations: A General Equilibrium Analysis," *Journal of Political Economy*, vol. 98, no. 4 (1990), pp. 853–73.

Earlier, Edward Denison had observed significant effects of expanding environmental rules on annual productivity growth. For 1967–69, 1969–73, 1973–75, and 1975–78, the productivity growth rate decreased 0.05, 0.10, 0.22, and 0.08 percentage points, respectively. In addition, Denison estimated that worker health and safety regulation reduced the annual growth rate of measured output by 0.1 of a percentage point in the 1973–76 period relative to earlier periods. See "Pollution Abatement Programs: Estimates of Their Effect upon Output per Unit of Input, 1975–78," *Survey of Current Business*, vol. 59 (August 1979), pp. 58–59; and *Accounting for Slower Economic Growth: The United States in the 1970's* (Brookings, 1979).

Drawing on a review of the available literature, Robert H. Haveman and Gregory B. Christainsen estimated that all federal regulations accounted for 12 to 25 percent of the slowdown in productivity growth experienced by the private sector between the early 1960s and mid-1970s. "Environmental Regulations and Productivity Growth," in Henry M. Peskin, Paul R. Portney, and Allen Kneese, eds., *Environmental Regulation and the U.S. Economy* (Washington: Resources for the Future, 1981), pp. 555–75.

Robin Siegel suggested that pollution control expenditures lowered the annual productivity growth rate by as much as half of a percentage point in 1965–73. See "Why Has Productivity Slowed Down?" *Data Resources U.S. Review*, vol. 1 (March 1979), pp. 1.59–1.65.

Sectoral and Industry Studies

In a paper examining numerous components of the productivity slowdown, J. R. Norsworthy, Michael J. Harper, and Kent Kunze found that spending on pollution abatement capital from 1973 to 1978 explained 13 percent of the decline in labor productivity growth experienced by the manufacturing sector. See "The Slowdown in Productivity Growth: Analysis of Some Contributing Factors," *Brookings Papers on Economic Activity*, 2:1979, pp. 387–421.

Analyzing both OSHA and EPA regulations, Wayne B. Gray determined that they may have accounted for 30 percent of the decline in productivity growth among manufacturing industries during the 1970s. See "The Cost of Regulation: OSHA, EPA and the Productivity Slowdown," *American Economic Review*, vol. 77 (December 1987), pp. 998–1006.

In a more recent paper, James C. Robinson also studied the impact of EPA and OSHA regulations. Examining 445 industries, he concluded that the "cumulative impact of regulation is analoguous to the cumulative impact of compound interest rates, but with the opposite effect on economic assets." Through 1986, multifactor productivity was lowered by 11.4 percent from the level it would have achieved absent the two sets of regulatory activities. "The Impact of Environmental and Occupational Health Regulation on Productivity Growth in U.S. Manufacturing," *Yale Journal on Regulation*, vol. 12 (1995), pp. 387–434.

Analyzing the effect of sulfur dioxide emission controls on the utility sector for 1973–79, Frank M. Gollop and Mark Roberts found the that annual average rate of productivity growth for utilities dropped by 0.59 of a percentage point per year. See "Environmental Regulations and Productivity Growth: The Case of Fossil-fueled Electric Power Generation," *Journal of Political Economy*, vol. 91 (August 1983), pp. 654–74.

Anthony J. Barbera and Virginia D. McConnell examined the effects of requirements to purchase abatement equipment in five industries. They estimate that these regulations reduced annual productivity growth rates in their sample by 9 percent to 55 percent between 1961 and 1980. "The Impact of Environmental Regulations on Industry Productivity: Direct and Indirect Effects," *Journal of Environmental Economics and Management*, vol. 18 (January 1990), pp. 50–65.

Wayne B. Gray and Ronald J. Shadbegian studied the effects of environmental compliance costs in paper, oil, and steel plants during 1979–85 and concluded that abatement costs reduced total factor productivity by 5.3 percent, 3.1 percent, and 7.6 percent, respectively. See "Environmental Regulation and Manufacturing Productivity at the

Plant Level," working paper 4321 (Cambridge, Mass.: National Bureau of Economic Research, April 1993). In a follow-up paper Gray and Shadbegian observed significant but smaller negative effects on productivity in the same industries for 1979–90. The authors noted that this is the result of the different time period and measurement procedure. However, they still concluded that a negative relationship exists between a plant's abatement costs and its total factor productivity level. "Pollution Abatement Cost, Regulation, and Plant-Level Productivity," working paper 4994 (Cambridge, Mass.: National Bureau of Economic Research, January 1995).

COMMENT BY ANNE O. KRUEGER

Pietro Nivola's chapter raises a great many questions of concern for public policy. Because a number of them are dealt with at greater length in other chapters in this volume, I want to focus on the relevance of social regulation for the American competitive position, the focal point around which Nivola has organized his thinking. For most issues in social regulation, the considerations are predominantly domestic: if costs and benefits are known and appropriately addressed, there may be international implications, but they should not be of concern (since the evaluation of costs and benefits will already have taken them into account).

To start at the beginning, there clearly are public goods, such as cleaner air or safe drinking water, for which harmful effects stemming from individual or firm behavior are an appropriate concern for public policy. Public policy should aim at minimizing the costs of reducing these effects (such as air pollutants). The decision as to how much reduction there should be will clearly be a function of the costs of the action as well as the benefits. When the situation generates a risk such as increased probability of death, efficient cost reduction entails equalizing at the margin the expected number of deaths prevented for the last dollar of expenditure on each source. When Nivola notes that the ruling limiting exposure to formaldehyde costs an estimated $93 billion per life saved while rulings requiring the use of seat belts cost $100,000 per life saved, he is pointing to an inefficiency in risk reduction. The benefits (in the form of reduced probability of death or other harmful effects on health) could be achieved with lower cost or, for the same costs, the probability of harm could be further reduced. Much of Nivola's concern is that litigation and other regulatory measures are yielding fewer benefits at higher costs than seems efficient.

Inefficiently achieved reductions in health threats impose an unnecessary cost on society and thus reduce welfare below its attainable level. But if they are dealt with in an economically efficient manner, reducing them increases welfare, even if it does not show up in measures of real national income. If measures to reduce the threats had been least-cost actions and had resulted in the decreased productivity and real wage growth that Nivola focuses on, they would nonetheless have improved welfare. Much of the complaint is that they are high-cost and inefficient ways of achieving stated objectives. Thus the author is implying that litigation is a costly way to achieve desirable outcomes, and that lower-cost ways could achieve the same objectives.

Let me now turn to the relationship between measures addressing health threats and international competitiveness. I agree with much that Nivola says. Certainly, the American propensity to attempt to regulate the rest of the world's behavior in the act of protecting its own environment is of dubious value and legality. Other countries are, after all, sovereign (and poor countries naturally question the motives of rich countries that despoiled their own environments during their struggle to develop their economies and now are perceived to be attempting to prevent developing countries from doing the same thing). In addition, it is often counterproductive to dictate their behavior (the excess costs of current regulation may retard developing countries' rate of growth and thus slow down the day when their citizens choose, because they are rich enough, to allocate more resources to offsetting environmental threats).

Beyond that, however, differences in tastes are a legitimate basis for comparative advantage and trade. For there to be comparative advantage, however, implies that there must be a differential impact on costs among tradable goods. If, instead, *all* industries' costs are affected proportionately, real wages in the country achieving cleaner air or water will go down (or, what is the same thing, the exchange rate will depreciate), but there will be no change in the relative comparative advantage of different industries.

If, however, some industries generate more health risks than others and the desired degree of pollution reduction imposes disproportionate costs on those industries, their comparative advantage will to that extent shift to countries willing to accept the higher real wage as compensation for reduced air or water quality. The empirical evidence as to the impact of environmental regulation on costs suggests that costs of individual industries have seldom been increased by as much as 1 or 2 percent. And even when they have been, some of the increase may have come from inefficient and therefore unnecessarily costly regulation. For example, there appears to be little doubt that the pharmaceutical industry in the United States has lost comparative advantage because of high manufacturing costs and delays in testing that may have achieved little, if any, increase in safety.

The main point is that if tastes in the United States are such that heavy costs are imposed on one or more industries and they therefore lose market share to foreign competition, real standards of living in the United States will go down less (for the same improvement in the environment) if imports replace some domestic production. America can achieve a higher level of consumption of goods and a cleaner environment through importing than through domestic production.

To be sure, there are activities that affect not only the national but the global environment, in which case it makes little sense for one country to restrict activities if other countries are not also doing so. International agreements are needed. A major impediment internationally for such agreements is the divide between developed and developing countries. The former believe that pollution rights should be allocated based on existing levels of emissions, or more or less proportionately to current shares of world GDP. By contrast, developing countries believe that pollution rights should be allocated more or less proportionately to a country's share in world population. Until a compromise is reached between these two positions, it will be difficult to achieve the necessary agreements, although the chlorofluorocarbon (CFC) agreement demonstrates that it can be done.

In the absence of such agreements, environmentalists have argued that trade-related measures should be used to impose compliance on other countries. The difficulties with this approach are several. The measures may be counterproductive to other countries' accepting responsibility for their environment, for reasons already mentioned. The trade weapon is a very blunt instrument, and it is almost impossible to use it in a way that is genuinely conducive to meeting environmental objectives without the weapon being seized by protectionists. Finally, there are many countries capable of producing any given good, and some of them are likely to be less influenced by sanctions (or, for that matter, extralegal trade in the commodity) than others. Use of trade measures in effect rewards with higher real incomes the countries that avoid the sanctions.

Within this framework of analysis, there is no doubt that Nivola is right. Many regulations could be replaced with measures that would achieve the same objectives at lower cost. Others would be at least partially rescinded if their costs (or lack of benefits) were recognized. But the chief burdens of these and other inefficiencies are lower living standards than could otherwise be achieved for the same level of environmental protection. They should be addressed because they are imposing unnecessary costs, regardless of whether those costs take the form of changing an industry's relative comparative advantage or raising costs for all industries uniformly.

COMMENT BY HENRY R. NAU

A tenet of popular wisdom is that the United States has a much lower level of regulation and direct taxation than Europe or Japan. For this reason, some analysts argue, the United States has room to tax and regulate (through smart industrial and technology policies) its way back to a balanced budget and global economic competitiveness.

In his chapter Pietro Nivola casts timely and justified doubt on this proposition. By some measures, such as the levels of central government regulation and taxation, the United States scores consistently below other OECD countries. But these measures do not take into account the enormous and rapidly growing costs to American business of the highly adversarial legal system in the United States, as well as local taxes and regulations imposed by states and municipalities. In 1991, as Nivola shows, U.S. tort costs absorbed more than 2 percent of GDP compared to a maximum of 0.7 percent in other OECD countries. In addition, U.S. tax laws and regulations are often more vigorously enforced and, given the greater diversity of American society, involve more severe measures against discrimination than those in other advanced countries. As this comment is being written, the Mitsubishi Motor Manufacturing Corporation is facing a massive legal challenge in the United States over sexual harassment, a form of discriminatory behavior that is seldom cited or enforced in Japanese law.

As Nivola argues, the high costs and inefficiencies of American regulations and litigating practices exact a significant toll on American competitiveness. They are partly to blame for slower growth in output per worker in the United States, which, between 1949 and 1992, grew at less than half the average rate in the other G-7 countries. They also discourage exports and foreign investment in the United States, and contribute to growing trade sanctions on imports as U.S. companies burdened by domestic costs seek protection against less regulated societies abroad by charging foreign companies with social dumping.

Nivola's analysis cannot be dismissed as another market-oriented swipe at government regulations. He is careful to point out that regulations bring many desirable and necessary results. Because no efficient market functions without public trust, confidence in product safety, contracts, and courts is imperative. But efficient markets also require consideration of costs. As Nivola points out, regulations that seek a risk-free environment and ignore the fact that many liability suits involve human error (such as the woman who sued McDonald's because she spilled coffee on her lap) are just as disruptive of efficient markets as companies that sell unsafe products. Nivola's perspective, in fact, helps to depoliticize the discussion of regulations and markets. He recognizes that it is demagoguery to argue that regulations always cost more than they return or that business is not trying to meet a payroll but is naturally racist, sexist, greedy, criminal, and immoral. The issue is more often the balance between the costs and benefits of regulations, not the existence of an arrogant government or a demonic business community.

Nivola's main point is that the balance between regulations and costs in the U.S. economy has shifted to the detriment of America's global competitiveness. This point is almost certainly true, especially since the late 1970s when U.S. regulatory laws exploded and productivity began to slow. Domestic policies are now the main source of U.S. companies' competition in global markets. So-called border policies, such as barriers to trade and investment or other obstacles to international economic exchanges, have been drastically reduced in recent decades. This lowering of separation fences makes countries increasingly sensitive to one another in so-called behind-the-border macroeconomic and microeconomic policies.

During the oil crises of the 1970s, industrial countries expanded fiscal and monetary policies to compensate for demand shocks. In recent years, however, these policies have become less flexible. Monetary policies in all the industrial countries are now focused on maintaining low inflation, and the European Union is moving, albeit in fits and starts, toward a single currency and common monetary policy. Fiscal policies face severe domestic political constraints, and no country any longer sees an expanding fiscal policy as a short cut to global competitiveness.

By default, microeconomic policies have become the principal arena of international competition among the industrialized countries. Ronald Reagan's and Margaret Thatcher's policies recognized this fact early in the 1980s, and the European Community picked up the idea with its Single Market Exercise of the late 1980s. Today, Japan is biting the bullet of deregulation after the disastrous bubble economy of the late 1980s.

Nivola's analysis highlights the importance of microeconomic policies but also underplays an important advantage of America's mixed public-private system of regulation compared with Europe's statist system. The U.S. system, while just as costly, may be more flexible. This flexibility is evident in both the growing and declining sectors of industrial change. Bankruptcy laws are more flexible in the United States and do not carry the stigma that still attaches to bankruptcy in many European countries. In the United States, companies not only go out of business more often, but they do so more quickly. Others downsize more vigorously, and there are no entrenched labor unions and corporatist business institutions to block such change as they do in Europe. In the growing sectors of industrial change, U.S. laws and institutions are more hospitable to small business and entrepreneurial capital that generate new businesses and jobs. Financial laws encourage a robust and risky venture capital and small-capitalization security markets. Many more Americans participate in these markets, both directly and through mutual funds, than do individual shareholders in Europe. Most important, the American ethos of placing more emphasis on individual responsibility and not trying to create a risk-free and permanently secure environment serves the country well in accelerating and exploiting the opportunities for change.

Not surprisingly, therefore, the United States has moved into the service and information economies at least a decade ahead of other OECD countries. Today, it employs less than 16 percent of its work force in manufacturing, while Germany employs 24 percent and Japan 30 percent. American manufacturing productivity has soared and in 1994 and 1995 topped that of Germany and Japan. This transition has reduced the net value-added contribution of manufacturing to U.S. growth, because the prices of manufactured goods have fallen more rapidly than the prices of services. But the shift to services does not signal the deindustrialization of America, any more than the shift to manufacturing a hundred years ago signaled the end of U.S. agricultural competitiveness.

It is true that labor productivity in services has been low and pulls the U.S. average down compared with that of Germany and Japan. But the U.S. economy, with its greater flexibility, provides jobs rather than high wages. Europe and Japan preserve high wages at the price of fewer jobs. Unemployment in OECD countries averages almost twice as much as in the United States. What is more, wages may not be the best measure of worker compensation. Benefits have increased significantly in the United States in the past fifteen years, and total compensation has not declined. Productivity and wages in the service sector may also be on the verge of rising. The U.S. economy has practically completed the task of absorbing new labor in services, a task Europe and Japan are only now beginning.

America has a unique advantage in its flexible microeconomy. That is all the more reason it should not squander this advantage, as Nivola warns, by ignoring the growing costs of its regulatory policies. Rather than imitate Europe or Japan, the United States should engage its industrial partners in a competition in the regulatory area. It should undertake a single-market exercise with other OECD countries, employing the same procedure of mutual recognition that the European Community applied in its Single Market Exercise. This procedure sets a certain floor for health, safety, and environmental regulations and then allows the consumers and the market place to decide the balance between the costs and benefits of regulations that are more strict than the basic ones. As Nivola points out, the marketplace raises regulatory standards as often as it lowers them. Both the United States and Europe would benefit. Europe and Japan would sensitize America to some of the excess costs of its more robust markets, while the United States would compel Europe and Japan to take into account the excess costs of their slowness to change.

NOTES

1. See, for example, Office of the United States Trade Representative, *National Trade Estimate Report on Foreign Trade Barriers* (GPO, 1996).

2. When fully implemented, the amended Clean Air Act is likely to cost an additional $29 billion to $36 billion annually. Its benefits, in terms of improved air quality, have been estimated as $14 billion to $16 billion. Thus costs appear to exceed benefits by a median margin of more than $17 billion. See Paul R. Portney, "Policy Watch: Economics and the Clean Air Act," *Journal of Economic Perspectives*, vol. 4 (Fall 1990), p. 179. C. Fred Bergsten and Marcus Noland's median estimate of the annual loss of U.S. exports caused by all formal and informal Japanese trade barriers is approximately $13.6 billion. See *Reconcilable Differences? United States-Japan Economic Conflict* (Washington: Institute for International Economics, 1993), p. 189.

3. The notable enactments were the Food Quality Protection Act of 1996 and the Safe Drinking Water Act of 1996. For a description of the Republican retreat on environmental regulation, see "The Great Environment Divide," *Economist*, April 6, 1996, pp. 23–24. Also, Margaret Kriz, "Not-So-Silent-Spring," *National Journal*, March 9, 1996, pp. 522–26.

4. With strong bipartisan support, Congress overrode Clinton's veto of the Securities Litigation Reform Act in December 1995. A few months later, however, the president killed the Product Liability Fairness Act, a bill establishing minimal standards for liability awards.

5. Interior Secretary Bruce Babbit, quoted in John H. Cushman Jr., "Congress Likely to Repeat Many Environmental Disputes as New Budget Takes Shape," *New York Times*, May 26, 1996, p. 16.

6. *Adarand Constructors, Inc. v. Pena, et al.*, 115 S. Ct. 2097 (1995); *BMW of North America, Inc. v. Gore*, 64 USLW 4335 (1996). No sooner was the ink dry on the latter decision than another Alabama jury awarded a record $150 million in damages in a case involving allegedly faulty door latches on a General Motors vehicle. Ronald Smothers, "Jury's $150 Million Award Against G.M. Touches Off Furor," *New York Times*, June 5, 1996, p. A17.

7. From the mid-1980s through the early 1990s, exports accounted for more than 40 percent of the growth in U.S. output. During the 1980s, foreign direct investment in the United States exceeded U.S. direct investment abroad. U.S. sales of foreign owned nonbank companies doing business in the United States rose from $194 billion in 1977 to $1.18 trillion by 1990. That year, foreign-owned units employed 4.7 million Americans, or approximately 4 percent of the civilian work force. F. M. Scherer, *Competition Policies for an Integrated World Economy* (Brookings, 1994), pp. 14–15.

8. Richard J. Herring and Robert E. Litan, *Financial Regulation in the Global Economy* (Brookings, 1994), pp. 23–24. On the new vulnerabilities of this dependency, as brought home by the crisis of the Mexican peso in early 1995, see for instance William Glasgall and others, "Hot Money," *Business Week*, March 20, 1995, pp. 47–48.

9. Robert A. Kagan, "Adversarial Legalism and American Government," *Journal of Policy Analysis and Management*, vol. 10, no. 3 (1991), pp. 369–406.

10. For the best cross-national comparison of systems of corporate governance, including regulatory structures, see Mitsuhiro Fukao, *Financial Integration, Corporate Governance, and the Performance of Multinational Companies* (Brookings, 1995), esp. pp. 116–17, for examples of U.S. stringency.

11. This is not a fictitious illustration. See the account in Max Boot, "A Rotten Fate," *Wall Street Journal*, November 3, 1995, p. A14.

12. The federal minimum wage, mandated under the Fair Labor Standards Act of 1938, also covers overtime work, which must be compensated at a rate one and one-half times the worker's regular rate of pay. In addition, the FLSA bans various activities, including some kinds of work, notably sewing and apparel making, in an employee's home without prior approval of the Department of Labor and certain kinds of hazardous work by people under the age of eighteen. Simon Rottenberg, *Mandates in Employment: A History of Added Burdens on the Unskilled* (Washington: Employment Policies Institute, 1994), p. 11.

13. Poor judgment was considered a symptom of mental or psychological disorder, and thus an impairment qualifying as a disability, in at least one ADA court case. Edward Felsenthal, "Potentially Violent Employees Present Bosses with a Catch 22," *Wall Street Journal*, April 5, 1995, p. B1. In another case a person with "body odor" sued Citicorp under the ADA, contending that the company should accommodate this disability just as it would any other handicap. Rochelle Sharpe, "A Mysterious Matter of Body Odor Turns into a Federal Case," *Wall Street Journal*, October 18, 1994, p. A1.

14. The Office of Federal Contract Compliance Programs has extensive jurisdiction. Federal contractors account for about 30 percent of private sector employment. David M. O'Neill and June O'Neill, "Affirmative Action in the Labor Market," *Annals of the American Academy of Political and Social Science*, vol. 523 (September 1992), p. 90.

15. Richard Edwards, *Rights at Work: Employment Relations in the Post-Union Era* (Brookings, 1993), p. 191, has commented, "Waiting in the wings are bills on 'cafeteria-plan' benefits, child care, the introduction of certain new technologies, privacy rights, health hazards from video display terminals, comparable-worth pay, and other issues."

16. Peter H. Lewis, "The Executive Computer: When Computing Power Is Generated by the Lawyers," *New York Times*, July 22, 1990, sec. 3, p. 4.

17. One study in the 1980s found that a handful of entrepreneurial California law firms routinely filed class action suits against *every* computer company if the value of its stock decreased substantially in the half-year following an initial offering. Janet Cooper Alexander, "Do the Merits Matter? A Study of Settlements in Securities Class Actions," *Stanford Law Review*, vol. 43 (February 1991), pp. 497–598. About these actions, Robert A. Kagan has written, "The plaintiffs' lawyers clearly filed suit merely on the basis of the stock decline, without any prior evidence of fraud or other securities laws vi-

olations, and then sought detailed pretrial discovery that probed for evidence that management had in some way exaggerated the company's product quality or sales prospects." "Do Lawyers Cause Adversarial Legalism? A Preliminary Inquiry," *Law and Social Inquiry*, vol. 19 (Winter 1994), pp. 42–43, note 143. Conditions were little better in the 1990s. Between 1990 and 1993, seventy-five shareholder class actions were filed in the Northern District of California, two-thirds against high-tech companies. More than half of the top 150 Silicon Valley companies were sued between 1990 and 1995. Nanette Byrnes, "Valley of the Pols," *Business Week*, August 28, 1995, p. 72.

18. Alexis de Tocqueville, *Democracy in America*, J. P. Mayer and Max Lerner, eds. (Harper and Row, 1966), p. 248.

19. Quoted in Charles Warren, *A History of the American Bar* (Buffalo: William S. Hein, 1990), p. 217.

20. Melinda Warren, "Reforming the Federal Regulatory Process: Rhetoric or Reality?" occasional paper 138, Center for the Study of American Business, Washington University, June 1994, p. 2; "America's Parasite Economy," *Economist*, October 10, 1992, p. 22; and Jonathan Rauch, "The Regulatory President," *National Journal*, vol. 23 (November 30, 1991), p. 2905. By 1991, Americans were spending an estimated 6.5 billion hours filling out forms and compiling records for the federal government. David M. Mcintosh and Murray Weidenbaum, "Will Clinton Let Republicans Help Him?" *Wall Street Journal*, February 23, 1995, p. A14.

21. Michael J. Boskin and others, "Reflections on the Bush Regulatory Record," *Regulation*, vol. 16, no. 3 (1993), p. 23. The 1970s saw the enactment of the Occupational Safety and Health Act, the Consumer Product Safety Act, the National Highway Safety Act, the Equal Employment Opportunity Act, section 503 of the Rehabilitation Act, the Employee Retirement Income Security Act, the Clean Air Act, and the amended Water Pollution Control Act. But in the 1980s Congress enacted amendments to the Age Discrimination in Employment Act, the Hazardous and Solid Waste Act, the Social Security Act, and the Fair Housing Act. It also passed the Asbestos Hazard Emergency Response Act, Civil Rights Restoration Act, another Highway Safety Act and Commercial Motor Vehicle Safety Act, the Lead Contamination Control Act, Ocean Dumping Ban Act, Migrant and Seasonal Agricultural Worker Protection Act, health insurance provisions for terminated workers in the 1985 Consolidated Omnibus Budget Reconciliation Act (COBRA), Immigration Reform and Control Act, Employee Polygraph Protection Act, Drug-Free Workplace Act, Worker Adjustment and Retraining Notification Act, Water Quality Act, and amendments to the Safe Drinking Water Act. The so-called Pollution Prevention Act and the Older Workers Benefit Protection Act, plus the Family and Medical Leave Act, the ADA, and the Clean Air Act amendments, were products of the 1990s.

22. Peter H. Stone, "Back Off!" *National Journal*, December 3, 1994, p. 2841.

23. Lisa Genasci, "Employment Practices: Does One Policy Undermine Another?" *Washington Post*, March 12, 1995, p. H6.

24. James V. DeLong, "The Criminalization of Just About Everything," *American Enterprise*, vol. 5 (March-April, 1994), p. 29.

25. For a perspective on the heavy hand of state and local regulation, see Philip K. Howard, *The Death of Common Sense: How Law is Suffocating America* (Random House, 1994).

26. General Accounting Office, *Workplace Regulation: Information on Selected Employer and Union Experiences*, vol. 1 (June 1994), p. 5.

27. Eugene Bardach and Robert A. Kagan, "Liability Law and Social Regulation," in Eugene Bardach and Robert A. Kagan, eds., *Social Regulation: Strategies for Reform* (San Francisco: Institute for Contemporary Studies, 1982), pp. 252–54; and American Assembly, *Tort Law and the Public Interest: Competition, Innovation, and the Consumer Welfare* (Columbia University, 1990), pp. 7–9. Federal product liability suits grew at an annual rate of 14 percent from 1976 to 1986. In California, tort cases (not including claims from automobile accidents) increased 74 percent. Deborah R. Hensler, "Reading the Tort Litigation Tea Leaves: What's Going On in the Civil Liability System?" *Justice System Journal*, vol. 16, no. 2 (1993), p. 143.

28. It is hard to tell how far state-level tort reform has actually gone. Proposed revisions have included caps on damage awards, modification of joint and several liability, regulatory approvals as a conclusive defense, changes in the collateral source rule, fee-shifting rules for attorney compensation, consumer contract law limiting tort liability, and insurance or compensation schemes in lieu of liability. In states famous for tort suits, the progress of any of these ideas has been uneven at best.

29. Brian J. Ostrom and Neal B. Kauder, *Examining the Work of State Courts, 1993: A National Perspective from the Court Statistics Project* (State Justice Institute, 1993), p. 19. Between 1984 and 1990, tort filings rose at a rate of 4 percent annually in the eighteen states for which detailed caseload data are available. The tort caseload in the federal courts rose 3.5 percent annually during the same period. For some reason, legal scholars call such rates of increase modest. Would that the U.S. economy consistently grew so well. Hensler, "Reading the Tort Litigation Tea Leaves," pp. 142–43.

30. There were fewer than 1,500 lawyers per 1 million Americans in 1970. By 1980 there were approximately 2,300, and by 1990 approximately 3,000. Jonathan Rauch, *Demosclerosis: The Silent Killer of American Government* (Times Books, 1994), p. 81. The United States has three times as many lawyers per 1,000 persons as Germany, ten times as many as Sweden, and twenty times as many as Japan. Derek C. Bok, "A Flawed System," *Harvard Magazine*, vol. 85 (May-June 1983), p. 40. Expenditures on lawyers in this country grew sixfold between 1960 and 1987, tripling the share of GNP devoted to legal services. Kagan, "Lawyers," pp. 11–12.

31. Mary E. Reid, "Words That May Later Haunt You," *Wall Street Journal*, December 20, 1993, p. C12; Barbara Whitaker, "Infertility Is a New Focus of Workplace Lawsuits," *New York Times*, April 21, 1996, sec. 3, p. 12; and Junda Woo, "Businesses Find Suits on Security Hard to Defend," *Wall Street Journal*, September 1, 1993, p. B1.

32. The United States has been the great job engine of the industrial world, with a 38 percent increase in employment from 1973 to 1990 compared with 19 percent in Japan and just 8 percent in Europe. Paul Krugman, *Peddling Prosperity: Economic Sense and Nonsense in the Age of Diminished Expectation* (Norton, 1994), p. 262.

33. Excessive bureaucratic control clearly bears relation to the recent stagnation of Japan's economy. Estimates suggest that deregulation could add perhaps half a percentage point to the country's economic growth. Daniel P. Hamilton, Michael Williams, and Norihiko Shirouzu, "Japan's Big Problem: Freeing Its Economy from Over-Regulation," *Wall Street Journal*, April 25, 1995, p. A13. For a catalogue of regulatory flaws that threaten to make Tokyo a financial backwater, see "Tokyo Rust Belt," *Wall Street Journal*, October 3, 1994, p. A20.

34. Albert Gore quoted in Fred Barnes, "What It Takes," *New Republic*, October 19, 1992, p. 24; and see also, "In Their Own Words; Transcript of Speech by Clinton Accepting Democratic Nomination," *New York Times*, July 17, 1992, p. A14.

35. Barry Bosworth and George L. Perry, "Productivity and Real Wages: Is There a Puzzle?" *Brookings Papers on Economic Activity*, 1:1994, pp. 329–30.

36. We tend to speak of Europe as if it were a monolith, obscuring the important variations in employment policies there. See, for instance, Martin Rhodes, "A Regulatory Conundrum: Industrial Relations and the Social Dimension," in Stephan Leibfried and Paul Pierson, eds., *European Social Policy: Between Fragmentation and Integration* (Brookings, 1995), especially pp. 91–94.

37. The trend in class action suits can be likened to a process of income redistribution. Dow Chemical's 1985 settlement of the Agent Orange suits involved payments to 250,000 claimants. Litigation bankrupted most asbestos manufacturers, including Johns-Manville, the largest, with legal bills and payments to 270,000 claimants. The Dalkon Shield controversy eventually forced $2.5 billion in payments to 327,000 claimants. And as of 1996, in the largest of all mass torts, the one over silicone breast implants, 480,000 claimants were in line for $325 million from 3M Corporation, $556 million from Baxter International, $1.15 billion from Bristol-Myers Squibb, and $2.02 billion from Dow Corning (which, having already spent $1 billion defending itself, declared bankruptcy). Joseph Nocera, "Fatal Litigation," *Fortune*, October 16, 1995, p. 75; Linda Himelstein and others, "A Breast-Implant Deal Comes Down to the Wire," *Business Week*, September 4, 1995, p. 89; and John A. Byrne, "Informed Consent," *Business Week*, October 2, 1995, p. 104.

38. Peter W. Huber, *Liability: The Legal Revolution and Its Consequences* (Basic Books, 1988), p. 150; and Kagan, "Adversarial Legalism," p. 55.

39. Jeremy Rabkin, *Judicial Compulsions: How Public Law Distorts Public Policy* (Basic Books, 1989), p. 187. Thus, following the 1962 amendments to the U.S. Food and Drug Act, four times as many drugs were pioneered in Great Britain during the 1970s as in the United States. The productivity of research and development (measured by new chemical entities introduced per dollar of R&D expenditures) declined sixfold among U.S. companies. Comparable

companies in the United Kingdom did not experience the same effect. Henry G. Grabowski, John M. Vernon, and Lacy Glenn Thomas, "Estimating the Effects of Regulation on Innovation: An International Comparative Analysis of the Pharmaceutical Industry," *Journal of Law and Economics*, vol. 21 (April 1978), p. 133. Quick approval of aseptic food packaging in Switzerland and Germany turned these countries into dominant suppliers for the U.S. market pending a U.S. regulatory decision that came a decade later. Michael E. Porter, *The Competitive Advantage of Nations* (Free Press, 1990), p. 649.

40. Office of Technology Assessment, *Industry, Technology, and the Environment: Competitive Challenges and Business Opportunities* (GPO, 1994), p. 214.

41. Ibid., pp. 184, 201–07. During the decade of the 1980s, for example, capital expenditures on pollution control equipment by Japanese manufacturers remained essentially unchanged, whereas expenditures by U.S. manufacturers rose sharply, more than doubling Japan's level of expenditures by 1990. The contrast in key industries, chemicals for instance, was even more striking. And the costs of compliance in Japan and other foreign countries may be, if anything, overstated owing to more generous tax incentives (accelerated depreciation, for example) for pollution controls.

42. See Piritta Sorsa, "Competitiveness and Environmental Standards: Some Exploratory Results," Policy Research Working Paper 1249, World Bank, Washington, February 1994, p. 22.

43. Pietro S. Nivola and Robert W. Crandall, *The Extra Mile: Rethinking Energy Policy for Automotive Transportation* (Brookings, 1995), p. 13.

44. See *Economic Instruments for Environmental Protection* (Paris: OECD, 1989); Joshua Duhl, *Effluent Fees: Present Practice and Future Potential* (Washington: American Petroleum Institute, 1993); and James J. Quinn, *Water Quality Management: Policy and Practice in Selected Countries* (Washington: American Petroleum Institute, 1992).

45. Robert J. Flanagan, "Labor Market Behavior and European Economic Growth," in Robert Z. Lawrence and Charles L. Schultze, eds., *Barriers to European Growth: A Transatlantic View* (Brookings, 1987), p. 211. We think of the United States as the only remaining industrial country clinging to strict employment-at-will doctrine. This is misleading. Only Delaware, Florida, Georgia, Louisiana, and Mississippi have remained strict employment-at-will states. See Cameron D. Reynolds and Morgan O. Reynolds, "State Court Restrictions on the Employment-at-Will Doctrine," *Regulation*, no. 1 (1995), pp. 57–66.

46. Audrey Choi and Maureen Kline "Fiat Has Designs on Future Big Markets," *Wall Street Journal*, June 20, 1995, p. A8; and Peter Gumbel and Audrey Choi, "Germany Making Comeback, with Daimler in the Lead," *Wall Street Journal*, April 7, 1995, p. A10. Cutbacks have been severe in Japan as well. As an extreme example, NKK Corporation slashed its work force by 40 percent between 1992 and 1996. "World Wire: Japan's NKK to Cut More Jobs," *Wall Street Journal*, March 15, 1996, p. A6.

47. Julia Flynn, "Finally, the Payoff from Thatcher's Revolution," *Business Week*, February 21, 1994, p. 48.

48. Richard B. Freeman, "How Labor Fares in Advanced Economies," in Richard B. Freeman, ed., *Working under Different Rules* (Russell Sage, 1994), p. 7.

49. And, one might note, the Japanese employers face virtually no age discrimination lawsuits. At the end of the 1980s, antiage bias suits, under the Age Discrimination in Employment Act of 1986, were costing U.S. companies almost three times as much as their race and sex bias cases combined. See Irene Pave, "They Won't Take It Anymore," *Across the Board*, vol. 27 (November 1990), pp. 18–23.

50. Employment Policy Foundation, "Compensatory and Punitive Damages under Title VII—A Foreign Perspective," Policy Paper (1992), pp. 3–11. See also Richard W. Stevenson, "Job Discrimination in Europe: Affirmative Laissez Faire," *New York Times*, November 26, 1995, p. 10.

51. What is more, parts of U.S. law can hold managers personally liable for the damages. Frances A. McMorris, "Boss May Be Personally Liable If Firing Violates Disability Law," *Wall Street Journal*, May 2, 1995, p. B1.

52. Cited in Employment Policy Foundation, "Compensatory and Punitive Damages," pp. 10–11. For an account of EEOC enforcement of "disparate impact" cases against small firms in the Chicago area, see James Bovard, "The Latest EEOC Quota Madness," *Wall Street Journal*, April 27, 1995, p. A14. The overall *direct* expenses incurred by businesses to comply with U.S. civil rights rules have been estimated at $5 billion to $8 billion a year. Murray Weidenbaum, "Regulations on Employers Repress the Willingness to Hire," *Los Angeles Times*, November 7, 1993, p. D2.

53. Rebecca Blank, "Does a Larger Social Safety Net Mean Less Economic Flexibility?" in Freeman, ed., *Working under Different Rules*, p. 184.

54. See Robert A. Kagan, "What Makes Uncle Sammy Sue?" *Law and Society Review*, vol. 21, no. 5 (1988), p. 721; also, Robert A. Kagan and John T. Scholz, "The 'Criminology of the Corporation' and Regulatory Enforcement Strategies," in Keith Hawkins and John M. Thomas, eds., *Enforcing Regulation* (Boston: Kluwer-Nijhoff, 1984). The evolving concept of environmental criminality is curious. For most crimes, prosecutors must demonstrate that an individual acted with specific intent. But in so-called environmental crimes the prosecution must only show that someone acted "knowingly." No proof of intent to cause injury or harm has to be established. Increasingly, it would appear, the interpretation of "knowing" approaches strict liability, in which individuals can be held liable even when no intended wrongdoing is involved. Murray Weidenbaum, "The Rising Presence of Government in the Workplace," Center for the Study of American Business, Washington University, November 1991, pp. 4–5.

55. David Vogel, *National Styles of Regulation: Environmental Policy in Great Britain and the United States* (Cornell University Press, 1986), pp. 74–78.

56. On the administrative paralysis resulting from lawyering and judicial activism, see Rabkin, *Judicial Compulsions*, chaps. 6 and 7. It is estimated that more than 80 percent of the EPA's regulations have been challenged in court. Lawrence Susskind and Gerard McMahon, "The Theory and Practice of Negotiated Rulemaking," *Yale Journal on Regulation*, vol. 3 (Fall 1985), p. 134; and Gary C. Bryner, *Bu-*

reaucratic Discretion: Law and Policy in Federal Regulatory Agencies (Pergamon Press, 1987), p. 117. Similarly, of the thirty health standards that OSHA issued since the early 1970s, twenty-seven were challenged in lawsuits. Stone, "Back Off!" p. 2843.

57. Michael S. Greve, "Environmentalism and Bounty Hunting," *Public Interest*, vol. 97 (Fall 1989), pp. 15–29. A number of U.S. regulatory statutes give citizens and advocacy groups the right to sue state and local governments for alleged underenforcement of federal laws, to sue the federal government for inadequate oversight of the states, and to sue regulatory violators directly if they seem not to have been adequately punished by government officials. The idea of "private attorneys general" filing citizen suits against government agencies to ensure enforcement of public regulations is largely an American invention. European and Japanese law sharply limits such forms of political participation.

58. See Alan O. Sykes, *Product Standards for Internationally Integrated Goods Markets* (Brookings, 1995), especially pp. 36–40. In the ensuing discussion I draw extensively on Christopher C. DeMuth, "Domestic Regulation and International Competitiveness," paper prepared for a Conference on United States Productivity, Brown University, February 1981, pp. 3–20.

59. DeMuth, "Domestic Regulation," p. 20.

60. Pietro S. Nivola, "More Like Them? The Political Feasibility of Strategic Trade Policy," *Brookings Review*, vol. 9 (Spring 1991), pp. 14–21.

61. Robert J. Samuelson, "Regulatory Juggernaut," *Washington Post*, November 2, 1994, p. A23; and John F. Morrall, "A Review of the Record," *Regulation* (November-December 1986), pp. 25–34.

62. W. Kip Viscusi, "The Dangers of Unbounded Commitments to Regulate Risk," in Robert W. Hahn, ed., *Risks, Costs, and Lives Saved: Getting Better Results from Regulation* (Oxford University Press and American Enterprise Institute, 1996), p. 155.

63. See W. Kip Viscusi, "The Impact of Occupational Safety and Health Regulation," *Bell Journal of Economics*, vol. 10 (Spring 1979), p. 136; Viscusi, "The Impact of Occupational Safety and Health Regulation, 1973–1983," *Rand Journal of Economics*, vol. 17 (Winter 1986), pp. 578–79; Robert S. Smith, "Have OSHA and Workers' Compensation Made the Workplace Safer?" in David Lewin and others, eds., *Research Frontiers in Industrial Relations and Human Resources* (Madison, Wis.: Industrial Relations Research Association, 1992), pp. 557–86; and Richard Edwards, "Reshaping Employee Protections for a Global Economy," *Challenge*, vol. 37 (January-February 1994), p. 36.

64. Paul H. Rubin, R. Dennis Smith, and Gregg Jarrell, "Risky Products, Risky Stocks," *Regulation*, vol. 12, no. 1 (1988), pp. 36–38. What CPSC product recalls do cause in many instances are sharp drops in stock prices of affected firms. See also W. Kip Viscusi, *Regulating Consumer Product Safety* (Washington: American Enterprise Institute, 1984); and Viscusi, "Consumer Behavior and the Safety Effects of Product Safety Regulation," *Journal of Law and Economics*, vol. 28 (October 1985), pp. 527–53.

65. See Stephen Breyer, *Breaking the Vicious Circle: Toward Effective Risk Regulation* (Harvard University Press, 1993), p. 29.

66. On the perceptibly deleterious effect of liability costs on innovation, see W. Kip Viscusi and Michael J. Moore, "Rationalizing the Relationship between Product Liability and Innovation," in Peter H. Schuck, ed., *Tort Law and the Public Interest: Competition, Innovation, and Consumer Welfare* (Norton, 1991), pp. 105–06; and Louis Lasagna, "The Chilling Effect of Product Liability on New Drug Development," in Peter W. Huber and Robert E. Litan, eds., *The Liability Maze: The Impact of Liability Law on Safety and Innovation* (Brookings, 1991), pp. 334–59. Also, Huber, *Liability*, chap. 10.

67. Marc K. Landy and Mary Hague, "The Coalition for Waste: Private Interests and Superfund," in Michael S. Greve and Fred L. Smith Jr., eds., *Environmental Politics: Public Costs, Private Rewards* (Praeger, 1992), pp. 77–78. In 1994 the Congressional Budget Office estimated costs of Superfund cleanup ranging from $106 billion to just under $463 billion. Katherine N. Probst and others, *Footing the Bill for Superfund Cleanups: Who Pays and How?* (Brookings and Resources for the Future, 1995), p. 18. Suffocating in litigation, the program managed to decontaminate only 52 of the 1,320 designated sites as of 1993. See also Thomas W. Church and Robert T. Nakamura, *Cleaning Up the Mess: Implementation Strategies in Superfund* (Brookings, 1993); and "America's Parasite Economy," *Economist*, October 10, 1992, p. 24.

68. Margaret Kriz, "The Superfund Saga," *National Journal*, October 21, 1995, p. 2594. In one case, *U.S. v. Ottati & Goss*, involving a waste dump in New Hampshire, a company spent an additional $9.3 million to settle a Superfund suit after the contested site was already clean enough for children playing on it to eat small amounts of dirt daily for seventy days a year without any significant harm. (There were no dirt-eating children playing in the area, which was a swamp.) Breyer, *Breaking the Vicious Circle*, pp. 11–12.

69. Robert Genetski, "The True Cost of Government," *Wall Street Journal*, February 19, 1992, p. A14; and Jay Mathews, "Disabilities Act Failing to Achieve Workplace Goals," *Washington Post*, April 16, 1995, p. A1. According to one survey, the employment rate among the disabled actually declined from 33 percent in 1986 to 31 percent in 1994. Steven A. Holmes, "In 4 Years, Disabilities Act Hasn't Improved Jobs Rate," *New York Times*, October 23, 1994, p. 22.

70. Robert W. Hahn and Thomas D. Hopkins, "Regulation/Deregulation: Looking Backward, Looking Forward," *American Enterprise*, vol. 3 (July-August 1992), p. 74. Between 1978 and 1987 no significant progress seems to have been made in traditional measures of quality such as the levels of dissolved oxygen and bacteria in water. Robert W. Hahn, "Clean Water Policy," *American Enterprise*, vol. 4 (November-December 1993), p. 67.

71. Hahn and Hopkins, "Regulation," p. 74; and Robert W. Hahn, "Regulation: Past, Present and Future," *Harvard Journal of Law and Public Policy*, vol. 13 (Winter 1994), pp. 167–229.

72. Robert W. Hahn, "Regulatory Reform: What Do the Government's Numbers Tell Us?" in Hahn, ed., *Risks, Costs, and Lives*, pp. 219, 239.

73. Henderson, "Green Eyeshades," pp. 83–84. It was estimated that EPA spent as much as 70 percent of its 1994 budget on environmental problems

that, according to the agency's own Science Advisory Board, caused low or indeterminate risks to human health. Compared to actions under the Clean Water Act, citizen suits to enforce air pollution rules were relatively infrequent. The 1990 amendments to the Clean Air Act, however, invited far more suits by private plaintiffs seeking civil penalty relief. See Scott M. Duboff, "The 1990 Amendments and Section 304: Spector of Increased Citizen Suit Enforcement," *Natural Resources and Environment*, vol. 7 (Fall 1992), pp. 34–37, 60.

74. Mark French and Peter Jarrett, "The United States: Restoring Productivity Growth," *OECD Observer*, no. 185 (December 1993-January 1994), p. 48.

75. In a systematic analysis, George Priest found little evidence that liability expansion has advanced its chief objective: improved safety. George L. Priest, "Products Liability Law and the Accident Rate," in Robert E. Litan and Clifford Winston, eds., *Liability: Perspectives and Policy* (Brookings, 1988), pp. 184–222.

76. Liability insurance companies typically pay out twice as much in administrative and legal costs as in compensation to injured claimants. Huber, *Liability*, p. 151. Also, *Product Liability and Legal Reform*, Hearing before the House Judiciary Committee, 104 Cong. 1 sess. (GPO, 1995), p. 50. But see also James S. Kakalik and Nicholas M. Pace, *Costs and Compensation Paid in Tort Litigation* (Santa Monica, Calif.: Rand, 1986).

77. The idea here ultimately derives from Olson's theory that differential rates of national economic growth have much to do with the extent to which a nation's economy is devoted to productive as opposed to rent-seeking activities. Mancur Olson, *The Rise and Decline of Nations: Economic Growth, Stagflation, and Social Rigidities* (Yale University Press, 1982). Countries with a high proportion of persons entering the legal profession appear to grow more slowly than countries generating more engineers. Kevin M. Murphy, Andrei Schleifer, and Robert W. Vishny, "The Allocation of Talent: Implications for Growth," *Quarterly Journal of Economics*, vol. 106 (May 1991), pp. 503–30. Also, Kevin M. Murphy, Andrei Shleifer, and Robert W. Vishny, "Why Is Rent-Seeking So Costly to Growth?" *American Economic Review*, vol. 83 (May 1993), pp. 409–14. Along similar lines, see David N. Laband and John P. Sophocleus, "The Social Cost of Rent-Seeking: First Estimates," *Public Choice*, vol. 58 (1988), pp. 269–75; Samar K. Datta and Jeffrey B. Nugent, "Adversary Activities and Per Capita Income Growth," *World Development*, vol. 14 (1986); and Scott M. Fuess Jr. and Hendrik van den Berg, "The Impact of Transactions Activities on U.S. Productivity Growth," *Economics Letters*, vol. 38 (1992), pp. 243–47.

78. Stephen P. Magee, "A Taxing Matter: The Negative Effect of Lawyers on Economic Activity," *Economic Insights*, vol. 2 (January-February 1991), p. 34. Magee's analysis, of course, has been the subject of much tempestuous debate. See, for example, Charles R. Epp, "Do Lawyers Impair Economic Growth?" *Law & Social Inquiry*, vol. 16 (Fall 1992); and Stephen P. Magee, "The Optimum Number of Lawyers: A Reply to Epp," *Law & Social Inquiry*, vol. 17 (Fall 1992).

79. See Jean-Pierre Courbois, "The Effect of Predatory Rent-Seeking on Household Saving and Portfolio Choices: A Cross Section Analysis," *Public Choice*, vol. 70 , no. 3 (1991), pp. 251–65.

80. As Robert Litan cautions, institutions such as the tort system cannot permanently affect the nation's overall trade balance unless they somehow affect domestic saving and investment. Robert E. Litan, "The Liability Explosion and American Trade Performance: Myths and Realities," in Schuck, *Tort Law and the Public Interest*, pp. 127–50. A tort "tax" somewhere between 2 and 3 percent of GDP, however, could be draining almost half the inadequate U.S. pool of net national savings.

81. A variety of biotechnology products, long considered safe in the United States, are still banned in the EU pending protracted safety tests. Current transatlantic trade negotiations are attempting to iron out more of these regulatory differences. Nathaniel C. Nash, "Showing Europe that U.S. Still Cares," *New York Times*, December 3, 1995, p. A20. See, in addition, John Schwartz, "FDA Revises Biotechnology Rules," *Washington Post*, November 13. 1995, p. 19; and Schwartz, "Study Says U.S. Has Better Barrier to Bad Drugs than Europe," *Washington Post*, February 3, 1995, p. 9.

82. Sykes, *Product Standards*, pp. 16–17. The Delaney clause was finally rescinded in 1996.

83. France's strict licensing of wines has been widely regarded as a market-enhancing quality guarantee. Michael Porter cites a number of examples of foreign-made products whose competitive advantage may stem in part from tough standards for product safety and environmental protection in countries such as Sweden and Japan. Michael E. Porter, *The Competitive Advantage of Nations* (Free Press, 1990), pp. 647–48. See also Porter, "America's Green Strategy," *Scientific American*, April 1991.

84. Robert W. Hahn, "The Politics and Religion of Clean Air," *Regulation* (Winter 1980), p. 21.

85. In 1992, for example, the government blocked exports of U.S.-made trucks to Iran to prevent possible military use. The big loser, of course, was not Tehran, which easily purchased its trucks from Europe and Japan instead, but American producers and workers that were frozen out of a $1 billion-a-year market. John Carey, "Export Controls: Clinton Draws a Line in the Sand," *Business Week*, April 18, 1994, p. 54. More than a few stories like this could be told about exports (and jobs) forgone due to cold war–era export controls. The most comprehensive assessment has put the cost of U.S. export disincentives as high as $40 billion annually. See J. David Richardson, *Sizing Up U.S. Export Disincentives* (Washington: Institute for International Economics, 1993), p. 2.

86. The general welfare loss from the Jones Act is in the multiple billions of dollars annually. See Gary Clyde Hufbauer and Kimberly Ann Elliott, *Measuring the Costs of Protection in the United States* (Washington: Institute for International Economics, 1994). On the potential export gains from deregulation of the merchant marine along with ending statutory prohibitions on exports of Alaskan oil (the Trans-Alaska Pipeline Act of 1973 and the Export Administration Act of 1979), see Richardson, *Sizing Up U.S. Export Disincentives*, p. 43. Legislation lifting the twenty-two-year export ban on Alaskan North Slope oil was finally enacted at the end of 1995.

87. Murray L. Weidenbaum, *Business and Government in the Global Market-place*, 5th ed. (Prentice-Hall, 1995), pp. 66–68.

88. Product liability travails at the end of the 1980s may have caused as much as $2.4 billion in export losses for the U.S. chemicals, machine tools, aircraft, and pharmaceuticals industries. Richardson, *Sizing Up U.S. Export Disincentives*, p. 130. Huber writes, "Between 1965 and 1985, the number of U.S. vaccine manufacturers shrank by more than half; by 1986 the nation depended on a single supplier for vaccines against polio, rubella, measles, mumps, and rabies. In the 1960s there were eight U.S. manufacturers of whooping cough vaccine; by 1986 there were only two. And only two major companies, Merck and Lederle Lab, were still investing heavily in vaccine research." See Huber, *Liability*, pp. 156, 166–67. The promising antipsychosis drug, clozypine, was costing four times as much to produce in the United States as in Europe because of liability fears in the U.S. market. Kagan, "Adversarial Legalism," p. 376. In California, biotechnology firms halted or delayed research on AIDs vaccines because of liability fears. Steven Hayward, "Gold Lawsuits in the Golden State," *Regulation*, vol. 17, no. 3 (1994), p. 30.

89. Robert Martin, "General Aviation Manufacturing: An Industry under Siege," in Huber and Litan, eds., *Liability Maze*, pp. 478–99; and Andrew Craig, "Product Liability and Safety in General Aviation," in Huber and Litan, eds., *Liability Maze*, pp. 456–77.

90. Showing what legal reform can do, the General Aviation Revitalization Act of 1994 has helped bring U.S. firms back from the grave by limiting the "long-tail" liability of planes older than eighteen years.

91. See Martin, "General Aviation Manufacturing," p. 486. Seventy percent of the accidents in light airplanes were the result of pilot error, not design or manufacturing defects. Yet plaintiffs and their lawyers ritually filed lawsuits as if manufacturing and design flaws caused all the accidents.

92. Alfred W. Cortese Jr. and Kathleen L. Blaner, "The Anti-Competitive Impact of U.S. Product Liability Laws: Are Foreign Businesses Beating Us at Our Own Game?" *Journal of Law and Commerce*, vol. 9 (1989), pp. 196–201. Du Pont used to supply small amounts of Teflon to the makers of jaw implants. But soon the company found itself spending an estimated $8 million a year for five years defending itself in 259 lawsuits involving these implants, even though it had nothing to do with their design or production. Du Pont won all of the cases but, burned by the litigation, decided to pull its product from the market. Manufacturers of the implants were left to scramble for a substitute. Joe Lieberman and John McCain, "Lifesavers and Lawsuits," *Washington Post*, April 3, 1996, p. A19. Similarly, Dow Plastics stopped supplying polyurethane for long-term implant applications because of the threat of lawsuits. Steve Walters, "Industry Sectors Feel Sting of Product Liability," *Rubber and Plastics News*, May 8, 1995, p. 1. In some instances, the commercialization of abandoned products was ceded to suppliers abroad. Union Carbide, for instance, sold its suitcase-sized kidney dialysis machine to a foreign company.

93. Paul Sweeney, "Full Siege Ahead," *Across the Board* (November-December 1994), pp. 30– 34

94. Between 1991 and 1994, companies that had been sued paid out about $2.5 billion, about one-third of which went to the lawyers. Robert J. Samuelson, "Lawyer Leash Law," *Washington Post*, January 10, 1996, p. A17. The average magnitude of settlements jumped from $5.8 million between 1988 and 1991 to $10.6 million during 1991–92. Frederick C. Dunbar, *Recent Trends in Securities Class Action Suits* (National Economic Research Associates, 1992), p. i.

95. Mike France, "Bye, Fraud Suits. Hello, Fraud Suits: New Federal Legislation Isn't Stopping Class Actions," *Business Week*, June 24, 1996, pp. 127–28.

96. William E. Nothdurft, *Going Global: How Europe Helps Small Firms Export* (Brookings, 1992), p. 3. Paul Krugman notes that even today "the shares of imports and exports in America's GDP are only about half of what they were in the United Kingdom thirty years ago; the U.S. economy is not now, and may never be, as dependent on exports as Britain was during the reign of Queen Victoria." See "Growing World Trade: Causes and Consequences," *Brookings Papers on Economic Activity, 1:1995*, p. 327.

97. Robert Z. Lawrence, *Single World, Divided Nations? International Trade and OECD Labor Markets* (Brookings and OECD Development Centre, 1996), p. 94. Lawrence's data are for 1989. According to Murray Weidenbaum, the figures are higher: foreign affiliates account for 40 percent of total manufacturing employment by U.S. multinationals and 25 percent of their service jobs. See "How Domestic Regulation Handicaps U.S. Global Business," occasional paper 142, Center for the Study of American Business, Washington University, September 1994, pp. 3–4. Most of the empirical research on the trade performance of regulated industries has concentrated on the effect of pollution abatement, the costs of which are more easily measured than are the costs of other kinds of social regulation. For the view that U.S. environmental regulations do little, if any, damage to the international competitiveness of U.S. firms see Robert Repetto, *Jobs, Competitiveness, and Environmental Regulation: What Are the Real Issues?* (Washington: World Resources Institute, 1995). But for a very different assessment, detecting a significant deterioration of net export performance in heavily regulated industries, see Joseph P. Kalt, "The Impact of Domestic Regulatory Policies on International Competitiveness," discussion paper 1141, Harvard Institute of Economic Research, Cambridge, Mass., March 1985.

98. Scherer, *Competition Policies*, pp. 14–15.

99. Gene Koretz, "America's Trade Ace in the Hole," *Business Week*, February 20, 1995, p. 26.

100. Keith Naughton and Amy Borrus, "America's No. 1 Car Exporter Is . . . Japan?" *Business Week*, February 26, 1996, p. 113.

101. After 1989 foreign direct investment flows into the United States fell off precipitously. Edward M. Graham and Paul R. Krugman, *Foreign Direct Investment in the United States*, 3d ed. (Washington: Institute for International Economics, 1995), pp. 2, 13–19. The inflow turned up again, however, in 1995. Fred R. Bleakley, "Multinational Firms Spent $325 Billion in 1995 on Foreign Direct Investment," *Wall Street Journal*, June 5, 1996, p. A2.

102. Philip M. Rosenzweig, "The New 'American Challenge': Foreign Multinationals in the United States," *California Management Review*, vol. 36 (Spring 1994), pp. 109, 111.

103. Some sectors are a lot more open than others. Requirements that at least 75 percent of the voting interest in a domestic airline company be U.S. citizens, for example, has posed a barrier to foreign mergers and acquisitions. See James E. Gjerst, "Crippling United States Airlines: Archaic Interpretations of the Federal Aviation Act's Restrictions on Foreign Capital Investments," *American University Journal of International Law & Policy*, vol. 7 (1991), pp. 173–74.

104. Walter E. Hoadley, "Excessive Litigation—Negative Force in the Economy," *Business Economics*, vol. 27 (October 1992), p. 14.

105. See Douglas J. Besharov, "Forum-Shopping, Forum-Skipping, and the Problem of International Competitiveness," in Walter Olsen, ed., *New Directions in Liability Law*, Proceedings of the Academy of Political Science, vol. 37, no. 1 (New York: Academy of Political Science, 1988), p. 143.

106. Cortese and Blaner, "Anti-Competitive Impact of U.S. Product Liability Laws," p. 199. Viscusi studied more than 10,000 product liability claims and found that plaintiffs had more difficulty suing foreign-based firms. See Paul Dykewicz, "Product Liability Scare Causes Business to Flee," *Journal of Commerce*, May 21, 1992, p. 8A.

107. Paul M. Barrett, "How a Bad Paint Job May Put Brakes on Big Punitive Rewards," *Wall Street Journal*, March 9, 1995, p. B1; and Barrett, "Top Courts Punitive-Damages Ruling Won't Help Defendants in Many Cases," *Wall Street Journal*, May 29, 1996.

108. Jay W. Waks and Patrick M. Muldowney, "Workers' Rights Now Extend Overseas: Applying U.S. Antidiscrimination Law to American Companies Abroad and Foreign Employers at Home," *Corporate Counsel's Quarterly*, vol. 8 (July 1992), p. 43.

109. One survey in 1989 found that more than half of all Japanese companies operating in the United States faced possible employee lawsuits over race, color, religion, age, sex and other types of employment bias. Lairold M. Street, "Helping Japanese Firms Cope with Employee Benefits and U.S. Labor and Employment Laws," *Howard Law Journal*, vol. 35 (1992), p. 383. A 1990 survey by SRI International found almost one in three Japanese firms reporting that they had been accused of discriminatory hiring and promotion practices. Daniel E. Bob, *Japanese Companies in American Communities: Cooperation, Conflict, and the Role of Corporate Citizenship* (New York: Japan Society, 1990), pp. 38–40.

110. Bob, *Japanese Companies*, p. 42; and Waks and Muldowney, "Workers Rights Now Extend Overseas," pp. 42–43.

111. Deborah L. Jacobs, "Costly Lessons in Discrimination," *Forbes*, May 27, 1991, p. 188.

112. Lindsay Chappell, "Alabama Politics Ensnare Mercedes Project," *Automotive News*, February 28, 1994, pp. 8, 36.

113. Pearl Stewart, "Japanese Banks: Bias?" *Black Enterprise*, June 1992, p.

33; and "Sumitomo's CRA Pledge Carries Lessons for Others," *Regulatory Compliance Watch*, February 1, 1993, p. 4.

114. James Risen, "Japanese Plants in U.S.: Is the Honeymoon Over?" *Los Angeles Times*, July 12, 1988, pp. 2, 3; and *Wall Street Journal*, January 10, 1996, p. A8. Maquiladora companies can hire and fire at will, can keep an employee on temporary status for three months, and can vary the length of the workday with ease. For interesting essays on the maquiladoras see Khosrow Fatemi, ed., *The Maquiladora Industry: Economic Solution or Problem?* (Praeger, 1990).

115. Milton Harris, CEO of Harris Steel Group, Inc., quoted in Brian Milner, "Canadian Firms Fear U.S. Justice," *Toronto Globe and Mail*, May 9, 1996, pp. B1, B17.

116. Office of the United States Trade Representative, *National Trade Estimate Report on Foreign Trade Barriers* (1995); Services of the European Commission, *Report on U.S. Barriers to Trade and Investment, 1995* (Brussels: European Commission, May 1995); Canadian Department of Foreign Affairs and International Trade, United States Trade Relations Division, *Register of United States Barriers to Trade, 1995* (Ottawa, 1995); and Mitsuo Matsushita, *Report on Unfair Trade Policies: 1994 Report of the Subcommittee on Unfair Trade Policies and Measures* (Tokyo: Ministry of International Trade and Industry, 1994).

117. European Commission, *Report on U.S. Barriers*, pp. 36–37.

118. The European Union, for instance, has argued that the CRA as modified by the Riegle-Neal Act applies differently to uninsured foreign and domestic institutions, with a potentially discriminatory impact on the former. For a full discussion of this issue, see David Vogel's chapter in this volume.

119. European Commission, *Report on U.S. Barriers*, pp. 55–56, 59–60. Some European companies, Peugeot for instance, have given up selling their products in the United States in part because of the costs of independent U.S. testing. Nash, "Showing Europe," p. 20. On the costs of FDA labeling regulations as a technical trade barrier, see Sykes, *Product Standards*, pp. 21–22.

120. John Zaracostas, "Panel Rules U.S. Fuel Act Operates as a Trade Barrier," *Journal of Commerce*, October 3, 1994.

121. Bhushan Bahree, "WTO's Procedures to Be Put to Test in Gasoline Dispute," *Wall Street Journal*, April 11, 1995, p. A16; and Greg Hitt, "Congress Moving to Block Venezuela Plea on Clean Air," *Wall Street Journal*, September 13, 1994, p. A6. See also Canadian Department of Foreign Affairs, *Register*, p. 16.

122. Cindy Webb, "Boiling Mad," *Business Week*, August 21, 1995, p. 32. Toy and sporting goods manufacturers have experienced similar difficulties, often with even higher stakes. In 1991, for example, a Wisconsin jury awarded $12.3 million, including $10 million in punitive damages, to a Green Bay man who had suffered serious injury on a Slip'n Slide. The plaintiff had alleged that the slippery lawn toy did not carry an adequate warning against adult use. Benjamin Weiser, "Tort Reform's Promise, Peril," *Washington Post*, September 14, 1995, p. A1.

123. *Adarand Constructors v. Pena*, June 12, 1995.

124. See, for instance, Jonathan R. Macey and Geoffrey P. Miller, "The Community Reinvestment Act: An Economic Analysis," *Virginia Law Review*, vol. 79 (March 1993), pp. 291–348. There is debate on this question. A 1984 study seemed consistent with Macey and Miller's subsequent analysis: the CRA seemed to retard branching activity into CRA-defined low-income areas. James R. Booth and Richard L. Smith II, "The Impact of the Community Reinvestment Act on Branching Activity of Financial Institutions," *Journal of Bank Research*, vol. 15 (Summer 1984). Some more recent reports suggest better results from the law, at least with respect to mortgage lending. John R. Wilke, "Mortgage Lending to Minorities Shows a Sharp 1994 Increase," *Wall Street Journal*, February 13, 1996, pp. A1, A8. However, recent reports also found a lenders' backlash. See, for instance, Albert R. Karr, "Federal Drive to Curb Mortgage-Loan Bias Stirs Strong Backlash," *Wall Street Journal*, February 7, 1995, p. A1.

125. Nivola and Crandall, *Extra Mile*, p. 112, estimate that a gasoline tax of 25 cents a gallon would have conserved at least as much oil as the CAFE standards did from their inception, but at one-third the social cost.

126. See David Vogel's chapter in this volume. See also Curt Suplee, "Dirty Air Can Shorten Your Life, Study Says," *Washington Post*, March 10, 1995, p. A1.

127. Examples abound of regulatory decisions and legal threats weighing on major firms in these industries. In 1983, while General Motors was being hammered by its Japanese competitors, the company settled an EEOC complaint by agreeing to spend at least $42.5 million to hire, train, and promote more women and minorities. Weidenbaum, *Business and Government*, p. 106. More recently, the Department of Transportation was poised to require a recall of 10 million GM pickup trucks with side-mounted fuel tanks on the theory that perhaps thirty lives would thus be saved. In the spring of 1996 the U.S. Justice Department took Chrysler Corporation to court to enforce an NHTSA order demanding the recall of 91,000 cars on grounds of alleged rear safety belt defects. According to Chrysler, however, there had not been a single incident of rear seat belt failure, injury, or complaint in the vehicles cited by NHTSA. Warren Brown, "U.S., Chrysler Going to Court over Seat Belts," *Washington Post*, June 5, 1996, pp. A1, A24. While this situation was unfolding, Chrysler was also a defendant in fifteen class action suits involving other kinds of allegations. Richard B. Schmitt, "Chrysler Bites Back at Class Action Lawyers," *Wall Street Journal*, March 27, 1996, p. B1. A regulatory and legal environment of this sort creates considerable uncertainties for firms. Not surprisingly, companies such as GM and Chrysler, like many others in the crunch, have periodically turned to trade redress, either on the import side or by demanding more access to export markets.

128. See Pietro S. Nivola, *Regulating Unfair Trade* (Brookings, 1993), p. 24. Tighter environmental controls, relative to the U.S. tariff structure, were associated with an increased exposure of various U.S. industries to foreign competition. See Carl A. Pasurka Jr., "Environmental Control Costs and U.S. Effective Rates of Protection," *Public Finance Quarterly*, vol. 18 (April 1985), pp. 174–75.

129. In 1979 the industry had estimated that it would need to spend $80 billion through 1985 to comply with the government's timetables for improving fuel economy along with safety and emission levels. Nivola and Crandall, *Extra Mile*, p. 93. On the costs of the automobile import quotas of the 1980s, see Robert W. Crandall, "Import Quotas and the Automobile Industry," *Brookings Review*, vol. 2 (Summer 1984), pp. 8–16.

130. For an account of how contracting works at Chrysler (or how "the competitive bid is no longer the center for the supplier selection process") see "The Problems Coming from Supplier-Base Downsizing," *Purchasing*, vol. 118 (February 16, 1995), pp. 101–03. During the early 1990s, while the U.S. trade representative's office was negotiating better penetration of the Japanese and Korean markets for American automobile companies, General Motors and Ford were fighting an expensive war on the home front: vast liability suits involving old models of light trucks and recreational vehicles. In a dispute that remained unresolved as of April 1996, Ford had already paid $113.4 million to settle 334 lawsuits regarding its Bronco II sport-utility vehicle. Saundra Torry and Warren Brown, "Ford Bronco Settlement Thrown Out," *Washington Post*, March 24, 1995, F1. In 1993 General Motors was ordered to pay $101 million in punitive damages in a single case involving the fuel tanks of certain pickup trucks. Weiser, "Tort Reform's Promise," p. A1.

131. Clarence E. Hagglund and Herbert A. Igbanugo, "Are U.S. Product Liability Laws Acting as a Trade Barrier to the Detriment of U.S. Companies?" *Federation of Insurance and Corporate Counsel Quarterly*, vol. 42 (Spring 1992), p. 353. Some of America's oldest machine makers have been sued into Chapter 11. *Congressional Record*, June 14, 1983, p. E2897.

132. Various industries facing the stiffest import competition are sometimes the most injured by domestic regulation. See, for instance, Ann P. Bartel and Lacy Glenn Thomas, "Predation through Regulation: The Wage and Profit Effects of the Occupational Safety and Health Administration and the Environmental Protection Agency," *Journal of Law and Economics*, vol. 30 (October 1987), pp. 239–64.

133. On the ease of obtaining antidumping sanctions and the reasons for it, see Richard Boltuck and Robert E. Litan, eds., *Down in the Dumps: Administration of the Unfair Trade Laws* (Brookings, 1991).

134. The WTO verdict seemed for the most part difficult to contest. Steve Charnovitz, "The WTO Panel Decision on U.S. Clean Air Act Regulations," *International Trade Reporter*, vol. 13 (March 13, 1996), p. 464. After the U.S. appeal was formally rejected, Washington duly promised to comply.

135. See I. M. Destler, *American Trade Politics*, 3d. ed. (Washington: Institute for International Economics, 1995), pp. 240–46.

136. On the case for international standards to internalize cross-border externalities, see Ralph C. Bryant, "Global Change: Increasing Economic Integration and Eroding Political Sovereignty," *Brookings Review*, vol. 12 (Fall 1994), p. 45. A classic example of a successful effort to generalize to the rest of the industrial world a collectively beneficial regulatory policy was the Montreal Protocol of 1987, establishing an international freeze on the use of chlo-

rofluorocarbons (CFCs). Robert L. Paarlberg, *Leadership Abroad Begins at Home: U.S. Foreign Economic Policy after the Cold War* (Brookings, 1995), pp. 79–80.

137. See Nivola, *Regulating Unfair Trade*, pp. 134–35.

138. Compliance with a workers' rights agenda has long been a precondition for granting the exports of developing countries duty-free status under the U.S. Generalized System of Preferences. Terry Collingsworth, F. William Goold, and Pharis F. Harvey, "Time for a Global New Deal," *Foreign Affairs* (January-February 1994), p. 12.

139. These and the ensuing examples are drawn from David Vogel, *Trading Up: Consumer and Environmental Regulation in a Global Economy* (Harvard University Press, 1995), pp. 208–17.

140. Bob Davis, "Free Trade Is Headed for More Hot Debate," *Wall Street Journal*, April 17, 1995, p. A1; Brushan Bahree, "U.S. Renews Controversial Bid to Tie Labor Principles to Trade Privileges," *Wall Street Journal*, April 5, 1995, p. A9; and Bruce Stokes, "The New Linkage," *National Journal*, June 25, 1994, esp. p. 1509. In a speech in Brussels at the end of 1993, the president stressed the importance of putting labor rights, along with the environment and other issues, on the list of topics that he wanted addressed by the new WTO. Clinton reiterated his intentions in a letter to AFL-CIO President Lane Kirkland in May 1994: "We are adamant that the WTO should address the relationship between internationally recognized labor standards and trade."

141. Vogel, *Trading Up*, p. 108.

142. See Paarlberg, *Leadership Abroad*, p. 43–44.

143. Asra Q. Nomani, "Sony Is Target in Rights Action Based on NAFTA," *Wall Street Journal*, February 18, 1994, p. A2.

144. Benn Steil, "'Social Correctness' Is the New Protectionism," *Foreign Affairs*, vol. 73 (January-February 1994), pp. 14–20. Also see Martha Nichols, "Third-World Families at Work: Child Labor or Child Care?" *Harvard Business Review*, vol. 71 (January-February 1993), p. 16.

145. G. Pascal Zachary, "Levi Tries to Make Sure Contract Plants in Asia Treat Workers Well," *Wall Street Journal*, July 28, 1994, pp. A1, A9.

146. Donald C. Dowling Jr., "Preparing for the Internationalization of U.S. Employment Law Practice," *Labor Law Journal* (June 1992), p. 354. See also Clay Chandler and Frank Swoboda, "A Union Rehabilitates NAFTA," *Washington Post*, February 27, 1996, pp. C1, C4.

147. Pollution is directly correlated with low per capita income. Gene M. Grossman and Alan B. Krueger have concluded that a nation's environmental quality improves after it reaches an annual per capita income of at least $8,000. See "Economic Growth and the Environment," working paper 4634 (Cambridge, Mass.: National Bureau of Economic Research, February 1994).

148. Ronald G. Ehrenberg, *Labor Markets and Integrating National Economies* (Brookings, 1994), p. 32. The amended Age Discrimination in Employment Act (like the rest of the civil rights laws) already extends the law's protections of U.S. citizens extraterritorially to discriminatory acts of foreign corporations if controlled by U.S. parents. James Michael Zimmerman, "Extraterritorial Application of Federal Labor Laws: Congress's Flawed Exten-

sion of the ADEA," *Cornell International Law Journal*, vol. 21 (Winter 1988), pp. 103–26. See also David A. Cathcart and Mark Snyderman, "The Civil Rights Act of 1991," *Labor Lawyer*, vol. 8 (1992), pp. 887–88; and Waks and Muldowney, "Workers' Rights Now Extend Overseas," pp. 40–47.

149. Waks and Muldowney, "Workers' Rights," pp. 96, 97, 98.

150. Stokes, "New Linkage," p. 1513. On the presence of sweatshops in the United States, see Susan Chandler, "Look Who's Sweating Now," *Business Week*, October 16, 1995, p. 91.

151. On the likelihood that the productivity comeback of the early 1990s was mostly cyclical, see Robert J. Gordon, "The Jobless Recovery: Does It Signal a New Era of Productivity-Led Growth?" *Brookings Papers on Economic Activity*, 1:1993, pp. 271–316. Total output per worker still grew at a rate of less than 1 percent between 1985 and 1992. Barry Bosworth and George L. Perry, "Productivity and Real Wages," *Brookings Papers on Economic Activity*, 1: 1994, p. 330. Amid a strong economic recovery in 1994, the productivity growth rate was said to have surged to just over 2 percent (a figure subsequently revised down to well under 2 percent). Gene Koretz, "How Fast Is the U.S. Growing?" *Business Week*, February 6, 1995, p. 28. But even under the most optimistic assumption that a leap to 2 percent holds up, the increase would still lag behind the rate of growth from 1960 to 1973, as well as the rate between 1947 and 1973. Bosworth and Perry, "Productivity," p. 330; and Alan S. Blinder, ed., *Paying for Productivity: A Look at the Evidence* (Brookings, 1990), p. 1. By 1996, even Morgan Stanley's Stephen S. Roach, an estwhile optimist about major productivity gains in services, had sobered. Louis Uchitelle, "A Top Economist Switches His View on Productivity," *New York Times*, May 8, 1996, p. D2.

152. Blinder, *Paying for Productivity*, p. 1; Louis Uchitelle, "In New Figures, Productivity Growth Slows," *New York Times*, February 9, 1996, pp. D1, D3; and James C. Cooper and Aaron Bernstein, "Suddenly, the Economy Doesn't Measure Up," *Business Week*, July 31, 1995, p. 75.

153. Martin Neil Baily, Gary Burtless, and Robert E. Litan, *Growth with Equity: Economic Policymaking for the Next Century* (Brookings, 1993), p. 1.

154. The consumer price index may overstate inflation by at least 0.5 percent. Systematically deflating income by that percentage over a twenty-year period lowers estimated median income by perhaps 8 percent. Income statistics also fail to report noncash benefits. Smaller households (owing to higher rates of divorce, late marriages, and longer life expectancies for the elderly) imply a somewhat lower median household income—perhaps as much as 12 percent lower—than prevailed when there were fewer singles in the population.

155. Notice, however, that the number of employees receiving health and life insurance, paid holidays, and other benefits has declined since 1980. Eric Schine, "Benefits Are Being Pecked to Death," *Business Week*, December 4, 1995, p. 42. Supposed gains in compensation, as distinct from cash wages, have been somewhat exaggerated. It is true that many employees have been receiving a greater share of their remuneration in the form of benefits, but the

data on this nonwage compensation can be misleading. The benefits from increased employer spending on social security, for instance, are not enjoyed until retirement. And many studies have found that the primary effect of increased spending on workmen's compensation and health insurance has been better wages for health care providers, not better medical coverage or care. See the readable discussion by Steven Pearlstein, "For Richer, for Poorer: An Election-Year Primer," *Washington Post*, May 5, 1996, pp. H1, H5.

156. Clifford Winston, "Economic Deregulation: Days of Reckoning for Microeconomists," *Journal of Economic Literature*, vol. 31 (September 1993), p. 1281.

157. As of mid-1995, inflation-adjusted wages and benefits were climbing at less than half the pace they set in previous economic expansions. Aaron Bernstein, "The Wage Squeeze," *Business Week*, July 17, 1995, pp. 55, 56.

158. G. Pascal Zachary, "Service Productivity Is Rising Fast—and So Is the Fear of Lost Jobs," *Wall Street Journal*, June 8, 1995, pp. A1, A10.

159. Although society is estimated to have netted at least $36 billion (1990 dollars) in annual savings from various experiments with economic deregulation in the past two decades, the net costs of social regulatory programs that expanded during the same period may well have offset these gains. On the estimated net benefits of economic deregulation, see Winston, "Economic Deregulation," p. 1284.

160. See Robert Z. Lawrence and Mathew J. Slaughter, "International Trade and American Wages in the 1980s: Giant Sucking Sound or Small Hiccup?" *Brookings Papers on Economic Activity, Microeconomics 2:1993*, pp. 161–210. Paul R. Krugman and Lawrence estimate that the likely wage loss from deindustrialization in the face of foreign competition has been less than 0.07 percent of national income. See "Trade, Jobs and Wages," *Scientific American*, vol. 270 (April 1994), p. 47. See also Gary Burtless, "Widening U.S. Income Inequality and the Growth in World Trade," paper prepared for the Tokyo Club Foundation for Global Studies, Dresden, September 1995.

161. Lawrence, *Single World*, p. 101.

162. Ibid., pp. 90, 94. Between 1977 and 1989 U.S.-based manufacturing employment in these multinationals plunged 14 percent, compared to a 1.2 percent decline of total manufacturing employment in the United States over the same period. Meanwhile, employment in their overseas affiliates in developing countries grew about 6 percent. Data for 1989 through 1991 continued to show a decline of approximately 5 percent in U.S.-based employment in multinational parents. By contrast, employment in majority-owned manufacturing affiliates increased by almost 2 percent.

163. See Barry Bosworth, "United States Economic Policy in Asia," paper prepared for a conference of the Tokyo Club Foundation for Global Studies, Dresden, September 1995.

164. Bernard Wysocki Jr., "Some Companies Cut Costs Too Far, Suffer 'Corporate Anorexia,'" *Wall Street Journal*, July 5, 1995, pp. A1, A5. According to a survey by the American Management Association, almost two-thirds of big companies that downsized between 1989 and 1994 experienced either no

improvement in worker productivity or an actual decline. See also Wayne F. Cascio and James R. Morris, "The Impact of Downsizing on the Financial Performance of Firms," working paper 1995-06, Graduate School of Business Administration, University of Colorado, Denver, 1995.

165. By 1988 lawsuits under statutes guarding employment rights were accounting for the largest single group of civil filings in federal courts. Edwards, *Rights at Work*, p. 191. As Thomas Burke shows in another chapter of this book, the litigiousness of employees subsequently intensified, due to the Americans with Disabilities Act and the amended Civil Rights Act.

166. Alarmed by the amount of workplace litigation, growing numbers of businesses are buying the latest species of insurance: employment practices liability. Leslie Scism, "More Firms Insure against Worker Suits," *Wall Street Journal*, November 15, 1996, p. A2. There is a remarkable lack of systematic empirical research on the costs of affirmative action programs and attendant litigation. But see Peter Griffin, "The Impact of Affirmative Action on Labor Demand: A Test of Some Implications of the Le Chatelier Principle," *Review of Economics and Statistics*, vol. 74 (May 1992), pp. 251–59; Joni Hersch, "Equal Employment Opportunity Law and Firm Profitability," *Journal of Human Resources*, vol. 26 (Winter 1991), pp. 139–53; John A. Barnes, "Does 'Diversity' Help Business?" *Investor's Business Daily*, May 17, 1995, pp. A1–A2; Doug Bandow, "Is Business Drowning in a New Regulatory Tide?" *Business and Society Review*, vol. 82 (Summer 1992), p. 48; Robert Frank and Eleena de Lisser, "Research on Affirmative Action Finds Modest Gains for Blacks over 30 Years," *Wall Street Journal*, February, 21, 1995, pp. A2, A6.

At considerable expense about 40 percent of American companies are said to have instituted some form of diversity training. Heather MacDonald, "The Diversity Industry," *New Republic*, July 5, 1993, pp. 22–25; and Brigid McMenamin, "Diversity Hucksters," *Forbes*, May 22, 1995. There are legal and regulatory pressures on companies to perform "culture audits" and create diversity plans. All firms with more than fifteen employees are covered by Title VII of the Civil Rights Act. All firms with more than one hundred employees must submit EEO-1 forms to the Equal Employment Opportunity Commission listing the numbers of each protected group employed at each occupational level. Federal contractors with more than $50,000 in contracts and fifty employees or more must maintain affirmative action programs and report how their payrolls break down by ethnic and racial group and occupation. Many businesses engage in what has been called defensive diversity management, aimed at shielding themselves from possible lawsuits.

"Liability for disparate impact" can be ambiguous and uncertain. Companies commission expensive disparity studies to fathom the concept. Nina Munk, "Fighting over the Spoils," *Forbes*, August 15, 1994, p. 50. Whether these efforts pay off with fewer legal problems, even for the most progressive companies, is not always clear. See, for instance, Laura Bird, "How Hechinger Co., Known for Diversity, Ended Up in Bias Suits," *Wall Street Journal*, February 10, 1995, p. A1; and Kara Swisher, "Diversity's Learning Curve," *Washington Post*, February 5, 1995, p. H1.

167. According to a survey of the literature, the evidence of industrial flight to developing countries is said to be "weak, at best," at least in response to environmental regulations. See Adam B. Jaffe and others, "Environmental Regulation and Competitiveness of U.S. Manufacturing: What Does the Evidence Tell Us?" *Journal of Economic Literature*, vol. 33 (March 1995), pp. 147–48, 159. Unfortunately, only two of the studies reviewed in this comprehensive article actually controlled for differences in "regulatory climate," and none tried to assess intensities of enforcement.

168. See Robert L. Rose, "Work Week: A Special News Report about Life on the Job," *Wall Street Journal*, January 17, 1995, p. A1; and Mathew Cooper and Allan Homes, "The Disaster That Never Happened," *U.S. News and World Report*, February 26, 1990, p. 47.

169. For some industries it is obviously inaccurate to assume that regulatory environments are not determinative. For the aircraft industry, for example, the institutional context is commonly decisive in locational and sourcing patterns. See Daniel Todd, "The Internationalization of the Aircraft Industry: Substance and Myth," in Gijsbert van Liemt, ed., *Industry on the Move: Causes and Consequences of International Relocation in the Manufacturing Industry* (Geneva: International Labour Office, 1992).

170. Peter Gumbel, "Job Losses Soar While Germans Fumble Real Reform," *Wall Street Journal*, February 2, 1996, p. A6. An OECD survey covering 1990–93 found two-thirds of German manufacturing firms intending to expand outside Germany. OECD, *OECD Economic Surveys: Germany* (Paris, 1995), p. 37.

171. Some of the best known American corporations have invested more of their assets overseas than at home: Gillette (66 percent), Mobil (63 percent), Digital Equipment (61 percent), Exxon (56 percent), IBM (55 percent), Chevron (55 percent), Bankers Trust (52 percent), Citicorp (51 percent). One half of Xerox's 100,000 employees now work on foreign soil. Murray Weidenbaum, "A Neglected Aspect of the Global Economy: The International Handicap of Domestic Regulation," *Business Economics*, vol. 30 (April 1995), pp. 38–39.

172. *Product Liability*, Hearing, p. 74. In 1986 Dow Chemical's legal bills and insurance expenses in the United States exceeded $100 million, compared to $20 million outside the country. The company, which does more business abroad than it does in the United States, faced 456 U.S. lawsuits but only 4 foreign suits in 1987."Product Liability in a Litigious Society," *Science*, June 17, 1988, p. 1589.

173. Wilkerson Group, *Forces Reshaping the Performance and Contribution of the U.S. Medical Device Industry* (New York, June 1995), pp. 3–4.

174. James Bovard, "First Step to an FDA Cure: Dump Kessler," *Wall Street Journal*, December 8, 1994, p. A18. Lipomatrix, a company that produced breast implants with a soybean oil derivative substitute for silicone that does not obstruct mammography, moved its entire operation from the West Coast to Neuchatel, Switzerland, following the U.S. breast implant controversy and delays in FDA approval.

175. General Accounting Office, *U.S.-Mexico Trade: Some U.S. Wood Furniture Firms Relocated from Los Angeles Area to Mexico*, GAO/NSAID-91-191 (April 1991), p. 1.

176. Elizabeth Horwitt, "EPA Hangs Tough: IS Escapes Federal Cuts by Passing on Layoffs to Outsourcer," *Computerworld*, December 21, 1992, p. 6.

177. Nivola and Crandall, *Extra Mile*, pp. 122–23; and Gregory A. Patterson, "Foreign or Domestic? Car Firms Play Games, the Categories," *Wall Street Journal*, November 11, 1991, p. A1.

178. See, for instance, the responses of more than 500 chief executive officers to a 1988 survey by the Conference Board. Steve H. Hanke and Stephen J. K Walters, *Social Regulation: A Report Card* (Washington: National Chamber Foundation, 1990), p. 26; and Alison Kittrel, "Tort System Costly Burden, Survey Finds," *Business Insurance*, May 9, 1988, pp. 3, 32. A statewide survey of business by Southern California Edison and annual surveys by the California Business Roundtable found that fear of lawsuits ranked high among the reasons companies have left the state. Hayward, "Golden Lawsuits," p. 29.

179. James N. Dertouzos and Lynn A. Karoly, *Labor-Market Responses to Employer Liability* (Santa Monica, Calif.: Rand Corporation, 1992), p. xii.

180. David Henderson, "The Europeanization of the U.S. Labor Market," *Public Interest*, no. 113 (Fall 1993). Several studies, including one by the Federal Reserve Bank of Cleveland, suggested that rising administrative costs associated with hiring or firing workers held down the growth of jobs from 1991 through 1993. Kristin M. Roberts and Mark E. Schweitzer, "Looking Back at Slow Employment Growth," *Economic Commentary*, Federal Reserve Bank of Cleveland (August 15, 1994), p. 5. The U.S. unemployment rate is low. However, the labor force participation rate stopped rising in 1990. Slow growth in the number of willing workers helps explain some of the low unemployment rate. See Bernard Wysocki Jr., "About a Million Men Have Left Work Force in the Past Year or So," *Wall Street Journal*, June 12, 1996, pp. A1, A6.

181. Even amid the robust economic expansion of 1994, corporate America slashed more than half a million jobs. Matt Murray, "Amid Record Profits, Companies Continue to Lay Off Employees," *Wall Street Journal*, May 4, 1995, p. A1. The average size of companies has shrunk since 1980, and the share of contingent workers as a share of total employment has climbed. The number of temporary workers, for example, tripled between 1982 and 1992. Marina V. N. Whitman, "Flexible Markets, Flexible Firms," *American Enterprise*, vol. 5 (May-June 1994), pp. 33, 36. See also Steven Pearlstein, "Large U.S. Companies Continue Downsizing," *Washington Post*, September 27, 1994, p. C1.

As one executive of a drug manufacturing outfit expained, "The question is, how do you limit risk? You do that by limiting the stuff that's easy to build but hard to get rid of, stuff like buildings and laboratories and big work forces." Kathleen Day, "Now, the 'Virtual Company,'" *Washington Post*, October 29, 1995, pp. H1, H5. Companies at or near statutory thresholds for compliance with various regulatory mandates have especially strong incentives to cease growing or to shrink to the thresholds. Clark S. Judge, "Thresholds of Pain," *Wall Street Journal*, August 10, 1994, p. A8.

182. John A. Byrne, "Has Outsourcing Gone Too Far?" *Business Week*, April 1, 1996, pp. 26–27.

183. John Mintz, "As Aerospace Firms Land Overseas Contracts, Unions Say U.S. Loses Jobs," *Washington Post*, November 26, 1995, p. A26.

184. Not surprisingly, outsourcing has triggered widespread labor unrest, including recent strikes in more than 70 percent of GM's North American assembly plants and against Boeing Company. G. Pascal Zachary, "Skilled U.S. Workers' Objections Grow as More of Their Jobs Shift Overseas," *Wall Street Journal*, October 9, 1995, p. A2. The issue has also dominated recent contract negotiations at Chrysler and Lockheed Martin, among other companies. Nichole M. Christian, "UAW Targets Outsourcing and Layoffs," *Wall Street Journal*, June 20, 1996, p. A2. On a number of occasions, management has gained negotiating leverage by threatening to outsource or exit. During a strike at Caterpillar, management warned openly that if forced to accept union demands, "We would have to move elsewhere, relocate some of our facilities outside this country or in this country." Phillip Siekman, "The War in Peoria," *American Enterprise*, vol. 6 (March-April 1995), p. 78. See also, Bob Davis, Neal Templin, and Brandon Mitchener, "Unions Threatened by Global Economy," *Wall Street Journal*, March 25, 1996, p. A11.

185. During his acceptance speech at the Democratic National Convention in July 1992, Clinton scarcely mentioned international relations. His opening congressional address in February 1993 was also practically devoid of references to the outside world. The same was true of his lengthy State of the Union address a year later. Clinton's campaign and his first-term agenda reflected his electoral slogan, "It's the economy, stupid." Ross Perot devoted much of his campaign to tapping an inchoate protest against globalism.

Both candidates were onto something; public unease with a perceived exportation of American jobs and an alleged American economic decline was discernible. The main 1992 exit poll found a substantial majority of voters convinced that U.S. trade with other countries destroyed more jobs than it created. Earlier polls uncovered other remarkable beliefs—for instance, that many more Americans consider Japan, not the United States, the world's leading economic power, and many more agree than disagree with the astonishing conclusion that "if the U.S. government doesn't do something soon, the Japanese will end up owning most of this country." See Ruy A. Teixeira and Guy Molyneaux, *Economic Nationalism and the Future of American Politics* (Washington: Economic Policy Institute, 1993), pp. 12, 14, 25. There was little reason to suspect that such sentiments had vanished in the mid-1990s, despite the economic recovery. In one of many indicators, a majority of respondents in a 1995 Harris poll blamed increasing global competition as a major reason why the incomes of working Americans "have stayed flat for fifteen years." Harris Poll, "Portrait of an Anxious Public," *Business Week*, March 13, 1995, p. 80.

186. In public opinion surveys the least popular item in the federal budget, by a large margin, has been foreign aid.

187. Guy Gugliotta, "Scaling Down the American Dream," *Washington*

Post, April 19, 1995, p. A21; Harris Poll, "America, Land of the Shaken," *Business Week,* March 11, 1996, p. 64; and Steven V. Roberts, "Workers Take It on the Chin," *U.S. News and World Report,* January 22, 1996, p. 44. As recently as May 1996, 51 percent of respondents in a *Wall Street Journal*/NBC News poll said their own family's income was falling behind. John Harwood, "Economic Insecurity Is Widespread, Poll Finds, But It's Unclear Which Party Can Capitalize on It," *Wall Street Journal,* May 16, 1996, p. A16.

188. Vice President Al Gore quoted in Mike McNamee, "Are You Better Off Now . . ." *Business Week,* March 4, 1996, p. 35.

189. For a broader indictment of unilateralism in U.S. trade policy than I am prepared to make, see Anne O. Krueger, *American Trade Policy: A Tragedy in the Making* (Washington: AEI Press, 1995), esp. chaps. 3 and 4.

190. Part of the difficulty was that many freshman members in the 104th Congress were more skittish about free-trade commitments than was the Republican rank-and-file of previous Congresses. Many new members had campaigned against NAFTA. A head count of eighty-six new House members in the spring of 1995 found only 25 percent in favor of approving fast-track negotiating authority for trade talks with Chile. An even slimmer 14 percent agreed that Congress ought to confer blanket fast-track authority to negotiate with any country. Ben Wildavsky, "Going Nativist?" *National Journal,* May 27, 1995, p. 1281.

191. Paul Lewis, "Is the U.S. Souring on Free Trade?" *New York Times,* June 25, 1996, pp. D1, D4. U.S. negotiators concluded that trading partners had offered inadequate reciprocity.

192. Quoted in Amy Borrus, "Free Trade: Republicans May Be Losing Faith," *Business Week,* February 19, 1996, p. 45; "Choking on Politics," *Wall Street Journal,* December 26, 1995, p. A6; and "NAFTA Gets Serious," *Washington Post,* September 10, 1992, p. A28.

193. "NAFTA Gets Serious," *Washington Post,* September 10, 1992, p. A28.

194. This is not to imply that all trade liberalization is grinding to a halt. The so-called Trans-Atlantic Marketplace framework concluded in December 1995 signalled further reductions of some nontariff barriers. See Mark M. Nelson, "Clinton and EU Will Sign Major Pact on Trade and Economic Cooperation," *Wall Street Journal,* December 1, 1995, p. A10. At the WTO meeting in Singapore in December 1996, countries representing most of the world's high-techonology trade agreed to lower tariffs on computers, software, and related products. Helene Cooper and Bhuchan Bahree, "Nations Agree to Drop Computer Tariffs," *Wall Street Journal,* December 13, 1996, p. A2. Most notably, a global agreement freeing trade in telecommunications services was consummated in February 1997.

195. Krueger, *American Trade Policy,* chap. 4.

196. Even Ronald Reagan chose to use this terminology. See Nivola, *Regulating Unfair Trade,* p. 59.

197. In 1986, for example, a quantitative trajectory for purchases of semiconductors in Japan was negotiated. In 1992 a numerical goal of $15 billion was set for Japanese orders of imported automotive equipment during the

succeeding two years. By 1994 some of the Clinton administration's trade tacticians sounded as if they wanted to negotiate in similar fashion results-oriented sales goals ("voluntary" import expansions) for automobiles, auto parts, supercomputers, medical equipment, and insurance services. For a general critique, see Douglas A. Irwin, *Managed Trade: The Case against Import Targets* (Washington: AEI Press, 1994), esp. pp. 8–17.

198. Clyde V. Prestowitz Jr., *Trading Places: How We Are Giving Our Future to Japan and How to Reclaim It* (Basic Books, 1989), p. 153. More recently, another former trade official used some similar language: "the Japanese government and industry should initiate a results-oriented affirmative action program with the goal of significantly reducing the current account surplus, increasing manufactured imports, and expanding inward foreign direct investment." Glen S. Fukushima, "Affirmative Action, Japanese Style," *Tokyo Business Today* (February 1994), p. 58.

199. As of mid-1995, inflation-adjusted domestic consumption expenditures per person had climbed at only 1.6 percent annually since 1991, compared with an average of 2.86 percent a year in previous expansions. Aaron Bernstein, "The Wage Squeeze," *Business Week*, July 17, 1995, pp. 55, 62.

200. Average personal income rose through the 1977–95 period, but much less rapidly than during 1959–77. Even adjusting the consumer price index downward by 1.1 percent a year does not bring the post-1977 rate of improvement in living standards close to the rate that had prevailed before 1977. See Gary Burtless, "The Progress and Distribution of U.S. Living Standards, 1959-1995," paper prepared for the 1977 annual meeting of the American Economic Association.

201. The Republicans seem to have greatly overestimated the public's eagerness for (and comprehension of) regulatory reform, particularly with respect to environmental policy. In 1974 surveys indicated that 34 percent of Americans believed stronger laws and regulations were needed to protect the environment. In 1994 the sentiment was even more widespread: 41 percent believed existing laws and regulations did not go far enough. See Everett Carll Ladd and Karlyn Bowman, "Opinion Pulse," *American Enterprise* (March-April 1995), p. 108.

202. Quoted in Mike Mills, "Gates Assails Bid to Curb Immigration," *Washington Post*, November 29, 1995, p. F1.

Chapter 3

Trouble for Us and Trouble for Them: Social Regulations as Trade Barriers

David Vogel

A S THE UNITED STATES becomes more integrated into the global economy, U.S. health, safety, antidiscrimination, and environmental policies increasingly have international as well as domestic consequences. Some U.S. social regulations not only impose substantial costs on American industry while yielding little or no net gain to society, but they also disproportionately burden foreign producers seeking to do business here. The two regulatory programs that constitute the primary focus of this chapter, namely, fuel economy standards and rules for reformulated gasoline, fall into this characterization. These regulations have been either inefficient or ineffectual in advancing legitimate domestic health, safety, and environmental policy goals. At the same time, they have discriminated against imports.

Originally enacted in 1975 and most recently revised for model year 1989, corporate average fuel economy standards represent the cornerstone of American energy conservation policy. But the CAFE standards are a dubious means of conserving energy, especially when compared with fuel taxes, the policy adopted by virtually all other advanced nations.[1] In 1993 the European Community, at the behest of European luxury car manufacturers, requested the convening of a dispute settlement panel to hear their complaint that U.S. rules for determining compliance with CAFE standards were discriminatory and therefore violated the General Agreement on Tariffs and Trade.

Another group of regulations, the 1963 Clean Air Act and its amendments in 1967, 1970, 1977, and 1990, constitutes the most costly and important component of U.S. environmental policy.[2] Some of the provisions of these complex statutes have been criticized for foisting substantial costs on producers and consumers while producing relatively meager environmental benefits.[3] For example, in 1990 amendments began to regulate the content of automotive fuel to improve air quality in urban areas. In 1995 Venezuela filed a complaint against the United States with the newly established World Trade Organization, claiming that the method chosen by the Environmental Protection Agency to measure fuel cleanliness under the 1990 amendments discriminated against its petroleum exports to the United States.

This chapter explores the legislative and administrative histories of these two regulatory policies in detail and evaluates their effectiveness in relation to the goals they were intended to accomplish. The cases illustrate the close connection between the regulatory burdens imposed on domestic interests and the emergence of new nontariff trade barriers. The chapter concludes by suggesting that the "least trade restrictive alternative" is often in the best interest not only of foreign producers but of the United States as well.

U.S. Fuel Economy Standards

In 1975 Congress faced the challenge of formulating a long-term plan to reduce the nation's use of oil. At the time, federal price controls on fuel encouraged excessive consumption. Nowhere was this more apparent than in automotive fuel usage, which accounted for 25 percent of American energy demand and the dominant share of domestic petroleum consumption.[4] However, fearful of a political backlash from allowing gasoline prices to rise to world market levels (let alone adding to the prices with an additional fuel tax), Congress chose to shift the burden of conservation onto motor vehicle manufacturers. Indeed, the legislation that authorized the Energy Policy and Conservation Act of 1975, also *extended* the government's price controls on oil.[5]

The legislation approved by Congress established fuel economy standards for all passenger vehicles sold in the United States. These standards were based on the average fuel efficiency of all vehicles sold by each manufacturer. Beginning with the 1978 model year, the average fuel economy standard for all cars produced by each company was set at 18 miles a gallon. A few years later, corporate fuel efficiency standards were set for light trucks as well. Manufacturers whose average fuel economy fell below these standards were subject to fines. All standards were subsequently strengthened; since 1990 the CAFE requirement for passenger cars has been 27.5 miles a gallon.[6]

The Political Economy of CAFE

From the outset CAFE standards sought not only to conserve fuel but to do so in a way that protected the market share of domestic automakers. Congress could have furthered fuel efficiency by combining a tax on gas guzzlers with tax incentives for the purchase of fuel-efficient cars. But like imposing a gasoline excise tax, this action might have reduced the sales of the three major American manufacturers and boosted the market share of their Japanese competitors. As a House Ways and Means Committee report on the CAFE legislation explained, "Currently, many fuel-efficient cars are imported, and [our] Committee did not want the auto efficiency tax to provide a stimulus to increased imports of autos in view of the depressed state of the U.S. auto industry."[7] Corporate averaging represented a way of preventing Japanese companies from taking advantage of their strong lines of fuel-efficient vehicles. The concession by no means satisfied the domestic industry, which continued to oppose any mandatory fuel economy requirement as well as a gasoline tax. But by basing standards on corporate averages rather than the performance of individual vehicles, and by regulating automobiles rather than taxing fuel, Congress did attempt to protect the U.S. firms.

Congress also wanted to design the CAFE system in a way that would protect American jobs. The simplest way for domestic manufacturers to improve the average fuel efficiency of their fleets would have been to import smaller, more fuel-efficient cars from their subsidiaries in Europe and Asia. But this would have reduced domestic employment in an already depressed industry. The United Automobile Workers was prepared to support CAFE standards, but only if it could be assured that they would not cost jobs. Legislators responded to UAW pressure by establishing separate but identical standards for domestic (defined as having at least 75 percent domestic content) and imported passenger cars.

Thus Chrysler, Ford, and General Motors, which manufactured vehicles in the United States and also sold imported cars, would be required to meet CAFE targets for *both* categories of vehicles. American firms would therefore be unable to meet CAFE standards by averaging the fuel economy of their imports with their less fuel-efficient, domestically produced vehicles. By calculating domestic and imported fleets separately, Congress sought to force domestic manufacturers not only to make more efficient cars but to make them in the United States.

Bad Policy

These competitive distortions aside, the CAFE standards have other unfortunate features. Not the least of these is that the standards focus the entire effort to reduce fuel consumption at the point of purchase. This means that once a consumer has bought a (relatively) fuel-efficient vehicle, he or she has no further incentive to conserve energy by, for example, driving less, driving more slowly, or carpooling. On the contrary, because a new vehicle achieves higher mileage per gallon, motorists have every reason to drive more. In other words, as long as gasoline prices remain low, strict CAFE standards reduce the marginal cost of each vehicle mile. In fact, the average cost of driving an extra mile in the United States in 1994 was one-third less than in 1973.[8] The average annual number of miles traveled per vehicle increased from 9,500 in 1980 to slightly more than 12,000 in 1995, a period during which oil prices steadily decreased in real terms.[9] Between 10 and 30 percent of the potential fuel savings from CAFE has been lost as a result of this increased vehicle use.[10]

In addition, reliance on CAFE mandates has not always spurred the transition of the American automotive fleet to more fuel-efficient vehicles. Compliance with the gradual increase in fuel-economy standards has been expensive for American automobile companies, an expense that has been passed on to consumers in higher prices for all new vehicles. Moreover, about 60 percent of the increase in fuel efficiency is due to either a reduction in car weight or to smaller engine displacement, attributes American motorists have tended to dislike.[11] Arguably, CAFE has played a role in slowing the vehicular turnover rate, leaving older, fuel-guzzling vehicles on the road longer.

The average age of cars "on the road" has increased by two full years since the mid-1960s. "Peak demand for new cars in the 1980s was no higher than in the early 1970s, despite higher real GNP and the larger population."[12] Ironically, any part played by CAFE standards in reducing new car sales would depress employment in the automobile industry, thus undermining one of the aims of the CAFE strategy.

The impact of CAFE on fuel consumption has also been tempered by the decision to establish different regulatory standards for different kinds of vehicles. Light trucks, which include pickups, vans, and sport utility vehicles, are required to meet standards of only 20.4 mpg, 7.1 mpg less than passenger vehicles.[13] In part because of this, they often offer a more favorable price-quality trade-off than do passenger cars, and their sales have therefore increased substantially. In 1995 more than 40 percent of the vehicles sold in the United States were in this category, thus helping to lower substantially the average fuel economy of all motor vehicles.[14] In 1994 the average fuel efficiency for the on-road fleet stood at 19.3 mpg, essentially unchanged from the mid-1980s.[15] Congress has made no effort to strengthen CAFE standards for the recreational vehicle category, which may in turn be related to the fact that American firms enjoy a comparative advantage in producing them.

Nearly twenty years of CAFE standards have certainly contributed to an improvement in overall fuel efficiency of new automobiles in the United States. Automobiles sold in the United States in 1990 averaged 28 mpg, twice the efficiency of vehicles produced during the 1974 model year.[16] CAFE deserves credit for this change, although higher gasoline prices in the late 1970s played a bigger role. But the energy conservation that CAFE has achieved could have been accomplished much more efficiently by a gasoline tax. Robert A. Leone and Thomas W. Parkinson concluded that a "gasoline tax required to match CAFE's conservation effect would have reduced producer and consumer welfare by 8 cents a gallon saved while the regulatory alternative actually reduced welfare by around 60 cents a gallon saved."[17] A study by Charles River Associates argues that a gasoline tax would have been far more effective than a fuel economy standard in both conserving petroleum and reducing carbon dioxide emissions.[18] Pietro Nivola and Robert Crandall estimate that a tax of (at most) 25 cents a gallon beginning in 1986 would have yielded as much, if not more, oil conservation as was achieved by CAFE through 1992.[19] Some critics argue that even a much smaller tax would have achieved the same results as CAFE has to date.[20]

Although CAFE has raised the fuel efficiency of new passenger vehicles, it has failed to lower fuel consumption below the levels of the early 1970s. Thanks to the steady increase in passenger miles driven since the early 1980s as well as the significant growth in sales of light trucks during the 1990s, both of which CAFE has perversely encouraged, or at least not discouraged, total fuel usage by all motor vehicles increased by 50 percent between 1970 and 1988.[21] Average motor fuel consumption per vehicle in the United States has remained twice as high as in Europe and Japan.[22] On a per capita basis, American motor fuel consumption is two to three times greater than in Europe and Japan, which imposed no fuel economy requirements on their automobile industries but have much higher gasoline prices. American gasoline consumption reached a record 7.79 million barrels a day in 1995.[23] As the centerpiece of the nation's energy conservation effort, CAFE has clearly fallen short.[24]

Consumer Safety

CAFE standards have also affected the safety of passenger cars. Automobile manufacturers have upgraded the fuel efficiency of new cars chiefly by reducing their weight. According to the National Highway Traffic Safety Administration (NHTSA), each 10 percent reduction in weight increases the fuel economy of new vehicle design by 8 percent.[25] Between 1974 and 1991 the weight of the average new car sold in the United States declined by 20 percent.[26] The doubling of fuel efficiency standards between 1975 and 1985 was due to a 1,000-pound reduction in average new car weight.[27]

But according to the NHTSA, large cars usually offer more protection in a crash than small cars. The greater vulnerability of the occupants of newer, lighter vehicles has been further heightened by the changing mix of vehicles on the road. In 1980 the NHTSA predicted that "with these smaller and lighter vehicles joining an increasing number of heavy trucks and older, heavier cars already on the road, the risk of death and serious injury will increase markedly."[28]

According to studies by Leonard Evans and by Crandall and John Graham, CAFE may have been indirectly responsible for perhaps 2,200 to 3,900 additional deaths for each model year's passenger cars in the ten years following their introduction.[29] Crandall and Graham predicted that cars produced under a standard of 27.5 mpg, which went into effect in 1990, would lead to a 14 to 27 percent increase in occupant deaths. Based on this estimate, the CAFE program is currently costing one additional fatality for every 2 million gallons of fuel saved. Doubtless, a tax on motor fuel would also have increased automobile deaths by inducing demand for lighter cars. But taxing fuel at least would not encourage owners of lightweight vehicles to increase their vehicle miles traveled. Unlike the less flexible CAFE solution, a tax would promote saving oil and lives by encouraging less driving, regardless of the weight of vehicles.

In 1985 the Council of Economic Advisers acknowledged CAFE's impact on automotive safety when it urged that the CAFE standard not be increased. Safety was subsequently raised in CAFE rulemaking hearings by the Insurance Institute for Highway Safety, the Competitive Enterprise Institute, and the National Safety Council. In a lawsuit by two public interest groups that challenged the EPA's decision to raise the fuel-efficiency level for the 1990 model year from 26.5 to 27.5, the plaintiffs argued that the Department of Transportation had not adequately addressed the linkage between CAFE and safety. Although the NHTSA has continued to doubt that CAFE might reduce motor vehicle safety, in 1990 it did cite the safety impact of fuel efficiency standards as grounds for opposing congressional proposals to increase the CAFE standard to 40 mpg. One administrator characterized the congressional initiative as sacrificing blood for oil.[30]

Distortions of Competition

Even the attempt by Congress to devise a way of protecting the American automobile industry while saddling it with additional regulatory costs has proven flawed. Initially, American firms considered CAFE preferable to a gasoline tax, since a tax might have abetted the market position of Japanese manufacturers. However, CAFE soon became a source of competitive advantage for the Japanese. Under its rules, companies are permitted to carry forward any excess credits over the 27.5 standard as potential offsets against future shortfalls and to carry back any excesses to compensate for past shortfalls. By the early 1990s, Japanese firms, which primarily produced small, relatively fuel-thrifty passenger vehicles, had accumulated large carry-forward credits, while General Motors and Ford incurred deficits. These accumulated credits enabled the Japanese producers to increase their sales of upscale cars without compromising fleet CAFE ratings. Japan, in other words, could export in much larger volumes precisely the kind of larger, more powerful models that claim the most profitable niche in the U.S. market. By contrast, the American companies have had to compromise on the designs of comparable vehicles in order to work off accumulated CAFE deficits. The upshot has been less overall fuel economy in the U.S. passenger car fleet but also further Japanese encroachment on the one market segment in which American manufacturers have been particularly competitive. So serious did this situation become that when Congress considered a proposal to raise CAFE standards in 1989, both the American automobile industry and the United Automobile Workers urged that the formula for calculating compliance with CAFE standards be altered.[31] The companies and the union demanded that all producers be required to improve the average fuel economy of their vehicles *proportionately*. This fix would have required Japanese producers to meet much higher standards than American firms because the average fuel economy of the cars Japan sold in the United States was higher to begin with. A spokesman for Chrysler explained, "The whole idea of the percentage increase is that everyone would be required to move upward."[32] Not surprisingly, the new formula was vigorously opposed by the Japanese automobile lobby. A representative of Toyota characterized it as "punishing people for good works."[33]

Not only did the proposed adjustment threaten to provoke another major Japanese-American trade squabble, but the requirement would likely have been flagrantly inconsistent with American obligations under GATT, because it would have required Japanese producers to meet a substantially higher standard than their American competitors. In any event, thanks to heavy pressure from domestic retailers and Japanese firms, Congress made no change in either the formula for calculating CAFE requirements or the requirements themselves. The Japanese continue to produce small to midrange vehicles in the United States, while using their credits to export high-performance luxury cars. (Japanese cars produced in the United States are counted as imports under CAFE because their domestic content is less than 75 percent, thus creating a further inducement for Japanese companies to keep the value added of their production facilities in the United States below the 75 percent threshold.) As Crandall commented, "the Japanese are being invited to compete in the highly profitable large and luxury car segments of the market by our own 'conservation' policies."[34]

CAFE and European Exports

The formula for establishing compliance with CAFE standards has improved the competitive position of the American automobile industry in one way: it has raised the price of European luxury cars sold in the United States. Because CAFE is calculated on the basis of the average fuel efficiency of the vehicles produced by each manufacturer, it has handicapped European makers who produce only the heavier, more powerful cars. Nearly all the vehicles manufactured by Jaguar, BMW, Volvo, Saab, Mercedes-Benz, Rolls-Royce, and Porsche are high-end products with relatively low mileage per gallon. As a result, these firms have been unable to comply with the increasingly strict CAFE criteria. In 1991, while cars exported by European manufacturers accounted for 4 percent of American sales, their manufacturers paid 100 percent of the CAFE penalties. Indeed, in the twenty-year history of the regulations, only European limited-line premium automakers have *ever* been subject to CAFE penalties.[35]

In 1985 the Environmental Protection Agency relaxed the fuel-economy standards for both passenger cars and light trucks after General Motors and Ford claimed they could not meet the original goals. The two companies were relieved of millions in penalties.[36] But European automobile firms have received no such solicitude. They have been required to pay the statutory fine of $5 for every tenth of a mile per gallon that their fleet average falls below 27.5, multiplied by the number of automobiles sold in the United States.[37] These fines have been substantial. In 1983 Jaguar missed the CAFE standard by over 7 mpg and was accordingly required to pay a CAFE penalty of $350 for each car it sold. Between 1985 and 1989 BMW paid CAFE penalties totaling $32 million, Mercedes-Benz $85 million, and Jaguar $27 million.[38] Only one major high-end European car exporter, Saab-Scania, met the 1989 CAFE standards, and that was because it offered cars with four-cylinder engines. Owing to these penalties, American customers were required to pay an additional $1,800 for a Jaguar XJ-S V-12 and $1,500 for the Mercedes 560 SEC sport coupe.

The GATT Trade Dispute

Matters came to a head in 1993. The European Union called for convening a GATT dispute settlement panel. In its complaint the EU charged that "the CAFE regulations are biased toward the full-line manufacturers [in other words, domestic manufacturers] that make both small, fuel-efficient and larger vehicles and limited-line manufacturers that produce mostly small vehicles."[39] The complaint also challenged two other American policies that it claimed discriminated against European automobile exports. One, the so-called gas-guzzler tax, is levied on passenger vehicles whose fuel economy is less than 22.5 miles a gallon. In contrast to the CAFE penalty, this tax is based on the fuel economy of particular models rather than on a corporate average. Established in 1978, the tax was doubled in 1991 and is now levied at a rate of $1,000 a vehicle.[40] To raise additional revenue the United States imposed in 1985 an excise tax on cars bought for business use and costing more than $16,000. In 1991 this impost was amended to apply to all cars costing more than $32,000.

That year the three taxes plus CAFE penalties raised a total of $558 million, of which $494 million was paid by European car manufacturers.[41] The cumulative financial impact was far from trivial. For example, in 1992 Mercedes-Benz paid $216 million in fines and taxes, approximately $3,500 for each car sold in the United States. The EU charged that all three taxes were protectionist because they "individually and collectively have a discriminatory incidence on car imports."[42]

Although the EU's complaint addressed all three American rules, its challenge to CAFE attracted the most attention. American environmental and consumer groups have always strongly supported CAFE, not only defending it against its critics but frequently advocating efforts to tighten its standards.[43] Friends of the Earth sharply attacked the EU's case: "the EC cannot claim to be concerned about the development of the trade and environment debate if it persists in attempting to define . . . whether or not the environmental laws of another country are simply disguised trade barriers."[44] Trade analysts in the United States expressed concern that a GATT ruling against the United States would add to the international body's reputation as antienvironment, given that two of the three laws under challenge were designed to encourage conservation. This in turn would make it more difficult to secure legislative ratification of the Uruguay Round of multilateral trade negotiations. One environmental trade expert predicted, "The CAFE standards are so central to [U.S. clean air safeguards] that it will do the GATT a lot of harm if it does rule against the United States."[45]

The GATT Panel Decision

In its decision in the fall of 1994, the dispute panel found the taxes on gas guzzlers and luxury cars to be consistent with U.S. obligations under the GATT, but held that the CAFE provision requiring separate calculations for domestic and imported vehicles was not. The panel's examination of CAFE focused on the GATT consistency of two of its components: the fleet averaging procedure and the separate fleet accounting requirements for imported and domestic cars.

The panel found that both rules violated the GATT's article III, section 4, its national treatment provision, because they effectively treated domestic and foreign producers differently. GATT rules do generally permit signatories to impose whatever regulatory standards they wish on products sold within a nation's borders provided they treat like foreign and domestic products alike, even though they may disproportionately burden imported products. But CAFE requirements were not based on the characteristics of a particular product, that is, the fuel efficiency of the cars themselves. Rather, the requirements were imposed on companies and varied in part according to their ownership and nationality.

However, the panel then went on to note that GATT contains an exception to the national treatment clause. Article XX(g) permits contracting parties to adopt or enforce measures that are necessary "to conserve exhaustible natural resources," provided the measures are not used to discriminate arbitrarily against imports or employed as a disguised restriction of international trade.[46] The panel determined that the primary goal of the fuel averaging requirement was indeed to protect and conserve natural resources, thus arguably bringing it within the scope of article XX.

The panel noted that the EU was correct in suggesting that the American policy objective of promoting fuel efficiency could be achieved in ways that were less restrictive of trade, especially by increasing the minimal U.S. tax on gasoline. But it declined to hold the United States to a "least trade restrictive" standard. Rather, it concluded, all the United States was required to do was to demonstrate that the regulations it imposed were necessary to improve fuel economy.

But the panel could find no such justification for CAFE's separate fleet accounting standards; distinguishing between cars produced in the United States and those produced overseas was clearly not necessary to promote conservation in the United States. Indeed, the panel observed that the use of separate foreign and domestic fleet accounting standards actually undermined domestic fuel conservation because it "prevented manufacturers of large domestic cars from meeting the CAFE requirement for their domestic fleet by adding to it small foreign cars, or small cars made from foreign parts." This "placed small foreign cars and foreign parts in a less favorable competitive position with respect to small domestic cars and domestic parts."[47]

The panel also noted that the two sets of accounting requirements "placed large foreign cars in a less favourable competitive position with respect to large domestic cars" because they prevented "manufacturers of large foreign, but not domestic, cars from meeting their CAFE requirements for their imported fleet by adding to it small domestic cars." In short, the separate accounting requirements not only violated article III's national treatment rule but did so in such a way as to undermine rather than achieve the ostensible purpose of the CAFE standards. Accordingly, the panel concluded that "the CAFE regulation is inconsistent with Article III:4 and, to the extent that it is based on separate foreign fleet accounting, cannot be justified under Article XX (g) or Article XX (d)."[48]

This finding was hardly surprising: the separate accounting provision had been deliberately included in the original legislation at the insistence of the United Automobile Workers Union. Indeed, without the provision it was unlikely that the CAFE legislation would have been approved in the first place. What *was* surprising was the panel's failure to discern protectionist motives behind Congress's decision to base fuel economy on corporate fleet averages.

The United States was extremely pleased with the GATT panel ruling and urged that it be formally adopted by GATT itself. U.S. officials claimed that the panel had upheld the "core provisions" of the CAFE law. "The panel has emphatically rejected the Europeans' claim that trade-neutral legislation intended to further energy conservation goals and protect the environment could be attacked because Chrysler, Ford, and GM invested and complied with the laws while Mercedes and BMW chose not to and had to pay penalties."[49]

U.S. officials also dismissed the significance of the one provision of CAFE that the GATT panel judged illegal. The trade representative's office indicated that it had no intention of changing the separate fleet accounting rule, claiming that the EU was not in a position to pressure the United States to make such a change because the rule in question did no economic harm to European manufacturers: "No European companies sell cars in the U.S. which qualify as domestic under CAFE, which sets a standard of 75 percent U.S. content."[50] Nor did the Japanese automobile producers appear to suffer as a result of this provision because even their American-made cars contained less than 75 percent domestic content.

The U.S. assessment of the GATT ruling, along with a refusal to modify the separate fleet accounting rule, was strongly criticized by the Europeans. An EU official stated: "We object to the fact that the U.S. appears unwilling to change the CAFE law, in the wake of a decision by a GATT panel that the law is discriminatory." He added that the U.S. posture did not bode well for the multilateral trade system or the World Trade Organization.[51]

Ironically, although both the American environmental groups and the Clinton administration expressed their delight, as well as their relief, at the outcome of the dispute, the episode ended up permitting the United States to continue an ill-conceived regulatory policy that not only distorts international trade but pursues conservation inefficiently. For in fact, the least trade-restrictive policy option is also the most sensible for American energy policy. A serious gasoline tax would not only lower fuel consumption at a fraction of CAFE's social cost, but would also avoid any discrimination among producers of European, American, and Japanese luxury vehicles. At the same time, the simple fuel levy would also benefit American manufacturers. Although substituting a tax for CAFE standards might reduce sales of oversized American cars, it would at least deprive Japanese competitors of the artificial competitive advantage CAFE inadvertently confers on them. Finally, by truly reducing the consumption of oil it would curb American dependence on foreign energy sources—a more useful policy objective than reducing American dependence on foreign cars.

The international dispute over the U.S. automotive fuel economy law did little to clarify or emphasize the shortcomings and contradictions of the U.S. approach to energy conservation in automotive transportation. An opportunity to better harmonize U.S. policy with the policies of major trading partners was lost. Neither the United States nor its trading partners are better off for this.

U.S. Clean Fuel Standards

Because automobiles are a major source of air pollution, especially in urban areas, reducing automotive emissions has been a major focus of the federal government's effort to improve air quality. During the 1970s the regulatory efforts of the federal government focused on mandating changes in engine technology. In the late 1980s, as Congress began another major revision of the Clean Air Act, the focus shifted: the government began contemplating further reductions in automobile emissions by mandating changes in the composition and content of motor fuels, which had not yet been subject to regulation.

The drive for a federal clean fuel policy was initiated by the Bush administration, for whom it represented a way of reducing the nation's dependence on foreign oil and demonstrating the administration's commitment to a dramatic new approach to pollution control. The technological feasibility of the new regulatory strategy received a significant boost in 1989 when the Atlantic Richfield Company (ARCO) announced that it had developed a reformulated gasoline for use in older cars (ones not equipped with catalytic converters) that would significantly reduce their emissions. ARCO's market share immediately increased by 10 percent, and the issue of clean fuels moved to center stage in the environmental policy drama.[52]

Unfortunately, there is no such thing as a perfectly clean fuel. Not only do all fuels emit some pollution when burned by an internal combustion engine, but there are harmful environmental consequences associated with the production of all energy sources. The challenge the administration and Congress faced was to decide which regulatory standards the government wanted automotive fuels to meet. The challenge was especially critical because designing a wholly fuel-neutral regulatory standard is virtually impossible. Whatever emission requirements the government selected would invariably favor some fuels and discriminate against others. Not surprisingly, the most heated conflict over the 1990 Clean Air amendments centered on fuels.

The Bush administration originally favored the use of methanol, an alcohol fuel typically made from coal or natural gas. Methanol appeared able to reduce significantly hydrocarbon emissions, which would in turn reduce smog. However, adding methanol to gasoline might also increase emissions of formaldehyde, which is a carcinogen. Thus it was not clear that methanol would provide net environmental benefits in comparison with conventional gasoline. Moreover, the new fuel would be expensive. Although it costs as much as conventional gasoline to produce, it is 30 percent less efficient. It is also more corrosive and would require substantial changes in engine technology.

The Politics of Ethanol

At the same time, policymakers found themselves under heavy political pressure to mandate the use of another alternative fuel, ethanol. Ethanol is produced by distilling corn into alcohol. It can be mixed in a ratio of one part ethanol to nine parts gasoline to produce gasohol. Support for federal tax breaks and rules facilitating the use of ethanol in the nation's gasoline supply was led by a number of lobbies, including the Renewable Fuels Association, the Clean Fuels Development Coalition, and the National Corn Growers' Association. However, the most influential role was played by the Archer Daniels Midland Company, the major domestic producer of ethanol, nearly half of whose profits come from products either protected or heavily subsidized by the federal government. Dwayne Andreas, ADM's chief executive officer, is one of the most politically active businessmen in the United States.[53] During the 1992 presidential campaign, Andreas contributed more than $1.4 million in soft money (which goes to party organizations rather than individual candidates) and gave an additional $345,650 to various congressional and senatorial candidates. He was a major contributor to the campaigns of both George Bush and Bill Clinton, giving Bush more than $400,000 and Clinton $270,000. Within Congress the use of ethanol was championed by senators and representatives from corn-producing states, including the Senate majority leader and 1996 Republican presidential candidate, Robert J. Dole, another major beneficiary of Andreas's largess.

A central strategy of ethanol's promoters was to back regulations requiring that automotive fuel contain a relatively high minimum oxygen content, one that could only be met by blending conventional gasoline with 10 percent ethanol. Opponents, led by the petroleum industry, argued that fuel content regulations are, in effect, ethanol mandates. The oil companies preferred to use an alternative fuel called MTBE (methyl tertiary butyl ether), which is a methanol-derived fuel oxygenate. Not only can they produce this oxygenate themselves, but it is substantially easier to transport because it does not mix with water. However, gasoline mixed with MTBE cannot attain the oxygen level of ethanol.

Ethanol and Conservation

Efforts to promote the use of ethanol in automotive fuels date from the late 1970s when the Carter administration believed it would help secure energy independence. Gasoline with 10 percent ethanol was exempted from federal fuel excise taxes, and in 1980 the Department of Agriculture provided $341 million in loans to finance the construction of gasohol plants. Notwithstanding the tax preference for gasohol and the production subsidies, the market for gasohol remained relatively modest: motor fuels blended with ethanol constituted less than 1 percent of the total fuels market in 1980, though the level increased to 7 percent by 1990.[54]

Although the use of ethanol was originally justified as a way of reducing oil imports, it is not an energy-inefficient fuel. Not only does it cost twice as much to produce as normal gasoline, but making it may actually consume more energy than it generates. According to an application for federal subsidy submitted by ADM in 1979, its ethanol plant required 1,284 barrels of natural gas to produce 1,485 barrels of ethanol, thus producing a net energy gain of less than 15 percent of the total fuel produced. Moreover, this figure excludes the substantial energy consumed by growing the corn in the first place. Although one gallon of ethanol contains the energy equivalent of 76,000 Btus, the Department of Energy estimated in 1991 that making a gallon of ethanol required 85,000 to 91,000.[55]

Ethanol also contributes to increased energy use by reducing fuel economy, since each gallon of ethanol contains only two-thirds as much energy as gasoline. According to the Department of Energy, gasohol-fueled vehicles average 4.7 percent fewer miles a gallon than vehicles fueled by standard gasoline.[56]

Ethanol and Clean Air

More recently, the case for adding ethanol to gasoline has come to be defended on environmental grounds. But this justification is equally dubious. In fact, the Clean Air Act amendments of 1977 banned products such as ethanol precisely to *protect* the environment. In 1978 the EPA announced that "recent EPA and Department of Energy tests . . . show slight increases in nitrogen oxide emissions and substantial increases in evaporative hydrocarbon emissions" from cars using gasohol. However, since ethanol then amounted to only a minuscule share of the nation's gasoline sales, the EPA concluded that "there is no significant environmental risk associated with its continued use."[57]

Alcohol blends improve gasoline combustion but are also significantly more volatile than alcohol-free gasolines. A 1986 USDA report concluded that "evaporative emissions reported for ethanol blends are 5 percent to 220 percent above emissions for straight gasoline." A subsequent study reported that while gasohol would reduce carbon monoxide emissions by 25 percent, hydrocarbons would increase by as much as 50 percent and nitrogen oxide by 15 percent. Ethanol may also contribute to ozone pollution (smog) because it evaporates relatively quickly, especially in hot weather. Thus the National Academy of Sciences concluded that "using ethanol as a blending agent in gasoline . . . would not achieve significant air-quality benefits and, in fact, would likely be detrimental."[58]

The 1990 Clean Air Act amendments require that gasoline sold in areas where ozone levels exceed federal standards must have a Reid vapor pressure (the standard measure of fuel volatility) of nine pounds per square inch because, as the Senate Committee on Environment and Public Works duly observed, "evaporative hydrocarbon emissions . . . are now the most significant source of vehicle hydrocarbon emissions during the summer, when ozone formation is at its peak."[59] However, the amendments actually *relax* the volatility requirements for fuels containing 10 percent ethanol. When even this concession was not sufficient to permit the use of ethanol in the summer in some of the nation's largest and most polluted cities, ethanol's supporters persuaded the EPA to issue a waiver that would permit the use of this "clean" fuel in all areas of the United States throughout the year.

Defining Reformulated Gasoline

Under the terms of the 1990 Clean Air Act, to reduce smog, "only reformulated fuel could be sold in the nine smoggiest cities."[60] This, however, begged a critical question: how would reformulated gasoline be defined? The answer provoked a bitter battle for market share between ethanol producers and the oil industry. The oil industry wanted to be allowed to determine the composition of cleaner fuels. In his testimony before the House Commerce Committee, Charles J. DiBona, president of the American Petroleum Institute, pleaded, "Tell us how much polluting emissions should be reduced. Don't dictate the recipe for making the fuel. We want to make the best fuel we know how, not 'government gas.'"[61] But the ethanol lobby feared that if given the flexibility in fashioning fuel composition, oil refiners would primarily rely on MTBE because this oxygenate could be produced by the refiners themselves.

For its part, the Clinton administration strongly favored the use of ethanol both to increase farm income and to reduce dependence on imported oil. To ensure a market for ethanol, the EPA issued a proposed rule in June 1994 requiring that at least 30 percent of gasoline contains a "renewable oxygenate" by 1996.[62] This regulation, in effect, mandated the use of ethanol or its derivatives, since MTBE is derived from fossil fuels and therefore is not considered renewable.

Following the announcement of the renewable oxygenate requirement, forty-eight senators sent a letter of protest to EPA administrator Carol Browner. "This RFG [reformulated gasoline] rule," they said, "will create chaos in the marketplace, cause serious deliverability problems, and unnecessarily increase the cost of RFG to consumers. Lastly, and most importantly, the rule will result in no clear environmental benefits."[63] The EPA's decision was also criticized by some environmentalists. A. Blakeman Early, the Washington representative for the Sierra Club, characterized the proposed rule as both illegal and bad policy, adding "It's not the role of the Clean Air Act to make mandatory markets for ethanol."[64] Senator Bill Bradley of New Jersey stressed that "no significant national environmental organization supports EPA's findings of environmental benefits" from the use of ethanol.[65] The administration's ethanol requirement was challenged on the floor of the Senate, where the vote primarily divided along geographic lines. Following a heated floor debate, the rule survived when Vice President Al Gore broke a tie vote in its favor.

The rule was subsequently struck down in federal court. In its decision the court reminded the EPA that "the sole purpose of the Reformulated Gasoline Program is to reduce air pollution," and that the agency itself had conceded that the use of ethanol might possibly make air quality worse.[66] What is more, the use of ethanol collided with the Clinton administration's commitment to reduce emissions of greenhouse gases because, in the words of EPA assistant administrator Mary Nichols, "the production of corn requires substantial amounts of energy, some of which results in greenhouse gas emissions."[67]

Although using ethanol would not benefit air quality and could harm it, its most important defect would be cost. According to the American Petroleum Institute, the EPA's ethanol mandate was projected to cost refiners $460 million a year, or 6 cents a gallon, to modify refinery facilities to blend ethanol for reformulated gasoline, to convert MTBE plants to produce ethanol-based oxygenates, and to modify product terminals and transport facilities. And this would be in excess of the extra cost of 5 to 10 cents a gallon to produce reformulated gasoline with MTBE. However, relatively few of these costs would have been visible to motorists comparing fuel prices because each gallon of ethanol sold in gasoline is exempt from part of the federal gasoline excise tax as well as part of state taxes. Indeed, the EPA's ethanol mandate was estimated to reduce federal and state taxes by $750 million a year.[68] As in the case of CAFE, the costs of the ethanol regime to the American public were hidden.

Subsidizing Farmers

The key to understanding the political economy of ethanol lies in the fact that requiring its use was, quite simply, a farm welfare program. Annual ethanol subsidies came to exceed $770 million. Such subsidies did increase farm income; demand for ethanol raised corn prices by an estimated 22 to 40 cents a bushel. But since most corn produced in the United States is used for feed grain, the ethanol program in fact increased costs to livestock producers by more than $1 billion a year, which in turn was passed on to consumers in the form of higher meat prices. Moreover, ethanol subsidies also harmed soybean farmers since corn by-products from ethanol production compete with soybeans. For a time, ethanol subsidies were depressing soybean sales by approximately $300 million. On balance, government-mandated ethanol production was costing farmers and taxpayers $4 for each $1 of extra farm income, making it a remarkably wasteful way of subsidizing farmers. According to a Department of Agriculture study, "Consumers would be much better off if they burned straight gasoline in their automobiles and paid a direct cash subsidy to farmers in the amount that net farm income would be increased by ethanol production."[69]

In sum, without extensive federal subsidies, which have amounted to approximately $550 million a year since 1978, little ethanol would be produced in the United States.[70] Pushing the use of ethanol in motor fuels not only distorts the marketplace for agricultural products, but by reducing tax revenues and requiring extensive government subsidies, contributes to the national budget deficit. Further, although they have been touted in part as a way to reduce oil imports, federal ethanol subsidies hurt U.S. exports of corn by raising its price. Thus even as a form of economic mercantilism, the promotion of ethanol in motor fuels is perverse: it reduces imports of one commodity by decreasing exports of another.

Protecting Ethanol

The commitment to subsidizing domestic ethanol production has also affected American trade policies. For even if there were substantial environmental dividends from using ethanol, it would be in the national interests to have it supplied as inexpensively as possible. Yet thanks to political pressure from ADM, the United States has restricted imports of ethanol, thus assuring that virtually all ethanol used will be heavily subsidized by American taxpayers.

In 1980 the Carter administration was persuaded to impose a prohibitive tariff on ethanol imports despite the absence of any evidence that these imports, which came primarily from Brazil, were damaging domestic producers. Three years later, Congress enacted the Caribbean Basin Initiative to improve the access of Caribbean products to the U.S. market and thus strengthen the economies of the countries in that region; as long as at least 35 percent of a product's value originated in the Caribbean, it would be allowed to enter the United States duty free. Consequently, companies invested a total of several million dollars to construct plants in Jamaica and Costa Rica that could convert surplus European wine into ethanol. In 1984 the Customs Service ruled that because the conversion of wine into ethanol added more than 35 percent of the value to the finished product, this ethanol could enter the United States duty free.[71]

Although imports of ethanol from the Caribbean never exceeded 3 percent of the U.S. ethanol supply, American producers, led by ADM, wanted to further limit foreign competition. Congress responded in 1986 by raising the local value-added requirement for Caribbean ethanol to 70 percent, which effectively restricted all imports because Caribbean countries lacked any surplus agricultural stocks. This clause was slightly modified by the lawmakers in 1989, when they established a staggered set of local feedstock requirements for ethanol produced in the Caribbean. These still discriminated against ethanol imports, however.[72]

Questioning the Clean Fuels Policy

Partiality to ethanol has not been the only dubious feature of the Clean Air Act regulations. A primary purpose of this legislation is to improve air quality for the nearly 89 million Americans as of 1990 who live in nonattainment areas (cities where air quality does not meet federal standards for ozone concentration). The law defines *nonattainment* strictly and precisely: if the fourth-highest daily one-hour reading recorded on any monitor during the preceding three years shows an ozone concentration greater than 0.12 part per million, the area is not in compliance with federal ozone standards. If compliance were instead measured by the average reading, the number of nonattainment areas would decrease significantly. The average readings in the majority of cities classified as nonattainment areas exceed the federal standard in less than 1 percent of the hours monitored.[73] In fact, with the exception of Los Angeles, almost all nonattainment areas meet federal standards more than 99.4 percent of the time. Moreover most ozone comes from emissions from pre-1983 cars, which are gradually being phased out.[74]

Even more important, the precise nature and extent of the health effects of prolonged exposure to ozone have yet to be demonstrated, while the costs of reducing VOC (volatile organic compounds) emissions that produce ozone are extremely high.[75] According to the Office of Technology Assessment, reducing VOC emissions by 35 percent (in 1989 dollars) from their 1990 levels will cost between $6.6 billion and $10 billion annually by 2004.[76]

Gasoline Standards as Trade Barriers

Although EPA's mandatory commingling of ethanol with gasoline was halted (at least for the time being) by a court order in April 1995, oil refineries had already begun to retool, at considerable expense, to produce reformulated gasoline, including ethanol-based fuel. Thus a legacy of the mandate, as well as of the fuel's long-standing differential tax treatment, was to saddle refineries with a sunk cost that they would soon try to offset. One way to do so would be by seeking relief from foreign competition.

On December 15, 1993, the EPA issued regulations implementing the reformulated gasoline provisions of the Clean Air Act of 1990. These rules required the sale of cleaner-burning gasoline in the nation's smoggiest areas beginning January 1, 1995.[77] Gasoline sales in a number of cities, including New York, Philadelphia, Washington, Hartford, Baltimore, Chicago, Houston, Los Angeles, and San Diego, were covered by this requirement. To avoid disrupting the fuel market and to provide refiners with enough time to adjust their production, the EPA decided to issue a five-year interim standard rather than a fixed one. During 1995, 1996, and 1997, refiners were required to reduce the amount of olefins (a chemical that leads to emissions of nitrogen oxide, which in turn contributes to ground-level concentrations of ozone). The reductions would be made on a percentage basis, using 1990 as the base year.

However, although American refiners were allowed to use their actual 1990 production as their baseline, foreign refiners were required to measure their improvement by using the U.S. average or statutory baseline. In addition, to prevent refiners from dumping high-emission RFG by-products into conventional gasolines, all non-RFG gasoline sold in the United States was required to be at least as clean in 1995 through 1997 as it was in 1990. Once again, the 1990 base was calculated differently for foreign and domestic refiners.

The EPA recognized from the outset that this rule would make it more difficult for gasoline produced by foreign refiners to be sold in the United States. In fact, EPA Assistant Administrator Nichols "told a Senate committee that she was motivated by a desire to lean in the direction of doing something that would favor the competitiveness of U.S. petroleum companies vis-à-vis Venezuelan companies."[78] Publicly, however, the agency claimed that it would be impossible to hold foreign producers to the same standard as the domestic firms because very few importers collected the data in 1990 needed to set their own baselines.[79] Accordingly, the EPA stated it had little choice but to employ a more "objective" standard, the 1990 domestic average. In practice, this meant that the standards applied to imported gasoline would in some cases be stricter and in other cases more lax than those for domestic producers.

Venezuela, one of the primary suppliers of imported gasoline to the United States, immediately filed a formal complaint with GATT on the grounds that the U.S. rule violated the trade agreement's national treatment clause, article III, by holding a like product to different standards, depending on its country of origin. Not eager to risk losing a trade dispute in the midst of the Uruguay Round negotiations, the Office of the U.S. Trade Representative pressured the EPA to modify its rule. Prudently, the office considered it "essential to try to make our country's environmental objectives and trade objectives compatible where possible."[80]

In exchange for convincing Venezuela to drop its complaint, the EPA proposed a corrective rule that would allow foreign refiners to establish their own baseline.[81] The agency stated it would approve the use of baselines for any foreign refinery that could supply it with the necessary data. This rule in effect exempted Venezuela because only its national oil company, Petroleos de Venezuela S.A. (PDVSA), appeared to have the data. At the same time, to ensure no significant deterioration in U.S. air quality, the new rule provided that any increase in the volume of gasoline imports from their 1990 levels would have to meet the statutory baseline as well.

This compromise outraged both environmentalists and the U.S. refining industry. The environmentalists chastised the EPA for sacrificing American environmental standards to gratify the State Department and the U.S. Trade Representative. EPA's amended rule appeared to confirm their fears that trade liberalization would compromise domestic regulatory standards.[82] Members of Congress also criticized the agency for bowing to pressures from the White House, claiming that the administration had been hoodwinked by Venezuela. For their part, the interests of the domestic refineries, mostly owned by the integrated oil companies, were straightforward: having been forced by the 1990 Clean Air Act amendments to invest billions of dollars in new technologies for refining gasoline, they now wanted federal regulations that would at least protect them from less expensive gasoline imports.[83] Industry representatives accused the EPA of tampering with the rules, claiming that its decision created "uncertainty" about the government's standards for reformulated gasoline, thus making it more difficult to deliver on schedule the new clean fuels required by law.[84]

Led by Sun Oil, a major marketer and refiner in the Northeast, where virtually all gasoline from Venezuela is sold, a coalition that included the National Petroleum Refiners Association, the American Petroleum Institute, and several major American oil companies lobbied to have Congress overturn the EPA's revised rule. The effort was strongly supported by environmental groups.[85] The alliance was effective. In August 1994 the Senate passed an amendment to the EPA's appropriations bill that prohibited the agency from implementing the new regulations. The amendment was later passed by the House. The EPA was compelled to reinstate its original rule. In effect, the domestic refiners had treated independent distributors and foreign refiners more or less the same way that corn farmers and ethanol producers had dealt with the refiners: each coalition had successfully lobbied in defense of an environmental regulation that would maintain its market share. The result was a regulatory apparatus that did little to improve environmental quality and also served as a trade barrier.

The World Trade Organization Dispute

Venezuela responded by resubmitting its complaint, first with GATT and then with the newly established World Trade Organization. The WTO convened its first dispute settlement panel to hear the case.[86] Subsequently, the panel agreed to examine a similar complaint from Brazil. Venezuela's financial stakes in the outcome of this dispute were considerable. Petroleos de Venezuela S.A. (PDVSA) had already embarked on a $1 billion refinery upgrading program, most of which was contracted to U.S. engineering and construction firms, to meet U.S. reformulated gasoline requirements and enabled it to double its gasoline exports to the United States. Unless the rule was changed, Venezuela's U.S. exports would decrease by 50,000 barrels a day, costing it $150 million a year in sales through 1997.[87] PDVSA would be faced with the choice of either modifying its refineries to produce gasoline that satisfied the U.S. statutory baseline or finding an importer that would blend Venezuelan gas with other gas to meet the U.S. standard. The first option would be extremely costly and would undermine Venezuela's ability to compete with U.S. refineries, which would not have to make similar modifications until 1998. The second option would also probably diminish the cost competitiveness of Venezuelan fuel.[88] All these difficulties would be avoided if, like its U.S. competitors, PDVSA were permitted to use an individual rather than a statutory baseline.

The environmental stakes in this trade dispute ranged from modest to nonexistent. The average olefins content of Venezuelan gasoline is two times higher than the Clean Air Act baseline. According to a federal report, "RFG produced to Venezuela's 1990 baseline would have as much as 13.9% greater NOx emissions than U.S. average RFG."[89] This in turn could significantly increase ozone levels in the Northeast, where nitrous oxide plays a major role in ozone formation.

However, in congressional testimony it was also reported that fifty-nine of eighty-eight domestic refiners had olefin levels higher than the statutory baseline to which foreign refineries were being held.[90] Only sixteen domestic refineries were able to meet the parameters of the statutory baseline. Indeed, in an internal memo, an EPA official admitted that "some domestic refiners have some individual gasoline baseline parameters that are as dirty or dirtier than PDVSA's," adding that the overall NOx increase from permitting PDVSA to use its 1990 baseline would be much less than 1 percent.[91]

Venezuelan gasoline is comparatively clean in other respects. PDVSA's planning manager for refining emphasized, for example, that "Venezuela exports only unleaded regular gasoline to the U.S. and, when compared with U.S. regular gasoline with which it competes, it has the same or lower sulfur and olefins content."[92]

Like the debate over the EPA's ethanol content mandate, the dispute over the health effects of Venezuelan gasoline appeared to have less to do with environmental protection than with the use of environmental rules to allocate market shares, internationally as well as domestically. Not surprisingly, PDVSA's demand that it be permitted to use its own baseline was strongly endorsed by the Society of Independent Gasoline Marketers of America. SIGMA represents 250 independent gasoline marketers and chain retailers throughout the United States, and its members account for 20 percent of domestic motor fuel retail sales. For these independent marketers, maintaining a diversity of supply sources, domestic as well as foreign, is essential to remain competitive with the fully integrated oil companies. According to a spokesman for CITGO, a major domestic marketing and oil transportation company owned by PDVSA, in overturning the EPA's revised rule, "Congress was duped by a few domestic refiners who saw an opportunity to unfairly seize a larger share of the government-mandated Reformulated Gasoline (RFG) market." The domestics, he continued, "were not worried about the environmental impact of foreign gasoline, they merely saw an opportunity to have Congress squeeze the supply of RFG thus causing a price increase and a shift of market share."[93]

A significant reduction in gasoline imports not only damages the interests of independent distributors, but also hurts American consumers. Only 3 to 7 percent of the gasoline used in the United States is imported, and of this about 50 percent comes from Venezuela, amounting to approximately 70,000 barrels a day.[94] However, gasoline markets are regional, and foreign refiners have supplied about 16 percent of the gasoline sold on the East Coast and 20 percent of the gasoline sold in the Northeast.[95] Restricting gasoline imports would limit competition and raise prices to consumers there.

In fact, this already has occurred. Because reformulated gasoline is less fuel efficient, more of it must be produced. By 1995 domestic refineries were operating at close to capacity. At the same time, thanks in part to the EPA rule, during January and February 1995 gasoline imports were 45 percent lower than during the comparable period in 1994. In June 1995 the price for a gallon of regular unleaded conventional gasoline in New York Harbor had increased by 19 percent from the previous year, while the price for super unleaded conventional gasoline had gone up 14 percent. The increase in prices for reformulated gasoline was equally significant: regular unleaded RFG was up 23 percent, while the price of super unleaded climbed by 16 percent.[96] So consumers in the region are paying considerably more for gasoline in return for little improvement in their air quality.

The WTO Decides

On January 17, 1996, the WTO dispute panel issued its decision. The panel began by noting that the U.S. standard clearly accorded imported gasoline less favorable treatment. It observed:

According to the United States, as of August 1995, approximately 100 US refiners, representing 98.5 percent of gasoline produced in 1990, had received EPA approval of their individual baselines. Only three of the refiners met the statutory baseline for all parameters. Thus, while 97 percent of US refiners did not and were not required to meet the statutory baseline, the statutory baseline was required of importers of gasoline.[97]

The panel then addressed the question of whether this difference in treatment was necessary for the United States to achieve the legitimate objective of cleaner air. It concluded that there was no such justification. The United States had not demonstrated that the nation's air quality would suffer if foreign refiners were allowed to use their individual baselines rather than the U.S. statutory average. Moreover, if doing so did result in adverse environmental impacts, then the appropriate policy for the United States was to impose slightly stricter requirements on both imported and domestic gasoline, not to hold them to different standards.

The panel concluded that holding gasoline produced by domestic and imported refineries to different standards violated American obligations under GATT's national treatment article. U.S. Trade Representative Mickey Kantor responded by stating, "Nothing related to this matter will undermine fulfilling the objectives of the Clean Air Act."[98] Environmentalists were incensed with the WTO: the panel's decision affirmed the "'right' of foreign oil companies to make profits in the U.S. market by selling dirty gasoline . . . over our right as citizens to pass laws protecting the quality of the air we are forced to breathe."[99]

The United States appealed the decision to a newly established WTO internal review board, which in April 1996 affirmed the panel's ruling. Under WTO rules, Venezuela and Brazil could either impose tariffs on U.S. imports equivalent to their losses from the disputed rule, estimated at $150 million, or demand the equivalent in compensation. However, on June 19, 1996, the Clinton administration announced it would propose changes in the application of clean air rules to imported gasoline to bring the United States into compliance.[100]

The Community Reinvestment Act

The two cases discussed in detail in this chapter are somewhat unusual. In each, U.S. social regulations were formally challenged through dispute settlement proceedings of GATT-WTO. But these two prominent stories do not exhaust the list of government rules that have been questioned by America's trading partners. Obviously, not all the criticisms are well founded. Just because a regulation imposes disproportionate strains on importers does not automatically make it protectionist. There are many legitimate reasons why it is often easier for domestic producers to comply with a particular national regulatory standard. Many regulations do make both domestic producers and consumers better off, even if they vex foreign firms.[101]

But what is striking is that more than a few regulations deemed abrasive by U.S. trading partners are also questionable as domestic policies. Consider another example, namely, the Community Reinvestment Act.

Best Intentions

The Community Reinvestment Act was passed in 1977 to address redlining, the practice in which banks draw lines around particular geographic areas, usually in central cities and populated by poor minorities, and deny financing to borrowers because they reside in these areas rather than because their credit histories are inadequate. Apart from violating people's civil rights, the alleged lending discrimination may accelerate urban decay.

The Community Reinvestment Act obligates commercial banks and savings and loan institutions to "meet the credit needs of the local communities in which they are chartered, consistent with the safe and sound operation of such institutions."[102] The law was, of course, broadly worded and did not aim specifically to allocate credit, create affirmative action in lending, or require depository institutions to support local charities.[103] It was based on the idea that depository institutions could make a profit in their local communities and thus help preserve them. This logic applied to institutions in low-income urban areas as well as those in wealthy suburbs.

Depository institutions were not automatically punished by regulators for noncompliance with the law. Although CRA compliance assessments were made at regular bank examinations, compliance was largely enforced at the point when an institution filed an application for acquiring another bank, merging with another bank, or establishing a new branch. Before 1989 both types of CRA assessments were confidential, but that year Congress amended the law, requiring regulators to prepare a public evaluation of an applicant's CRA record. These resulted in stricter CRA enforcement, mainly because the evaluations could be used by urban community activists to put political or legal pressure on regulators, indirectly exacting concessions from lending institutions. With the 1989 amendments it became easier for regulators and local advocacy groups to obtain funds and services (for example, pledges to offer more checking services, pledges of loans to specific neighborhoods, or changes in terms of credit).

Problems

There has been considerable criticism of the CRA. First, direct compliance costs are high. Bankers claim that this latest regulatory venture requires massive paperwork, an especially onerous burden for small community banks. Two surveys by banking associations found the law to be the most costly of all regulatory burdens imposed on banks.[104] Second, it is claimed that the CRA conflicts with the soundness of depository institutions by forcing loans on terms that would not be normally available, thus heightening risk. Being required to hold such loans also reduces the ability of an institution to diversify its loan portfolio, adding systemic risk for the institution. Third, by effectively raising the costs of doing business in low-income neighborhoods, the law may chase away as much capital as it obtains for such areas. Fourth, by enforcing the law at the time of an application for expansion, merger, or branching, the CRA places a tax on the banking industry's restructuring and consolidation. This complication has resulted at times in delays of proposed mergers and consolidations and the abandonment of acquisitions altogether. Finally, because the CRA affects only banks, it places them at a relative disadvantage vis-à-vis credit unions, pension funds, life insurance companies, and the fast-growing mutual fund industry.

Behind all these doubts is the proposition that the banks can ill afford added regulatory baggage.[105] Implicit in the logic of the CRA is that banks can use high profits from other areas of business to subsidize the riskier loans. But in an era of increasing international competition in financial services, the banks' capability for such cross-subsidization is weakening.[106]

For years the Community Reinvestment Act was solely a domestic matter. With the passage of the Riegle-Neal Interstate Banking and Branching Act in 1994, however, the CRA began to assume an international dimension.

The CRA applies only to insured retail banks. Because the European banking presence in the United States largely consists of uninsured, wholesale banks that are not covered by the Federal Deposit Insurance Corporation, the European banks at first were mostly exempt from the law's requirements. As federally insured institutions, however, U.S. wholesale banks were required to comply with it.

The relaxation of interstate banking restrictions opened new opportunities to branch across the United States. Because the branches of foreign wholesale banks would seldom be bound by the CRA, the United States feared a growing inequity: that European bankers might develop a competitive advantage in the U.S. market. The concern found sympathy in the Senate, where legislation was introduced requiring foreign banks to use a U.S. subsidiary to take advantage of the new interstate branching authority. The House version, however, allowed foreign banks to branch freely, without the U.S. subsidiary proviso. In conference the final bill generally followed the House's rendition, but to assuage the concerns raised by senators, several compromises were made. Most notable was a stipulation that a foreign wholesale bank acquiring a retail bank and then converting it into an uninsured branch must keep its branches in compliance with the CRA.[107] The difficulty here is that national treatment standards are violated because foreign wholesale banks are not FDIC insured but are being asked to assume some additional credit risks when branching across state lines by acquiring U.S. banks.[108]

Conclusions

These three cases illustrate situations in which the imposition of new regulations on a domestic industry has led to policies that create new and sometimes unequal burdens for foreign competitors.

Thus significant additional rules imposed on the U.S. automobile industry that were aimed at furthering energy conservation were also structured to protect U.S. producers. Wholly intended or not, the protective components of CAFE were a necessary price for its passage. CAFE's domestic deficiencies and its protectionist consequences are directly linked to one another. A better energy conservation policy—

for example, a straightforward tax on automotive fuel—would not discriminate against vehicles on the basis of where they were manufactured or on the range of a manufacturer's product lines. In effect, CAFE has been a disappointment on shore as well as off: it has not conserved energy efficiently, and it has managed to antagonize producers from America's largest trading partner, the European Union.

A similar irony pervades U.S. policy regarding reformulated gasoline. As in the case of CAFE, serious doubts have been raised as to whether the reformulated gasoline requirement in general and the subsidization of ethanol in particular have been effective means of improving public health by restricting pollutants produced by motor vehicles. Yet once again, when faced with significant compliance costs, a major U.S. industry reached for an import restriction. And in the end, American motorists in the Northeast are paying higher prices for gasoline with no discernible improvement in air quality.

In this instance, the protection of both domestic ethanol producers and domestic refineries has been paid for not by manufacturers of luxury products in advanced countries but by the producers and workers from less developed nations in the Caribbean and Latin America. The manufacturers of expensive European automobiles have experienced some marginal reduction in sales in the United States as a result of CAFE. But the effect of U.S. trade restrictions on the exports of Caribbean nations, Venezuela, and Brazil have carried a much more significant economic penalty relative to the developmental needs of their economies. Although the trade disagreement with Venezuela and Brazil may have attracted little public attention in the United States, in the Latin American countries the matter was serious. Venezuela in particular depends on petroleum exports to the United States to service its massive foreign debt. The European Union and Norway also watched the dispute closely.

Both the domestic and international implications of the Community Reinvestment Act are far less dramatic. But here, too, a regulation is imposing substantial costs on a U.S. industry, costs that are not clearly offset by social benefits, and the rule has become the subject of international criticism.

Finally, it is important to note that in each of these cases the efforts to shift some of the costs of regulatory requirements from domestic firms to their foreign competitors was supported by public interest groups. CAFE has always been enthusiastically applauded by consumer and environmental organizations; they have spear-headed every effort to raise the fuel economy requirements. These same organizations also strongly criticized the European Union's challenge to CAFE through GATT. Environmental advocates did not promote the ethanol mandate, but they have been vigorous proponents of the quest for rules mandating clean fuel at almost any cost. And they have worked closely with the domestic oil industry to secure different standards for gasoline refined in Venezuela. Likewise, both the Community Reinvestment Act and the decision to extend its provision indirectly to foreign banks were backed by community groups.

If there is a lesson in all this it is that trade liberalization and regulatory reform can be mutually reinforcing. At least in the case studies examined in this chapter, the interests of the American public would have been better served had the United States chosen to accomplish its legitimate policy objectives by adopting the least trade-restrictive alternative. In the cases of both CAFE and reformulated gasoline, the interests of foreign producers and of American consumers actually complemented one another. Thus the complaints of America's trading partners about the discriminatory effects of some U.S. regulatory policies warrant serious reflection. Trade agreements can help improve domestic regulatory policies because they can highlight rent seeking that is masquerading as consumer or environmental protection. Just as U.S. efforts to pressure Japan to open its markets have frequently reinforced internal Japanese efforts to reform that country's economy, so might America's trading partners become equally constructive in bettering some U.S. regulatory practices. What may be good for them is sometimes also better for us.

COMMENT BY I. M. DESTLER

David Vogel has written an interesting and informative paper. It is impressive how the U.S. government tied itself in knots by trying to promote fuel economy without a gasoline tax. It is dismaying, but hardly surprising, that the case for cleaner fuel became transmuted into a battle over economic rents among regional economic interests and between them and foreign economic interests. In any case, it is hard to retain much enthusiasm for CAFE as even a second- or third-best measure for fuel conservation or as a venture into the regulation and subsidization of motor fuel content.

The author needs to highlight the constructive tension between the paper and the apparent premise (and provocative title) of the conference. "Comparative *dis*advantage" is a label reinforcing the common perception that U.S. regulations are a burden on U.S. producers, cutting into their capacity to compete. That hypothesis also requires, of course, that analysts find disproportional impact on a particular industry—otherwise regulation will not affect *comparative* advantage, though it may reduce overall national welfare.

In any case, Vogel's stories do not conform to the hypothesis, for these regulations were certainly not burdens borne atypically by U.S. producers alone; they applied, not always equally, to all major players in the U.S. market. One major reason is that unlike many environmental laws they were not regulations of the production process but of the product going into the U.S. market. In intent, and in some respects in their specific language, these regulatory programs were closer to the opposite: burdens on foreign producers. In effect, CAFE—the more interesting case—was mixed, as Vogel notes. This highlights the enormous difficulty of crafting indirect protectionist measures in a world where Robert Reich's question "Who is us?" remains a vexing one, implying a tension between the interests of companies and the interests of favoring home production.

The treatment of CAFE in Vogel's chapter is powerful, even devastating, but sometimes the heat of the argument impedes the shedding of light. As Vogel catalogues the nefarious effects of this unusual law, I find myself repeatedly asking "Compared to what?" or "Was CAFE the *only* reason?" or "What is the balance here?" Let me offer a few examples.

Early in the chapter the reader learns that with a gas tax out of political reach, Congress decided to shift the burdens of reducing gasoline consumption onto the manufacturers of motor vehicles. One might infer that manufacturers responded by supporting a gas tax because it would shift the burdens onto consumers. But wait. A gas tax surely burdens the manufacturers as well and would likely have had the same effects as a tax on low-efficiency cars in increasing the market share of Japanese models. There was no way to deal with the issue without burdening the U.S. manufacturers, and on a comparative basis, CAFE was probably better for them than a gasoline tax.

Similarly, Vogel then stresses—no doubt accurately—that CAFE standards drove the Big Three to reduce the weight of their motor ve-hicles, increasing occupants' vulnerability in case of accidents. But wouldn't a raising of gasoline prices to European levels have had a similar impact? Which route, comparatively, was better for auto safety then? The chapter doesn't even ask the question, much less address it.

Instead, the argument against CAFE takes on the character of piling on. One is told, on one page, that CAFE, together with other new-vehicle regulatory standards, is entirely responsible for an in-crease of two full years in the average age of cars on the American road. Nothing is said about quality improvement as a possible cause, or income stagnation among American auto buyers, or price rises with causes other than those cited.

Subsequently, the author notes that CAFE drove Detroit to shift gas-guzzler production overseas, because the fleet average for imports allowed it. But he does not balance this result against the earlier-noted effect (and intention) of concentrating economy car pro-duction in the United States because the fleet average for domestic production demanded it. Thus the assertion that it "costs American jobs" is dubious, since no comparison is made of the two opposite effects.

My point is not to question the conclusion that CAFE standards and the requirements for reformulated gasoline were an inefficient means of reducing energy consumption or of improving air quality. My purpose is only to urge greater restraint and proportionality in the argument. I, too, favor the gas tax alternative, but there is no sense pretending that it would not have had some of the same negative impacts that Vogel attributes to CAFE. As often as possible, therefore, he needs to show that the means he is critiquing do more damage than other plausible means.

Vogel also makes a persuasive case on trade policy: CAFE did dis-criminate against foreign firms, and in some respects, against foreign-owned production. It would have been better, in my view, had the GATT panel also found the fleet-averaging requirement inconsistent with U.S. trade obligations, though I can sympathize with throwing this bone to the largest GATT member—given the inefficacy of CAFE as a protectionist instrument, which the chapter documents. But let me close my comments with broader reflections on how to define protectionism and how one would like the necessary future debate on U.S. trade policy to proceed.

I start with a suspicion I have: the Ways and Means Committee members who drafted CAFE would vigorously deny that they were protectionists. They had no plan to block imports; they just wanted to keep Toyota and other companies from gaining additional advantage—and General Motors and other companies from further injury—by way of gasoline conservation measures. But by one simple and logical standard Congress was undoubtedly protectionist, just as it is when it enacts antidumping (AD) laws or countervailing duty laws that "offset" subsidies granted by Canadian provinces but not subsidies granted by American states. The logical definition of protectionism is: *any* law that treats goods produced abroad—and by extension, production by foreign-owned companies—less favorably than goods produced within the fifty states. Since the United States does not have a domestic antdumping law, the law for foreign trade is protectionist.

This definition is different from the question of GATT consistency. The main provisions of the AD law are GATT consistent, though Mickey Kantor and Congress may have stepped over the line in certain provisions of the 1994 Uruguay Round implementing legislation. The definition is also different from the view of the broad liberal-trade consensus in the United States that tolerates or even endorses numerous measures that in fact discriminate against non-U.S. production. But it seems to me that we need a clear intellectual delineation of free trade, a principle that advocates can argue with conviction, not just pragmatism, even if it will not always prevail. In today's politics, the Office of the U.S. Trade Representative cannot take this line, and perhaps it will never be able to.

Finally, in some cases, what is protectionist by this standard will also be GATT-inconsistent. Venezuela should probably win its World Trade Organization case on the merits, as the initial panel finding suggests it will. In others, the standard put forward here will clearly go beyond current international trade agreements but might help the United States in framing future ones. It may help, therefore, to curb or limit domestic regulations that apply different roles to domestic and foreign producers.

COMMENT BY SHARYN O'HALLORAN

David Vogel's essay addresses the use of nontariff barriers, disguised as social and economic regulations, to limit imports into the

United States. The paper presents three examples in which environmental regulations serve to hinder free trade, principally through CAFE standards on fuel economy for cars and the provisions of the 1990 Clean Air Act dealing with ethanol-based fuels and with reformulated gasoline.

Vogel argues that while the intent of these regulations may have been well meaning, the end result has been to hurt American consumers and the public by raising domestic prices and limiting imports. Furthermore, these measures have proved rather ineffective in achieving their original intent of improving overall environmental quality. The explanation for these policies, according to Vogel, is that they are the result of special interest groups wielding undue influence in the political process. To overcome the natural tendency for law makers to misuse social policies to protect well-organized domestic producers, Vogel suggests that following the rule of "least restrictive trade" when setting environmental regulations would lead to a more efficient and effective regulatory setting.

However, if these policies are so inefficient and run counter to American consumers and the public interest at large, how did they get enacted in the first place? In my comments, I want to offer the following explanation of how we got here and where a policy of strict adherence to "least restrictive trade" might lead us. In the American system of government, passing broad regulatory policies requires broad-based social coalitions. Often, attracting the support of different groups requires concessions that are not in themselves efficient. However, given political constraints, these concessions may be necessary to achieve *second best* policy outcomes. Furthermore, these outcomes may improve overall social welfare even though they do not follow the course of least restrictive trade. In the end, a policy of least restrictive trade may lead to a reinforcement of status quo policies by eliminating the possibility of coalition building among key political actors.

In the following paragraphs, I briefly review the three cases analyzed by Vogel and offer an explanation of why trade restrictions were implemented hand-in-hand with environmental reforms. In each case, a persuasive argument can be made that the real choice was not between social regulation that was trade restrictive and social regulation that was less restrictive, but rather between social regulation with trade concessions or no regulation at all.

CAFE Standards

The first case is corporate average fuel economy standards. To examine the politics of CAFE standards, figure 3-1 shows two policy dimensions: the level of CAFE standards and the degree of protection afforded U.S. industries. In this policy space, the status quo CAFE standard as of the late 1980s was set at 27.5 mpg. That is, every car maker had to achieve an average of 27.5 mpg for the entire fleet. Vogel notes that this policy was slightly protectionist in favor of U.S. auto producers, owing to the requirement that each producer meet the CAFE standard for its domestic and imported fleets separately.

There are three major actors to consider in passing higher CAFE standards: the House, the Senate, and environmentalist groups. Figure 3-1 shows indifference curves running through the status quo policy for all three players. Here I assume that the environmentalists care only about increasing CAFE standards and are unconcerned about protecting U.S. industries. The House answers to more local concerns and would thus be expected to react strongly to U.S. auto makers' demands for protection. In particular, the chair of the House Commerce Committee during this time was Representative John Dingell from Detroit, making it unlikely that any legislation that did not confer some protection on the auto industry would pass through the House. The Senate, having broader constituencies and therefore being better equipped to supply public goods than the House, shared both environmental and protectionist concerns. These competing demands are represented in the indifference curves by the relative willingness of each actor to trade off some protection for higher CAFE levels.

Under this particular configuration of preferences and status quo policy, what are the possible coalitions that could form in favor of a new policy? In the figure, region I represents deals that could be made between environmentalists and the Senate. Note that this includes areas with higher CAFE standards and disadvantages for U.S. car makers in the form of lower protection. Region II represents House-Senate deals, all of which give higher protection for car makers. And region III represents the intersection of all three groups; this area represents the set of policies that environmentalists would endorse and Congress would enact. Note that all points in region III have both higher CAFE standards and higher protection for U.S. car

FIGURE 3-1. *1990 Clean Air Act CAFE Standards*

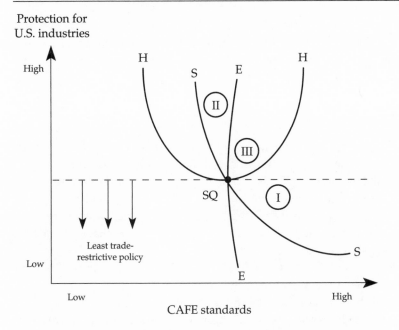

I   = Coalition between Environmentalists and Senate
II = Coalition between House and Senate
III = Coalition among all three groups

makers. In fact, throughout the discussions of raising CAFE standards in the late 1980s, automakers suggested options like the percentage approach and antibacksliding provisions, both of which would discriminate against foreign producers.

Vogel's policy prescription suggests that the United States should adhere to the policy of least restrictive trade. If this condition is added to the figure, then the constraint is that no regulations can further disadvantage foreign importers, meaning that any policy enacted must lie below the dotted line. Note, however, that this would also cut out any possibility of policy movement, as the intersection of all four sets is empty.

The implication of the preceding analysis is that the price of any policy movement in this area—improvement in environmental standards—is higher protection. To put it another way, given the current political configuration, the requirement of least restrictive trade policy will end up enforcing the status quo. It may be that this is the best outcome for all concerned. But there may be some welfare-improving policy options (like those represented in area III) that cannot be achieved under the policy of least restrictive trade.

Ethanol

The second big case discussed in the chapter refers to fuel standards that favor the use of ethanol as a gasoline additive to create what are called clean fuels. Whereas CAFE standards do have some redeeming public policy merits, I do agree with Vogel's assessment that it is hard to justify the ethanol program on good policy grounds. However, this raises the question of why these pro-ethanol standards were ever adopted.

Again Vogel's response relies on the privileged position of powerful interests groups in the political process. But as figure 3-2 shows, the number of groups who stood to gain from ethanol mandates—farmers and corporations like Archer Daniels Midland—were certainly outnumbered by the forces arrayed against ethanol—the auto industry, the oil industry, and essentially the rest of the nation. If we take the size of these humps as an indication of the relative size of the two groups, the pro-ethanol forces were clearly in the minority. Thus a median voter argument would predict that the antiethanol forces would prevail and ethanol would remain unprotected.

So why were pro-ethanol standards adopted? This is an issue that cannot be studied in a vacuum, as the ethanol standards were implemented as part of the 1990 Clean Air Act. By examining the larger picture, literally as well as figuratively, the following scenario emerges.

In the bottom half of figure 3-2, the dimensions are pro- or antiethanol, as above, and overall levels of environmental reform. The status quo represents the current level of environmental standards and a slightly pro-ethanol policy. The two ovals represent the set of ideal points of the antiethanol and pro-ethanol legislators, who are assumed to represent antiethanol and pro-ethanol groups, respectively.

The politics surrounding the enactment of the Clean Air Act produced three distinct groups. The opponents of ethanol were divided into group A, who favored stronger environmental standards, and

FIGURE 3-2. *1990 Clean Air Act Clean Fuels: Ethanol*

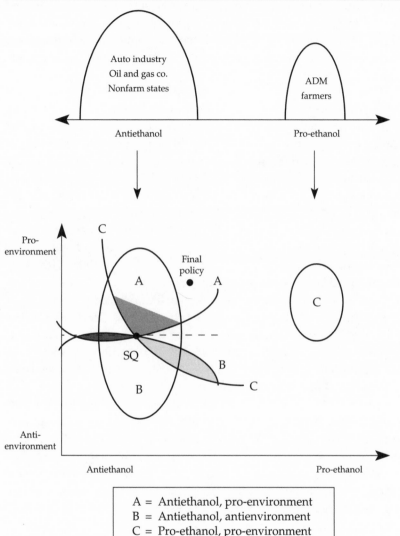

A = Antiethanol, pro-environment
B = Antiethanol, antienvironment
C = Pro-ethanol, pro-environment

group B, who favored weaker environmental standards or the status quo. The ethanol promoters are labeled group C and, as the diagram shows, they were more on the pro-environment side of the debate.

The key to the politics of the Clean Air Act is that passing any policy required two out of the three groups; no group alone had a clear majority. As in figure 3-1, I have drawn indifference curves through the status quo for each group. Groups A and B are indeed antiethanol, but they care relatively little about this dimension compared with larger environmental issues. By contrast, the indifference curve of group C opens up and to the right, indicating their pro-environment and pro-ethanol stance.

What were the possible coalitions? As usual with spatial diagrams, the set of points that beat the status quo are represented in the petals that are the intersection of any two win sets. So one coalition that could have formed would be the purely anti-ethanol forces, groups A and B, represented by the shaded area. But then not much would happen environmentally. Second, we could have seen concessions made for the ethanol forces by the antienvironmentalists, a coalition between B and C, as shown in the area with vertical lines.

In the end, the coalition that formed, after a marathon series of negotiations, was between the pro-environmentalists and the ethanol supporters, groups A and C, indicated by horizontal lines. This probably resulted because the pro-ethanol forces included a number of legislators close to the chamber median, such as Senators Robert J. Dole from Kansas and Charles E. Grassley from Iowa. The final bill thus contained the pro-ethanol provision. But it also included a number of important environmental gains: acid rain provisions, phase-out of chlorofluorocarbons (CFCs), limits on motor vehicle emissions, regulation of toxic air pollutants, and a reduction of urban smog.

Thus the overall policy gains made in the 1990 Clean Air Act were not inconsequential, even though the act did include provisions to appease the ethanol producers. Again, the bottom line of the story is that given political realities, concessions had to be made to special interests in order to achieve broader policy goals. The policy that resulted may not have been "first best," but the alternatives were either the environmental bill that was passed or no bill at all.

Reformulated Gasoline

Finally, let us take a look at the other side of the fuel standards issue, which is the reformulated gasoline debate. The 1990 Clean Air Act left a number of questions open for future determination by the Environmental Protection Agency (EPA). One of these was the phase-in requirements for reformulated gas in nine major cities. In 1994 the

FIGURE 3-3. *1990 Clean Air Act Reformulated Gasoline*

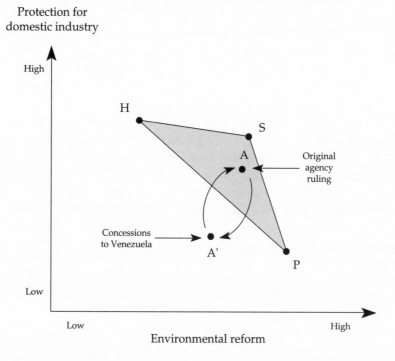

EPA issued regulations that strengthened gas standards but required foreign producers to improve their standards more quickly than domestic producers.

I represent the EPA ruling graphically in figure 3-3 by again considering a policy space with two dimensions—environmental reform and protection for domestic industry. The ideal points of the House, Senate, and president are shown, with the House preferring the highest level of protection and the president preferring the most reform for the environment. Again this story is consistent with the size of the constituencies of the three branches. Note that passing new policy requires the assent of all three actors. Thus it is only those points inside the shaded triangle that cannot be overturned by any viable condition. However, policies outside this triangle can be overturned by a coalition of all three branches. The policy originally promulgated by the EPA is shown as point A, inside the Pareto triangle—cleaner gas but some protection.

After Venezuela protested that the new regulations were discriminatory, the EPA responded by exempting Venezuela from the faster phase-in requirement, thereby shifting policy to point A' in the figure. While this policy was less discriminatory, it also weakened the environmental component of the regulation, as Venezuela, one of the major suppliers to the United States, produced somewhat dirtier gas than American reformulated fuels. These concessions, however, moved policy outside the Pareto triangle, breaking the coalition necessary to sustain environmental reform. This action, in turn, provoked a congressional response overturning the EPA's ruling and returning policy to point A.

The moral of this story is that even when policy is made by apparently neutral administrators, who may try to promote freer trade, outcomes may still be trade restrictive. Regulatory policy is ultimately made by the elected branches of government, and any regulations that stray too far away from their preferences will merely be overturned. Again, there are political limits to what can be obtained from social regulations.

Conclusion

The political reality in all three cases is that domestic regulations are made by domestic politics. This implies, first of all, that certain policy instruments will not be feasible, even if they are economically desirable. For instance, David Vogel correctly notes that significantly higher gas taxes or a carbon tax may be more efficient than CAFE standards, but such taxes would have no realistic chance of passing. (Note the current debate over eliminating the 4.3 cents a gallon gas tax.) It also implies, given the American system of separate powers, that enacting broad social regulations requires a broad-based coalition of interests. In some cases, this may mean that domestic industries will receive policy concessions in the form of phase-in periods or relief from foreign competition. But the requirement of "least trade restrictive" policies that do not disadvantage foreign producers may eliminate the possibility of policy movement altogether. Thus the original CAFE standards bill and the 1990 Clean Air Act could not have been passed without some degree of policy concessions. In the world of second best, where political constraints effectively prevent states from adopting the most efficient policy solution, the price of two steps forward on environmental issues may be one step back on trade.

NOTES

1. The most comprehensive analysis of CAFE is Pietro S. Nivola and Robert W. Crandall, *The Extra Mile: Rethinking Energy Policy for Automotive Transportation* (Brookings, 1995). See esp. pp. 22–42.

2. For an overview of the politics of clean air legislation through 1981, see David Vogel, "A Case Study of Clean Air Legislation 1967–1981," in Betty Bock and others, eds., *The Impact of the Modern Corporation* (Columbia University Press, 1984), pp. 309–86. For the 1990 amendments, see Gary C. Bryner, *Blue Skies, Green Politics: The Clean Air Act of 1990* (Washington: Congressional Quarterly Press, 1993).

3. See, for example, Lester B. Lave and Gilbert S. Omenn, *Clearing the Air: Reforming the Clean Air Act* (Brookings, 1981).

4. John D. Graham "Saving Gasoline and Lives," in John D. Graham and Jonathan Baert Wiener, eds., *Risk versus Risk: Tradeoffs in Protecting Health and the Environment* (Harvard University Press, 1995), pp. 88–89.

5. "Ford Ends Stalemate, Signs Energy Bill," *1975 Congressional Quarterly Almanac* (1975), pp. 220–43.

6. Nivola and Crandall, *Extra Mile*, p. 23.

7. Quoted in Daniel C. Esty, *Greening the GATT: Trade, Environment, and the Future* (Washington: Institute for International Economics, 1994), p. 45.

8. Matthew L. Wald, "How America Perpetuates Its Gas Crisis," *New York Times*, May 5, 1996, p. E4.

9. Agis Salpukas, "What's Next, Tail Fins: Fast Speeds and Big Cars Send Gas Consumption Up?" *New York Times*, February 15, 1996, p. C1.

10. Graham, "Saving Gasoline and Lives," p. 90.

11. Ibid.

12. Robert W. Crandall, "The Changing Rationale for Motor Vehicle Fuel-Economy Regulation," *Regulation* (Fall 1990), p. 11.

13. Nivola and Crandall, *Extra Mile*, p. 23.

14. William K. Stevens, "Trying to Stem Emissions, U.S. Sees Its Goal Fading," *New York Times*, November 28, 1995, p. B8.

15. Wald, "How America Perpetuates Its Gas Crisis," p. E4.

16. Nivola and Crandall, *Extra Mile*, p. 8. This figure has remained relatively stable through 1995. See Stevens, "Trying," pp. A1, B8.

17. Quoted in Nivola and Crandall, *Extra Mile*, p. 33.

18. Ibid., pp. 33–34.

19. Ibid., pp. 49–50.

20. See, for instance, Thomas Gale Moore, "A Hidden Culprit in Auto Imports," *Wall Street Journal*, January 14, 1992, p. A14.

21. Paul A. Eisenstein, "Automakers Are Being Pushed toward Fuel Economy," *Christian Science Monitor*, March 23, 1989, p. 9.

22. Nivola and Crandall, *Extra Mile*, p. 11.

23. Wald, "How America Perpetuates Its Gas Crisis," p. E4.

24. Nivola and Crandall, *Extra Mile*, p. 5.

25. Sam Kazman, "Death by Regulation," *Regulation* (Fall 1991), p. 20.

26. Graham, "Saving Gasoline and Lives," p. 95.

27. Kazman, "Death by Regulation," p. 20.

28. Ibid., p. 21.

29. Nivola and Crandall, *Extra Mile*, p. 41; and see also Kazman, "Death by Regulation," p. 21.

30. Kazman, "Death by Regulation," p. 21.

31. See David P. Baron, *Business and Its Environment* (Prentice-Hall, 1996), pp. 221–27. See also Neal Templin, "Fuel Economy Law That Would Stymie Japanese Is Sought by U.S. Auto Makers," *Wall Street Journal*, December 5, 1989, p. A11.

32. Templin, "Fuel Economy Law," p. A11.

33. "Fuel-Efficiency Effort Defeated in Senate," *1990 Congressional Quarterly Almanac*, vol. 46 (1991), p. 280.

34. Crandall, "Changing Rationale," p. 12.

35. Frances Williams, "Brussels Wins U.S. Car Tax Probe," *Financial Times*, May 13, 1993, p. 6; and Nancy Dunne, "EC Challenge over U.S. Fuel Economy Tax," *Financial Times*, May 11, 1993, p. 5.

36. Reginald Stuart, "Car Makers Are Getting Back in the Driver's Seat," *New York Times*, July 21, 1985, p. E2.

37. "GATT Rules against CAFE, Opens Door to Conservation Exception," *Inside U.S. Trade* (October 4, 1994), p. S-4.

38. John Griffiths, "Fuel Economy Rule May Hit Jaguar," *Financial Times*, February 28, 1983, p. 1; and David Vogel, *Trading Up: Consumer and Environmental Regulation in a Global Economy* (Harvard University Press, 1995), p. 132.

39. Dunne, "EC Challenge," p. 5.

40. "EC Seeks GATT Panel on U.S. 'Gas Guzzling' Taxes," *Reuter European Business Report*, May 11, 1993.

41. "EC Threatens Formal Action against U.S. Car Taxes," *Reuter European Community Report*, February 11, 1993.

42. "U.S. Blocks EC Bid for GATT Dispute Panel on Car Tax," *Reuter European Business Report* (March 24, 1993).

43. See, for example, Doron P. Levin, "Detroit's Assault on Mileage Bill," *New York Times*, May 11, 1991, p. L35.

44. Quoted in Dunne, "EC Challenges," p. 5.

45. Quoted in Peter Behr, "Trade Case Could Endanger Environmental Law, GATT: Europeans Contend That Gasoline Consumption Standard Is Unfair to Their Auto," *Washington Post*, June 10, 1994, p. F1.

46. "GATT Rules against CAFE," p. S-5.

47. Ibid.

48. Ibid., pp. S-5, S-6.

49. Ibid., p. S-1.

50. Ibid., p. S-7.

51. Ibid., p. S-7.

52. Bryner, *Blue Skies, Green Politics*, p. 134.

53. Dan Carney, "Dwayne's World," *Mother Jones*, July–August 1995, pp. 44–47.

54. James Bovard, "Corporate Welfare Fueled by Political Contributions," *Business and Society Review*, no. 94 (Summer 1995), pp. 24, 26.

55. Ibid., p. 26.

56. Ibid., p. 28.

57. Quoted in ibid., p. 26.

58. Quoted in ibid., pp. 26–27.

59. Jonathan H. Adler, "Clean Fuels, Dirty Air: How a (Bad) Bill Became Law," *Public Interest*, no. 108 (Summer 1992), pp. 128–29.

60. "Fuel Efficiency Effort," p. 229.

61. Testimony of Charles J. DiBona, "Clean Air Act Amendments," Hearing before the House Subcommittee on Oversight and Investigations of the Committee on Commerce, 104 Cong. 1 sess. (Government Printing Office, 1995), p. 42.

62. Jeffrey L. Katz, "Home State Interests Prevail as Ethanol Rule Squeaks By," *Congressional Quarterly Weekly Report*, August 6, 1994, p. 2259.

63. Bovard, "Corporate Welfare," p. 28.

64. Quoted in Margaret Kriz, "Fight over Clean Fuels Gets Dirty," *National Journal* (April 16, 1994), p. 898.

65. "EPA's Ethanol Additive Proposal Draws Fire," *Oil and Gas Journal* (May 23, 1994), p. 31.

66. Quoted in James Bovard, "Dole, Gingrich and the Big Ethanol Boondoggle," *Wall Street Journal*, November 2, 1995, p. A18.

67. Bovard, "Corporate Welfare," p. 27.

68. "Corn Growers Preserve Energy Rule," *Congressional Quarterly Weekly Report*, August 6, 1994, p. 2260; and Bob Williams, "MTBE, Ethanol Advocates' Squabble May Complicate RFG Implementation," *Oil and Gas Journal* (February 13, 1995), p. 22.

69. Quoted in Bovard, "Dole," p. A18.

70. Senator Malcolm Wallop quoted in "EPA's Ethanol Additive Proposal Draws Fire," *Oil and Gas Journal*, May 23, 1994, p. 30.

71. Bovard, "Corporate Welfare," pp. 28–29.

72. Ibid., p. 29.

73. Kenneth Chilton and Anne Sholtz, "A Primer on Smog Control," *Regulation* (Winter 1990), pp. 31–40.

74. Ed Rubenstein, "Clearing the Air," *National Review* (March 5, 1990), p. 15.

75. See, for example, Chilton and Sholtz, "Primer on Smog Control," pp. 31–40; and Kenneth Chilton and Christopher Boerner, "Smog in America: The High Cost of Hysteria," Center for the Study of American Business, Policy Study 128 (Washington University, January 1996), pp. 1–28.

76. Chilton and Boerner, "Smog in America," p. 20.

77. Steve Charnovitz, "The WTO Panel Decision on U.S. Clean Air Act Regulations," *International Trade Reporter*, vol. 13 (March 13, 1996), p. 459.

78. Ibid.

79. "U.S. Defends Gas Rules in WTO against Charges of Discrimination," *Inside U.S. Trade*, vol. 13 (July 7, 1995), p. 8.

80. Testimony of Ira Shapiro, "Reformulated Gasoline," Hearing before the House Subcommittee on Oversight and Investigations of the Committee on Energy and Commerce, 103 Cong. 2 sess. (GPO, 1995), p. 67.

81. Letter to Office of General Counsel, Office of the U.S. Trade Representative, from Steven R. Berlin, CITGO Corporation, May 12, 1995.

82. Steve Charnovitz, "The Environment vs. Trade Rules: Defogging the Debate," *Environmental Law*, vol. 23 (April 1993), pp. 475–517.

83. David E. Sanger, "World Trade Group Orders U.S. to Alter Clean Air Act," *New York Times*, January 18, 1996, p. C5.

84. "Venezuela Defends Its EPA Exemption for RFG," *Oil and Gas Journal*, vol. 92 (May 30, 1994), p. 30.

85. Caleb Solomon, "Venezuela's Pressure on Clean Air Act Stirs Environmental, Trade Controversy," *Wall Street Journal*, November 9, 1993, p. A5.

86. Frances Williams, "WTO Sets Up First Disputes Panel," *Financial Times*, April 11, 1995, p. 6.

87. "RFG Exemption for Venezuela Gasoline Comes under Fire," *Oil and Gas Journal*, vol. 92 (May 2, 1994), p. 54; and Guy de Jonquieres, "WTO Receives First Calls to Settle Disputes," *Financial Times*, February 11, 1995, p. 3.

88. "U.S. Defends Gas Rules in WTO against Charges of Discrimination," *Inside U.S. Trade* (July 7, 1995), p. 8.

89. Summary of NEC meeting on PDVSA reprinted in "Reformulated Gasoline," Hearing, p. 116.

90. Letter to Office of General Counsel from Berlin, May 12, 1995.

91. Meeting with Petroleos de Venezuela, S.A., "Reformulated Gasoline," Hearing, p. 163.

92. "Venezuela Defends Its EPA Exemption," p. 30.

93. Letter to Office of the General Counsel from Berlin, May 12, 1995.

94. Solomon, "Venezuela," p. A5.

95. John Gilardi, "Drivers in Northeast May Face Soaring Gasoline Prices," *Reuter European Business Report*, September 13, 1994, pp. 10–11.

96. Prepared Statement of the Society of Independent Gasoline Marketers of America, "Clean Air Act Amendments," Hearing, June 7, 1995, p. 58.

97. "WTO Panel Report on US-Venezuela Gasoline Dispute," January 17, 1996, p. 8.

98. Alan Tonelson and Lori Wallach, "Overruled by the World Trade Organization," *Washington Post National Weekly Edition*, May 13–19, 1996, p. 23.

99. Kevin Danaher and Rick Rowden, "Trade vs. Our Environment," *San Francisco Chronicle*, February 21, 1996, p. A17. See also Tonelson and Wallach, "Overruled," p. 23.

100. Richard W. Stevenson, "U.S. to Honor Trade Ruling against It on Foreign Fuel," *New York Times*, June 20, 1996, p. C3.

101. This theme is developed in Vogel, *Trading Up*.

102. Quoted in Lawrence J. White, "The Community Reinvestment Act: Good Intentions Headed in the Wrong Direction," *Fordham Urban Law Journal*, vol. 20 (Fall 1993), pp. 281–92.

103. For a description and history of the CRA see Jonathan R. Macey and Geoffrey P. Miller, "The Community Reinvestment Act: An Economic Analysis," *Virginia Law Review*, vol. 79 (March 1993), pp. 291–348.

104. Grant Thornton, *Regulatory Burden: The Cost to Community Banks*

(New York: Independent Bankers Association of America, January 1993); and Barbara A. Rehm, "ABA: Cost of Compliance Equals 59% of Bank Profits," *American Banker* (June 18, 1992), p. 1, cited in Macey and Miller, *Community Reinvestment Act*, p. 325.

105. This argument should not be taken lightly. Revenue growth in the banking industry has stalled and profits have thinned as nonbank rivals apply new competitive heat and costs increase. Since 1987 Congress has imposed some forty major regulatory measures on banks and thrifts. The ultimate cost of the paperwork and red tape has been estimated to be perhaps as much as $14 billion annually. See Toby Roth, "Perfect Time for a New Banking Era," *Wall Street Journal*, January 16, 1996, p. A14; and Kelley Holland with Zachary Schiller, "Bankers' Hours Don't Look So Good: Slowing Profit Growth Is Forcing Banks to Pass Out Pink Slips," *Business Week*, December 19, 1994, pp. 102–03.

106. For this and the above argument see Macey and Miller, *Community Reinvestment Act*.

107. For a basic layout of the debate and compromises reached see Andrew Taylor, "Interstate Banking Law," *Congressional Quarterly* (December 3, 1994), p. 3462–63; and *International Banking Focus*, vol. 16 (August 4, 1994) and vol. 16 (September 23, 1994).

108. See European Commission, *1995 Report on US Barriers to Trade and Investment* (Brussels: Services of the European Commission, May 1995), p. 55.

Chapter 4

Adversarial Legalism: An International Perspective

Robert A. Kagan and Lee Axelrad

"MY ANCESTORS were Puritans from England. They arrived here in 1648 in the hope of finding greater restrictions than were permissible under English law at that time."[1] Contemporary Americans who smile at this gibe from Garrison Keillor suspect they, among all peoples, may be uniquely entangled in a proliferating web of laws and regulations. In some ways they are right, but in other ways they are not. In *all* economically advanced democracies, legal rules and liabilities now penetrate deeply into economic and social life.[2] Many European nations have heavier taxes than does the United States and far more restrictive rules concerning land use, dismissal of employees, and market entry of new businesses. Moreover, in an increasingly integrated global economy, national regulatory systems often seem to be converging.[3]

In at least one important respect, however, law and regulation in the United States does tend to be especially burdensome. Even when basic American policies and laws are similar to those in other countries, the United States has a distinctive legal style. American methods of implementing legal and regulatory norms and resolving related disputes are often unusually legalistic, adversarial, and expensive. To the

Interviews and research for this chapter were conducted by the authors and by the following researchers affiliated with the Comparative Legal Systems Project, Center for the Study of Law and Society, University of California, Berkeley: Kazumasu Aoki, John W. Cioffi, John P. Dwyer, Tatsuya Fujie, Lori Johnson, Martine Kraus, Alan C. Marco, Laura Beth Nielsen, Charles J. Ruhlin, and Deepak Somaya. Jeb Barnes contributed to the literature review portion of the paper.

direct costs of complying with laws and regulations, therefore, U.S. adversarial legalism, as we label it, generally adds *friction costs* that are not characteristic of other economically advanced democracies.[4]

Economists have begun to calculate cross-national differences in costs of complying with environmental regulations and expenditures on legal services.[5] Little systematic research has been done, however, concerning the pervasiveness and economic significance of U.S. adversarial legalism, the costs of which are often indirect and difficult to measure. This chapter reports on some preliminary research in that direction. We report on the findings of existing studies. We also draw on our own interviews with people in multinational corporations, where we asked company representatives to compare their experiences in the United States with their experiences in other countries.

Our interview responses confirm a conclusion of previous research. In most spheres of business and public policy, U.S. legal and regulatory processes are more complex, punitive, unpredictable, and costly than are their counterparts abroad. Moreover, the international differences in legal and regulatory *processes* often are more important to multinational enterprises than are differences in the nominal requirements of national laws and regulations. The extra costs and delays associated with adversarial legalism, while difficult to quantify, matter. Finally, the results of our interviews suggest that America's adversarial legalism does not consistently generate offsetting social benefits when compared with the less adversarial, less legalistic methods of regulation and dispute resolution in other democracies.

These findings, while illustrating certain inefficiencies in U.S. legal and regulatory processes, do not permit us to draw broad inferences about the overall impact of adversarial legalism on the U.S. economy. Nevertheless, in a more competitive world economy, developing less wasteful, less uncertain, and less alienating ways of carrying out regulatory and legal requirements may be nearly as important as developing more efficient means of producing goods and services. Understanding that there are some desirable alternative models among trading partners would seem to be a necessary first step toward reform.

Convergence and Divergence

In a global economy, the costs of doing business imposed by a nation's domestic laws and adjudicatory processes acquire greater significance.[6] European welfare states now worry about whether rules that provide high levels of security for workers have an adverse effect on growth and national competitiveness.[7] In the United States, politicians and academics have debated whether the U.S. civil liability system impairs economic growth.[8] A recent Japanese government report expressed concern over whether Japanese regulation of land use is "holding back Japan's future development and progress."[9]

Paradoxically, concern about the consequences of national regulatory differences arises in the context of considerable policy convergence, at least among industrialized countries.[10] The electorates of these societies often share values and expectations about environmental protection, product safety, nondiscrimination, fair business practices, and compensation for personal injury. Increasingly, policymakers share the same knowledge about technological and environmental risks; they employ similar modes of economic analysis and have comparable conceptions of justice. Policy convergence increases as delegations of regulators and legal scholars visit other countries in search of better ways of achieving similar goals.

Thus, international treaties demand harmonizing national laws on disposal of wastes in the ocean, eliminating ozone-depleting chemicals, patent protection, and liability for cargo damage. The list grows longer each year. The new "accounting directives" promulgated by the European Union rely on U.S. models for policing corporate disclosure.[11] The Council of Europe's directive on product liability law incorporates basic principles that are remarkably similar to the common law standards crafted by U.S. state court judges.[12] International networks of scientists, public health officials, and policy advocates have pushed most rich democracies to develop similar regulatory norms for the safety of commercial aircraft, labeling and packaging of chemical products, control of polyvinyl chloride fumes from plastics factories, and the restriction of cigarette smoking.[13] Deregulation of trading commissions by the U.S. stock exchange convinced British authorities to adopt similar rules so that London would not lose stock trading activity to New York.[14]

A focus on increasing policy harmonization nevertheless may lead one to ignore many important variations. Even when national policies are similar, the specific regulations and legal practices that operationalize policies often diverge strikingly. For example, the United States and western European countries strictly regulate the same kinds of emissions from new combustion facilities (for example, sulfur dioxide and nitrogen oxides), but the German, Dutch, and Swedish standards are considerably stricter than those issued by the U.S. Environmental Protection Agency.[15] Within the OECD, large differences persist in tax rates on corporate profits, statutorily guaranteed employee benefits, maximum truck sizes, and many other policies.[16] American law imposes much greater restrictions on the lines of business that banks can engage in and on bank ownership of industrial enterprises.[17] Germany and Japan, in contrast to the United States, have complex bodies of regulations protecting local shopkeepers, thereby impeding the efforts of discount chains to open new stores. Meanwhile, in the United States large retailers are subject to much greater exposure to product liability lawsuits.[18]

The persistence of legal differences, however, can coexist with an overall trend toward transnational harmonization of legal and regulatory policies. The dynamic proceeds more rapidly in some sectors than in others. According to Karen Palmer, Wallace Oates, and Paul Portney, "Although U.S. environmental regulations are arguably the most stringent in the world, the *differentials* between U.S. standards and those of our major industrialized trading partners are not very great."[19] In our research, multinational enterprises that have parallel operations in the United States and other OECD countries report relatively few significant differences in the basic policies embodied in environmental, safety, patent, and commercial laws they encounter. In other fields, such as labor law, tax law, and competition policy, powerful domestic political constituencies battle the leveling influence of international pressures, sometimes more successfully, sometimes less so. Thus, distinctions persist.[20] And in an increasingly integrated global marketplace, those distinctions can loom large for firms competing head to head.

Perhaps most resistant to harmonization are national institutional arrangements and practices aimed at effectuating regulatory goals, enforcing legal norms, and resolving disputes. National legal or regulatory styles are crucial intervening variables, muting, amplifying, or transforming the laws on the books. By *style* we mean such matters as the propensity to employ courts and formal legal procedures to implement governmental policy; the detail, specificity, and complexity of the legal rules or regulations that embody general policy; the severity of legal penalties imposed on violators; institutional arrangements for regulatory enforcement and adjudication; and the finality, uniformity, and predictability of case-by-case legal and regulatory decisionmaking.[21] It is in these respects that the United States appears to be distinctive.

American Adversarial Legalism

In the past twenty years, social scientists and legal scholars have conducted many detailed comparative case studies of legal and regulatory processes (table 4-1). Most focus on a particular arena of public policy or law—compensating injured people; regulating pollution; equalizing educational opportunity; adjudicating civil lawsuits; regulating workplace safety; deterring malpractice by physicians, chemical companies, nursing homes, or policemen. Across this array of sectoral studies one finding recurs. The relevant American legal process tends to be characterized by more complex and detailed bodies of rules; more frequent recourse to formal legal methods of implementing policy and resolving disputes; more adversarial and expensive forms of legal contestation; more punitive legal sanctions (including larger civil damage awards); more frequent judicial review, revision, and delay of administrative decisionmaking; and more malleability and unpredictability.

We summarize here just a few of these studies.

—Comparing social controls on corporate governance in the United States, the United Kingdom, France, Japan, and Germany, Jonathan P. Charkham found, "Litigation only figures in one of the countries studied. . . . The unheavenly trio of derivative suits, class actions, and contingency fees is unique to the USA."[22]

—Comparing methods for selection of labor union representation in the United States and eleven other countries, Derek C. Bok found that the U.S. National Labor Relations Act created a uniquely decentralized and adversarial method of unionizing and a singularly complex and detailed regulatory scheme to govern unions' and employers' behavior. "The result has been a level of regulatory activity and litigiousness in labor relations that is without parallel in the rest of the world."[23]

—Thomas W. Church and Robert T. Nakamura studied the cleanup of toxic waste sites in the United States, Denmark, and the Netherlands. They found that the U.S. regulatory regime, governed

TABLE 4-1. *Cross-National Socio-Legal Studies*

Study	Policy area	Countries compared with United States
Badarraco (1985)	Exposure to chloride	France, Germany, Japan, Great Britain
Bayley (1976)	Policing	Japan
Bok (1971)	Selecting labor representatives	Several west European countries
Braithwaite (1985)	Coal mine safety regulation	Australia, France, Germany, Great Britain, Japan
Braithwaite (1993)	Nursing home regulation	Australia, Great Britain
Brickman, Jasanoff, and Ilgen (1985)	Hazardous chemicals regulation	Several west European countries
Charkham (1994)	Corporate governance	France, Germany, Japan, Great Britain
Day and Klein (1987)	Nursing homes	Great Britain
Flanagan (1987)	Labor	Canada, Japan
Glendon (1987)	Regulating abortion; providing child support	Several European countries
Jasanoff (1986)	Regulating carcinogens	Several west European countries
Kelman (1981)	Workplace safety	Sweden
Kirp (1982)	Special education	Great Britain
Kirp (1979)	Racial discrimination in schools	Great Britain
Langbein (1985)	Civil litigation methods	Germany
Litt and others (1990)	Banking regulation	Japan
Lohof (1991)	Hazardous waste cleanup	Several west European countries
Lundqvist (1980)	Air pollution regulation	Sweden
Quam and others (1987)	Medical malpractice	Great Britain
Reich (1985)	Corporate bailouts	Germany, Great Britain, Japan
Schwartz (1991)	Product liability	Several west European countries
Tanase (1990)	Compensation for motor vehicle accidents	Japan
Teff (1985)	Pharmaceuticals regulation	Great Britain
Vogel (1986)	Environmental regulation	Great Britain
Wokutch (1992)	Occupational safety and health	Japan

Sources: See the "Bibliography of Cross-National Socio-Legal Studies" in this volume.

by the federal Superfund statute, is by far the most punitive, imposing strict and retroactive liability on almost any party associated with the polluted site, regardless of fault or contribution to the overall level of contamination or whether any serious risk to the public ensued. The result is an extraordinary level of costly litigation at each site, delaying cleanup efforts: "Most Superfund negotiations can be characterized as adversarial, coercive, and combative." They go on to say that cleanup of hazardous waste sites in The Netherlands and Denmark almost certainly operates with less acrimony and more cooperation than in the United States.[24]

— In a comparative study of coal mine safety regulation, John Braithwaite found that while Great Britain and France have moved "from prosecution and toward persuasion as the best way of achieving mine safety," the United States embraced a legalistic and punitive approach, resulting in "an inspectorate that spends more time in court than in mines, and an [alienated] industry . . . resisting any improvement not achieved by legal compulsion."[25]

To characterize the overall thrust of such descriptions of the American legal and regulatory style, we use the summary term *adversarial legalism*.[26] Figure 4-1 distinguishes its most prominent characteristics. Adversarial legalism differs first of all from informal methods of resolving disputes or making policy decisions, such as mediation, expert professional judgment, or bargaining among political authorities. Second, in adversarial legalism, litigants and their lawyers play active roles in the policy implementation and decisionmaking process; hence the style differs from governance that is legally formal but more hierarchical or bureaucratic. In western European courts, bureaucratically organized judges dominate fact gathering and selection of expert witnesses.[27] In U.S. adversarial legalism, attorneys for the parties dominate the process.

Even when compared with the British legal system from which they descended, U.S. methods of adjudication are more party influenced and less hierarchically controlled. Judges in the United States are more diverse than British judges, more political, more autonomous, and their decisions are less uniform.[28] Law in the United States is more malleable, open to novel legal and policy arguments put forth by parties and their lawyers. In the United States, lay jurors still play a large and important role in civil cases, which in turn magnifies the importance of skillful legal advocacy by the parties and reduces legal certainty.[29]

FIGURE 4-1. *Methods of Policymaking and Dispute Resolution*

Degree of legal formality

		Informal	Formal
Structure of decisionmaking authority	*Hierarchical*	Expert or political judgment	Bureaucratic legalism
	Party influenced	Negotiation/ mediation	Adversarial legalism

Similarly, compared to most European democracies, where central governments are accorded stronger hierarchical authority, regulatory rulemaking in the United States (where hierarchical authority is mistrusted) entails many more legal formalities: public notice and comment, open hearings, restrictions on informal contacts, legalistically specified evidentiary and scientific standards, mandatory official findings, and responses to interest group arguments. These devices facilitate interest group participation and judicial review of administrative decisions. In the regulatory policymaking bodies of western Europe and Japan, by contrast, a combination of expert and political judgment prevails, lawyers rarely participate, and appeals to the courts are infrequent.[30]

The difference, the case studies in table 4-1 indicate, shows up in regulatory implementation and enforcement as well. In the United States, governmental authority is fragmented and subject to challenge, both by regulated companies and proregulation advocacy groups. Thus U.S. regulatory implementation more often follows a pattern of adversarial law enforcement: regulated entities are treated with mistrust; desired behaviors are closely specified in detailed regulations; detected violations are punished; recourse to courts, by both the regulators and the regulated, is common; and a spirit of adversarial gamesmanship often prevails. Comparable agencies in other economically advanced democracies, where hierarchical authority is less questioned, tend to employ a more informal, cooperation-seeking or educational implementation style. Disputes are resolved through negotiation or informal appeal to higher political authorities, and recourse to the courts and to formal legal contestation is comparatively rare.

The United States accords unusual prominence to tort law in compensating victims of highway, medical, and product-related accidents. Thus the U.S. compensation system is far more contentious and driven by litigant activism than are European systems, which operate primarily through hierarchically organized benefit-payment bureaucracies. In the 1970s and 1980s, for example, the incidence of asbestos-related diseases among Dutch workers was five to ten times higher than in the United States. Dutch law permitted tort claims against employers. Yet as of 1992, whereas an estimated 200,000 asbestos-based tort cases had been filed in the United States, circumventing administratively based workers' compensation systems, fewer than 10 cases had been filed in The Netherlands from 1981 to 1991, where diseased workers had access to a publicly funded compensation program.[31] In Great Britain, where asbestos victims' medical costs and lost earnings are handled by the National Health Service and by government-provided disability pensions, the rate of asbestos-related tort suits has been far lower than in the United States. British tort recoveries are about half as large, and asbestos firms have not been driven into bankruptcy.[32]

For the United States, adversarial legalism is not an arbitrary choice. It reflects a political tradition that from the nation's beginnings harbored antipathy for hierarchically organized, concentrated governmental power. The U.S. Constitution and its state-level counterparts fragment and constrain governmental authority and invite a broad judicial role in the protection of individual rights. Courts, lawyers, and juries are prominent institutions of governance.

However, the reach and intensity of contemporary adversarial legalism is something new, far surpassing its status in the decades before the mid-1960s—an era of less active government.[33] The adversarial legalism described in the studies listed in table 4-1 springs from a new force in American politics: a public preference for comprehensive governmental protections from harm, injustice, and environmental dangers. But the demands for an activist agenda are channeled through governmental and economic structures that reflect the traditional mistrust of concentrated power and a reluctance to pay the high taxes that support European-style bureaucracies and welfare programs. In effect, Americans have asked policymakers to transform and improve society and to compel widespread changes in business behavior without relinquishing a penchant for fractioning and checking authority, public and private, through detailed laws, procedural safeguards, and privately activated adversarial action. Lawsuits, rights, penalties, lawyers, courts, and juries thus are the U.S. substitutes for the powerful central bureaucracies, corporatist bodies, central banks, and *keiretsu* that dominate the social regulatory regimes of other advanced democracies.

Within the United States, the extent of adversarial legalism varies. Some policy arenas, administrative systems, communities, and business sectors are relatively free of it.[34] Most problems and losses are dealt with through private or public insurance, not by litigation.[35] Quite a few U.S. regulatory agencies emphasize flexible and cooperative procedures rather than punitive modes of enforcement.[36]

Even in arenas where adversarial legalism is rife, full-scale legal contestation may be uncommon. The costs and uncertainties of litigation impel most disputants to negotiate settlements or to structure their conduct to minimize the risk of a regulatory violation or of cause for a lawsuit. In recent years, moreover, state legislatures have enacted dozens of laws designed to restrict tort litigation and to encourage more cooperative forms of environmental law enforcement.[37] Politicians have streamlined some administrative procedures for new projects, such as the regulatory approval of new drugs. Hospitals, securities firms, and many other businesses have scrambled to build alternative dispute resolution procedures into their contracts and personnel management systems.

In addition, some legal scholars have suggested that adversarial legalism is on the rise in other countries and that the United States may end up being less of an outlier. As regulatory authority in Europe has shifted to bureaucracies in Brussels, European business executives have begun to complain about encountering more formalistic, procedurally complex modes of regulation in the European Union. Amid intensifying economic competition and the dismantling of state-owned enterprises and state-supported cartels, Europeans are witnessing the arrival of large corporate law firms, more aggressive approaches to litigation, and inch-thick, defensively worded American-style contracts. Some legal scholars now speak of the "Americanization" of European commercial law.[38]

A recent study of land development disputes in Germany, France, and the United States found that major construction projects were challenged in court in European countries nearly as often as they are in the United States.[39] In Belgium and Germany, where many citizens carry insurance for legal costs, litigation rates for automobile accidents are high.[40] In Germany, where the law provides workers extremely strong protections and generous rights to severance pay, litigation in labor tribunals regarding termination of employment is common.[41] European legal scholars and judges, facing political demands for transparency and participation akin to those that have driven the evolution of American administrative law, are calling for more formal legal techniques of controlling administrative policy-making and implementation.[42]

Notwithstanding such developments, studies indicate that adversarial legalism is significantly more prevalent in U.S. law and regulation than it is elsewhere. Our interview-based research confirms this proposition.

Further Explorations

During 1995 and early 1996 we interviewed representatives of multinational corporations that conduct "parallel" business operations in the United States and other economically advanced countries. Nearly one hundred in-depth interviews were conducted with corporate executives, attorneys, consultants, representatives of trade associations, and government officials. In the case of seven corporations, initial interviews have developed into more intensive case studies. The companies interviewed do not constitute a statistically representative sample distributed across all standard industrial classification codes. But our respondents, as indicated in table 4-2, include executives and lawyers in a number of industries, and our discussions focused on a variety of legal or regulatory topics. Some respondents are from U.S.-based corporations, and some are from corporations based in Japan, The Netherlands, Great Britain, Canada, or Germany.

Legal Style versus Substantive Standards

When asked to compare their companies' legal and regulatory experience among countries, the representatives of multinational corporations that we interviewed emphasized differences in national

TABLE 4-2. *Interviews Conducted*

Industry	Number of interviews	Areas of discussion
Automakers	11	Environmental, product liability
Banking	8	Regulation, debt collection, contract, bankruptcy
Chemicals	16	Health, safety, environmental, contract, liability, patents, project development, transportation
Consulting	8	Employment discrimination, product liability, environmental, liability, transportation, land use, permitting
Consumer products	1	Investor suits, intellectual property
Government	6	Product liability, patents, environmental, project development
Electronics	7	Contracts, patents, arbitration, environmental
Engineering and planning	2	Land use, energy, water quality
Food	4	Labeling, testing, trademarks
Health care	1	Patents
Law firms	7	Product liability, employment, construction, petroleum transportation, environmental, commercial transactions, energy production
Metal parts	5	Environmental
Mining	1	Employment
Petrochemicals/ petroleum	20	Environmental, transportation, safety, liability, occupational health, antitrust, land use, commercial law
Petroleum equipment	3	Environmental safety
Pharmaceuticals	12	Employment, product approval
Trade associations	6	Environmental, employment discrimination, product liability
Video games	2	Intellectual property

legal style rather than differences in the substance of national laws and rules. In environmental and safety regulation, company officials indicated that both the substantive standards embodied in official regulations and the actual control or prevention measures that have to be implemented are basically similar in the OECD countries. The same goes for comparative experience with respect to commercial law, patent law, and safety standards for the licensing and manufacturing of genetically engineered biological products.

In our interviews we encountered little criticism of the United States for enacting more stringent health, safety, or environmental rules than do other countries. European representatives of an international petrochemical company told us that safety regulations in Europe and the United States concerning the labeling, packaging, and land transportation of hazardous chemicals were fundamentally the same. When we interviewed engineers from a Japanese chemical firm that is refitting a recently purchased plant in the United States to mimic certain processes successfully pioneered at its factory in Japan, they told us that with two or three minor exceptions, the substantive rules on fire safety and air pollution control were essentially the same in both countries, and that only minor adjustments in equipment had to be made to meet U.S. standards.[43] An official from a chemical and pharmaceutical manufacturer with operations in Europe, Japan, the United States, and elsewhere said that regarding required levels of safety and environmental protection, "in the industrial world, the playing field is reasonably level."

The chief contrast between the legal systems of the United States and those of other industrial nations, according to the chief environmental attorney for a multinational chemical company, is not that the laws or standards are different but that "cultural processes" are different.[44] The salient features of the U.S. process, this official observed, are the familiar ones of adversarial legalism: more complex bodies of legal rules; a dispersion of authority, forcing a company to satisfy many agencies and respond to scattered claims in different courts; greater uncertainty concerning legal requirements; and longer decisionmaking delays. For example, this respondent noted that the U.S. air pollution permit process for new or renovated chemical manufacturing facilities involves more jurisdictional stops, more opportunities for local opponents to appeal, and more stages at which both federal and state regulators must agree. In other countries, the official stated, the emission standards are comparable but there is nothing quite like this kind of procedural legal maze for gaining regulatory approval.[45]

Adversarial legalism seemed to be less salient to corporate managers who deal with U.S. regulatory agencies that specialize in a single industry and technology. For example, officials from the shipping division in a multinational petrochemical company described their relationship with the tank car safety section of the Federal Railroad Administration (FRA) as generally nonadversarial and nonlegalistic. A pharmaceutical company's regulatory affairs official described his encounters with the biological products office of the U.S. Food and Drug Administration as somewhat legalistic (in the sense that this agency is a stickler for strict compliance with rules) but not adversarial; disputes rarely end up in court.

However, the petrochemical company's shipping safety procedures are driven in part not only by the FRA but also by the omnipresent threat that a tank car or truck accident will result in a tort suit, a prospect far less likely for the same company's shipping department in Europe. Similarly, in designing manufacturing processes, the pharmaceutical company's U.S. officials worry about the possibility of tort litigation more than their counterparts abroad do.

Companies operating in other countries are not wholly free of concerns about adversarial legalism. A U.S. chemical company that sought to obtain patents for a breakthrough invention in the United States, Japan, and the European Union experienced a great deal of time-consuming and unpredictable legal contestation in all three venues. American procedures for granting a patent, in fact, were less adversarial, since U.S. patent law does not provide for pregrant "oppositions" in the same way as the Japanese and European patent offices. But the legal processes for enforcing a patent in the United States are much more adversarial, partly because U.S. litigation entails extensive (and expensive) pretrial discovery, dueling expert witnesses, and the threat of treble damages.[46]

In sum, while multinational companies occasionally run into comparable regulatory complexity in Europe, our interviewees confirmed that the American regulatory style is often exceptionally legalistic. The threat of litigation looms larger in the United States, and litigation in American courts is more combative, costly, and menacing.

Legalistic Regulatory Enforcement

To corporate personnel with international experience, perhaps the most disturbing and striking procedural feature of U.S. law is the prevalence of legalistic enforcement of environmental and safety regulations.[47] Time and again, persons charged with managing regulatory affairs in multinational corporations told us of incidents in which unintentional violations of "prophylactic" regulations (reporting, labeling, design of storage containers, and so on) that entailed no actual harm to workers or to the environment were met with automatic fines amounting to many thousands of dollars.

For example, a regulatory compliance official from a U.S. chemical plant reported a meeting in London with her counterparts from corporate plants in the United Kingdom, Canada, and Australia. All these nations have laws requiring chemical companies to maintain detailed inventories of chemicals in the production process and in shipment. Given the volume and speed of shipments, said the U.S. official, it is "extremely easy to make a mistake." When a British regulatory compliance official discovered such an error, his attitude, the bemused American told us, was, "Oh dear, I think I'll have to do something about that," suggesting that a report or a call to the relevant agency would take care of such a nonwillful violation. If the U.S. subsidiary's regulatory compliance office discovered a similar error, we were told, "We'd panic. We'd start calculating the fine we owed," because self-reporting can reduce the statutory fine (up to $25,000 a day) by half.[48]

Multinational corporate managers repeatedly told us that regulators in Europe and Japan rarely resort to formal punishment in response to relatively trivial or unintentional offenses. Instead, the foreign regulators are much more inclined to sit down with company representatives to work out agreements on technically appropriate remedial measures.[49]

U.S. regulatory agencies' hair-trigger resort to formal enforcement is far from uniform, but it is unpredictable. And it is doubly troublesome to corporate officials, given the detail and complexity of U.S. regulations. Firms are often unsure whether they have actually achieved compliance. Officials from a U.S. chemical firm said that when they encountered an ambiguous TSCA regulation and sought guidance from the EPA on whether the firm needed to submit certain paperwork, the agency issued a $23 million fine against the company.

The Distinctiveness of American Liability Law

Our interviews also underscored the unique risks of the U.S. liability law regime, particularly tort suits and civil cases brought pursuant to environmental statutes. Its distinctiveness lies not in substantive standards for corporate liability, but rather in litigants' readiness to mobilize, the unpredictability and potential magnitude of damage awards (due to the vagueness of legal rules for damages and the use of juries), and the costs of the litigation process itself. Consider the following examples.

— One of our corporate case studies involved a multinational company that prescribed identical personnel management policies and procedures for the United States and for its Canadian branches; the company even shifted human resources personnel back and forth to try to ensure uniform compliance. Yet, in a recent year, almost 23 percent of "forced separations" of employees in the United States resulted in a lawsuit against the company, compared with 7 percent in Canada, where the law protecting employees against arbitrary dismissal is more comprehensive and more protective of workers than is U.S. law.

— A legal counsel for a foreign motor vehicle manufacturer told us that no country in which his firm sells vehicles comes close to the United States in terms of the incidence and cost of product liability litigation.[50] Canada is perhaps the closest, he noted, but still remains a very distant second for several reasons. First, Canada requires losing plaintiffs to pay some or all of the defendant's lawyer fees, and in Ontario, the most populous province, contingency fees are banned.[51] This "chills the filing of frivolous cases in Canada," unlike in the United States, where a significant number of cases are filed without much investigation in hopes of getting a quick nuisance settlement. Second, in civil cases, Canada does not use juries. In the United States, jury trials in auto product liability cases typically involve complex and conflicting expert witness testimony on such issues as "accident reconstruction, body mechanics, and motor vehicle design engineering and decisionmaking," and befuddled juries, the corporate counsel believed, often are swayed by clever lawyering. Third, Canada has much more specific damage rules and does not impose punitive damages (which even in the United States are actually paid in only a small percentage of claims, but are important, the corporate counsel said, because 10 percent of the liability cases generate 90 percent of the firm's financial exposure). Fourth, Canada has a rule that if the injured plaintiff was contributorily negligent as a result of alcohol or drug abuse, no recovery is permitted. Fifth, Canada does not have the highly organized litigation machine created by entrepreneurial lawyers in the United States. Here plaintiffs' lawyers draw on (and help fund) data bases, litigation kits, workshops on particular vehicles, and expert witnesses—all provided by the American Trial Lawyers Association and the Center for Automotive Safety.

In sum, although our sample of business sectors and areas of law is not comprehensive, the cumulative findings of our interviews reinforce the thrust of earlier research: adversarial legalism pervades the U.S. business climate.

Economic Consequences

By exalting lawyers and courts, Americans empower activist organizations, businesses, and even ordinary citizens to challenge corporate malfeasance and the arbitrary exercise of governmental authority. Access to the courts makes public policy more responsive to new ideas, local conditions, and the interests of political minorities. Using the courts, the National Association for the Advancement of Colored People (NAACP) successfully attacked racial segregation, disabled children won rights to better education, and innovative companies cracked open telecommunications and financial monopolies. Plaintiffs' lawyers can help uncover evidence of negligence or fraud. Civil suits can encourage safer technologies and sounder financial markets. By putting teeth into environmental policies, private rights of action have pushed private enterprise to take environmental problems seriously, thereby reducing some harmful pollution. Fierce adversarial litigation makes U.S. courts more effective than those of other countries for certain kinds of claims and remedies. Consider:

—A New Zealand corporation, attempting to recover assets pirated by former employees, brought almost identical legal actions against them in four jurisdictions in which the defendants operated corporate shells: Hong Kong, New Zealand, Great Britain, and California. The California judge, the New Zealand corporation's lawyer told us, was the most pragmatic and the quickest to issue a preliminary injunction. The California judge issued rulings from the bench directly after oral arguments, rather than taking decisions under advisement. U.S. courts, in the opinion of that experienced commercial lawyer, may be less legally precise and reliable, but they are often more creative and responsive than their counterparts abroad.

—As suggested earlier, experienced patent lawyers note that U.S. litigation, although costly, offers far more potent tools for attacking infringers than do the courts of Japan and Germany. Among the greatest difficulties faced by firms seeking to enforce patent rights in Japanese courts are lack of discovery, long court proceedings (a series of short hearings occurring at intervals over a long period of time), and greater difficulty obtaining preliminary injunctions.[52] Perhaps this helps explain why in 1990 there were 1,236 patent infringement suits filed in the United States compared with only 141 filed in Japan.[53]

So, notwithstanding the attention we are about to pay to the economic costs of the U.S. legal style, we also recognize its advantages. Some unknown proportion of the U.S. system's total costs is worth paying. Some scholars have offered estimates of the aggregate "friction" costs that U.S. regulation and legal culture impose on the U.S. economy.[54] Aggregate estimates of the social benefits are made less frequently. Problematically, for our purposes, none of these studies attempts to separate the costs and benefits attributable to adversarial legalism from those attributable to substantive legal obligations. Our strategy in analyzing costs and benefits is to view the U.S. legal and regulatory model from a comparative perspective, focusing on specific policy areas in which some cross-national information is available or in which we have been able to interview company officials with cross-national experience.

It seems reasonably clear that U.S. adversarial legalism generates higher costs than do some alternative modes of governance. Yet there is little evidence in the policy areas covered by our research that the higher expenditures imposed by the system yield better environmental protection, more safety, and so on than the results that prevail in other sophisticated democracies. In other words, our comparative interviews with corporate officials suggest that a significant share of the costs of U.S. adversarial legalism is not fully offset by its benefits. We proceed by identifying several categories of such costs, then by reviewing the comparative literature on the subject and reporting conclusions from our interviews with multinational enterprises. At the end we return to the question of whether adversarial legalism confers adequate compensatory benefits.

Costs of Litigiousness

U.S. lawyers who have litigated abroad perceive litigation costs in the United States to be considerably greater than those in foreign countries.[55] Comparisons of the basic procedures suggest that American-style litigation, with its pretrial discovery and its cumbersome jury trials, poses complications that other highly developed legal systems generally avoid.[56]

— In routine auto accident lawsuits in the United States, payments to lawyers account for 37 percent of total liability insurance payouts.[57] In Japan and The Netherlands, a variety of alternative dispute resolution and legal mechanisms compensate motor vehicle accident victims at much lower transaction costs. (The lawyers' take in more complicated tort cases is even larger.)[58]

— Claims agents who deal with cargo damage disputes arising from transatlantic shipments say that their lawyers' bills are far higher if a legal dispute is processed in the Port of New York instead of in Rotterdam, even though the relevant substantive law in the two countries is essentially identical.[59]

— Patent attorney James Maxeiner has written that because patent litigation in the United States is singularly adversarial, "Expert testimony in U.S. patent litigation is much more costly than in Germany."[60] The American Intellectual Property Law Association estimated in 1994 that in patent infringement cases, the median litigation cost *for each side* was $280,000 through pretrial discovery and $518,000 through trial.[61]

— According to a 1992 survey, in shareholders' lawsuits against corporate officers and directors, the median legal defense costs in cases that were settled before trial was about $250,000, an expense foreign corporations typically have not had to worry about.[62]

— In lawsuits filed by individual employees alleging unjust dismissal, the average cost of legal defense in a sample of cases brought to trial in California between 1980 and 1986 was more than $80,000. The average plaintiff was forty-five years old and made $36,000 annually, but the median verdict in the 67.5 percent of cases that plaintiffs won was $177,000. Plaintiffs' lawyers generally collected 40 percent of the ultimate recovery.[63] Although studies of labor courts in Germany, Great Britain, and the Netherlands do not provide comparable quantitative data, detailed sociolegal descriptive studies indicate that legal costs there in dismissal cases are far lower and that remedies, while frequently granted, are far less punitive.[64]

If U.S. litigation is more costly, does the extra expenditure deliver intangible social benefits, such as more justice? For some kinds of issues, the answer must be yes. Contingency fees and sharp pretrial discovery tools, for example, allow American plaintiffs with meager resources to obtain voluminous information, some of which may prove essential to their claims; their counterparts abroad may not do as well in that regard. In a large range of cases, however, the answer is probably not. The same U.S. discovery norms and attorney compensation rules increase the costs of defending, and hence the nuisance value, of many ill-founded lawsuits. Conversely, the expense and unpleasantness of U.S. litigation also deters or diminishes the settlement value of many legally valid claims.

Legal Unpredictability

On December 28, 1983, Pennzoil Corporation offered to purchase 20 percent of Getty Oil Company's outstanding stock for $100 a share. Getty Oil's management feared that Pennzoil would join forces with large dissident Getty shareholders, but after some negotiations, an apparent verbal agreement was reached on January 2, 1984, to sell Pennzoil three-sevenths of Getty's stock at $112.50 a share. A joint Pennzoil-Getty press release stated that they had an "agreement in principle" that was "subject to execution of a definitive merger agreement." Pennzoil, however, declined to withdraw its pending tender offer of $100 a share until "a definitive merger agreement is executed."[65] Getty Oil's board frantically sought a better price for the company from other sources. After being assured by leading corporate takeover professionals that Getty Oil was free to deal, Texaco offered to buy all of Getty Oil's outstanding stock at $125 a share. After the offer was increased to $128, it was formally accepted by Getty's management on January 7, 1984.[66]

When a Delaware court rejected Pennzoil's request to enjoin the sale to Texaco, Pennzoil, a Houston-based company, sued Texaco (a New York company) in a Houston court, alleging intentional interference with Pennzoil's "contract" with Getty. Texaco argued that there was no contract under either New York or Texas law. The relevant laws of the two states differ in some respects, and it was not clear, legal experts agree, which state's law was properly applicable.[67] Legal analysts do agree, however, that under either state's law and in light of the facts presented, Texaco had not acted wrongfully, since no formal contract had been concluded. Nevertheless, the Houston jury found for Pennzoil, which was represented by a famous Texas trial lawyer. What is more, the jury awarded Pennzoil the astronomical sum of $7.53 billion in actual damages and $3 billion in punitive damages.[68] The trial judge refused to hear Texaco's request for a new trial, but a Texas appeals court reduced the punitive damages to a mere $1 billion. Legal analysts point out that under both Texas and New York law, the maximum actual damages Texaco should have been compelled to pay, assuming it really had been liable, were $422 million.[69] Even Texaco could not easily afford to write a check for $8.5 billion and had to file for bankruptcy, from which it eventually emerged. Still, Texaco suffered from a fire sale of $5.1 billion in assets. Business relationships were impaired, and the livelihoods of thousands of workers were threatened.

How could a sophisticated company such as Texaco, with its legion of well-paid, experienced attorneys and investment advisers, fail by such a wide margin to discern the legal risks to which it was exposed? The answer is that in the decentralized U.S. judicial system, constantly being shaped and reshaped by adversarial argument, legal rules are malleable and litigative outcomes are highly uncertain. The legal terrain is unstable.

This is not an endemic feature of all legal regimes. When asked about transatlantic cargo damage disputes that reach adjudication, shipping line and insurance firm representatives whom we interviewed asserted that outcomes in the Dutch courts are much more predictable than the results in U.S. courts.[70] For a number of reasons, civil adjudication tends to be more predictable in many western European nations and in Japan than it is in the United States. Professional judges, never amateur juries, decide civil cases, and their decisions are explained in writing and are therefore reviewable. Judges, not lawyers, dominate the production and evaluation of evidence. Damage awards in tort cases are moderate and more constrained by law. Judges are less "creative," and more dedicated to legal consistency than are their American counterparts.[71] The decisions of European regulatory bureaucracies, too, are more stable, not because European bureaucrats are more reasonable, but because they are more insulated from ad hoc political pressures and less subject to judicial reversals.

American-regulated entities and litigants, faced with unpredictable and potentially massive legal penalties, often feel compelled to settle highly contestable regulatory demands and civil lawsuits.[72] So obvious did this become with respect to class action suits alleging securities fraud that in 1996 Congress finally moved to shield corporate management from extortionate claims.[73] The legislation stipulated that plaintiffs that lose at trial will have to pay the defendant's counsel fees.[74]

Peter Huber compared verdicts by juries in product liability cases concerning Bendectin (a morning sickness drug), alleged defects in Audi motor cars, and various other allegedly dangerous products. Most juries, in accordance with the weight of the scientific evidence presented, found that the products in question were not defective or not responsible for the plaintiffs' injuries. However, in each sequence of trials concerning a particular product, one or two juries, hearing the same evidence as those that found no liability, decided otherwise and awarded the plaintiff huge compensatory and punitive damages. The modal jury award was zero, but the average was in the multiple millions of dollars. For the manufacturers in question, the degree of uncertainty was great enough to dictate a settlement strategy for subsequent legal threats.[75]

When the city of Boston sought to build a new highway and tunnel, an environmental group threatened litigation. Boston officials could not be sure that a judge would find the suit groundless and were sure that the litigative process could stall the project to death. Boston felt compelled to offer 1,100 "mitigation projects" (for greenspace, transit, research, and environmental improvements) at a staggering cost of $2.8 billion. Of the 113 largest mitigation commitments, fewer than 50 were directly related to the transportation project.[76]

Such settlements can be detrimental to the U.S. economy because they represent questionable wealth transfers exacted by legal extortion, not by carefully deliberated public choices, and because a disproportionate share of such transfers goes to plaintiffs' lawyers. As Marc Galanter has shown, the higher the costs and uncertainties of litigation in relation to the stakes, the further pretrial settlements will deviate from the outcome likely to result from adjudication.[77] Various studies, as well as abundant anecdotal evidence, indicates that in countless smaller claims, too, insurance companies and other defendants routinely pay to settle nuisance suits in order to avoid the high litigation costs and uncertainties associated with adversarial legalism.[78]

Lawyering

Direct outlays for legal services in the United States have been estimated to exceed $100 billion a year.[79] Economists have estimated that in terms of value added (an industry's gross receipts minus its purchases from other economic sectors), the U.S. legal industry in 1987 was larger than the U.S. steel industry, the textile industry, and even the domestic auto industry.[80] In some recent years, legal services purchased by foreign businesses and governments reportedly have been New York City's largest "export."[81]

Much of that expenditure is socially beneficial; any modern society needs lawyers to help communicate the requirements of complex and changing legal rules, to structure contracts, and to defend the accused. Nevertheless, although accurate comparative data are hard to come by, adversarial legalism drives people in the United States to spend much more on legal services than is spent by people in other industrial countries. Ordinary observation leaves little doubt that U.S. business executives engaged in negotiating sales franchises, seeking approval for real estate projects, acquiring other companies, issuing stock, and launching new products surround themselves with larger phalanxes of high-priced attorneys than do business managers anywhere else.[82]

In our interviews with multinational enterprises, respondents often mentioned that they pay much more for legal counsel in their U.S. operations than in their similar operations elsewhere. Generally, this cost difference reflected the number of legal experts (as opposed to higher hourly rates) needed to conduct business operations in the United States. The value, frequency, and duration of consultations with in-house and outside counsel are especially great for matters such as selecting pollution control equipment, managing problem personnel, and conducting sales transactions.

The bill for lawyering runs high in the United States partly because in seeking social control U.S. society is especially inclined to place its bets on the presumed deterrent effects of harsh civil sanctions and regulatory penalties. Whatever the actual deterrence obtained (a matter we will return to later), the throw-the-book-at-'em strategy seems to produce a heightened state of legal defensiveness. The legalistic enforcement style stimulates many more legal appeals than do the cooperative enforcement styles pursued by English and Swedish regulators.[83] One case study found that when a pharmaceutical firm terminated individual employees in the United States, the firm consulted its attorneys earlier, more frequently, and more substantively than when terminating employees in Canada. In the

United States an in-house attorney was involved full-time in employment matters. In Canada company human resources officials spoke infrequently to their outside counsel by telephone.

A corporate general counsel in the U.S. office of a multinational chemical company told us that in the U.S. subsidiary, unlike in its European corporate parent, a wide variety of documents are routinely reviewed by the legal department. One stimulus to this procedure was a lawsuit for breach of contract in which a drawing made by a company sales representative was held, much to the company's surprise, to have been evidence of a contract. The suit cost the company roughly $500,000 in damages and $500,000 in legal expenses. Now, the lawyer said, "Half of our salesmen are scared to death to do anything without consulting a lawyer." The U.S. subsidiary employs six specially trained nonlawyers who spend at least half their time fielding legal questions that salespeople routinely ask about sales contracts. To further avoid legal problems, "When European people [from the parent firm] come over here," the corporate attorney added, "we have to forbid them from talking or writing letters to anyone."

The law in most western European countries, as in the United States, incorporates a "polluter pays" principle for cleaning up defunct hazardous waste sites. But whereas European regulatory administrators often moderate those obligations and employ public funds for the initial cleanup, the U.S. Environmental Protection Agency administers the Superfund law by imposing massive cleanup costs on a handful of larger private companies and municipalities whose wastes find their way into the sites.[84] The EPA expects them to seek contributions from other users of the sites. The resulting legal infighting among potentially responsible parties and their insurance companies has equaled an estimated 24 to 44 percent of the funds expended on actual cleanups.[85]

Accountability

U.S. regulatory regimes impose more extensive and specific requirements for reporting, record keeping, testing, employee education, certifications, and so on than do regulatory regimes elsewhere. In addition to the costs of complying with substantive standards, therefore, regulated companies spend more on proving that they are complying. In addition to explicitly mandated accountability measures, many enterprises feel compelled to invest heavily in further proof of compliance because regulatory rules in the United States are more complex and are often enforced in an uncompromising manner. A threatening liability system often has the same effect.[86]

Thus our interviews with multinational corporate officials indicate that specialized intracorporate regulatory compliance staffs and payments to outside firms specializing in compliance services are substantially larger in the United States than in parallel operations abroad. A vice president of an engineering and planning firm operating in the United States and Germany told us that a company seeking development approvals can employ fewer persons to handle regulatory matters in Germany since there are fewer agencies with which the firm must interact.[87] We interviewed an attorney with a multinational petroleum exploration and production company who claimed that one of the more burdensome aspects of regulation in the United States, as compared with Great Britain, is the larger number of people that need to be employed just to perform compliance tasks.[88]

The dynamic was revealed by our visit to a U.S. plastic products plant in Texas that was modeled on its corporate owner's factory in Japan. The relevant air pollution control standards in the two nations, Japanese engineers in the Texas plant told us, are roughly the same. So are the basic pollution control systems in the two installations. There is little variation, moreover, in the equipment (gauges, flanges, and valves) used to control fugitive emissions from the complex system of pipes and ducts. But firms in the United States are required to keep detailed records of emissions and to file lengthy reports to the state agency that enforces federal regulatory standards. In the Texas factory, there are at least four thousand points in the manufacturing process at which emissions can leak out. Each one must be tagged, monitored, and recorded with time and date, and total emissions must be estimated quarterly. The Texas plant hires outside consultants to do this time-consuming task. In Japan, we were told by corporate officials with experience in both countries, government audits are less frequent and fines for detected noncompliance are levied only in instances of continued violations. Once a company has acquired a good reputation for compliance, as this firm's Japanese plant had, it need not invest in the extra layer of monitoring required in the Texas plant.[89] Nor did the officials think fugitive emissions in their Japanese plant were any worse than in the Texas facility.

Liability Insurance

In a system that relies on lawsuits rather than social insurance systems for injury compensation, privately purchased liability insurance (or self-insurance) costs are steep. In fiscal year 1991 New York City reportedly paid out $229 million to settle lawsuits for medical malpractice, auto accidents, sidewalk mishaps, and so forth, much more in the aggregate than the city spent to operate all its parks and libraries.[90]

It is difficult to be precise about what proportion of U.S. liability insurance costs might be considered excessive, but it is illuminating to look at some comparative figures. In 1986 the average American physician's malpractice premium was 11.5 times the average Canadian doctor's premium.[91] Peter Huber estimates that in the late 1980s liability insurance added $300 per birth to the cost of maternity and obstetrical care in New York City.[92] Dow Chemical stated that its 1986 legal and liability insurance expenditures in the United States were five times its overseas costs for a comparable volume of business.[93] Tillinghast, an insurance consulting firm, published estimates that in 1991 aggregate private tort costs (compensation paid to injured persons plus legal and claims administration) came to 2.3 percent of the U.S. gross domestic product, compared with an average of less than 1 percent in other OECD countries.[94] How much credence to lend to some of these estimates is an open question. And one should bear in mind that businesses and employees in other countries typically pay higher taxes to support the government programs that funnel funds to accident victims. However, the basic shape of the Tillinghast estimates seem entirely plausible.

Moreover, it is likely that the tort system is more costly than are social insurance arrangements for compensating accident victims. It wastes far more money on resolving disputes. A large proportion of tort damages, and thus liability insurance costs, covers discretionary noneconomic damages ("pain and suffering"). In many American states, in contrast to most other countries, tort law requires defendants to compensate plaintiffs even for losses already covered by the plaintiffs' own medical and disability insurance. Thus Stephen Sugarman points out, "When payments for losses already covered by collateral sources and for pain and suffering are subtracted, one finds that only about 10–15 percent of the costs of the tort system go to compensating victims for out-of-pocket medical expenses, lost income, and the like."[95] A careful 1988–89 survey of accident victims by the RAND Institute for Civil Justice indicated that most Americans who experience personal injuries seek payment for their medical bills and lost wages from employer-provided health insurance, workers' compensation insurance, government-provided medicaid or disability insurance, and so on.[96] Net of attorney fees, the tort system ends up compensating only 7 percent of total economic loss for injuries (that is, excluding payment for pain and suffering). If one includes payments for pain and suffering, tort claims yield about 11 percent of compensation received by the victims.[97]

Further, the authors of another RAND report point out, "The availability of general damages for pain and suffering and the fact that they are usually calculated as some multiple of economic losses provide the incentive to submit claims for nonexistent injuries and to build medical costs." The RAND scholars' cross-state comparisons led them to estimate that "about one-third of the automobile industry medical costs submitted to insurers appear to be excess."[98] Not surprisingly, another RAND study concluded, if California voters had adopted a ballot measure barring tort suits for motor vehicle injury claims in return for a mandatory self-insurance (no-fault) system, auto insurance premiums would decrease an estimated 11 to 29 percent, which provides some sense of the relative efficiency of social insurance compared with tort litigation as a method of compensation.[99]

Defensive Medicine

Adversarial legalism's heavy sanctions, combined with its uncertainty, also drives many producers and providers to make significant expenditures—some socially useful, some surely excessive—in hopes of avoiding litigation. Most notorious are the arguably unnecessary hospitalizations, laboratory tests, caesarean sections, and other procedures aimed at warding off malpractice suits. Some practitioners, fearful of having to deal with lawsuits, tend to avoid performing certain medical procedures entirely.[100]

The equivalent of defensive medicine occurs in many other arenas. According to a 1992 survey of 500 public accountancy partnerships in the United States, more than half have limited their audit services, or have shunned certain clients engaged in higher-risk markets, to protect themselves from lawsuits by disappointed investors.[101] Manufacturers of some generally safe but easy-to-misuse products such as child care equipment, vaccines, contraceptive devices, and small aircraft have withdrawn from the market to avoid tort suits and unaffordable liability insurance.[102] Even some products that, according to epidemiological evidence, are safe (for example, Bendectin, a drug that had been widely used by pregnant women suffering from morning sickness) or have not been shown to be unsafe (such as breast implants and other medical devices made of silicone) have been withdrawn from the market owing to actual or potential lawsuits.[103] According to a news account, Clozapine, an important antipsychosis drug, costs more than four times as much in the United States as in Europe because liability fears induced the supplier to insist on costly monitoring schemes for patients when the drug is prescribed in the United States.[104]

Another common defensive strategy, according to our interviews, is to farm out the work on risky activities to other companies. For example, all international marine insurance and regulatory bodies have stringent safety rules designed to prevent petroleum spills in oceans and harbors. The U.S. Oil Pollution Act of 1990, enacted in the wake of the *Exxon Valdez* spill, added a special dose of adversarial legalism to the U.S. market. Several multinational petroleum companies told us that liability risks associated with the act led them to contract out ocean transportation of petroleum to specialized shipping firms. Although the desire not to be publicly associated with an oil spill seems to be one factor in this particular decision, the firms are also attentive to the greater uncertainties and sanctions of the U.S. regulatory system. Under the U.S. law, liability could be hundreds of millions of dollars; states are not preempted from enacting their own, more protective legislation (California has already done so); and the enormous number and diversity of people and interests affected by oil spills can lead to large numbers of separate lawsuits. One wonders whether the oil companies' decision to contract out, in the face of legal risks posed by U.S. law, will end up increasing the danger of environmental damage by shifting preventive responsibility to less reliable shipping firms.

Corporate hedging against the distinct risks imposed by U.S. regulatory and liability law often means spending more money on monitoring outside contractors. Sometimes this tactic might be construed as "positive defensive medicine." A petrochemical company that we spoke to incorporated periodic audit-and-inspection provisions in its contracts with over-the-road trucking companies in an effort to guard against negligence by the truckers. At the same time, the petrochemical company also bombards its customers with lengthy, complex descriptions of the chemicals involved in each shipment, including data on potential hazards, while acknowledging that the information is so voluminous and technically worded that many customers are unlikely to read it or to comprehend the real nature of the hazards involved. The company hopes that the detailed disclosures and warnings might protect it from lawsuits in the event of an accident.

Opportunity Costs

In their quest for consumer safety and environmental protection, regulatory systems impose necessary delays on new construction and infrastructural projects, the marketing of new products, and the application of new technologies. Regulatory delays, however, also entail opportunity costs. For every ninety seconds that a state environmental permitting process stalls an auto assembly line, we were told, the plant forgoes the production of one vehicle. For every month that a Food and Drug Administration review kept a certain new genetically engineered product off the market, we were told, the manufacturer had to forgo serving a market that may be worth more than $13 million in monthly sales.

Sometimes, of course, foreign legal systems impose even greater delays than do U.S. procedures. A U.S. General Accounting Office study found that it took six to seven years, on average, to win approval of a patent in Japan, compared with about nineteen months in the United States.[105] A European study indicated that it would take more than a year longer to complete a research and development project in an automobile assembly company in Germany than in the United States, largely because of employment regulations that curtail working hours.[106] When a pharmaceutical company sought to license a biotech product through the European Union's Committee for Proprietary Medicinal Products and then through the relevant agencies of the member states, the process took about as long and involved at least as many detailed regulatory demands as it did in the United States, where the FDA granted a manufacturing license 31 months after application, slightly less than the FDA's average (35.3 months) for new biological products.[107]

Nevertheless, U.S. legal and regulatory processes generally are more fragmented, complex, and legalistic. Compared with port authorities of commercial seaports in Europe and Japan, U.S. port authorities seeking to dredge their harbors are much more likely to get bogged down in development-delaying litigation.[108] While a jumble of regulatory agencies and courts debated for years where to dispose of dredged harbor sediments, the Port of Oakland, unable to accommodate larger ships, lost shipping business and the surrounding community lost employment and port-generated contributions to municipal services.[109] The same kind of adversarial legalistic deadlock has led to loss of shipping business at the Port of New York.[110]

An environmental consultant with a great deal of international experience told us that for comparable industrial development projects, the regulatory permitting process in the United States, compared with that in western Europe, entails more legal formality and complexity, a higher incidence of redundant multiagency demands for additional studies, greater bureaucratic caution, and lack of finality.[111] Consequently, "it takes less time overseas. The cost for initial studies is less. We are not required to accumulate as much information. In Europe [the time from application to permit averages] one-third less."

Automobile manufacturers in both the United States and Japan are obligated to control volatile organic compound (VOC) emissions that occur in the course of applying paint and other surface coatings to car bodies. In Japan the VOC standards are specific and in some cases very stringent. Companies are not required by law or regulation to use any particular technology to achieve those goals, although memorandums from regulatory officials often alert manufacturers to standards applicable to their particular plants and suggest particular technologies. Nonetheless, the choice of technology and configuration of the assembly line is not locked in by permits and regulations; modifications to existing permits are not difficult to obtain, according to knowledgeable industry officials. U.S. regulations, by contrast, contain detailed specifications concerning VOC and other emission control technologies. But production and coating technologies are constantly changing, so automakers in the United States encounter rigidities, delays, and uncertainties in applying for permit modifications. As a consequence, closely coordinated changes in major models are sometimes thrown off schedule, and EPA regulations have prevented or delayed use of some attractive paint finishes that are common on vehicles made in Japan.

One chemical industry executive told us that for some industries regulations have to accommodate small frequent process changes; if the regulators cannot keep up, he said, "you go to Singapore."[112] A London-based official of a multinational chemical company, while telling us that there were few national differences in transportation safety regulations for chemicals, also said, "The most notable exception is U.S. liability law, which I would judge to be a major discouragement to doing business in the U.S." Of course, because the United States is such a large and important market, a great many firms, domestic and foreign, remain eager to do business here. Gritting their teeth, they treat adversarial legalism as the price to be paid. Moreover, some academic analyses suggest that the burdens of U.S. environmental regulation, viewed in relation to other economic factors, do not have a large effect on industrial location decisions.[113] Nevertheless, the aggregate data are not very good. It seems likely that because adversarial legalism adds significantly to the costs and uncertainties of doing business in the United States, it can sometimes operate as a nontariff barrier to some firms and as an inducement to transfer operations abroad.

Finally, adversarial legalism tends to corrode personal and institutional relationships. When regulators and regulated enterprises become locked in legalistic confrontations, the cooperation and exchange of information so essential to effective regulation are jeopardized.[114] As a National Academy of Science analysis of EPA policymaking observed, when regulatory rulemaking is only a prelude to litigation, contending interests are more likely to resist compromise.[115] Steven Kelman has noted that "adversary institutions . . . fail to create any relationship among the parties to a policy disagreement. Participants in adversary institutions . . . remain separate individuals, physically proximate only in order to argue in front of a third party. They do not talk with each other."[116] By rendering legal and regulatory processes complicated, frustrating, or threatening, adversarial legalism tends to alienate citizens and business executives and to undermine respect for governmental institutions, including essential administrative and regulatory organs and the judiciary itself.

Compensatory Social Benefits?

Are the costs of the U.S. legal and regulatory style—defensive tactics, litigation, unjust settlements, large liability premiums, armies of lawyers and consultants, opportunity costs—offset by its assets, especially its powerful deterrent punch? This is an inherently vexing question, mainly because the empirical data needed to answer it are inadequate.

Yet a number of thoughtful scholars have come to the conclusion that the vaunted deterrent effect of the fierce U.S. tort regime is in fact minimal or only erratically significant. Stephen Sugarman has observed that the liability system's deterrent threat is muted by liability insurance, which means that tortfeasors do not bear the full cost of the harms they do, and by the uncertainty and delayed fuse of tort liability, which cause potential tortfeasors to discount the threat and to regard tort suits as random lightning bolts rather than as a source of systematic guidance about what precautions to take.[117]

With respect to the relevant research, there are only a few studies comparing the quality of medical care in the United States with the quality or amount in other economically advanced countries that feature lower liability law threats, and those studies have been inconclusive.[118] Case studies of the motor vehicle and small aircraft manufacturing industries, in a book edited by Peter W. Huber and Robert E. Litan, disputed the presumed safety-enhancing effect of U.S. product liability litigation.[119] However, one often hears anecdotal accounts of precautions instituted to avoid running afoul of liability law. Perhaps the most exhaustive and thoughtful review of the relevant empirical studies is by Gary Schwartz, who, although emphasizing the insufficiency of the evidence, tentatively concludes that U.S. tort law does provide an extra measure of deterrence in some spheres of activity, but that those effects are partial and erratic.[120]

In our own research, representatives of multinational enterprises, although keenly alert to U.S. liability law, usually could not point to more extensive precautions in their U.S. sites than in their installations abroad. One exception was the shipping official in a petrochemical company who noted that its U.S. branch took special precautions, beyond those called for in regulations, in cleaning trucks and railcars, auditing the safety practices of outside truckers, and training emergency response teams to rush to the site of any chemical spill. These managers suspected, but were not sure, that liability risks (as opposed to general corporate concern for its public reputation) had led to these practices.

Still, the dominant finding of our case studies is that adversarial legalism does not appear to produce significantly greater protections in the United States. Interviewed for our water pollution case study, a consultant with twenty-five years of experience helping manufacturers comply with water pollution regulations around the world said that, "while regulation is similar [among countries], enforcement is quite a bit different. In the U.S., we have strong legal constraints. If you [mess] up, you can have stiff fines. You can readily get sued. We're the only country in the world where that's true." Yet despite this, he emphasized that in the 1990s innovative "treatment technology is implemented simultaneously worldwide."

Personnel managers in a U.S.-based multinational pharmaceutical company told us that detailed corporate procedures to ensure fairness in terminating unsatisfactory employees originally stemmed in part from the company's desire to avoid lawsuits in U.S. courts. However, the same personnel practices are followed in the company's Canadian subsidiary, where the law is just as protective as in the United States but the incidence of lawsuits experienced by the company is lower.

Quality control officials in a multinational company that makes biotechnology products recognize the enormous liability risks that would arise in the United States from the sale of a contaminated product. When the company sought manufacturing licenses from the FDA and the European Union's regulatory body, however, it was the EU that insisted on more probing analyses of quality control, leading the company to establish certain controls that had not been stimulated by the more legalistic U.S. legal and regulatory system.

Such tales comport with the comparative literature on regulatory enforcement, cited in table 4-1. More legalistic and punitive modes of occupational safety enforcement in the United States, for instance, do not appear to lead to higher levels of safety than those achieved by more cooperative administrative methods employed in various European nations. Similarly, John Braithwaite found that whereas regulations concerning quality of care in nursing homes are enforced more legalistically (with stiff monetary fines and the threat of court orders) in the United States than in Australia, quality of care in U.S. facilities is on average worse because legalistic enforcement has led to the development of large corporate-run homes (that can better afford to comply with costly regulations concerning facilities) and to a mechanical, penalty-avoiding approach to service delivery.[121]

Of course, one might turn up countervailing examples. Some observers believe the much greater frequency of securities lawsuits in the United States "adds further authenticity to the firm's disclosures and enhances the attractiveness of U.S. markets to foreign investors."[122] Enforcement and legal coercion in some areas of U.S. environmental regulation, some of our interviewees pointed out, occasionally push U.S. companies to take the lead in developing control technologies that firms overseas employ later at lower cost and with less pressure. In a global economy, regulatory legalism in one location can facilitate regulatory cooperation in others.

It should be noted also that our own research focuses on large, multinational companies that partly because of their visibility and their interest in their reputations tend to have better regulatory compliance records than small firms lacking specialized in-house compliance staffs. (There is some evidence that aggressive OSHA enforcement leads to lower accident rates in medium-sized firms but not in large firms.)[123] Large automobile manufacturers in Japan, Richard Wokutch found, have better occupational safety and health practices than comparable U.S. plants. But working conditions in small Japanese subcontractors were comparatively worse.[124] Our findings based on large multinational corporations therefore may overstate the social benefits of avoiding adversarial legalism. At the same time, the U.S. regulatory style undoubtedly bears down even more heavily on smaller firms that lack a typical multinational company's army of lawyers, consultants, and regulatory affairs specialists.[125]

U.S. firms are generally regarded as more combative and less deferential to governmental authority than are Japanese and European firms. Indeed, the more rambunctious U.S. business style is one reason why U.S. tort and regulatory law is more legalistic, contentious, and deterrence oriented. One might argue, therefore, that regulatory compliance in the United States would be worse if the deterrent effect of adversarial legalism were moderated. Yet there is little evidence that compliance deteriorated in the 1980s when, for a time, the Reagan administration lowered the heat of formal enforcement actions by federal environmental and safety agencies.[126] More fundamentally, even assuming that adversarial legalism contributes to deterrence, the overall size and distribution of this putative welfare gain is uncertain and may not be large enough to compensate for the substantial costs.

Conclusion

Compared with the practices in other prosperous democracies, U.S. methods for enforcing regulatory policies and resolving disputes involve more formal and burdensome legal contestation. Regulatory programs in the United States often carry more detailed rules and stiffer penalties for infractions. And a particular form of social regulation—liability law and civil litigation—is employed more frequently here than in Europe, Japan, and British Commonwealth nations. Americans pride themselves on pragmatism, yet the U.S. style of regulation can be costly and exasperatingly unpredictable compared with some alternative modes of securing the same social objectives. Productive enterprises operating in this country do not view these drawbacks as trivial problems, even if they are tolerated because of the opportunities provided by America's comparatively open economy.

Of course, legal systems have always posed transaction costs. When Hamlet soliloquized about shuffling off this mortal coil, he cited "the law's delay" in the same breath as "the insolence of office" and "the pangs of dispriz'd love." Nevertheless, comparative studies suggest that the law's delay, and its costs, tend to be greater in American courts and regulatory bodies than in those of most other industrial countries. Moreover, for all the lengthy proceedings, legal bills, and penalties associated with American social regulation, the European and Japanese operations of multinational enterprises often achieve levels of environmental protection and product safety that are comparable to, if not better than, those met by the firms' facilities in this country. These observations imply that moderating the harder edges of the U.S. legal and regulatory style could net important social gains.

The trick is to find ways of reducing the burdens of adversarial legalism without losing its virtues. The same features that increase America's litigiousness and regulatory red tape—easy recourse to the courts, entrepreneurial lawyering, strong remedies, judicial activism, transparent proceedings, extensive legislative oversight, and so on—are also powerful instruments for holding public and private institutions accountable.

Some conservative proposals would fix the U.S. system by curtailing regulatory obligations, providing business with broad immunities from private lawsuits and from some legitimate regulatory constraints. An alternative reform strategy, however, is suggested by the findings reviewed in this chapter. Some other democracies manage to impose stringent regulatory standards with far less legalistic conflict by according governmental officials greater discretion in applying rules and responding to violations. Following that strategy would require not a weaker, more legally constrained government but better trained bureaucrats, more resources for administrative agencies, wider grants of authority, and less legislative and judicial micromanagement.

Other countries limit the rights of both regulated enterprises and proregulation advocacy groups to appeal administrative decisions to court. Legal quagmires, such as the Superfund program, are avoided by placing greater emphasis on publicly funded cleanup of fundamental problems. Likewise, many European governments have side-stepped the waste and abuse of tort liability law by extending to accident victims automatic coverage of their medical needs and of lost earnings through national health care systems and generous disability benefits. In sum, curbing adversarial legalism may not always be easy to reconcile with a quest for smaller government. However difficult the path to reform, an essential first step is to recognize that a number of other democratic nations appear to achieve more cost effectively some of the objectives strenuously sought by U.S. plaintiffs's lawyers and regulators.

Comment by S. Lael Brainard

Robert Kagan and Lee Axelrad focus on an issue of growing salience: are U.S. regulations a comparative disadvantage? As traditional barriers to goods and services trade are progressively dismantled, the emphasis increases on differences in domestic legal and regulatory institutions and standards as important determinants of cost differences between countries. Such regulatory cost differences could be important drivers of competitiveness and of corporate location and configuration decisions.

Main Conclusions

Kagan and Axelrad adopt an interesting approach to address this issue. Relying primarily on interviews in a qualitative, case study approach, they examine multinationals operating in the United States and other industrialized economies to control for differences in products and processes across firms. This research yields a number of interesting insights.

The insight that is perhaps most interesting and most robust is that the United States diverges most dramatically from other industrialized economies not in its standards but in the system by which laws and regulations are implemented, disputes are settled, licenses are approved, and compliance is enforced. The U.S. system is characterized by more and costlier legal contestation, more punitive legal sanctions, more frequent judicial review and revision of governmental decisions, and more legal discretion. In sum, this system imposes higher costs and higher uncertainty to impose the same regulatory standards.

Second, Kagan and Axelrad conclude the costlier U.S. system is socially unproductive and indeed wasteful. The litigious system found in the United States creates additional social costs that are not outweighed by additional social benefits. Companies operating in the U.S. market incur additional costs for legal staffs and defensive documentation. Yet these additional expenditures yield no social value: actual control and prevention measures are basically the same across countries.

Third, Kagan and Axelrad observe that these systemic differences are likely to endure, even as convergence in standards across countries grows, reflecting the influence of globalization and international trade.

Finally, the differences in systems do not fundamentally alter firm location or production decisions. Executives at a number of companies surveyed argued that the allure of the U.S. market compensates for the costly systemic differences.

A Second Look

These results are both interesting and somewhat surprising. For that reason, they bear closer examination. The most troubling claim is that the United States is simply wasting resources: its "uniquely inefficient method of resolving legal disputes" yields no net increase in social benefits. Because it has such profound implications, this claim bears very close scrutiny and corroboration—by those who bear the social costs not of meeting the regulation but when regulations are not met.

The researchers rely for their evidence on social costs solely on evaluations by the firms who are required to meet the regulations. But they might find somewhat different results if they asked consumers to evaluate the social costs and benefits in product liability cases. Similarly, we should be a little suspicious when corporate executives report that their companies provide equal levels of protection across countries regardless of the system of enforcement. When one examines regulations that are perceived to benefit U.S. firms, the anecdotal evidence suggests that corporate executives do not feel equally protected from anticompetitive behavior or patent infringement in all industrialized countries.

The conclusion that social benefits do not differ across enforcement systems depends centrally on the claim (by corporate executives) that the same product and process is adopted regardless of the legal-regulatory system. But this standardization could be explained by cost minimization rather than by the similarity of product standards across markets. Many companies may initially develop products to meet the most stringent compliance requirements in the U.S. market, and then transfer them to other, more lax environments without modification because this is the least-cost approach. It should be possible to investigate this response by comparing companies that are located only in Europe and Japan with multinationals that are also in the United States.

A second experiment to address the same question might focus on a case in which regulatory systems are similar across markets but standards differ. That should provide a nice contrast with the approach in this research, which effectively takes cases for which the standard is similar across markets and examines how firms respond to different enforcement systems. For instance, it should be possible to compare operations within firms operating in two U.S. states that have different standards but share the same basic legal and regulatory approach. It is possible that, just as companies use the same products and processes across different systems with the same standards, so too companies produce to the same standard across markets with different standards for reasons of cost minimization. If similarities in the compliance rate across countries reflect similarities in the standard despite differences in enforcement systems, then the United States is wasting resources. But if similarities in the compliance rate are also immune to differences in standards, then it suggests that companies design products and processes to meet the highest standard and then transfer it to other markets. In that case, it would suggest the United States is using its large market to raise standards worldwide.

In addition, the conclusion that globalization is creating pressures for convergence of standards but not for convergence of enforcement systems bears some examination. To the extent that systemic differences create substantial cost differences, one would expect general pressures for convergence, as firms adjust their business systems to exploit national differences. Further, in the area of patents, Kagan and Axelrad suggest that the system of adversarial legalism is spreading from the United States to Japan and the EU. If indeed adversarial legalism is the most inefficient and costly system, the question arises of why there are pressures for convergence to the most rather than least costly system, unless it is producing benefits for either consumers or producers.

On the flip side, another important conclusion is that differences in the cost of regulatory-legal systems (as opposed to standards) have no effect on U.S. competitiveness. This argument rests on the observation that the U.S. market is sufficiently attractive to outweigh high regulatory costs. But that begs an important question. Obviously, the U.S. market has a number of features that attract companies even at the cost of paying a penalty to operate here. But what we really want to know is whether adversarial legalism on the margin shifts more production or innovative activity toward or away from the U.S. market or otherwise disadvantages U.S. companies, holding other market characteristics constant.

COMMENT BY ROBERT E. LITAN

The central premise of this chapter is that the substance of law in the United States is less distinctive than are the differences in the ways the United States compels compliance, mostly through legalistic regulations and tort litigation. To support this proposition, the chapter undertakes novel research on the operations of multinational companies in various countries. The chapter reports only limited, initial results from interviews, and the authors do not pretend to have studied a scientific sample of firms.

A casual reading of the chapter strikes a chord, though on closer inspection, I am by no means convinced that the process of regulatory compliance in the United States is more costly than in other industrial nations. In fact, a recent study by the OECD shows just the opposite. The OECD did not include civil liability–related costs; here Kagan and Axelrad may be closer to the mark.

The interesting question, however, is not just whether Kagan and Axelrad's rough inferences about comparative costs are right or wrong. Suppose the authors are right: overall the United States is on the high end. What difference does that make?

The authors themselves are tentative, acknowledging that in the context of the economy as a whole, they are not at all sure. On a micro level, they are on surer footing. Excessive litigation has sometimes severely hurt particular industries.

Fortunately, I did not have to think too hard about this issue, because I spent much time several years ago on a paper prepared for a volume entitled *Tort Law and the Public Interest*.[127] My focus was on the comparative effects of U.S. liability law on the U.S. trade balance—a question that is (or ought to be) related to the questions posed by Kagan and Axelrad. In brief, here is what I found.

The trade balance, as virtually all economists know, is determined by the relationship between a country's saving and investment. There is scant evidence that liability law, or for that matter any other regulatory proceedings, affects overall saving or investment, so long-run, aggregate trade flows have little to do with the issues of legal process that Kagan and Axelrad identify. Of course, as the authors recognize, law can and does affect the trade performance of individual firms or even industries. This might lead to aggregate trade effects in the very short run. Such effects, however, are soon canceled out by adjustments in exchange rates, so again, the trade balance over the long haul has little or nothing to do with laws or lawsuits.

A more relevant matter is whether differences in law affect domestic living standards. This is what most good economists mean by competitiveness. Put another way, how well does a nation live when its trade is balanced? Other things equal, it is better to balance trade with a higher exchange rate than with a lower one, because a stronger dollar allows one to purchase imports more cheaply.

Kagan and Axelrad observe that the country spends approximately $100 billion on lawyers each year, or about 1.5 percent of GDP. Let us assume, further, that the Tillinghast estimates for 1989 are more or less correct: the U.S. liability system has imposed an additional "tax" of about $117 billion annually, or approximately 2.6 percent of GDP. Ballpark: the United States spends a total of, say, 3.5 percent of GDP on legally related expenditures (including compensation for victims and their attorneys but not counting compliance costs imposed by government regulations). Maybe, in fact, the total figure should be closer to 4 percent to 5 percent, because the above estimates do not count the time that business people must divert from their regular activities to legal problems.

Now, does this mean that if the United States fixed its legal system—or carved its costs down to something like those seen overseas—U.S. living standards would rise by 4 percent? Of course not. First, other nations spend money on compensating victims, too, though they rely on government compensation mechanisms. Kagan and Axelrad do not tell us much about the expense, and often the wastefulness, of these mechanisms.

Second, other societies, too, spend money on lawyers. I do not have precise figures on the differentials, but even if they are much lower, the other societies do not necessarily have their living standards enhanced as a result. Legal expenditures buy some social benefits. Liability law, for example, presumably buys some deterrence. How much is a matter of much debate. Kagan and Axelrad suspect the deterrence value has been oversold. Many consumer advocates would disagree; they are convinced that the benefits of liability litigation exceed its costs.

I am not going to resolve the cost-benefit debate today. That debate will continue long after I'm gone. But let's take the critics' view and say, for the sake of argument, that the United States only receives fifty cents of social benefits for every dollar of liability bills. This would imply that for gross costs to the economy of 3.5 percent or 4 percent, the United States has net social costs of about 2 percent of GDP (or about $500 a person). That is, the nation would be better off as a society by only that per-capita amount if it did not have this burden.

And this would be true regardless of whether or not other countries' liability costs and benefits are better balanced.

The impact of higher liability and legal costs can be more pronounced for particular industries. Here the key question is whether the higher costs fall on inputs or on product design. Ignore the exact magnitudes; just worry about getting the signs right. Input costs might be higher for certain U.S. industries because of various regulations or liability-related costs. And regardless of whether the higher costs are offset by social benefits, they hurt U.S. exports abroad, while also making it easier for foreigners to sell their goods in America (though foreign-owned businesses in the United States presumably do not get this advantage unless they are screwdriver plants, which purchase all their basic inputs abroad).

The story is different for effects on product design. In this case, foreigners must meet U.S. standards, whether imposed by regulation or by liability suits, and thus American firms face no disadvantage. As for U.S. exports, if American firms are able to differentiate their products for the home and foreign markets (right- and left-side drive on autos, for example), then the variations in product standards should make no significant difference.

There are two important qualifications to these results, however. First, if it costs U.S. firms money to make different product designs, whether because of higher R&D expenses or other development costs, then the differences in law that lead to variations in design do put U.S. exports at a disadvantage (unless foreign firms seeking to export their design to the U.S. market suffer corresponding costs).

Second, and potentially more important, the U.S. legal process may create uncertainties that stifle innovation, thereby harming exports, reducing the U.S. equilibrium exchange rate, and thus damaging living standards. The general aviation industry appears to be a clear case in point. Another is the pharmaceutical industry. To my knowledge, however, there is little reliable evidence of an across-the-board impact on innovation.

In short, what I concluded several years ago, and what I still think to be true, is that legal differences affecting inputs costs can put U.S. companies at a competitive disadvantage, at home or abroad, but that differences affecting product design are less likely to have this consequence. All told, from the little empirical evidence I was able to find using data from 1978 through 1984, I could not discern a statistically

significant effect of differences in liability costs on export performance across industries.

Indeed, Kagan and Axelrad repeatedly mention the complexity of
U.S. legal procedures. But if Americans are more likely to be familiar
with the complexities than foreigners are, the more "costly" legal
process here acts as an invisible entry barrier to foreign investors. At
the margin, this would have the effect of protecting U.S. firms from
competition.

Finally, suppose the perverse or unnecessary legal and regulatory
costs that the authors stress definitely exist and do have at least some
deleterious impact on specific industries. What are the possible solutions? One obvious answer is executive branch review of major regulations to ensure better cost effectiveness. This process has been
subject to ups and downs, and perhaps for that reason, interest in
Congress has mounted to legislate a cost-benefit test, backed by judicial review. The Clinton administration has opposed this legislation
on the grounds that it would only fuel the litigation fire. I do not
know where the authors stand on this subject, but if they think there
are big, consequential differences in legal processes between the
United States and the rest of the world, then I suspect they too should
be concerned about an approach that would judicialize cost-benefit
determinations.

A second possible remedy is to put a "social tariff" on incoming
goods, ostensibly to level the playing field between the United States
and foreign competitors. We hear this from the left (Ralph Nader) and
from the right (Pat Buchanan). I hope I do not have to convince this
audience that this route would be a big mistake, for several reasons.

For one, as the authors of this chapter demonstrate, there are no
precise data on the extent of legal and regulatory handicaps, that is,
the net social costs that U.S. firms incur. One can be sure that the advocates of the social tariff would ignore such intricacies by setting
any tariff much too high. Further, setting a social tariff amounts to
making value judgments on the appropriate level of regulation
abroad, since the United States would be punishing foreigners for
being less stringent than itself. Who does the United States think it is
to do that? And last, the social tariff only affects imports and thus
really masks protectionism, pure and simple. A social tariff does
nothing to help U.S. exports and sales in third markets (unless
America provides an offsetting export subsidy, which no one could

consider seriously in this budgetary climate). If anything, such a tariff would hurt U.S. exports, since it would raise the U.S. exchange rate. This would be even more true if other countries retaliated by setting social tariffs of their own, as many would surely do.

In sum, I found this chapter a useful addition to our meager knowledge of the impacts of national legal regimes. I would urge the authors not to overstate the effects. I welcome their research method and look forward to the results of their future case studies.

NOTES

1. Garrison Keillor, quoted in Jon Winokur, ed., *True Confessions* (Penguin Books, 1992), p. 4.

2. Marc Galanter, "Law Abounding: Legalisation around the North Atlantic," *Modern Law Review*, vol. 55 (January 1992), pp. 1–24. See also Union of Industrial and Employers' Confederations of Europe (UNICE), *Releasing Europe's Potential through Targetted Regulatory Reform: The UNICE Regulatory Report* (Brussels: September 1995). The report noted that 79 percent of European firms surveyed responded that there are too many regulations confronting them; 55 percent said that European regulations were too complex (p. ii).

3. Martin Shapiro, "The Globalization of Law," *Indiana Journal of Global Legal Studies*, vol. 1 (Fall 1993) pp. 37–64; and Brigitte Unger and Frans van Waarden, eds., *Convergence or Diversity? Internationalization and Economic Policy Response* (Aldershot, U.K., and Brookfield, Vt.: Avebury, 1995).

4. Robert A. Kagan, "Adversarial Legalism and American Government," in Marc K. Landy and Martin A. Levin, eds., *The New Politics of Public Policy* (Johns Hopkins University Press, 1995), pp. 88–118; also published under the same title in the *Journal of Policy Analysis and Management*, vol. 10, no. 3 (1991), pp. 369–406.

5. See, for example, Karen Palmer, Wallace E. Oates, and Paul R. Portney, "Tightening Environmental Standards: The Benefit-Cost or the No-Cost Paradigm?" *Journal of Economic Perspectives*, vol. 9 (Fall 1995), pp. 119–32.

6. Herbert Giersch, "Europe 1992 in an Open World Order" (Hamburg, 1988), quoted in Sylvia Ostry, *Governments and Corporations in a Shrinking World: Trade and Innovation Policies in the United States, Europe and Japan* (New York: Council on Foreign Relations Press, 1990), p. 81. See also UNICE, *Releasing Europe's Potential*, p. 10.

7. The OECD identified the relative inflexibility of Europe's labor markets as one of the reasons unemployment is higher in Europe than in the United States or Japan. UNICE, *Releasing Europe's Potential*, p. 43, citing Organization for Economic Cooperation and Development, "The OECD Jobs Study: Facts Analysis Strategies," Paris, 1994. See also UNICE, *Releasing Europe's Potential*, p. ii.

8. See "Debate: Do Lawyers Impair Economic Growth?" *Law and Social Inquiry*, vol. 17 (Fall 1992), pp. 585–711.

9. Economic Planning Agency, Government of Japan, *Economic Survey of Japan (1993–1994): A Challenge to New Frontiers Beyond the Severe Adjustment Process* (Tokyo), p. 336.

10. See, generally, Lee E. Preston and Duane Windsor, *The Rules of the Game in the Global Economy: Policy Regimes for International Business* (Norwell, Mass.: Kluwer, 1992).

11. Wolfgang Wiegand, "Americanization of Law: Reception or Convergence?" in Lawrence M. Friedman and Harry N. Scheiber, eds., *Legal Culture and the Legal Profession* (Boulder, Colo.: Westview Press, 1996), pp. 137–52.

12. Gary T. Schwartz, "Product Liability and Medical Malpractice in Comparative Context," in Peter W. Huber and Robert E. Litan, eds., *The Liability Maze: The Impact of Liability Law on Safety and Innovation* (Brookings, 1991), p. 41.

13. Joseph L. Badaracco Jr., *Loading the Dice: A Five-Country Study of Vinyl Chloride Regulation* (Harvard Business School Press, 1985); and Robert A. Kagan and David Vogel, "The Politics of Smoking Regulation: Canada, France, the United States," in Robert L. Rabin and Stephen D. Sugarman, eds., *Smoking Policy: Law, Politics, and Culture* (Oxford University Press, 1993), pp. 22–48.

14. Steven K. Vogel, *Freer Markets, More Rules: Regulatory Reform in Advanced Industrial Countries* (Cornell University Press, 1996), pp. 93–117; and Michael Moran, *The Politics of the Financial Services Revolution: The USA, UK, and Japan* (St. Martin's Press, 1991), p. 86.

15. Susan Rose-Ackerman, *Controlling Environmental Policy: The Limits of Public Law in Germany and the United States* (Yale University Press, 1995), p. 28.

16. Unger and van Waarden, *Convergence or Diversity?*

17. Mark J. Roe, "A Political Theory of American Corporate Finance," *Columbia Law Review*, vol. 91 (1991), p. 11.

18. Bob Davis, Peter Gumbel, and David P. Hamilton, "Red-Tape Traumas: To All U.S. Managers Upset by Regulations; Try Germany or Japan," *Wall Street Journal*, December 14, 1995, pp. A1, A5.

19. Palmer, Oates, and Portney, "Tightening Environmental Standards," p. 130.

20. Unger and van Waarden, eds., *Convergence or Diversity?*; "Books in Europe: Read All About It," *Economist*, April 6, 1996, p. 69; "Not at Any Price," *Economist*, April 6, 1996, p. 70 (on retailing in France); and Timothy Aeppel, "Europe's 'Unity' Undoes a U.S. Exporter," *Wall Street Journal*, April 1, 1996, p. B1 (on divergent national standards for gas hoses for commercial stoves).

21. See also Frans van Waarden, "Persistence of National Policy Styles: A Study of Their Institutional Foundations," in Unger and van Waarden, eds., *Convergence or Diversity?* pp. 333–72.

22. Jonathan P. Charkham, *Keeping Good Company: A Study of Corporate Governance in Five Countries* (Oxford: Clarendon Press, 1994), p. 357.

23. Robert J. Flanagan, *Labor Relations and the Litigation Explosion* (Brookings, 1987), p. 3. See also Derek C. Bok, "Reflections on the Distinctive Char-

acter of American Labor Laws," *Harvard Law Review*, vol. 84 (1971), pp. 1394, 1449; and Joel Rogers, "Divide and Conquer: Further 'Reflections on the Distinctive Character of American Labor Laws,'" *Wisconsin Law Review*, no. 1 (January-February 1990), pp. 1–147.

24. Thomas W. Church and Robert T. Nakamura, "Beyond Superfund: Hazardous Waste Cleanup in Europe and the United States," *Georgetown International Environmental Law Review*, vol. 7 (1994), p. 56. See also Andrew Lohof, "The Cleanup of Inactive Hazardous Waste Sites in Selected Industrialized Countries, Discussion Paper 69 (Washington: American Petroleum Institute, August 1991); Marc K. Landy and Mary Hague, "The Coalition for Waste: Private Interests and Superfund," in Michael S. Greve and Fred L. Smith Jr., eds., *Environmental Politics: Public Costs, Private Rewards* (Praeger, 1992), pp. 67–87; and Thomas W. Church and Robert T. Nakamura, *Cleaning Up the Mess: Implementation Strategies in Superfund* (Brookings, 1993). Litigation and related government and private transaction costs add up to at least one-third of the funds actually expended on cleanup. Timothy Noah, "Clinton, Facing Conflicting Advice on Superfund, May Attempt to Ease the Burdens on Business," *Wall Street Journal*, December 2, 1993, p. A16; and Peter S. Menell, "The Limitations of Legal Institutions for Addressing Environmental Risks," *Journal of Economic Perspectives*, vol. 5 (Summer 1991), pp. 93–113.

25. John Braithwaite, *To Punish or Persuade:Enforcement of Coal Mine Safety* (State University of New York, 1985), pp. 4, 114; and Steven Kelman, *Regulating America, Regulating Sweden: A Comparative Study of Occupational Safety and Health Policy* (MIT Press, 1981).

26. See Kagan, "Adversarial Legalism," *Journal of Policy Analysis and Management*, p. 1.

27. John H. Langbein, "The German Advantage in Civil Procedure," *University of Chicago Law Review*, vol. 52 (1985), p. 823.

28. P. S. Atiyah and Robert S. Summers, *Form and Substance in Anglo-American Law: A Comparative Study of Legal Reasoning, Legal Theory, and Legal Institutions* (Oxford University Press, 1987).

29. Surveys and experiments have shown that attorneys and insurance claims managers assign widely different settlement values to the same or similar civil cases. See Marc Galanter, "The Quality of Settlements," *Journal of Dispute Resolution*, vol. 1988 (1988), pp. 76–77; Gerald K. Williams, *Legal Negotiation and Settlement* (St. Paul: West Publishing, 1983), pp. 6, 111–14; Douglas E. Rosenthal, *Lawyer and Client: Who's in Charge?* (Russell Sage Foundation, 1974), pp. 202–07; and Michael J. Saks, "Do We Really Know Anything about the Behavior of the Tort Litigation System—And Why Not?" *University of Pennsylvania Law Review*, vol. 140 (April 1992), pp. 1215, 1223.

30. Badaracco, *Loading the Dice*; Ronald Brickman, Sheila Jasanoff, and Thomas Ilgen, *Controlling Chemicals: The Politics of Regulation in Europe and the United States* (Cornell University Press, 1985); David Vogel, *National Styles of Regulation: Environmental Policy in Great Britain and the United States* (Cornell University Press, 1986); and Harvey Teff, "Drug Approval in

England and the United States," *American Journal of Comparative Law*, vol. 33 (1985), pp. 567–610.

31. Deborah Hensler and Mark A. Peterson, "Understanding Mass Personal Injury Litigation: A Socio-Legal Analysis," *Brooklyn Law Review*, vol. 59 (1993), p. 1004; and Harriet Vinke and Ton Wilthagen, "The Non-Mobilization of Law by Asbestos Victims in The Netherlands: Social Insurance versus Tort-Based Compensation," Hugo Sinzheimer Institute, University of Amsterdam, 1992.

32. William L. F. Felstiner and Robert Dingwall, *Asbestos Litigation in the United Kingdom: An Interim Report*, ABF Working Paper 8807 (Chicago: AB Foundation, 1988).

33. Kagan, "Adversarial Legalism." See also van Waarden, "Persistence of Styles," pp. 333–72.

34. Carol J. Greenhouse, *Praying for Justice: Faith, Order, and Community in an American Town* (Cornell University Press, 1986); Robert C. Ellickson, "Of Coase and Cattle: Dispute Resolution among Neighbors in Shasta County," *Stanford Law Review*, vol. 38 (February 1986), pp. 623–87; and Stewart Macaulay, "Non-contractual Relations in Business: A Preliminary Study," *American Sociological Review*, vol. 28 (February 1963), p. 55.

35. Richard E. Miller and Austin Sarat, "Grievances, Claims, and Disputes: Assessing the Adversary Culture," *Law and Society Review*, vol. 15, nos. 3–4 (1980–81), pp. 525–66; Marc Galanter, "Reading the Landscape of Disputes: What We Know and Don't Know (and Think We Know) about Our Allegedly Contentious and Litigious Society," *UCLA Law Review*, vol. 31 (October 1983), pp. 4–71; Robert A. Kagan, "The Routinization of Debt Collection: An Essay on Social Change and Conflict in the Courts," *Law and Society Review*, vol. 18, no.3 (1984), p. 323; and Deborah R. Hensler and others, *Compensation for Accidental Injuries in the United States* (Santa Monica, Calif.: RAND Corporation, 1991).

36. Joseph V. Rees, *Reforming the Workplace: A Study of Self-Regulation in Occupational Safety* (University of Pennsylvania Press, 1988); and Robert A. Kagan, "Regulatory Enforcement," in David H. Rosenbloom and Richard D. Schwartz, eds., *Handbook of Regulation and Administrative Law* (Marcel Dekker, 1994), pp. 383–422.

37. Joseph Sanders and Craig Joyce, "Off to the Races: The 1980s Tort Crisis and the Law Reform Process," *Houston Law Review*, vol. 27 (March 1990), pp. 207–96; and John H. Cushman Jr., "Many States Give Polluting Firms New Protections," *New York Times*, April 7, 1996, pp. A1, A12.

38. Wolfgang Wiegand, "The Reception of American Law in Europe," *American Journal of Comparative Law*, vol. 39 (Spring 1991), p. 235; Weigand, "Americanization of Law"; Yves Dezalay and Bryant Garth, "Merchants of Law as Moral Entrepreneurs: Constructing International Justice from the Competition for Transnational Business Disputes," *Law and Society Review*, vol. 29 (February 1995), pp. 27–64; and David M. Trubeck and others, "Global Restructuring and the Law: Studies of the Internationalization of Legal Fields and the Creation of Transnational Arenas," *Case Wetern Reserve Law Review*, vol. 44 (1944), pp. 407–98.

39. Jefferey M. Sellers, "Litigation as a Local Political Resource: Courts in Controversies over Land Use in France, Germany, and the United States," *Law and Society Review*, vol. 29, no. 3 (1995), pp. 475–516.

40. Basil S. Markesinis, "Litigation-Mania in England, Germany and the USA: Are We So Very Different?" *Cambridge Law Journal*, vol. 49 (July 1990), pp. 233–76.

41. Erhard Blankenburg and Ralf Rogowski, "German Labour Courts and the British Industrial Tribunal System: A Socio-Legal Comparison of Degrees of Judicialisation," *British Journal of Law and Society*, vol. 13 (Spring 1986), pp. 67–92.

42. Shapiro, "Globalization of Law," pp. 37–64.

43. The Japanese engineers noted that certain U.S. regulations were more stringent. U.S. air pollution regulations, unlike those in Japan, required them to build flare stacks on the U.S. plant to burn certain organic wastes. The U.S. plant was required to install scrubbers to reduce emissions of low concentration organics from waste material; Japan has strict regulations on high-concentration organics (greater than 10 percent), but not on low concentrations. In addition, in response to national fire safety standards in the United States, enforced by insurance companies, the U.S. plant had to be equipped with more extensive and powerful sprinkler systems in warehouse areas than did the similar Japanese factory.

44. Interview with chief attorney for environmental affairs, chemical company, September 29, 1995.

45. Interview with chief attorney for environmental affairs, chemical company, September 29, 1995. The air pollution permit for a U.S. clone of a Japanese factory, Japanese officials told us (with some dismay), was one inch thick (not counting the three to six inches of supporting drawings), compared with ten pages in Japan. Interview with an environmental manager and engineers, chemical company, September 15, 1995.

46. See James Maxeiner, "The Expert in U.S. and German Patent Litigation," *IIC— International Review of Industrial Property and Copyright Law*, vol. 22, no. 5 (1991), pp. 595–605.

47. This experience, as noted earlier, is not universal. Referring to their dealings with the Department of Transportation's regulation of railroad tankcar safety, officials in a petrochemical corporation told us that inspectors are usually flexible and are not inclined to impose fines for minor violations by regulated companies they regard as "good firms." Moreover, when the company has problems with particular regulations, it usually can work out a modification in the context of a committee that includes representatives of the American Association of Railroads and the Department of Transportation. For a survey of the literature on variation in regulatory enforcement styles, see Kagan, "Regulatory Enforcement," pp. 383–422. See also Eugene Bardach and Robert A. Kagan, *Going by the Book: The Problem of Regulatory Unreasonableness: A Twentieth Century Fund Report* (Temple University Press, 1982).

48. Interview with a product safety official of a petrochemical firm, September 16, 1995. A number of the instances of legalistic and punitive enforce-

194   Robert A. Kagan and Lee Axelrad

ment that we heard of in our interviews involved state officials who were implementing state compliance programs pursuant to federal laws. Interviewees
said that the state officials were less inclined to be flexible and nonlegalistic
because of the federal oversight to which their decisions were subjected.

49. According to a director of safety, health, and environment for a multinational chemical company, European regulatory enforcement officials use
their discretion to make regulations more reasonable at the site level. In the
United States "the laws are extremist . . . and the interpretation is ultracon-
servative." Interview, director for safety, health, and environment, September
20, 1995.

50. See also Schwartz, "Liability and Malpractice."

51. See David E. Bernstein, "Procedural Tort Reform: Lessons from Other
Nations," *Regulation*, no. 1 (1996), pp. 71–81.

52. General Accounting Office, *Intellectual Property Rights: U.S. Companies'
Patent Experiences in Japan*, GAO/GGD-93-126 (July 1993), pp. 63–66.

53. Ibid., p. 67.

54. See, for example, Murray Weidenbaun, "Reforming Government Regulation to Promote Prosperity," presentation to the Colorado Council on Economic Education, Denver, September 20, 1995, reprinted in *Vital Speeches of
the Day*, vol. 62 (November 1, 1995), p. 51 (estimating "an aggregate hidden
tax of regulatory costs of at least $400 billion a year or more" in the United
States); Thomas Hopkins, "The Cost of Federal Regulation," *Journal of Regulation and Social Costs*, vol. 2, no. 1 (1992), p. 5, cited in UNICE study, p. 7,
n. 11 (estimating a gross cost of federal regulations borne by U.S. companies
and citizens of at least $600 billion a year, equivalent to about 10 percent of
U.S. GDP); Hopkins, "Cost of Regulation: Filling the Gaps," report prepared
for the Regulatory Information Service Center, Washington, August 1992 (estimating aggregate costs of U.S. federal regulation of $500 billion in 1992, or
about $5,000 per household), cited in "Control and Management of Govern-
ment Regulation", *PUMA*, vol. 95 (October 12, 1995), p. 4, and sources cited
in notes 94–96.

Regarding product liability, see Man C. Maloo and Benjamin A. Neil,
"Products Liability Exposure: The Sacrifice of American Innovation," *Journal
of Product Liability*, vol. 13 (Fall 1991), pp. 361–72, 368 (estimating direct and
indirect costs of product liability to American businesses of $380 billion an-
nually), cited in William A. Worthington and David H. Timmins, "Empirical
Effects of Restatement (Second) and Other Versions of Modern Product Liability Doctrine," *Journal of Products and Toxics Liability*, vol. 15 (1993), pp. 315,
322. Regarding securities disclosure requirements, see Susan M. Phillips and
J. Richard Zecher, *The SEC and the Public Interest* (MIT Press, 1981), p. 51 (estimating the costs in 1980 of the U.S. disclosure system for publicly traded
firms at no less than $1 billion), cited in James D. Cox, "Rethinking U.S. Se-
curities Laws in the Shadow of International Regulatory Competition," *Corporate Practice Commentator* (1990–91), p. 900, n. 61. Regarding environmental
law, see Congressional Budget Office, *Environmental Regulation and Economic
Efficiency* (Washington, 1985), estimating the adverse impact of environmen-

tal regulations on annual productivity growth in Japan (0.06 percent) compared with that in the United States (0.28 percent), and saying (p. xvi) that this difference might be because of the greater flexibility of the Japanese regulatory system: "The actual standards set by the regulatory process may be less important . . . than is the manner in which the regulations are carried out." Quoted in Richard B. Stewart, "Environmental Regulation and International Competitiveness," *Yale Law Journal*, vol. 102 (June 1993), p. 2069.

55. Report of a Task Force, *Justice for All: Reducing Costs and Delay in Civil Litigation* (Brookings, 1989), p. 6.

56. Langbein, "German Advantage"; Herbert L. Bernstein, "Whose Advantage after All?: A Comment on the Comparison of Civil Justice Systems," *University of California Davis Law Review*, vol. 21 (1988), pp. 587–603; and Atiyah and Summers, *Form and Substance*. Regarding the Japanese system for litigation, see Ko-yung Tung, Heather R. Evans, and Kosei Watanabe, "Dispute Resolution in U.S.-Japanese Commercial Transactions: A View from the Japanese Side," in *Private Investments Abroad* (Matthew Bender, 1991), pp. 11-6, 11-7, 11-11, 11-12, n. 46, citing Yamane, "Resolving Disputes in U.S.-Japan Trade: The Japanese Perspective," *Arbitration Journal*, vol. 39 (1984), pp. 5–6.

57. Deborah R. Hensler and others, *Trends in Tort Litigation: The Story behind the Statistics* (Santa Monica, Calif.: RAND, 1987), p. 27; James S. Kakalik and Nicholas M. Pace, *Costs and Compensation Paid in Tort Litigation* (Santa Monica, Calif.: RAND, 1986), p. xiii; Task Force on Medical Liability and Malpractice, *Report of the Task Force on Medical Liability and Malpractice* (Department of Health and Human Services, 1987), p. 16; and Kenneth S. Abraham and Lance Liebman, "Private Insurance, Social Insurance, and Tort Reform: Toward a New Vision of Compensation for Illness and Injury," *Columbia Law Review*, vol. 93 (January 1993), pp. 75–118.

58. Takao Tanase, "The Management of Disputes: Automobile Accident Compensation in Japan," *Law and Society Review*, vol. 24, no. 3 (1990), pp. 651–89; Erhard Blankenburg, "The Infrastructure for Avoiding Civil Litigation: Comparing Cultures of Legal Behavior in The Netherlands and West Germany," *Law and Society Review*, vol. 28, no. 4 (1994), pp. 789, 803–04; and E. Blankenburg and J. R. A. Verwoerd, "The Courts as a Final Resort? Some Comparisons between the Legal Cultures of The Netherlands and the Federal Republic of Germany," *Netherlands International Law Review*, vol. 35, no. 7-28 (1988), pp. 13–15.

59. Robert A. Kagan, "What Makes Uncle Sammy Sue?" *Law and Society Review*, vol. 21, no. 5 (1988), p. 717.

60. Maxeiner, "The Expert in U.S. and German Patent Litigation," p. 604.

61. Andrea Gerlin, "Patent Lawyers Forgo Sure Fees on a Bet," *Wall Street Journal*, June 24, 1994, p. B1. Ultimately, therefore, the costly U.S. patent enforcement process is influenced as much by the relative economic staying power of the parties as it is by the law, which, as is common under U.S. adversarial legalism, is rendered uncertain by a diverse, weakly coordinated judiciary and by the use of juries. Recently, in *Markman v. Westview Instruments*,

Inc., no. 95-26, the Supreme Court diminished the role of juries in patent litigation, ruling that the determination of patent scope is a matter for judges to decide. Linda Greenhouse, "Ruling Curbs Jury's Role on Patents," *New York Times,* April 24, 1996, p. D1.

62. Charkham, *Keeping Good Company.* See generally Roberta A. Romano, "Corporate Governance in the Aftermath of the Insurance Crisis," in Peter E. Schuck, ed., *Tort Law and the Public Interest: Competition, Innovation, and Consumer Welfare* (Norton, 1991), pp. 151–75. Japan's recent reductions in the costs of initiating such derivative suits, increasing shareholder access to legal remedies, was partly driven by pressure from U.S. negotiators in the Japan-U.S. Structural Impediments Initiative trade talks. This seems to be a clear instance of adversarial legalism being deliberately spread by U.S. officials. See Hiroshi Oda, "Business and the Law: Liable to a Flood of Litigation," *Financial Times,* December 21, 1993, p. 10.

63. James N. Dertouzos, Elaine Holland, and Patricia Ebener, *The Legal and Economic Consequences of Wrongful Termination* (Santa Monica, Calif.: RAND, 1988), pp. vii, 24–27, 37–38.

64. Blankenburg and Rogowski, "German Labour Courts"; and Robert Knegt, "Regulating Dismissal from Employment: Administrative and Judicial Procedures in the Netherlands," *Law and Policy,* vol. 11 (April 1989), pp. 175–87.

65. Roger M. Baron and Ronald J. Baron, "The Pennzoil-Texaco Dispute: An Independent Analysis," *Baylor Law Review,* vol. 38 (Spring 1986), pp. 254–56.

66. Thomas Petzinger Jr., *Oil and Honor: The Texaco-Pennzoil Wars* (Putnam's, 1987). See also Robert H. Mnookin and Robert B. Wilson, "Rational Bargaining and Market Efficiency: Understanding *Pennzoil v. Texaco,*" *Virginia Law Review,* vol. 75 (March 1989), pp. 295–315.

67. Baron and Baron, "Pennzoil-Texaco Dispute," p. 260. The primary difference between Texas and New York on tortious interference with contractual relations is that in Texas the issue of whether parties intended an oral agreement to be immediately binding is a question of fact for the jury (p. 262).

68. The jury's damage verdict was based on Pennzoil's novel claim that it was entitled to the exploration costs for finding as much oil as Getty had in proven reserves—$10.87 a barrel—minus the $3.40 a barrel it had been willing to pay Getty. Petzinger, *Oil and Honor,* p. 321.

69. According to Baron and Baron, "Pennzoil-Texaco Dispute," p. 268, the measure of damages should have been the difference between the fair market value of Getty's shares at the time of the "breach of contract" ($128 per share) and the contract price ($110), or $422 million at most.

70. Kagan, "Uncle Sammy," p. 65.

71. On the unpredictability of U.S. civil adjudication, see John H. Langbein, "Will Contests," *Yale Law Journal,* vol. 103 (May 1994), pp. 2039–48; Atiyah and Summers, *Form and Substance;* George L. Priest, "Justifying the Civil Jury," in Robert E. Litan, ed., *Verdict: Assessing the Civil Jury System* (Brookings, 1993), pp. 103–36; Marc Galanter, "The Regulatory Function of the Civil Jury," in Litan, ed., *Verdict,* p. 70.; and Peter Huber, "Junk Science and the

Jury: The Role of the Jury in Civil Dispute Resolution," *University of Chicago Legal Forum* (1990), pp. 273–302. "Japan-based companies are shocked by the enormous and unpredictable damages awarded by American (and especially California) juries in employment cases. If an employer in Japan is found to have terminated an employee without 'just cause,' the primary remedy is job reinstatement and monetary damages are limited to small severance payments. In the United States, however, juries have recently" awarded over $15 million to a single discharged employee, and verdicts in excess of $100,000 have become fairly common." David M. Lofholm, "Legal Implications of Japanese-Style Labor Relations in the United States," internal memorandum, Graham & James, Human Resources Group, November 18, 1991, p. 14.

72. This is not to say that the modal instance of litigation involves an extreme or unjust outcome. The majority of product-related claims, for example, are dropped or settled before trial, and punitive damages awards are rare. Kenneth Jost, "Tampering with Evidence," *ABA Journal* (April 1992), pp. 45, 49. The notable point is that defendant firms are uncertain whether theirs will be in the minority of cases in which companies are hit with enormous judgments. To foreclose the risk of catastrophic loss, they are likely to settle out of court more often than they would if there were less uncertainty regarding catastrophic loss as being avoidable.

73. See Janet Cooper Alexander, "Do the Merits Really Matter? A Study of Settlements in Securities Class Actions," *Stanford Law Review*, vol. 43 (February 1991), pp. 497, 513; and Roberta Romano, "The Shareholder Suit: Litigation without Foundation?" *Journal of Law, Economics, and Organization*, vol. 7, no. 1 (1991), pp. 55, 65.

74. *Private Securities Litigation Reform Act of 1995*, P.L. 104-67.

75. Huber, "Junk Science."

76. Thomas C. Palmer Jr., "Commitments to Foes Raise Artery Price Tag," *Boston Globe*, September 13, 1994, pp. 1, 6.

77. Galanter, "Quality of Settlements."

78. The best research has been done in the area of medical malpractice claims. In an intensive review of claims against anesthesiologists, an expert panel concluded that in 46 percent of the examined cases the claimant had received appropriate care. However, 42 percent of the claimants who received appropriate care also received compensation, although not as much as those claimants with comparable injuries for whom the care was found to be inadequate. Frederick W. Cheney and others, "Standard of Care and Anesthesia Liability," *Journal of the American Medical Association*, vol. 261 (March 17, 1989), pp. 1601–02. A study of medical malpractice claims in Hawaii found that in 24 percent of the claims for which a screening panel deemed "no liability" the claimant filed suit. Of the fifty-one closed cases in that category, plaintiffs received some compensation in thirty cases (or 60 percent), and in ten cases more than $100,000. Jean Kadooka Mardfin, *Medical Malpractice in the State of Hawaii: A Report to the 1986 Legislature* (Honolulu: Department of Commerce and Consumer Affairs, 1986), cited in Thomas B. Metzloff, "Researching Litigation: The Medical Malpractice Example," *Law and Contempo-*

rary Problems, vol. 51 (Autumn 1988), pp. 223–24. See also Henry S. Farber and Michelle J. White, "Medical Malpractice: An Empirical Examination of the Litigation Process," *RAND Journal of Economics*, vol. 22 (Summer 1991), pp. 199–217, 205 (a panel review of 252 cases from one hospital found that of 95 cases found to involve good quality care, one-fourth received some payment); Frank A. Sloan and Stephen S. van Wert, "Cost and Compensation of Injuries in Medical Malpractice," *Law and Contemporary Problems*, vol. 54 (Winter and Spring 1991), pp. 131–68; and Patricia M. Munch, *Costs and Benefits of the Torts System If Viewed as a Compensation System* (Santa Monica, Calif.: RAND, 1977), pp. 76–81. At the same time, many of these malpractice studies show that significant numbers of malpractice victims and some legal claimants who did receive inadequate care, according to expert review panels, received relatively little compensation or none.

79. Richard H. Sander, "Elevating the Debate on Lawyers and Economic Growth," *Law and Social Inquiry*, vol. 17 (Fall 1992), p. 665.

80. Richard H. Sander and E. Douglass Williams, "Why Are There So Many Lawyers? Perspectives on a Turbulent Market," *Law and Social Inquiry*, vol. 14 (Summer 1989), pp. 434–35.

81. William E. Nelson, "Contract Litigation and the Elite Bar in New York City, 1960–1980," *Emory Law Review*, vol. 39 (Spring 1990), pp. 413, 446.

82. Sellers, "Litigation as Resource."

83. Keith Hawkins, *Environment and Enforcement: Regulation and the Social Definition of Pollution* (Oxford: Clarendon Press, 1984); Kelman, *Regulating America, Regulating Sweden*; Vogel, *National Styles*; and Braithwaite, *Punish or Persuade*.

84. Thomas W. Church and Robert T. Nakamura, "Beyond Superfund: Hazardous Waste Cleanup in Europe and the United States," *Georgetown International Environmental Law Review*, vol. 7, no. 1 (1994), p. 56.

85. Menell, "Limitations of Institutions," p. 108.

86. William T. Barker, "Managing the Discovery Process: Some Thoughts for In-House Counsel," *Corporate Practice Commentator* (1990–91), pp. 603–14. Barker suggests that firms with no current litigation under way take the following steps to prepare for discovery requests that may arise in conceivable future litigation: first, systematically and consistently retain documents reaching back as long as any pertinent statutes of limitations (fifteen years or longer in some cases), and second, "instill a bias toward documentation" among company employees (pp. 604–05).

87. Telephone interview with the vice president of an engineering and planning firm, July 31, 1995.

88. Telephone interview with an attorney of a petroleum exploration and production firm, June 21, 1995.

89. Interview with engineers of a chemical company, September 15, 1995.

90. Allen R. Myerson, "Soaring Liability Payments Burdening New York," *New York Times*, June 29, 1992, p. B1.

91. Donald N. Dewees, Michael J. Trebilcock, and Peter C. Coyte, "The Medical Malpractice Crisis: A Comparative Empirical Perspective," *Law and Contemporary Problems*, vol. 54 (Winter and Spring 1991), pp. 217, 221; and

Peggy Berkowitz, "In Canada, Different Legal and Popular Views Prevail," *Wall Street Journal*, April 4, 1986, p. 21.

92. Peter W. Huber, *Liability: The Legal Revolution and Its Consequences* (Basic Books, 1988), pp. 3–4.

93. Franklin W. Nutter and Keith T. Bateman, *The U.S. Tort System in the Era of the Global Economy: An International Perspective* (Schaumberg, Ill.: Alliance of American Insurers, 1989), p. 20.

94. Robert W. Sturgis, *Tort Cost Trends: An International Perspective* (Valhalla, N.Y.: Tillinghast, 1992), p. 14. See also Mark French and Peter Jarrett, "The United States: Restoring Productivity Growth," *OECD Observer*, no. 185 (December 1993-January 1994), pp. 46–48.

95. Stephen D. Sugarman, *Doing Away with Personal Injury Law: New Compensation Mechanisms for Victims, Consumers, and Business* (Quorum Books, 1989), p. 40.

96. Hensler and others, *Compensation*, p. 54.

97. Ibid., pp. 107–08, note 53.

98. Stephen Carroll, Allan Abrahamse, and Mary Vaiana, *Documented Briefing: The Costs of Excess Medical Claims for Automobile Personal Injuries* (Santa Monica, Calif.: RAND, 1995).

99. Stephen Carroll and Allan Abrahams, "The Effects of a Proposed No-Fault Plan on the Costs of Auto Insurance in California: An Updated Analysis," issue paper, Santa Monica Calif., RAND Institute for Civil Justice, January 1996, p. 1.

100. Task Force on Medical Liability and Malpractice, *Report of the Task Force on Medical Liability and Malpractice*; Roger A. Reynolds and others, "The Cost of Medical Professional Liability," *Journal of the American Medical Association* (May 22–29, 1987), pp. 2776–2781; and David M. McIntosh and David C. Murray, *Medical Malpractice Liability: An Agenda for Reform* (Indianapolis: Competitiveness Center of Hudson Institute, 1994), pp. 26–29, 34–37.

101. Lee Berton and Joann S. Lublin, "Seeking Shelter: Partnership Structure Is Called in Question as Liability Risk Rises," *Wall Street Journal*, June 10, 1992, p. A1; and Lee Berton, "Big Accounting Firms Weed Out Risky Clients," *Wall Street Journal*, June 26, 1995, pp. B1, B6.

102. Luigi Mastroianni Jr., Peter J. Donaldson, and Thomas J. Kane, eds., *Developing New Contraceptives: Obstacles and Opportunities* (Washington: National Academy Press, 1990); and Robert Martin, "General Aviation Manufacturing: An Industry under Siege," in Huber and Litan, eds., *Liability Maze*, 478–99.

103. See prepared statement of Robert T. Clarke, president and CEO, Memorial Health System on Behalf of the Health Care Liability Alliance, "Health Care Reform Issues: Antitrust, Medical Malpractice Liability, and Volunteer Liability," Hearings before the House Committee on the Judiciary, February 27, 1996, 104 Cong. 2 sess. (Government Printing Office, 1996) (regarding Bendectin), p. 240; Susan Hershberg Adelman, "Liability a Threat to Future of Biomedical Materials," *American Medical News*, vol. 38 (August 14, 1995), pp. 19–20 (regarding silicone); and "Dow Chemical Receives Setbacks

in Breast Implant Litigation," *Liability Week*, vol. 10 (June 5, 1995) (regarding silicone).

104. Kenneth Prager, "Clozaril: Torts' Dangerous Side Effects," *Wall Street Journal*, December 6, 1990, p. A18.

105. The GAO report attributed the longer delays in the Japanese patent office to the larger number of applications (because Japanese patents are more narrowly drawn), the smaller number of examiners, and the pre-grant opposition system in Japan. General Accounting Office, *Intellectual Property Rights*, pp. 4–5. Recently, the Japanese government has instituted changes to speed up the process.

106. UNICE, *Releasing Europe's Potential*, p. 19.

107. The average FDA approval time for genetically engineered biologics is based on a U.S. Pharmaceutical Manufacturers Association study. Mark Mathieu, "CBER and the Biological IND Review," in Mark Mathieu, ed., *Biologics Development: A Regulatory Overview* (Waltham, Mass.: Parexel International, 1993), pp. 77–99.

108. Robert A. Kagan, "The Dredging Dilemma: Economic Development and Environmental Protection in Oakland Harbor," *Coastal Management*, vol. 19 (1991), pp. 313–41.

109. Ibid.

110. Andrew C. Revkin, "Curbs on Silt Disposal Threaten Port of New York as Ships Grow Larger," *New York Times*, March 18, 1996, pp. A1, A7.

111. "In western Europe," the environmental consultant explained, "there are several levels of implementation. You sit with them and work through the process. U.S. bureaucrats are overly cautious and want to attach too much cost to impact assessments. Furthermore, they never want to make a real decision. I think the problem is that they always want more information." This presumably reflects the fact that American regulators, operating under more specific statutes, enjoy less administrative discretion and are more susceptible to political criticism, court challenge, and judicial review.

Similarly, a Japanese lawyer who represents Japanese firms in the United States noted that his clients complain about the legal fees required in starting operations here. The main problem, he thought, is legal uncertainty: "In the U.S. the process is never ending. There is no one-time deal; it is always conditional on future process. For a Japanese company, there is always a fear of uncertainty and lack of finality. It comes down to the word 'responsibility'— can government agencies commit to a final decision without asking for more action?"

112. Telephone interview with the chief attorney for environmental affairs of a chemical firm, September 29, 1995.

113. See William D. Gunther, "Plant Locations and Environmental Regulation," in David L. McKee, ed., *Energy, the Environment, and Public Policy: Issues for the 1990s* (Praeger, 1991), pp. 55–64. "Only a relatively small number of U.S. industries [such as copper mining and smelting] appear to have had their international location patterns significantly affected by environmental regulations in the United States. . . . Most . . . have been able to adapt . . . [by]

changing their production processes or by using different raw materials." H. J. Leonard, *Are Environmental Regulations Driving U.S. Industry Overseas?* (Washington: Conservation Foundation, 1984), p. 131, quoted in Gunther, "Plant Locations," p. 62.

114. Bardach and Kagan, *Going by the Book*.

115. Commission on Natural Resources, National Research Council, *Decision Making in the Environmental Protection Agency*, vol. 2 (Washington: National Academy of Sciences, 1977), pp. 79–81.

116. Steven Kelman, "Adversary and Cooperationist Institutions for Conflict Resolution in Public Policymaking," *Journal of Policy Analysis and Management*, vol. 11, no. 2 (1992), p. 186.

117. Sugarman, *Doing Away*, pp. 3–18.

118. Compare Patricia M. Danzon, "Malpractice Liability: Is the Grass on the Other Side Greener?" in Schuck, ed., *Tort Law and Public Interest*, pp. 176–204 ("informed observers believe that the elimination of liability [in New Zealand] has led to laxer standards of medical care" [p. 203]); and Walter Gellhorn "Medical Malpractice Litigation (U.S.)—Medical Mishap Compensation (N.Z.)," *Cornell Law Review*, vol. 73 (January 1988), pp. 170, 200 ("No study has shown that, as a consequence [of New Zealand's 1974 reform], the quality of medical service has suffered."). See also Don Dewees and Michael Tribilcock, "The Efficacy of the Tort System and Its Alternatives: A Review of Empirical Evidence," *Osgoode Hall Law Journal*, vol. 30 (Spring 1992), pp. 57, 59–60; Mark Grady, "Why Are People Negligent? Technology, Nondurable Precautions and the Medical Malpractice Explosion," *Northwestern University Law Review*, vol. 82 (Winter 1988), pp. 293, 305–06; Rose Anne Devlin, "Liability Versus No-Fault Automobile Insurance Regimes: An Analysis of the Experience in Quebec," pp. 499–520, and Marc Gaudry, "Measuring the Effects of the No-Fault 1978 Quebec Automobile Insurance Act with the Drag Model," pp. 471–98, in Georges Dionne, ed., *Contributions to Insurance Economics* (Boston: Kluwer Academic Publishers, 1992). See also B. Dunlop, "No-Fault Automobile Insurance and the Negligent Action: An Expensive Anomaly," *Osgoode Law Journal*, vol. 13 (1975), p. 439; and Christopher J. Bruce, "The Deterrence Effects of Automobile Insurance and Tort Law: A Survey of the Empirical Literature," *Law and Policy*, vol. 6 (January 1984), pp. 67–100.

119. Martin, "General Aviation Manufacturing"; Andrew Craig, "Product Liability and Safety in General Aviation," pp. 456–77; John D. Graham, "Product Liability and Motor Vehicle Safety," pp. 120–90; and Murray Mackay, "Liability, Safety, and Innovation in the Automotive Industry," pp. 191–223, all in Huber and Litan, eds., *Liability Maze*.

120. Gary T. Schwartz, "Reality in the Economic Analysis of Tort Law: Does Tort Law Really Deter?" *UCLA Law Review*, vol. 42 (December 1994), pp. 377–444.

121. John Braithwaite, "The Nursing Home Industry," in Michael Tonry and Albert J. Reiss, eds., *Beyond the Law: Crime in Complex Organizations*, vol. 18: *Crime and Justice* (University of Chicago Press, 1993), pp. 11–54.

122. One of every fourteen companies listed on the "Big Board" New York Stock Exchange was the subject of a securities fraud suit between 1988 and 1991. Vincent E. O'Brien, "The Class-Action Shakedown Racket," *Wall Street Journal*, September 10, 1991, p. A20, quoted in Cox, "Rethinking U.S. Securities Laws," p. 915. In a sample of 330 cases, 75 percent of those sued had been in existence for more than ten years, indicating that this is not a problem unique to new issuers. Perhaps as a consequence of the securities disclosure regime in the United States, in 1989 only 8 Japanese corporations listed their shares on the U.S. stock exchanges, while 93 Japanese firms listed shares on the London Stock Exchange. O'Brien, "Class-Action Shakedown," p. 907. "Private sanctions for misleading statements adds further authenticity to the firm's disclosures and enhances the attractiveness of U.S. markets to foreign investors. At the same time, the fear of being the target of such a suit makes U.S. securities markets less attractive to foreign issuers and is very much a part of a U.S. company's decision to raise its capital abroad" (p. 916).

123. Wayne B. Gray and John T. Scholz, "Analyzing the Equity and Efficiency of OSHA Enforcement," *Law and Policy*, vol. 13 (July 1991), pp. 185–214.

124. Richard E. Wokutch, *Worker Protection, Japanese Style: Occupational Safety and Health in the Auto Industry* (Ithaca, N.Y.: ILR Press, 1992), pp. 8, 223, 225, 228.

125. UNICE, *Releasing Europe's Potential*, p. 29. The observation that the economic consequences of adversarial legalism may fall disproportionately onto the shoulders of small and medium-sized businesses is made more troubling by the fact that environmental regulation in the United States is moving into a new phase. Beyond large sources of pollution, regulatory focus has broadened to include the very large number of small sources. "These affect people . . . who don't have the habit of hiring lawyers, engineers and consultants and have not been confronted with the environmental control apparatus before. They are confused, in many cases angry about it, and in some cases terrified." "William K. Reilly," interviewed by Alex Barnum, *San Francisco Chronicle*, February 4, 1996, p. 3.

126. B. Dan Wood and Richard W. Waterman, *Bureaucratic Dynamics: The Role of Bureaucracy in a Democracy* (Boulder, Colo.: Westview Press, 1994).

127. Robert E. Litan, "The Liability Explosion and American Trade Performance: Myths and Realities," in Peter H. Schuck, ed., *Tort Law and the Public Interest: Competition, Innovation, and Consumer Welfare* (Norton, 1991), pp. 127–50.

Chapter 5

U.S. Environmental Regulation in a More Competitive World

Marc Landy and Loren Cass

PROTECTION of the environment has been one of the most impressive efforts of public policy in the United States in the past quarter century. Certainly no other advanced nation has been more energetic in promulgating hard-hitting environmental rules and regulations. Yet a number of major environmental programs have proven to be inefficient, either imposing costs greater than the recognizable benefits to society or yielding net benefits but at an unnecessarily steep cost. Because global trade patterns are subjecting the U.S. economy to new and intense competitive pressures, flawed domestic regulatory activities are becoming less affordable. Now perhaps more than ever, cost-effective alternatives need to be explored so that Americans can continue to enjoy the fruits of a cleaner environment but with less economic sacrifice.

The first part of this chapter contends that inefficiencies in U.S. environmental policies constitute a significant drag on productivity growth, particularly for some internationally prominent U.S. industries. We then analyze the pollution control policies of two of this country's trading partners, Germany and Great Britain. Do their regulatory styles offer some valuable lessons? At the end, we probe the conceptual and political roots of shortcomings in U.S. policy and, on the basis of this assessment, sketch a corrective strategy.

The Problem

It often seems easy to play down the economic impact of environmental regulatory programs. The sky is not falling. Only 2.1 percent of GDP is said to be touched by environmental compliance costs.[1]

Studies that have focused directly on the relationship between U.S. environmental regulation and economic competitiveness claim only negligible effects.[2] And while some U.S. environmental rules are notoriously wasteful, our international competitors often indulge in forms of regulation that are as bad or worse.

Moreover, the U.S. government has become more attentive to regulatory inefficiency. Since the mid-1980s, the Environmental Protection Agency has made efforts to lessen needlessly expensive and ineffective rules. Attempts have been under way, for example, to perform comparative risk analyses to evaluate whether the agency's interventions are being targeted at the most severe problems. The Clinton administration's "reinventing government" initiative has encouraged the EPA to grant companies some leeway to deviate from the letter of some rules in order to achieve acceptable results more cheaply.

Obviously, it is misleading to dwell on the costs of environmental regulation without duly recognizing the economic gains that result. As Michael Porter suggests, there may be considerable "green gold" in pollution abatement: "Strict environmental standards do not inevitably hinder competitive advantage against foreign rivals; indeed, they often enhance it. Tough standards trigger innovation and upgrading."[3] Specifically, two types of benefits can result. When forced by government to reduce pollution, companies may rethink their production strategies in ways that improve productive efficiency or product mix. Environmental control technologies also offer export opportunities. Properly encouraged, parts of the U.S. pollution control industry are well positioned to market equipment abroad. For example, the adoption of the Montreal protocol created a competitive advantage for E. I. Dupont de Nemours, a company that had a readily available substitute for the banned chlorofluorocarbons.

It is almost certainly true that requiring businesses to invest in more pollution-controlling devices will lead to job growth and higher wages in the pollution control sector. It is also likely that if other countries adopt similar standards, American firms that are already producing the devices may have an advantage.

Cause for Concern

Although pollution abatement costs may seem small in relation to U.S. economic output as a whole, they are substantial in important industries: chemicals, petroleum products, coal, paper, stone, clay, glass, and primary metals.[4] These industries employ almost one-fifth of all production workers in the manufacturing and mining sectors. Average weekly wages are at least 50 percent higher than average service industry wages and well above even the average for manufacturing.[5] But these are also the industries suffering the greatest productivity losses from the weight of environmental regulations. It is far from clear that the losses have been wholly offset by the social benefits of increasingly stringent compliance.

In industries in which operations are already subject to strict regulation, future costs are likely to far exceed current ones. The revised Clean Air Act, for example, places many industries on tight timetables that will force companies to make much larger expenditures much faster to achieve diminishing percentage reductions in emissions.

This is not to say that all the cheap and easy pollution reductions have been achieved. Opportunities still exist for cutting emissions substantially and affordably. But current regulatory schemes are not well designed to focus on these cost-effective opportunities. The emphasis on technological mandates forces firms to make expensive equipment changes even when cheaper methods may be available. Overall regulatory compliance costs in manufacturing industries have grown both in absolute terms and relative to overall manufacturing costs and revenues.[6]

The relationship between environmental strictures and slower productivity growth can pose a significant trade-off. James C. Robinson examined data for 445 U.S. manufacturing industries from 1974 to 1986. Finding scarce evidence that regulations prod companies to develop more efficient methods and products, Robinson observed a diversion of "economic resources and managerial attention away from productivity-enhancing innovation."[7] Wayne Gray and Ronald Shadbegian examined slightly more recent data (through 1990) and also found that plants with higher abatement costs experienced lower productivity.[8]

The effects, Robinson stresses, are cumulative. "Small annual effects snowball into more substantial productivity deficits."[9] Over a dozen years, culminating in 1986, EPA and Occupational Safety and Health Administration (OSHA) regulations accounted for substantial shares of the industrial productivity slowdown: about 32 percent for primary metals, 25 percent for petroleum products, 28 percent for chemicals, and 27 percent for paper. Overall, the U.S. manufacturing sector's multifactor productivity was down 11.4 percent from the level it would have achieved without the environmental and, to a lesser extent, occupational health regulations after 1974.[10] It strains credulity to suppose that effects so noticeable have posed no hindrance to the competitiveness of some U.S. tradable goods in world markets, especially during interludes of unfavorable currency exchange rates. Amid increasing globally generated competition, even marginal increments in domestic regulatory burdens cut closer to the bone.

These traces of a link to sectoral productivity problems raise doubts that environmental standards imposed during the 1970s typically forced product or process innovation that promoted growth. More likely, as J. Ladd Greeno, senior vice president of Arthur D. Little, concluded,

> Most companies focus on compliance, not competitive advantage—for good reason. Environmental managers would welcome a world in which they could "search exclusively for win-win solutions." In reality, however, they concentrate on ensuring compliance with current environmental regulations, remediating environmental problems caused by past operations, and anticipating the impact of proposed regulations.[11]

Managers who were unable to find more efficient processes before onerous regulations were imposed have had even less time to spend on the problem as they rush to comply with new regulatory standards and timetables. Of course, anecdotes can be found in which the imposition of some new regulation was a bucket of cold water in the face, rousing managers from apathy and provoking experimentation with improved production processes. But if this has been the norm, it implies an implausible degree of organizational slack pervading U.S. manufacturing. It would seem odd to assume that government regulators and outside consultants know more about opportunities to improve productive efficiency than do businesspeople working daily in the trenches. Further, as Robinson points out, regulatory mandates that supposedly induce innovative attempts to reduce pollution compete for the same engineering resources that would otherwise focus on reducing industrial costs. Companies' investments in research and development may decrease as managerial energies are diverted from developing new products and processes into complying with regulations.[12]

Making matters worse, some recent environmental regulatory initiatives are hazardous not only for industrial productivity growth but for the environment itself. Aspects of the Clean Air Act are illustrative. Because new sources of air pollution have been subject to much more stringent controls than have existing sources, polluters have a strong incentive to keep existing equipment working rather than replace it with newer, cleaner equipment.[13] Section 111 of the law gave the EPA responsibility to set new source performance standards (NSPS) for all new sources of air pollution for which ambient air standards had been established. The NSPS were required to be based on the "best technological system of continuous emission reduction." As strict as this standard is, it is even stricter for new equipment located in areas that are currently not in compliance with the standards of the law (so-called nonattainment areas) where new sources must achieve "the lowest achievable emissions rate."[14]

By contrast, existing pollution sources, even those in dirty areas, have not had technology-based standards imposed on them. Companies have had an incentive to keep their existing smokestacks puffing and to do so in the dirtiest places. The old-source bias discourages firms from buying new equipment that, except for the added cost imposed by NSPS, can make plants more productive.

Likewise, the Comprehensive Environmental Response, Compensation, and Liability Act (Superfund) is riddled with perverse side effects. Superfund's greatest environmental harm stems from its impact on firms' decisions about where to locate. Because the program's liability scheme is so menacing, land near hazardous waste sites that have been placed on the Superfund list or that might be so designated becomes virtually unsalable. Vast stretches of urban real estate have been written off.

Urban land that is not put to productive use is detrimental to the environment. Litter accumulates, vandalism spreads, the property value of adjacent real estate declines, and a cycle of blight begins. This deterioration is often much worse than what might be wrought by new manufacturing facilities, even if they are similar to those that had existed in the vicinity for decades. Would-be investors locate facilities elsewhere, on "green fields," often spoiling areas that had been relatively clean.

Recent initiatives could change some of these unintended effects. The amended Clean Air Act is more vigorous in its treatment of nonattainment areas. The law forces states and localities to attack existing sources more aggressively. But this victory has been achieved largely by applying command-and-control regulatory methods. To remove the cloud of Superfund liability, the EPA has recently announced potential sites that will not be placed on the Superfund list. This action would be even more reassuring if the agency were not at the same time creating disincentives for industrial recycling via its Resource Conservation and Recovery Act (RCRA) corrective action program.

Comparing Risks

In the past few years important studies have compared different types of health and safety regulations on the basis of how much they cost per human life saved. Of course, some regulations have beneficial attributes beyond saving lives. But the regulations that were evaluated all have that as their primary rationale. What stands out in the evaluations are the enormous differences in the costs of environmental regulations compared with other forms of public health intervention.

As John Graham points out, the health plan the Clinton administration proposed in 1993 limited mammographies to one every two years because more frequent screenings would have cost more than $100,000 per life saved. By contrast, a very large number of the EPA's toxin control rules cost hundreds of millions of dollars per life saved. Regarding the EPA's reformulated gasoline rule, Graham estimates the cost per cancer case avoided to be $6 million for the projected reductions of volatile organic compounds (VOCs) and $35 million for the reductions in nitrogen oxide.[15] When the Harvard Center for Risk Analysis compared 273 of the federal government's public health programs, it found that the median toxin control policy run by the EPA costs ten times as much per life saved as did the health and safety regulations administered by the Department of Transportation or the Occupational Safety and Health Administration. At the extreme, benzene emission controls specified for rubber tire manufacturing plants are estimated to cost $20 billion per life saved. But even if this figure is anomalous, five other kinds of benzene controls were together estimated to cost more than $90 million per life saved.[16]

Robert Hahn's extensive review of the government's own figures on costs and benefits of environmental health and safety regulations is consistent with the Harvard study. Using agency estimates by the EPA, OSHA, the Consumer Product Safety Commission, and the National Highway Traffic Safety Administration between 1990 and 1995, Hahn found that only half of the final rules promulgated met a net benefit test. Only twelve of the forty final regulations issued by the EPA passed such a test. On average, environmental regulations are less cost effective than other forms of health and safety regulation.[17]

Just how costly many EPA mandates have become can best be appreciated by trying the following mental experiment. Suppose the United States chose to spend its entire GNP on reducing cancers and accidental deaths. The maximum available to be spent would be $65 million per life saved. Yet more than 40 percent of the EPA's regulations exceed that average sum. "In other words," Hahn comments, "for a significant number of regulations, we would spend money at a rate that would exhaust the GNP simply on investments aimed at reducing fatal accidents and a small proportion of cancers."[18]

This realization does not by itself provide a formula for determining which regulations to adopt and which to abolish. But it does suggest the existence of widespread wasteful mistakes in the design of some environmental regulatory programs. And it points out the need for a more strategic approach to public health regulation. There is clearly considerable room to achieve economic savings without compromising the nation's health and safety.

One Size Fits All

To understand why too much current environmental regulation places unnecessary burdens on industry, it is helpful to unpack the hackneyed phrase "command and control." Central to these terms are the specific limitations on emissions and the technological mandates imposed on sources. Companies that may face very different market conditions and that have adopted very different business strategies are required to respond uniformly. It is the failure of this type of regulation to take into account the diversity of circumstances that accounts for much of the discomfort of firms with some environmental sanctions.

Command and control takes varying forms. In some instances it requires adopting specific equipment. All sources of a hazardous air pollutant might be required to use the technologies employed by the 10 percent of all sources that emit the least. In other instances the regulations specify emissions limitations, but in practice, only certain types of equipment exist that will satisfy the limits. Other regulations are technology forcing, which means that the equipment necessary to meet the emissions requirement does not yet exist. The assumption behind technology forcing is that by mandating a search for a solution, and threatening to penalize those who fail to find it, an acceptable technological fix will emerge.

From an environmental standpoint, the problem with emissions limits or technological mandates is that they set maximums as well as minimums. They act as if there were a precise, scientifically determined safe limit to be achieved. In fact, the designated limits are largely arbitrary. When a firm meets the limit, it has little incentive to do better.

The bias against further improvement should not be overstated. Even after a particular limit has been established, pollution control firms may still develop new products and then lobby for tighter standards based on the pollution reduction capabilities of those products. But such initiatives require legislative and bureaucratic institutions to do what they do not do well: make clever technological and economic gambles. Pollution control firms engage in political rent seeking rather than a market test of their merchandise.

The productivity loss to firms from command-and-control regulation stems not only from the often inordinate cost of mandated hardware, but also from the constraints that rigid requirements place on creative management.

The Second Battle of Yorktown

The severity of the problems we have discussed was starkly illustrated in the Yorktown Project, a joint research effort by the EPA and Amoco that sought to analyze comprehensively the relationship between regulatory efforts and industrial emissions emanating from a single facility. The first objective was to identify the types, amounts, and sources of emissions into the air, land, and water from Amoco's Yorktown, Virginia, facility and to determine the relative risks they posed to human health. The second objective was to develop cost-effective ways to reduce the pollutants and to identify factors that encourage or discourage pollution prevention.

The greatest significance of this experiment was the discovery of an enormous gap between the most efficient control options and the EPA-mandated controls confronting Amoco. Volatile organic compound emissions were found to be the greatest health hazard. Emissions could be significantly reduced with capital investments of $10 million, or $510 per ton of VOC reduction. By contrast, the mandated capital investments under relevant EPA regulations were estimated to cost $41 million, more than four times the cost of the study's recommended solutions.[19]

The study concluded that the greatest VOC reductions could be achieved by controlling emissions primarily during the off-loading of barges. The EPA did not require that. Instead, it was requiring the oil company to construct a new sewer system to control benzene emissions, a course of action that the Yorktown study found to be of minimal consequence.

No statutory means existed for adjusting the EPA's requirements in response to the study's findings. So Amoco was forced to invest in a new sewer treatment system and to make other mandated but inefficient capital expenditures. Amoco did implement several cost-effective strategies for reducing emissions as suggested by the report. But it did not act on controlling emissions from the off-loading of barges. It chose to manage defensively, deeming it unwise to undertake a major investment in control technologies that were not yet covered by EPA policy.

Although Amoco had assumed that roughly 3 percent of its operating costs (other than pumping crude oil) were devoted to complying with environmental regulations, the Yorktown study showed that compliance represented 22 percent of operating costs, not including any future liability for environmental cleanup. The report estimated that if the company had been allowed to approach pollution control strategies cost effectively, the same level of control could be achieved at 25 percent of the current cost.[20]

The EPA and the White House are not unaware of these difficulties. The EPA has initiated projects to enable companies and municipalities to match resources and risks more closely. Among these have been the Toxics Integration Project, the Unfinished Business Report, the report of the EPA Science Advisory Board entitled *Reducing Risk,* the State Comparative Risk Project, Project XL, and the Common Sense Initiative.

But at the same time, Congress and the agency have embarked on new command-and-control regulatory schemes that dwarf these reform experiments in both size and importance and show every sign of replicating and exacerbating the inefficiencies that the EPA is striving to address as it wears other hats. The Resource Conservation and Recovery Act's corrective action program is expected to cost $240 billion over the next thirty years, or about $8 billion a year. By the year 2005 the 1990 version of the Clean Air Act is anticipated to cost $29 billion to $36 billion more per year than it does today but provide recognizable benefits of only $14 billion to $16 billion.[21] What follows is a detailed discussion of these two expensive new initiatives.

The Clean Air Act of 1990

The 1990 Clean Air Act takes up 314 pages of the Federal Register and is almost seven times longer than the original statute it amended. It is full of deadlines, "hammers," and timetables to limit the discretion and flexibility of bureaucrats and of regulated sources. For all the added complexity and expense the act introduces, the preexisting standard-based structure remains unchanged. There were only marginal modifications in the national ambient air quality standards, the prevention of significant deterioration regions, and the new source performance standards.[22] The changes adopted represent a kind of perverse learning by Congress, which concluded that the command-and-control structure itself was not fundamentally in need of reform and that the EPA had been insufficiently energetic and punitive.

As one of the chief congressional drafters, Representative Henry Waxman, Democrat of California, explained:

> To an extent unprecedented in prior environmental statutes, the pollution control programs of the 1990 Amendments include very detailed mandatory directives to EPA, rather than broad grants of authority that would allow for wide latitude in EPA's implementation of the CAA programs. In addition, statutory deadlines are routinely provided to assure that the required actions are taken in a timely fashion. More than two hundred rule-making actions are mandated in the first several years of

the 1990 Amendment's implementation. . . . The specificity in the 1990 Amendments reflects the concern that without detailed directives, industry intervention might frustrate efforts to put pollution control steps in place. This could happen either directly, through EPA inaction, or indirectly, through interference with EPA rule making efforts by White House entities such as the OMB or, more recently, the White House Council on Competitiveness. History shows that even where EPA seeks to take strong action, the White House will often intervene at industry's behest to block regulatory action.[23]

Perhaps the most significant change in the 1990 act was that it forbids *any* consideration of cost in setting national ambient air quality standards. This has virtually eliminated state discretion over how to bring nonattainment areas into compliance, which had been an avenue for addressing cost concerns. The new rules replace discretion with mandates and short deadlines. For example, regarding ozone pollution, the act establishes six categories of nonattainment areas ranging from moderate to extreme. The severity of the regulatory action required varies depending on the category: more actions are required for more severe problems. In the most severe areas the act calls for regulation of sources emitting as little as twenty-five tons, a level that can include gas stations, auto paint shops, and dry cleaners.

Whereas the original act required states to make "reasonable progress" toward meeting timetables, the new act specifies what percentage reduction must be met each year.[24] While this increasing intervention in nonattainment areas may indeed push state enforcers to treat old sources more harshly, it does so only at great expense and intrusiveness.

The commitment to command and control is evident in the act's provisions governing hazardous air pollutants. The 1970 Clean Air Act had given the EPA authority to list toxic chemicals and establish emission standards for them that provided "an ample margin of safety to protect the public health."[25] By 1990 the EPA had succeeded in listing only 8. To show its dissatisfaction with this rate of progress, Congress declared 189 chemicals to be toxic, set emissions limits for them, and mandated the technology to be used to achieve those limits.[26]

To gain the ambitious reductions in hazardous air pollutants envisioned in title III, the EPA mandates the use of "maximum achievable control technology" in regulated processes, which is defined as the best-performing 12 percent of technology currently in use by industry. The EPA provides reference technologies for each of its rules as a minimum for compliance. Individual rules continue to govern each step of the production process, including emission standards for process vents, storage vessels, transfer racks, and wastewater operations, as well as leak detection and remediation.

Regulating hazardous air pollutants can impose enormous costs. The original national emissions standard for hazardous air pollutants, covering fugitive emissions of benzene, cost $3.4 million for every premature death averted. Three subsequent revisions of the standard have increased its cost from $6.1 million to $32.9 million to $168.2 million per premature death averted. Other hazardous air pollutant standards are even more expensive: $13.5 million per life saved for the arsenic emissions standard for glass plants and $23 million for the arsenic-copper standard.[27]

The aspect of the act with the greatest potential for imposing additional paperwork, managerial burdens, and legal entanglement is title V, the permitting requirement. Previously, the EPA could bring an enforcement action only if it could demonstrate that a company was out of compliance with an emissions regulation. Title V reverses the burden of proof: all emitters of at least ten tons a year of a hazardous air pollutant or one hundred tons a year of any regulated air pollutant (twenty-five tons in ozone nonattainment areas) must obtain a permit that demonstrates compliance. To obtain such a permit it is first necessary to catalog every emission from a plant. The next step is to identify all federal and state regulations that apply to each emission source. As Charles Malloch, director of regulatory management for the Corporate Environmental Health and Safety Department of Monsanto County, Missouri, puts it, "The hard part comes when you have to match up each of the thousands of emissions points with its applicable requirement."[28] These requirements will vary state by state. Many states have adopted more stringent requirements for some emissions or added additional chemical compounds to be regulated.

The third step is to determine and demonstrate compliance with each relevant regulation. This will involve testing to ensure that emissions are within limits. Where emissions exceed the relevant limits, the company must either invest in the necessary pollution control technology or find alternative pollution prevention solutions to comply with the rules. Each facility must develop a monitoring and record-keeping plan to demonstrate compliance and calculate fees.[29] The monitoring, record-keeping, and reporting requirements are likely to force a company to hire additional staff. Many of the rules require continuous monitoring of emissions leading to extensive investments in monitoring equipment. Finally, states may open the applications to public comment and provide for public hearings, for which facilities will have to prepare.

Like many regulatory endeavors that later prove perverse, the premise of the permit system appears sensible. Firms *should* know what they are emitting, and it makes more sense for them to show beforehand that they are in compliance than to face the uncertainty of an EPA inspection after the fact. Superfund was based on equally plausible assumptions: the polluter pays, and cleanup should precede litigation.[30] But premises do not make a policy. Like Superfund, the policy design for the permit program may well entail long delays, uncertainty, inflexibility, legal pettifogging, and bureaucratic intrusion.

The minimum tonnage figures that force a company to file for a permit are based not on a plant's actual emissions but on the potential to emit from its various production processes. This is calculated on the basis of what a piece of equipment would emit if it were operating at full throttle 24 hours a day, 365 days a year. In some plants, some equipment may be run that hard and long, but most production occurs in batches, with significant downtime in between. Thus many plants that do not come close to emitting the amounts of pollutants required for a permit will be obligated to obtain one. Their alternative is to seek an exemption by accepting specific limits on the use of their equipment, restrictions that could prove costly by limiting the flexibility of the production process.

The permit application process is cumbersome. As Gale Hoffnagle, vice president and technical director of TRC Environment Corporation, notes, "Without question, Title V is more complicated than the U.S. tax code."[31] One petroleum refinery's application ran to more than 10,000 pages.[32] Preparing a permit will cost as much as $400,000, not including filing fees, testing for emissions, or investments in compliance measures.[33]

The permit programs are run by the states, each of which has developed its own permitting process that has been approved by the

EPA. The result has been significant variation in the complexity, coverage, and application deadlines. New Jersey, California, and Wisconsin have some of the most complex and demanding regulatory requirements. New York and Ohio have adopted simpler programs.[34] The result is that companies with facilities in several states could face very different permitting requirements and considerable difficulty transferring permits among states. The winners, of course, are the environmental consultants and lawyers that coach companies on how to navigate the regulatory shoals.

The permits are rigid. They last for five years and require firms to incorporate any potential process changes into the original permit or else request a modification at a later date, which can take more than a year to approve. For maximum production flexibility, firms must attempt to anticipate changes that might have an impact on emissions over the five-year period. These possibilities must be contained in the permit as "alternative operating scenarios." Once they are approved, the facility can shift to them after notifying state authorities. Still, the hurdles can be daunting for industries that must alter production to match innovations or frequent changes in product demand.

The current permitting process poses difficult choices for individual firms. Innovations in pollution control can lead to more efficient and cost-effective abatement, but they may also lead to delays in the permitting process and uncertainty regarding final approval. Room for experimentation is limited because any failure in emissions control risks criminal charges. The system creates a bias in favor of standard approaches and locks in a level of protection without providing incentives for further innovation in emissions reduction.

The 1990 Clean Air Act also contains a provision for citizen lawsuits that, in coordination with the permit program, provides fertile ground for adversarial legalism. In the past, citizen suits focused more on the Clean Water Act, largely because of its publicly accessible national pollutant discharge monitoring reports that document companies' permit violations. Courts have generally accepted the reports as admissions of guilt and have often provided summary judgments on liability. Under title V of the Clean Air Act, companies must file biannual reports of all compliance data in pounds per hour of emissions. Any violations of the relevant permit will become readily apparent. It will therefore be much easier for private parties to sue for compliance.

Also, before 1990 there were no provisions in the Clean Air Act for civil penalties. Amendments to section 304 now allow such awards, a portion of which can be allocated to pollution mitigation programs. These programs are popular with many of the groups that initiate lawsuits. An additional incentive for litigation is the law's awards program, which pays up to $10,000 to anyone furnishing information leading to a successful legal action against a company violating the Clean Air Act. The result could be a proliferation of environmental bounty hunters.[35]

RCRA's Corrective Action Program

Hazardous waste regulation has two distinct components: abandoned site cleanup—Superfund—and regulation of hazardous waste control practices at current manufacturing, transport, and disposal facilities. The law governing Superfund has proved so expensive and counterproductive that it has become an effigy for proponents of environmental regulatory relief. However, even as the EPA and Congress grapple with means for making Superfund less onerous, regulation of existing facilities under the RCRA is becoming increasingly conflictual and costly.

The most controversial and potentially expensive aspect of this current effort is known as corrective action. It is targeted at facilities that treat, store, or dispose of hazardous waste (TSDFs). The $234 billion price tag attached to this program is $80 billion greater than that of the Superfund.[36]

Corrective action has four components. The first, facility assessment, is conducted by agency staff using existing documentary evidence and site visits to determine whether corrective action is required. If so, the facility owner must next conduct a facility investigation that identifies the character and extent of all hazardous waste releases and their pathways of exposure. If a site is found to exceed specific soil, groundwater, air, or surface water standards, a study of remedial measures is required. Although EPA retains the right to choose the remedy, firms are urged to participate in the study to encourage the choice of the most efficient alternative. Finally, the owner implements the designated solution.

This description of the corrective action process glosses over the crucial analytic question. What is a waste? To many in the industrial community, a waste is what gets thrown away. If an input is separated out of one production process and reused in another, it has not been wasted and is not a waste. This is true even if it is not reused immediately but needs to be stored for some period of time. Indeed, a great deal of manufacturing activity is of this type. Chemicals are culled from one process and used later for some other purpose.

The EPA interprets the same reality differently. The agency considers that a waste occurs any time a stream of inputs divides and some are cast aside. Whatever is removed is a waste, even if at a later stage it is reincorporated. So if a solvent is poured first on machinery and then wiped by a rag, the rag becomes a hazardous waste. But if the solvent is first poured on the rag and then the rag is used to wipe the machinery, the rag is not considered a hazardous waste. The difference presumably is that in the first instance the solvent is being "emitted" by the machinery.

Amusing though it might be, this conceptual controversy has great practical import. Currently, the EPA's presence on the factory floor is limited. It is restricted, on the whole, to monitoring a factory's external emissions. But if every tank and pipe on the premises has the potential of being defined as a transporter, storer, or disposer of waste, even if no emissions extend beyond the factory gate, the agency has a rationale for maintaining a continual investigatory presence in the workplace and a mandate to interfere in everyday production decisions regardless of how disruptive such interference might become.

Because corrective action is considered potentially intrusive, companies have a strong incentive to evade it through defensive management. Because action is triggered by the application for an RCRA permit, the trick is to keep from having a facility defined as needing a permit. The easiest way to keep something from being declared a hazardous waste is to avoid reusing it and therefore avoid being defined as a "treater or storer" of such material. Instead one simply ships the material off to a licensed hazardous waste disposer who either incinerates it or places it in a landfill. In the process a valuable opportunity to recycle is lost, a high disposal fee is paid, and more hazardous waste is either emitted into the atmosphere via incineration or dumped into the ground.

International Contrasts

An examination, albeit cursory, of German and British air and hazardous waste remediation policies offers instructive comparisons with U.S. policy. German regulation shares the American predilection for technological mandates but does so without the adversarial legalism that the U.S. system generates. The British rely on a much more flexible approach to regulation in general.

The German and British Models

German air pollution rules rely on a licensing system with many similarities to the U.S. permitting process under title V of the 1990 Clean Air Act amendments. The German environmental licensing system is, in fact, more comprehensive. Except for laws affecting water, nuclear energy, and mining reclamation, it integrates all environmental laws with licensing provisions into a single license application. German air quality standards cover approximately 200 substances and 80 processes, half as many substances as the 400 covered by U.S. law. But the stringency of emissions limits is comparable to that of U.S. standards and in some cases more ambitious.

The primary German air pollution law is the Federal Air Quality Protection Act (Bundes-Immissionsschutzgesetz, or BImSchG) of 1974. The BImSchG relies on ambient quality and emission standards, but in practice ambient standards are set by default through the use of mandated technology for regulated industries. The ambient standards are more relevant if a company wishes to expand production or build in an area that fails to meet ambient air quality requirements. If the facility will worsen the local airshed, the license request may be denied.

Just as the U.S. Clean Air Act requires the use of maximum achievable control technology, German law mandates the use of the "best available technology," which is defined in the *Technische Anleitung Luft* (technical instructions on clean air maintenance).[37] The *TA Luft* sets the emissions limits for specific waste gases and technical requirements for processing techniques.

German air pollution regulations are very detailed. Facilities seeking licenses must be able to certify that they are complying with best available technology requirements and are meeting all relevant emissions standards. Facilities must submit an emissions declaration describing emissions levels over a given period. But once a facility receives a license, the reporting and monitoring requirements are much simpler than under title V of the U.S. act. Under the BImSchG, continuous emissions monitoring may be required of any regulated facility, if the relevant regulating body has reason to believe that emission limits may have been exceeded. In practice, continuous monitoring is rare. For example, in Lower Saxony less than 5 percent of regulated facilities are required to invest in continuous monitoring equipment.[38] Other facilities may be required to pay for an independent monitor to test air quality for short periods.

German environmental policy is relatively free of adversarialism. Under German law, state and district governments are responsible for carrying out environmental regulations. The federal government has few powers to force the states to implement federal policies.[39] Industries do not frequently challenge environmental rules in court. In part, this may be because the German central government frequently provides subsidies and tax breaks as incentives for industries to meet standards.

German administrative courts largely confine themselves to procedural issues, deferring to regulators on matters of substance. Under federal law, there are no provisions for private rights of action to force compliance with regulations, although environmental groups have had standing to sue for damage to health or property in a number of German states courts. On the whole, the system is weighted against excessive litigation.

Because state and local governments implement environmental regulations, enforcement efforts vary. Common to all states, however, is a cooperative approach. There are no criminal penalties for the contravention of a license. Regulators typically issue an order for a company to correct a pollution problem. If the company fails to do so, the regulatory authority may impose a monetary fine of up to DM 100,000.

Germany's Constitutional Court has ruled that "the mere risk of harm must be avoided or at least reduced in proportion to the probability, kind, and extent of risk," but it has specifically denied that this creates a *right* to a safe and healthy environment.[40] The polluter is forced to bear the costs of pollution control, but the principle that the polluter pays is qualified by the *Gemeinlastprinzip*, or principle of public responsibility, which holds that the government has a responsibility for bearing the costs of certain environmental threats. Environmental policy must be effectuated with the cooperation of business and labor. As Eckard Rehbinder has noted, "It is safe to state that the procedure for the preparation of regulations and administrative rules for environmental protection are not adversarial, but are oriented toward the gathering of consensus through an informal, rather intransparent, process of interest accommodation."[41]

Throughout the process there is a conscious weighing of scientific evidence, public health concerns, practicability of standards, cost of regulation, and effects on competitiveness. Business, labor, and government attempt to coordinate a workable, cost-effective approach to pollution control. The result is a system of pollution abatement with operating costs and standards largely comparable to those in the United States, but with fewer hidden costs and surprises for businesses, many of which have participated in devising policy at every stage. Legal expenses are much lower. Issuance of permits is streamlined. Intense conflict between regulators and industry is unusual, and the nature of future regulatory interventions is often predictable.

The traditional approach to controlling industrial air pollution in Great Britain was to build higher smokestacks and let the pollutants to be carried away by the wind.[42] Stricter measures have been adopted in recent years, but the British system is characterized by an absence of regulatory commands and controls. In 1990 the British Parliament undertook a dramatic rewriting of its air pollution statutes at approximately the same time as the United States. As important as these changes are, they do not alter the conclusion that, overall, the British system remains highly discretionary.

Part I of the Environmental Protection Act of 1990 established a national system of integrated pollution control (IPC), covering approximately 5,000 of the largest pollution sources, plus a system of local air pollution control (APC) administered by local authorities for approximately 27,000 smaller-scale pollution sources. IPC combines the regulation of all pollution media into a single permitting process intended to minimize the pollution emitted into any environmental medium. APC applies only to airborne emissions.

IPC requires the use of the best practicable environmental option, which is "the outcome of a systematic consultative and decision-making procedure. . . . The BPEO procedure establishes, for a given set of objectives, the option that provides the most benefit or least damage to the environment as a whole, at acceptable cost, in the long run as well as the short term."[43] In applying this procedure, facilities are required to use the best available technique not entailing excessive cost (BATNEEC). The Department of Environment has accepted that there is no absolute BATNEEC for a particular process. Her Majesty's Inspectorate of Pollution guidance provides information to firms regarding the environmental quality standards for each regulated process and a number of ways to meet the relevant standards. These guidelines are typically drafted in consultation with representatives from the affected industries. If a firm chooses not to use the best technique as described by the inspectorate, the onus is on the firm to justify that the selection of another technique either will provide commensurate pollution control or that the best available technique would involve excessive cost. To demonstrate excessive cost, the firm must show that the increased cost of producing the product is grossly disproportionate to any public environmental benefits. In the permitting process, regulators and the facility may take into account geographic variables such as high winds or high volumes of water that would sufficiently dilute the emissions so as to pose little hazard to the public. Thus different BATNEECs are possible in various areas of the country. The application process requires negotiations between individual facilities and regulators.

Regulators continue to have significant discretion in the permitting process. The strength of this approach is that it looks to the needs of individual facilities and communities. But limited public participation in permitting weights the process in favor of business interests, which may result in suboptimal pollution control. Air quality management includes few deadlines, few references to public health, no public hearings before the promulgation of environmental standards, no citizen suits, and no civil penalties. Environmental impact statements are optional. Scientific analysis by government relies heavily on industry scientists.

The British pollution control effort goes out of its way to promote cooperative business-government relations. The parties rarely sue one another. In fact, environmental bureaus in Britain typically have few lawyers on staff. There was only one reported lawsuit (in 1985) concerning the air pollution laws of 1956 and 1968 before passage of the 1990 Environmental Protection Act.[44] British law limits the possibilities for litigation. Courts generally defer to the decisions of regulators. To sue, a potential litigant must be able to prove an unambiguous connection between pollution and harm to health or property. Environmental groups are seldom granted standing unless their property interests are involved. The legal system does not allow contingency fees, and the losing side must reimburse the winning side for fees.

Policy Outcomes

Germany has been extremely successful in reducing emissions of sulfur oxides, nitrogen oxides, and volatile organic compounds from power plants, manufacturing facilities, and other stationary sources. Britain has also reduced emissions of sulfur oxides and nitrogen oxides, though it has not controlled VOC emissions as effectively. For these three pollutants emanating from stationary sources, the United States has a fair record for VOCs and sulfur oxides but a disappointing one for nitrogen oxides. A study comparing sulfur oxide, nitrogen oxide, and particulate concentrations in a single polluted city in each of the three countries showed Germany outperforming the United States and United Kingdom in improving air quality.[45]

The important point is that Germany does not appear to sacrifice air quality even though it relies on local administration, accepts less aggressive enforcement, and experiences fewer acrimonious confrontations with industry. The United Kingdom has also made some significant strides in several areas of pollution control without resorting to heavy-handed legal deterrents, relying instead on congenial business-regulator relations and a facility-by-facility approach to remediation.

Companies manufacturing in other OECD countries face only a small fraction of the reparations and transaction costs borne by U.S. firms under Superfund. In Germany, cleaning up has taken second place to containment. German environmental cleanup law is based on health risks to the community. As long as industry can contain the pollution and limit the risks, further action is not required. Even when the government does issue an order to force a cleanup, the order is usually based on negotiations between government authorities and the polluter. These negotiations involve the time frame for the task, the methods to be used, and guidelines for how clean "clean" must be.

German industry has been fairly cooperative with state-sponsored remediation efforts. In Bavaria industry groups have formed the Industry Committee for Hazardous Waste Cleanup to contribute to voluntary projects. The postcleanup use of the property is considered in setting the standard for determining the appropriate amount of abatement. U.S. Superfund legislation, by contrast, sets specific targets for detoxification regardless of how the site might be used in the future or what degree of abatement might suffice.

It has been estimated that 27,000 hectares (67,000 acres) of land in the United Kingdom are potentially contaminated.[46] British environmental law has no explicit statute for the restoration of contaminated land. The most applicable area of law is nuisance law. If contaminated land poses a threat to health or property, British law permits government action to relieve the statutory nuisance. But mandated cleanups only require that the contamination be bounded so that it does not pose a threat to the health or property of neighbors.

The British and German abatement efforts have been much less expensive than those in the United States, but neither have they been on the same scale. Much more public money has been spent on the problem in Europe, where mechanisms for suing polluters for damage are weaker. Thomas Church and Robert Nakamura concluded in their study of comparative hazardous waste cleanup:

> At the risk of oversimplification, we can characterize the American system, with its "big stick" liability system and substantial administrative powers, as producing expensive cleanups, financed by private parties, and achieved at the price of substantial transaction costs. And because the public frequently benefits without paying directly, the value they assign to high levels of cleanup may overstate what they would be willing to provide for themselves on a voluntary basis. European systems produce a different constellation of results. The "little stick" liability systems . . . force greater reliance on negotiation with a smaller set of private parties than in the United States. . . . The results, not surprisingly, are lower levels of cleanup and a large portion of the bill being picked up by the public.[47]

German and British firms face fewer hidden costs in environmental regulation. Less litigation means fewer legal bills and less uncertainty in investment and production decisions.

By involving businesses early and throughout the decisionmaking process, the British and German systems also seem to smooth resistance to the implementation of new environmental policies. The environmental laws of these countries further illustrate the value of flexibility. In Germany, returning a contaminated site to a pristine pre-industrial state is not regarded as the best use of pollution control resources. What is important instead is limiting the risk to future users of the site. This bit of common sense alone, if emulated in the United States, could possibly save tens of billions of dollars. Why have such lessons largely eluded the U.S. environmental policy process?

Barriers to Progress

With some notable exceptions, such as the 1990 Clean Air Act's highly innovative marketable permits systems for sulfur dioxide emissions, national environmental protection in the United States has not attached enough importance to experimenting with alternative administrative methods that could cut costs. Although the EPA performs various kinds of programmatic cost-benefit evaluations and risk assessments, resource allocation decisions are not regularly made on the basis of comparative risk or the maximization of net benefits. Congressional micromanagement has erected tall barriers. Clauses in several of the major environmental statutes explicitly forbid the weighing of economic costs or the ranking of policy options according to the magnitudes of risk they purport to reduce.

Cost-sensitive experiments are also inhibited by the nature of public support for the environmental laws. Although the public is scarcely conscious of the unnecessary statutory rigidities and arcana, it routinely perceives efforts to trifle with existing law as an assault on the environment. Thus the Republican-controlled 104th Congress achieved precious little change in the environmental policy status quo. Backed strongly in opinion polls, the Clinton administration successfully painted any and all of the GOP's regulatory reforms as "extremist." By the mid-1990s, the Republican agenda was in full retreat.

Yet it remains somewhat surprising that critics (including some constructive ones among the Republican "revolutionaries") have been so generally unsuccessful in making a case that the nation might secure excellent environmental quality at a lower price. Their frustration has to do, no doubt, with the fundamental difficulty of accepting policy alternatives that, however cost effective, require greater tolerance of risk. Public preferences appear remarkably inflexible on this point. Even a modest degree of risk stemming from pollution seems far less acceptable than the much higher known risks associated with traffic accidents, smoking, swimming, or owning handguns.[48]

It is natural, of course, for people to tolerate greater risk of injury from voluntary activities than from involuntary exposures, such as pollution, even if the benefits are judged to be equal. But to be as much as one thousand times more risk averse about environmental hazards—even when the hazards are uncertain and the costs of minimizing them immense—may seem irrational.[49] What helps account for some of this bias is the widespread perception that the costs of environmental cleanup are concentrated, while the benefits are diffuse. Industries, not consumers, pay the bill. And if the polluter pays, why care how much or whether the risk in question is trivial?

But there is another, no less fundamental part of the story. The most important and expensive pieces of U.S. environmental legislation propound, in effect, a doctrine of health *rights*. It is not too much to say that these statutes promise not only to diminish the risks posed by pollutants but to defend everyone's right to live in an environment essentially free of such risks. Framing public discourse on environmental policy in terms of rights (in contrast to, say, living standards) greatly complicates a serious introduction of cost considerations. Invoking a right trumps other values. For rights, by definition, are not meant to be abridged, segmented, or subjected to trade-offs.

Air Rights

Before 1970 air pollution standards were set on a state basis, with the federal role limited to that of reviewing state plans. This system had been formalized in a 1967 law whose primary author was Senator Edmund Muskie, Democrat of Maine.[50] The states proved slow to meet their responsibilities under the 1967 act, and critics soon called for federal regulators to assume primary responsibility for setting air quality standards. Muskie, however, felt it was premature to judge the existing arrangement. He prepared a revision of the act that sought to strengthen its enforcement provisions but left its essential framework intact. [51]

Muskie's plan was derailed by a report from a Ralph Nader study group that bitterly assailed the existing law and accused the senator of "selling out" to business.[52] Also, the Nixon administration issued its own clean air proposal, which incorporated national ambient air standards and was therefore much more ambitious than Muskie's amendments. Muskie responded by upping the ante. He scrapped his proposal and endorsed national standards that were even more severe than those Nixon had proposed. The Muskie plan now required that economic considerations be ignored in setting standards. Human health alone would be the determinant: standards would be set at a level "allowing an adequate margin of safety . . . requisite to protect the public health."[53]

Muskie's trump card formed the core of the 1970 act. In his speech introducing the revised bill on the Senate floor, he proclaimed the right of every citizen to clean air:

> 100 years ago the first board of health in the United States, in Massachusetts, said this: We believe that all citizens have an inherent right to the enjoyment of pure and uncontaminated air . . . 100 years later it is time to write that kind of policy into law. . . . Anybody in this nation ought to be able at some specific point in the future to breathe healthy air.[54]

Later revisions of the Clean Air Act reaffirmed these principles and exacerbated some of their worst flaws. Because regulation of nonattainment areas was more exacting than for areas in compliance, the Clean Air Act seemed to abet dispersal of industrial activity from highly populated eastern and midwestern metropolitan areas toward locations in the South and West.[55] Such dispersion was staunchly opposed by environmentalists and by the congressional delegations from nonattainment zones. The former did not want unspoiled areas to be degraded. The latter were unwilling to obtain a deconcentration of polluters at the price of decreased economic activity, diminished tax rolls, and higher unemployment in their districts. If the basic principles of the law, particularly the national ambient air quality standards (NAAQS), were to survive intact, some means would have to be found to diminish the incentive for firms to move from dirty to clean regions.

Further, the new source performance standards (NSPS), as applied to coal-burning power plants, threatened to drastically change in a politically unacceptable manner the regional pattern of coal production. Many power plants were finding that they could meet the standards more cheaply by importing low-sulfur coal from the West than by installing the scrubbing equipment needed to achieve the standards with the high-sulfur eastern or midwestern coal that most plants were using. Such a switch threatened to close large parts of the coal mining industry in West Virginia, Kentucky, Indiana, and Ohio. To uphold an "inherent right" to healthy air, proponents had to address both these difficulties. They succeeded in doing so, but at considerable cost both to the economy and to the environment.

The interests of nonattainment areas were served in two ways. First, the deadlines for attainment were delayed. The 1970 act had called for reaching the NAAQS by 1975. As of that date, most nonattainment areas were still violating one or more of the standards, but in anticipation of a major overhaul of the law in 1977 the EPA overlooked these failures. The 1977 revision then extended the deadlines to 1982. Second, a policy of prevention of significant deterioration (PSD), which made it more difficult and expensive for firms to degrade the air in areas that were in compliance, was fashioned. PSD won the endorsement of Ohio, the state with the most severe stationary source pollution problems in the nation, and of the National Association of Counties. The National League of Cities also endorsed PSD as a way to address "the need to protect against massive industrial migration to clean air regions."[56]

Representatives from the high-sulfur coal-producing states were placated by amending the NSPS for coal-fired power plants; they were now required to achieve a percentage reduction in the sulfur content of the coal they burned, whether clean or dirty. As interpreted by the EPA, this change in the statute required *all* coal-burning power plants to install scrubbing equipment, regardless of the type of coal they used. Since they had to scrub anyway, many plants would not have an incentive to buy low-sulfur coal. Thus the economic position of high-sulfur coal was preserved.[57]

Stretching the attainment deadlines for another five years, in turn, meant that standards would continue to be flouted. Firms were encouraged to adopt a rather cynical posture toward compliance; if failing to comply could succeed in obtaining a delay this time, why not again and again, perhaps ad infinitum? In fact, deadlines were lengthened repeatedly throughout the ensuing decade.[58]

The PSD provision increased the cost of environmental compliance well beyond what could be justified on the basis of the NAAQS. Thus it biased firms in favor of continuing to make use of older, dirtier equipment in highly populous urban areas where the risks of pollution-related illness were greatest. Requiring "scrubbers for everybody" had the same negative environmental consequence. Because it added greatly to the cost of building new power plants, utilities were encouraged to continue to use existing, dirtier plants. The fix also redistributed millions of dollars from the utility rate payers to certain coal companies and their employees.

Entitlement to Superfund

At first glance, abandoned hazardous waste sites would hardly seem to justify federal intervention. Unlike air or water pollution, these sites do not move; they do not cross state boundaries. The problems they pose are local in origin and local in impact. Yet they came to be defined not as hazards or nuisances to be addressed by the immediate community but as violations of basic rights of citizens to a clean and safe environment. Nationally defined rights, perforce, must be federally protected.

The initial impetus for Superfund came from the widely publicized Love Canal scandal: the discovery in 1978 of a massive abandoned toxic waste dump beneath a suburban upstate New York neighborhood. To make the case for federal action, the EPA first had to demonstrate that similar disasters existed nationwide. It commissioned a task force charged with uncovering evidence that "ticking time bombs" were to be found across the land, in as many congressional districts as possible. Dutifully, the task force completed its mission. Sites were found and congressional offices were so informed.[59]

Having made the case for nationwide intervention, the EPA implicitly framed its legislative proposal as an entitlement. The proposal avoided the question of how much cleanup a given site should receive. To ask the question would imply that a trade-off existed between the degree of risk reduction to be achieved at a site and the amount spent on cleaning it up. At some point, the costs of further cleanup might outweigh the benefits of further reduction. Instead, the law implied that all sites would be cleaned up to a degree that guaranteed everyone's right to safety. In order to ensure that this guarantee of protection did not impose great burdens on the taxpayers, and thus cause them to inquire if such a right was really worth creating, Superfund, like the Clean Air Act, kept the funding of the program off budget. It relied on liability law to impose the bulk of cleanup costs on culpable private parties.[60]

The slow progress under Superfund led not to a reconsideration of its overreaching philosophy, but rather to the adoption of more draconian means for invoking it. Because no formal standard existed for determining how much cleanup to do at a particular site, each site's cleanup was done on an ad hoc basis. This lent credence to the charge that sites with politically powerful constituencies received more attention and those not so lucky got less. Instead of adopting a risk-benefit approach, the revised Superfund protects a universal right to safety by establishing uniform cleanup standards. All cleanups must meet all "applicable or relevant and appropriate" state and federal environmental air and water quality standards.[61] To appreciate how sweeping this requirement is, note that virtually all the standards to be met were not written with hazardous waste cleanup in mind. They required treatment and *restoration* of sites, often at staggering expense. The new law allows no real room to ask what possible benefits might be obtained from, say, spending lavishly to return a site, lodged amid other dirty and smelly land uses, to a pre-industrial condition.

What Is to Be Done?

A society that has grown accustomed to thinking of environmental protection as something close to a legal birthright, not merely a public preference competing for resources with other valued goods, is no fertile ground for fundamental regulatory reform. If everyone is *entitled* to "green" conditions, the costs of attainment are not to be weighed impartially against the perceived benefits, but typically to be subordinated to those benefits, often regardless of their relative magnitude.

Yet Americans are also growing impatient with corporations that, facing stiffer international competition, have been laying off employees and depressing wages. Regulatory reformers might make a little more headway by clarifying the basic predicament in a number of key industries: competing in a global economy, fewer firms can readily return to their workers a higher standard of living while also scrambling to satisfy (among a host of other legal demands) the maximal expectations of environmental policy instruments that are often ill designed. Surely, legislators are not likely to overturn, say, laws that expressly prohibit environmental rulemakers from considering economic consequences—until such hidden taxes in these statutes become more transparent to the public.

A Regulatory Budget

One modest way to begin to introduce greater transparency would be through a regulatory "budget." This device would resemble the annual federal budget in that it would estimate the costs of each regulatory program, but it would differ in that its estimates would include the costs to the society at large, not just the costs imposed on the federal government. Its virtue would be the same as that of any budgetary exercise: to provide some framework in which to compare the worth of different programs based on their relative cost. A regulatory budget would not purport to measure the benefits of programs. (The existing federal budget provides no scoring of benefits, either.) But by setting a ceiling on spending, similar to the regular budget reconciliation procedure, congressional deliberations would at least compel some comparisons of relative risk reduction and cost effectiveness among regulatory items.

Decentralization

National regulatory budgeting could nudge policymakers closer to asking the right questions about particular environmental regulations, but much more than that will be needed to bring home to voters the burdens along with the benefits implicit in controversial programs. Since a number of major environmental issues—such as urban smog, toxic waste dumps, habitat conservation, and safe drinking water—are mostly localized problems, more of their management ought to be devolved to regional, state, or local authorities. Their taxpayers, not the nation's, ought to have greater responsibility in ranking environmental policies amid other priorities, in selecting alternative modes of intervention, and in footing a larger share of the bill. Decentralization would ensure, so to speak, the environmental equivalent of a health insurance copayment.

Of course, the characteristics of some environmental woes preclude them from being treated effectively on a subnational basis.

(Stratospheric ozone depletion and acid rain are examples where even national solutions do not suffice.) But the current environmental regulatory regime does not limit itself to such contingencies. In fact, the landmark environmental laws of the 1970s and 1980s were motivated largely by dissatisfaction with state and local action, whether or not significant interstate or international spillovers were at stake. This dissatisfaction had both a technical component (state and local agencies were allegedly incapable of performing the requisite administrative tasks) and a political component: lack of national uniform standards supposedly encouraged states and localities to "race to the bottom," relaxing their requirements in an effort to attract business.

Whatever the merits of these arguments when the initial federal statutes were enacted, the pertinent question is whether they remain valid a quarter of a century later. State and local administrative capacity has improved substantially, and even where it remains deficient, the relevant comparison is to federal administrative capacity, which is not always exemplary, not to the capacity of some utopian bureaucracy. Likewise, the extent of any race to the bottom is an unsettled empirical question. Business is not necessarily drawn to a foul environment. States have diverse economic interests, some of which (tourism, for instance) require high levels of environmental amenity. In sum, it is by no means obvious that the states, in their self-interest, will wantonly disregard a broad consensus that the abatement of egregious pollution is a legitimate role of government.

Some of America's political institutions could prove uniquely supple and inventive in meeting the economic challenges of a more competitive world. One such institution is federalism, which encourages innovative experimentation and mitigates the centralist proclivity for "one-size-fits-all" approaches to more and more of the tasks of public policy. Any serious quest for a more cost-conscious environmental policy would do well to rediscover this asset.

COMMENT BY BARRY RABE

Marc Landy and Loren Cass correctly call for a more balanced assessment of the "green gold" hypothesis and effectively take aim at some of the biggest examples of regulatory overreach in environmental policy. But in lamenting the current state of environmental affairs in America, I fear they lurch toward embrace of three suspect propositions. First, almost all aspects of the federal role in environmental policy can be lumped together and dismissed as fundamentally misguided. Second, devolution of regulatory authority to states should be energetically pursued as inherently superior to current practices of environmental federalism. Third, other Western democracies demonstrate that more consensual approaches deliver comparable or greater environmental protection at less cost.

As I will suggest, each of these propositions has some merit. My concern stems from a growing tendency in environmental policy debates, reflected to some degree in this chapter, to embrace them as proven principles that can reliably direct future policy in the United States. I would submit that the greatest challenge facing environmental policy analysts is avoiding the tendency for sweeping generalization and instead seeking a more systematic understanding of what does—and does not—work.

The Federal Role

Alongside the familiar tales of Superfund and Clean Air Act rigidities, a series of significant changes have occurred in federal environmental policy during the past decade. Actively promoted by the last four administrators of the Environmental Protection Agency, a host of initiatives have been launched that offer considerable promise of simultaneously delivering environmental improvement and regulatory flexibility.

Examples such as the emissions trading program of the 1990 clean air legislation and the celebrated Amoco refinery case have tended to receive most of the scholarly and journalistic notoriety. But these have been supplemented with a series of federal efforts that address virtually every dimension of the regulatory process. Challenge regulation programs, such as 33/50 and Green Lights, have involved a minimum of federal oversight but led to far-reaching successes. Pollution prevention efforts, thought to be beyond federal capacity as recently as a decade ago, have been actively promoted through 1990 legislation and related grant and technical assistance programs. Some regional offices have begun to work closely with state agencies attempting to foster greater integration of permitting and enforcement functions across traditional medium-specific boundaries of air, land, and water. Through such collaboration, single, facilitywide permitting is now a very real possibility in some states. New initiatives, such as Project XL and the National Environmental Performance Partnership System, offer unprecedented flexibility to participating firms and states in exchange for demonstrable performance improvement and clear commitments to pollution prevention. Thirty-three states now participate in the National Environmental Performance Partnership System, which is encouraging federal and state authorities to revisit every aspect of the regulatory process in search of creative alternatives to medium-based, command-and-control strategies. Many of these initiatives are attributable to policy entrepreneurship within the EPA, suggesting that conventional depictions of that agency as hopelessly fragmented and resistant to innovation may need to be revisited.

Perhaps the best illustration of this promise involves the continuing evolution of federally mandated information disclosure. For all the opprobrium that has appropriately been heaped on Superfund, the 1986 reauthorization of that program was also responsible for creation of the toxics release inventory (TRI). This effort to mandate public disclosure of the release of 320 toxic materials to air, land, and water has evolved into a key ingredient in virtually all federal, state, local, and corporate pollution prevention initiatives of the past decade. Expanded through the 1990 Pollution Prevention Act, the TRI not only contributes to a common metric on toxic releases but also allows for careful assessment of whether reductions in releases from year to year are attributable to actual reductions consistent with pollution prevention goals or instead reflect paper compliance.

The TRI has revolutionized American environmental policy in at least two ways. First, the mere publication of annual reports on toxic releases revealed unexpectedly large numbers of major sources across the nation. Many of these sources were previously unregulated, and releases went unobserved by firms and regulators. This form of "regulation by embarrassment" prompted hundreds of firms to seek technical assistance, often from state and federal authorities, in addressing major problems. Indeed, the growing literature in industrial ecology is littered with case studies of prominent firms that were unaware of major toxic releases and the often-substantial costs associated with their loss of expensive chemicals and materials. Time and again, TRI data has contributed to a new way to look at environmental contamination and facilitate a search for economical ways to reduce releases.

Second, TRI data has stimulated substantial environmental policy innovation at both federal and state levels. Challenge regulations, such as EPA's 33/50 program, utilized TRI data as hundreds of participating firms achieved substantial reductions in toxic releases within a few years. Many of these easily exceeded the program goal of a 50 percent reduction in specified releases over a seven-year period. At the state level, many of the most promising pollution prevention initiatives, such as toxics-use reduction and regulatory integration strategies in Massachusetts, Minnesota, and New Jersey, are largely inconceivable without TRI data.

The State Role

Landy and Cass are correct to note that decentralization may be a desirable goal, particularly in those areas of environmental policy where problems can be confined within individual state boundaries. But devolution of authority is best viewed with some degree of caution rather than as a magical elixir that can cure what ails American environmental policy.

The track record of states in recent decades does indeed reflect growing capacity and innovation. But it also includes numerous instances in which delegation has clearly backfired. For example, the nation's approach to low-level radioactive waste disposal was largely dictated to Congress by states in 1980. It called for far-reaching decentralization, allowing multiple states to form regional compacts to resolve common disposal problems. More than fifteen years later, this strategy can be viewed as a disaster that rivals the worst failures of federal policy. No new disposal facilities have been opened, little creative collaboration has occurred, and states have proven remarkably inept in overseeing this process. States have encountered similar problems in managing other areas of waste, often pursuing "out of sight, out of mind" strategies that emphasize waste export over internal management approaches. These regularly lead to bitter conflicts involving states and regions that often must be settled by federal institutions.

Decentralization strategies are also suspect because of an enduring reality of American federalism: uneven state capacity and commitment. Even states with similar traditions of commitment to environmental protection tend to diverge markedly in many respects, particularly in their willingness to pursue more creative alternatives. At one extreme, Minnesota has systematically reviewed all aspects of its environmental activities under the auspices of its 1990 Toxic Pollution Prevention Act. It has attempted to reshape each regulatory tool, including permitting, monitoring, and enforcement to promote pollution prevention, minimize cross-media transfers, and maximize compliance flexibility for regulated parties. The state has also made aggressive use of financial incentive systems and provides an array of heavily utilized technical assistance services. And, contrary to its image as an unyielding regulatory Leviathan, the federal government has politically encouraged, technically assisted, and financially underwritten a good deal of this innovation. Overall, Minnesota may well be closer to the popular depictions of European nations such as Britain and Germany than actual regions within those nations.

At the other extreme, Michigan has moved in a starkly different direction. Most pollution prevention and regulatory integration efforts are purely symbolic, as the state has pursued an aggressive campaign to politicize all aspects of the regulatory process. Political connections tend to drive regulatory decisionmaking, and substantial staff cuts have contributed to huge delays in tending to basic regulatory functions. Regulatory innovation is increasingly seen as a luxury for which resources are lacking. Indeed, were some scholar eager to update the late Grant McConnell's classic account of regulatory capture, Michigan environmental policy would be an excellent starting point.

Such uneven performance would be little cause for concern if most environmental problems were reliably confined within state boundaries. But growing evidence from the physical sciences, perhaps best demonstrated in Chesapeake Bay and the Great Lakes Basin, underscores the relentless capacity of many contaminants to migrate with unexpected ease across medium and jurisdictional boundaries. Any strategies of decentralization must reflect a careful consideration of what functions are best handled by states and localities, rather than driven by a singular assertion that states know best.

Comparative Policy

Much of the literature comparing national styles of environmental regulation properly concludes that the United States has a great deal to learn from other Western democracies. But while much of the comparative analysis accentuates what is good abroad and lamentable in the United States, there are other lessons to be considered. Canada constitutes a potentially rich comparative case, given its proximity to the United States, long tradition of joint regulatory efforts, and heavy reliance on decentralization of regulatory authority to individual provinces. Moreover, Canada possesses many other features attractive to critics of the American system, including a confined role for the judiciary and far greater discretion granted to bureaucratic agents by legislative principals.

In practice, the Canadian experience offers some warning flags rather than a blueprint for the United States. In the absence of significant central authority, individual provinces have been very slow to adopt the sorts of innovative, incentive-based regulatory approaches now being developed in the United States. Instead, they have tended to adhere to conventional, medium-based strategies, backed by a very sketchy record of enforcement or technical assistance for regulated parties. Bureaucracies tend to be extremely resistant to change, remarkably insulated from legislative pressures, judicial challenges, and either environmental or industry groups. In recent years, both Ottawa and a few provinces have demonstrated some movement in more creative directions, and they consistently turn to American federal and state experiences as models for their own departures. Canada's new information disclosure program, the National Pollution Release Inventory, borrows heavily from the American TRI. This lag in innovation may partly explain why most efforts to compare environmental outcomes in these neighboring nations conclude that Canadians generate considerably more solid, hazardous, and radioactive wastes and more toxic releases per person than their American neighbors.

Looking Ahead

These points of caution are in no way intended to suggest wholesale vindication of the American approach to environmental policy. But they do underscore a long-standing concern that much environmental policy analysis involves exaggerated criticisms of the most glaringly flawed programs, something akin to shooting fish in a barrel. The greater challenge, in my view, is carefully separating policy failure from policy success and drawing appropriate lessons from both types of cases.

NOTES

1 Martin L. Weitzman, "On the Environmental Discount Rate," *Journal of Environmental Economics and Management*, vol. 26 (May 1994), pp. 200-09.

2. For two very good reviews of the literature on the effects of environmental regulation and competitiveness, see Adam B. Jaffe and others, "Environmental Regulation and the Competitiveness of U.S. Manufacturing: What Does the Evidence Tell Us?" *Journal of Economic Literature*, vol. 33 (March 1995), pp. 132-63; and Richard B. Stewart, "Environmental Regulation and International Competitiveness," *Yale Law Journal*, vol. 102 (June 1993), pp. 2039-2106.

3. Michael E. Porter, "America's Green Strategy," *Scientific American*, vol. 264 (April 1991), p. 8.

4. James C. Robinson, "The Impact of Environmental and Occupational Health Regulation on Productivity Growth in U.S. Manufacturing," *Yale Journal on Regulation*, vol. 12 (Summer 1995), p. 423.

5. Average weekly wages figures are from Bureau of Labor Statistics, *Employment, Hours, and Earnings, United States, 1909-94*, vols. 1, 2 (September 1994). The figures from May 1992 were chosen to correspond with the May 1992 employment data. Total employment and total production workers' data for manufacturing industries are from Bureau of Labor Statistics, *Occupational Employment in Manufacturing Industries, 1992* (February 1994). Total employment and total production workers' figures for mining and service industries are from Bureau of Labor Statistics, *Occupational Employment in Mining, Construction, Finance, and Services, 1993* (March 1995).

6. Robinson, "Impact of Environmental and Occupational Health Regulation," p. 415.

7. Ibid., p. 389.

8. Wayne B. Gray and Ronald J. Shadbegian, "Pollution Abatement Costs, Regulation, and Plant-Level Productivity," working paper 4994 (Cambridge, Mass.: National Bureau of Economic Research, January 1995).

9. Robinson, "Impact of Environmental and Occupational Health Regulation," p. 416.

10. Ibid., pp. 413–16.

11. "The Challenge of Growing Green," *Harvard Business Review*, vol. 72 (July-August 1994), p. 39.

12. Robinson, "Impact of Environmental and Occupational Health Regulation," p. 396.

13. Ibid., p. 395.

14. Paul R. Portney, *Public Policies for Environmental Protection* (Washington: Resources for the Future, 1990), pp. 37–38.

15. John D. Graham, "The Future of Risk Regulation," in Charls E. Walker, Mark A. Bloomfield, and Margo Thorning, eds., *Strategies for Improving Environmental Quality and Increasing Economic Growth* (Washington: American Council for Capital Formation, Center for Policy Research, August 1995), p. 3.

16. Tammy O. Tengs and others, "Five Hundred Life-Saving Interventions and Their Cost Effectiveness," *Risk Analysis*, vol. 15 (June 1, 1995), pp. 369–89.

17. Robert W. Hahn, "Regulatory Reform: What Do the Government's Numbers Tell Us?" Washington: American Enterprise Institute, January 2, 1996, especially abstract and pp. 11–12.

18. Ibid., p. 21. Hahn assumes that about 1 percent of cancer deaths are caused by environmental pollution.

19. Ronald E. Schmitt, "The Amoco/EPA Yorktown Experience and Regulating the Right Thing," *Natural Resources and Environment*, vol. 9 (Summer 1994), p. 13.

20. Vernon Rice, "Regulating Reasonably," *Environmental Forum*, vol. 11 (May-June 1994), p. 19.

21. Paul Portney, "Policy Watch: Economics and the Clean Air Act," *Journal of Economic Perspectives*, no. 4 (Fall 1990), pp. 173–81.

22. A detailed summary of the act appears in "Clean Air Act Rewritten," *1990 Congressional Quarterly Almanac* (Washington: Congressional Quarterly News Features, 1990), pp. 248–74. For a broad discussion of the act, see Gary C. Bryner, *Blue Skies, Green Politics* (Washington: Congressional Quarterly Press, 1993).

23. Henry Waxman, "An Overview of the Clean Air Act Amendments of 1990," *Environmental Law*, vol. 21, no. 4, pt. 2 (1991), pp. 1742–44.

24. "Clean Air Act Rewritten," pp. 248–49.

25. *Clean Air Act Amendments of 1990 (H.R. 3030)*, H. Rept. 101-490, pt. 1, 101 Cong. 2 sess. (Government Printing Office, 1990), p. 322.

26. "Clean Air Act Rewritten," pp. 247, 275. See also Mark M. Hultman, "A Practical Approach to Compliance with the HON MACT," *Chemical Engineering*, vol. 102 (March 1995), pp. 90, 93.

27. Office of Management and Budget, *Regulatory Program of the United States Government: April 1, 1991–March 31, 1992*, p. 12.

28. Quoted in Kent Christensen, "Title V Sends Shock Waves through the CPI," *Chemical Engineering*, vol. 102 (January 1995), p. 35.

29. The fees that firms must pay are based on emissions. The fee can be set by the states, but the minimum is $25 per ton of emissions.

30. See Marc Landy and Mary Hague, "The Coalition for Waste: Private Interests and Superfund," in Michael S. Greve and Fred L. Smith, eds., *Environmental Politics: Public Costs, Private Rewards* (Praeger, 1992), pp. 67–87.

31. Quoted in Christensen, "Title V," p. 35.

32. Ibid.

33. Vincent A. Rocco, "New Requirements under the Clean Air Act," *Risk Management*, vol. 42 (March 1995), pp. 25–28.

34. Ibid., p. 28.

35. The term *bounty hunter* is taken from Michael Greve, "Environmentalism and Bounty Hunting," *Public Interest*, no. 97 (Fall 1989), pp. 15–29. For details on the citizen suit provisions of the act, see Scott M. DuBoff, "The 1990 Amendments and Section 304: The Specter of Increased Citizen Suit Enforcement," *Natural Resources and Environment*, no. 7 (Fall 1992), pp. 34–37, 60.

36. Milton Russell, E. William Colglazier, and Mary R. English, *Hazardous Waste Remediation: The Task Ahead* (Knoxville, Tenn.: Waste Management Research and Education Institute, 1991), p. 16.

37. Article 3. VI. 1 of the Bundes-Immissionsschutzgesetz (the federal emissions protection law) defines "best available technology" as "the developmental level of advanced procedures, installations or operating methods which makes certain the practical suitability of a measure for limiting emissions appear certain." Quoted in Gerd Winter, ed., *German Environmental Law: Basic Texts and Introduction* (Boston: Martinus Nijhoff/Graham and Trotman, 1994), p. 7. The German standard does not require that a technology is in common use, but only that it has been proven to be viable. German environmental law is technology forcing.

38. Ibid., p. 59.

39. In the United States federal funding is tied to state environmental actions. The federal government also has oversight authority over state implementation, which allows the government to sue states to force the implementation of federal law. In Germany federal transfers to the states occur in lump sums, and the federal government is prohibited from tying financial transfers to state implementation of federal programs. Under article 37 of the Basic Law, the federal government has the power to compel a state to enforce federal laws, but this power is rarely used and has never been used in environmental policy.

40. Eckard Rehbinder, "The Federal Republic of Germany," in Turner T. Smith and Pascale Kromarek, eds., *Understanding U.S. and European Environmental Law: A Practitioner's Guide* (Boston: Graham and Trotman, 1989), p. 11.

41. Ibid., p. 18.

42. Britain is endowed with fast-flowing rivers and high winds that create the opportunity for pollutants to be flushed out of the country with relative ease.

43. Simon Ball and Stuart Bell, *Environmental Law: The Law and Policy Relating to the Protection of the Environment*, 2d ed. (London: Blackstone Press, 1994), p. 259.

44. Richard Macrory, "The United Kingdom," in Smith and Kromarek, eds., *Understanding U.S. and European Environmental Law*, p. 41.

45. For comparative environmental performance data, see *OECD Environmental Data: Compendium 1993* (Paris: OECD, 1993).

46. Ball and Bell, *Environmental Law*, p. 338.

47. Thomas W. Church and Robert T. Nakamura, "Beyond Superfund: Hazardous Waste Cleanup in Europe and the United States," *Georgetown International Environmental Law Review*, vol. 7 (Fall 1994), p. 56.

48. At the generally low doses in which most airborne and waterborne pollutants are found in the environment, only a small percentage of people exposed develop disease.

49. See Rick Weiss and Gary Lee, "Pollution's Effect on Human Hormones: When Fear Exceeds Evidence," *Washington Post*, March 31, 1996, p. A14. A number of studies comparing public risk aversion toward voluntary

and involuntary dangers have suggested that involuntary dangers may exceed voluntary ones by a thousandfold.

50. For an account of Muskie's political career, see Theodore Lippman Jr. and Donald C. Hansen, *Muskie* (Norton, 1971).

51. Charles O. Jones, *Clean Air: The Policies and Politics of Pollution Control* (University of Pittsburgh Press, 1975), p. 204.

52. John C. Esposito and others, *Vanishing Air* (Pantheon, 1970), pp. 306–10.

53. R. Shep Melnick, *Regulation and the Courts: The Case of the Clean Air Act* (Brookings, 1983), p. 239.

54. *A Legislative History of the Clean Air Amendments of 1970*, Committee Print, Senate Committee on Public Works, 93 Cong. 2 sess. (GPO, 1974), pp. 231, 227.

55. Melnick, *Regulation and the Courts*, p. 99.

56. Ibid.

57. Bruce A. Ackerman and William T. Hassler, *Clean Coal/Dirty Air: Or How the Clean Air Act Became a Multibillion-Dollar Bail-Out for High-Sulfur Coal Producers and What Should Be Done about It* (Yale University Press, 1981), pp. 79–103.

58. R. Shep Melnick, "Pollution Deadlines and the Coalition for Failure," in Greve and Smith, eds., *Environmental Politics*, pp. 89–104.

59. Marc K. Landy, Marc J. Roberts, and Stephen R. Thomas, *The Environmental Protection Agency: Asking the Wrong Questions* (Oxford University Press, 1990), pp. 141–42.

60. Landy and Hague, "Coalition for Waste," pp. 68–71.

61. Ibid., pp. 73–75.

Chapter 6

On the Rights Track: The Americans with Disabilities Act

Thomas F. Burke

O PENING the legislative debate on the Americans with
Disabilities Act of 1990, one of the bill's sponsors,
Senator Tom Harkin, predicted that the act would "help strengthen
our economy and enhance our international competitiveness" by
bringing disabled people into the labor force.[1] In reality, the disabilities law has done nothing of the kind. What the law has enhanced
instead is the volume of litigation in the workplace. How this came
about is a saga that is best begun with the experience of one potential
beneficiary.

In 1990 Lori Vande Zande began work as a program assistant for
the Wisconsin state housing office. She was paralyzed from the waist
down because of a tumor in her spinal cord. Her duties were mainly
clerical, and she was able to perform them while in a wheelchair. The
agency that employed her made several adjustments to help her carry
out her work. It modified the bathrooms in her office. It bought
special adjustable furniture. It paid for one-half the cost of a cot that
she used for personal care and adjusted her schedule so that she
could attend medical appointments.

But Vande Zande became convinced her employer had not done
enough. When she commented that the kitchenette at her workplace
was too high to use from her wheelchair, her supervisor told her to
use the bathroom sink, a solution she found unsatisfactory. Later,
when a bout of ulcers forced her to stay home, she asked for a
desktop computer so that she could do her work from there. Her supervisor refused this request and offered her only fifteen to twenty

hours of work that she could do at home. The rest, her supervisor said, would have to be made up with sick leave or vacation time.

To Vande Zande, these incidents, along with some comments made by her supervisors, demonstrated insensitivity. She filed a complaint with the Equal Employment Opportunity Commission and eventually sued her employer in federal court. The state of Wisconsin, she claimed, had discriminated against her on the basis of her disability. To those unfamiliar with disability rights law, the claim might seem puzzling.[2] What, they might ask, makes the failure to provide a computer an act of discrimination? Yet Vande Zande's lawsuit, whatever its merits, was fully in keeping with the logic of disability rights law.

The ADA and Disability Rights

Although the concept of disability rights has lately begun to migrate to other nations, nowhere has it been implemented as fully as in the United States. Beginning with the passage of section 504 of the 1973 Rehabilitation Act, Congress and the states have created an array of disability rights laws, many of them giving those aggrieved the right to sue in court for discrimination. The Americans with Disabilities Act (ADA), the law under which Vande Zande sued, marks the culmination of this trend. Passed in 1990 by a wide margin in Congress and signed by an enthusiastic President Bush, the ADA prohibits barriers to disabled people in a wide range of activities. Title I of the act, the part under which Vande Zande sued, requires employers to provide "reasonable accommodations" to "otherwise qualified" disabled workers.[3] Title II applies nondiscrimination requirements to state and local governments and their agencies, and mandates that public transit systems be made accessible to disabled people. Title III requires that nearly all facilities and programs, from bars and bowling alleys to parks and zoos, be made as accessible as is "readily achievable" and that new facilities be designed to be accessible unless it is "structurally impracticable" to do so.[4]

Complainants under the ADA can bring their claims to the Equal Employment Opportunity Commission and various other federal agencies, but the ADA also gives disabled people the right to sue those who fail to live up to its provisions. Under Title I, employers found guilty of discrimination can be made to provide back pay, attorney's fees, and, in some cases, punitive and compensatory damages.[5] Under Titles II and III, managers of facilities and programs can be sued to force them to make the facilities and programs accessible to disabled people. Title III lawsuits can also result in fines and "pain and suffering" damages against those judged guilty of discrimination.[6] Thus the ADA's sweeping mandates are to be enforced by lawsuits—and the threat of lawsuits—like Lori Vande Zande's.

This chapter examines the causes and consequences of the turn to litigation in disability policy. First, why has the United States taken a uniquely litigious, rights-oriented approach to the problem of disability? Second, what are the costs of this approach? Third, and perhaps most important, is there a better way? The final section of the chapter compares the U.S. approach with those taken by other economically advanced Western nations. Drawing on this comparison, it examines how implementation of the ADA might be improved and evaluates the political feasibility of an improvement.

The ADA's rights orientation and litigiousness are typical of U.S. public policy. They reflect what has been called "adversarial legalism," a style of dispute resolution that pervades much social regulation in the United States. This style involves formal adversarial procedures, punitive sanctions, costly forms of legal contestation, and complex legal rules that are subject to frequent controversy and change.[7] As the example of disability policy suggests, the tendency toward adversarial legalism in U.S. social policy creates unique costs that are not borne by other economically advanced nations, even those with more extensive regulatory and welfare programs.

The ADA was advertised not just as a civil rights measure, but as a way to take disabled people off welfare and get them onto the employment rolls.[8] It would be nice to believe that the specification and enforcement of rights leads directly to jobs and thus to greater productivity, as participants in the ADA debate seem to have assumed. But in fact rights-based policies turn out to be a problematic method of promoting employment, one that in the United States suffers from all the inefficiencies and inequities of court-based enforcement. The dependence on rights in disability policy reflects a strange American amalgam: a deep distrust of bureaucratic welfare-state approaches to social problems combined with a seemingly boundless faith in the capacity of courts and rights to change society for the better. Because no other nation shares this combination of values to the same extent, it is especially important for Americans to consider the costs of rights-based policies like the ADA.

Adversarial Legalism

The Americans with Disabilities Act illustrates several characteristics of adversarial legalism. The law itself is complex and subject to many interpretations, and the system of enforcement is mainly complaint driven, with easy access to courts. The ADA's provision for pain and suffering and punitive damages allows for high penalties for noncompliance. But most important, the ADA makes disability policy a matter of rights—duties that are owed to disabled people and so can be legally enforced—rather than of needs, problems that society chooses to pay for collectively.

The costs of a regime of adversarial legalism in disability policy are considerable.

— *Uncertainty.* One of the hallmarks of adversarial legalism is that the decisionmaking process is unpredictable, variable, and reversible. In Vande Zande's case, for example, no one could know in advance what a federal court would consider a "reasonable accommodation." Further, no one could be certain that an appeal to a higher court would result in the same decision. Even after the decision in *Vande Zande*, a plaintiff with a similar case might still prevail in another court.

— *Delay.* In an adversarial legal system a final decision may be delayed in seemingly endless ways. After filing her claim in federal district court, Vande Zande had to wait for two years to have her case decided.[9] She moved on to another job before her case was resolved.

— *High Transaction Costs.* Because of uncertainty, delay, and the expense of legal assistance, transaction costs in an adversarial legal system are high. Vande Zande and her employer undoubtedly invested many thousands of dollars to bring their dispute all the way to a federal appeals court. Transaction costs deter plaintiffs from challenging even blatantly illegal policies and drive defendants to settle claims they consider unwarranted.

— *High Penalties.* An adversarial legal system uses the threat of high penalties to achieve compliance. By contesting Vande Zande's claims, the employer risked a court award of pain and suffering damages and legal fees that would vastly outstrip the costs of the accommodations she had asked for. Of course many would argue that high penalties are appropriate for acts of discrimination, but the costs of such penalties generally get passed on to the public in the form of higher prices. The threat of such penalties also leads defendants to settle claims that may be legally dubious.

— *Defensiveness and Distrust*. The formality of adversarial legal processes can breed distrust and disagreement where other processes might reach accommodation. When an ADA lawsuit is filed, it is likely to put great strain on workplace relationships. Moreover, the threat of ADA litigation may lead employers to fear and distrust (or even refuse to hire) disabled workers.

— *Scattershot Enforcement*. A system of implementation by litigation depends on the ability of private parties to mount their own campaign to enforce the law. Those without the knowledge, resources, or motivation required to contest violations will simply try to live with the violations. At the same time, potential plaintiffs with resources can afford to make tenuous claims that stretch the law. Thus the pattern of litigation is bound to be at war with the purposes of the statute. Underenforcement *and* overenforcement are to be expected.

The Scope of the Law

These potential problems in ADA enforcement are important simply because the law itself touches so much of American life. According to one estimate, more than 600,000 businesses, 5 million places of public accommodation, and 80,000 units of state and local government are covered by the law.[10] The highest estimate of the number of disabled people in the United States approaches 50 million, though more conservative assessments put it somewhat lower: one figure suggested by an expert on the demographics of disability is 36 million.[11] According to even the low estimate, at least one of eight Americans is disabled, which means nearly everyone has a disabled relative or friend.

The magnitude of these estimates of the disabled population may seem surprising until one considers the range of people designated "disabled." The ADA defines disability as "(a) a physical or mental impairment that substantially limits one or more of the major life activities; b) a record of such an impairment; or c) being regarded as having such an impairment."[12]

What this definition actually entails depends, of course, on how courts interpret these phrases. Recent court decisions suggest that the range is much narrower than 50 million, but how much narrower is difficult to determine. In any case, the law clearly covers a broad spectrum of conditions, including some, such as drug addiction and emotional disorders, that fall outside popular conceptions of disability.

Not surprisingly, then, disability discrimination has already become one of the leading categories of claims at the EEOC. But job discrimination complaints like the one Vande Zande brought are just one aspect of the ADA. Because of ADA mandates, state and local governments, transit authorities, nonprofit agencies, and businesses face the prospect of spending billions of dollars to remake their physical environments. Beyond this, litigants have used the ADA to challenge a broad array of institutions and practices. ADA lawsuits have resulted in rulings that courts cannot bar blind people from serving on juries, bar associations cannot ask applicants about their history of treatment for mental illness, and insurers cannot limit benefits for people with AIDS.[13] The ADA's mandates and ADA lawsuits seek to literally reshape American society.

The ADA reflects a typically American approach to the problem of disability, one that emphasizes *rights* and litigation over *needs* and governmental assistance. Yet the turn to rights and litigation in disability policy has been relatively recent. Its causes can be best illustrated by a brief history of modern disability politics.

The Rise of Disability Rights

Until the 1960s disability policy centered on welfare, institutionalization, and rehabilitation programs. With the important exception of blind and deaf people, few raised discriminatory attitudes or architectural barriers as an issue, and the rhetoric of disability rights was mainly confined to academic treatises.[14] Disability politics was mostly animated by the nondisabled, especially physicians, rehabilitation therapists, and other service providers. The idea behind disability policy was charity: disability was an unfortunate condition, and society had an obligation to extend a helping hand to the afflicted.

The politics of disability was changed forever by the rise of a new generation of disabled people in the 1960s, the result of improvements in medical technology, the polio epidemic of the 1950s, and the Vietnam war. The new generation was larger, better educated, often less likely to be congenitally disabled, and perhaps as a result more determined than its predecessors.

Out of this generation grew the modern disability movement. Starting in centers of radical political activity, especially Berkeley, Boston, and New York, groups such as Disabled in Action, the United Handicapped Federation, SO FED UP (Students Organization for Every Disability United), MIGHT (Mobility Impaired Grappling Hurdles Together), and WARPATH (World Association to Remove Prejudice against the Handicapped) spread throughout the nation. These groups rejected charity and traditional rehabilitation therapy as hopelessly paternalistic. Advancing such slogans as "You've Given Us Your Dimes, Now Give Us Our Rights!" they demanded more power for people with disabilities to control their own lives.[15]

The Independent Living Movement

The first focus of the wave of disability activism was the creation of independent living centers. The concept of independent living centers was a reaction to the limitations of the vocational rehabilitation system, which disability activists had experienced firsthand. Vocational rehabilitation programs had aimed from their beginnings in the 1920s at getting their clients into the job market as efficiently as possible. Vocational rehabilitation directors justified their programs with cost-benefit statistics showing that they more than paid for themselves in increased tax revenues from gainfully employed disabled people. Thus the bureaucratic imperative within the program was to make people employable at the lowest cost. Because the rehabilitation programs generally had far more applicants than they could serve, they "creamed," taking the younger, the whiter, and the less disabled, and rejecting the rest.[16]

Vocational rehabilitation programs had little use for severely disabled people, who were deemed unemployable. Moreover, oriented as they were to job placement, the programs paid little attention to myriad other problems faced by disabled people. Surmounting architectural barriers, finding and paying for personal attendants, arranging accessible transportation, and dealing with the various welfare bureaucracies were all basic difficulties faced by people with disabilities, yet the rehabilitation programs were useless in these matters. Independent living centers were places where these needs could be met. As disabled people, attracted by the array of services provided, gathered at them, the centers became forums for discussion and headquarters for political activism.

Many in the first wave of the independent living movement embraced a radical critique of the ideology of rehabilitation. The critique grew out of personal experiences with rehabilitation professionals and exposure to various currents of thought in the 1960s and 1970s. In an influential analysis of its ideological origins, Gerben DeJong described the movement as a response to what he and other observers called the "medical model" of disability. In the medical model the physician is the expert who uses his knowledge to make decisions for the patient. The patient is expected to fulfill what Talcott Parsons called the "sick role." The patient is exempted from normal social activities and responsibilities and likewise from blame for his illness. In exchange, the patient is obligated to define his condition as undesirable and to follow the doctor's advice to get well. Disabled people, DeJong argued, often fall into a variant of the sick role, the "impaired role" as described by Siegler and Osmond, in which the patient gives up the hope of recovery and continues as a dependent, relieved of all normal responsibilities of life.[17]

Unlike medical rehabilitation, vocational rehabilitation attempted to restore some of those responsibilities, but it also tended to reinforce the belief that the problem of disability lay with the individual. According to the precepts of independent living, this belief in itself limited the lives of disabled people. The advocates of independent living redefined success for people with disabilities. Instead of advocating their fitting in by learning to overcome their disabilities, the independent living philosophy stressed that disabled people should control their own lives as much as possible. Independent living was premised on the belief that success for disabled people was a matter more of changing attitudes and removing barriers than of rising above one's physical condition.

Thus, as DeJong summarized, rehabilitation was part of the problem, not the solution.[18] Accordingly, independent living centers aimed above all to remain independent of disability professionals—physical therapists, occupational therapists, vocational rehabilitation counselors, even physicians. One of the leaders of the disability movement, Ed Roberts, was proud of the fact that he seldom went to a doctor.[19] Instead, services were to be controlled by disabled people themselves. Independent living centers strongly favored in-home personal attendants hired by disabled people themselves over services provided by nurses in institutional settings. Disabled people, according to the independent living philosophy, should be treated as capable adults, not sick children.

Section 504

Ideas about disability rights had been floating around even before the changes in disability politics in the late 1960s and early 1970s. Academics such as Jacobus tenBroek, a professor of political science who was blind, had written articles exploring the application of rights concepts to people with disabilities, or comparing the situation of the "cripple" to that of blacks.[20] Moreover, litigation in matters of deinstitutionalization, patient rights, and education of people with disabilities had invoked rights concepts. Two important lower federal court decisions even entertained the possibility of considering disability a special "suspect" or "semisuspect" category under the equal protection clause of the U.S. Constitution, thus according people with disabilities the same constitutional rights extended to blacks and women.[21]

For many in the disability movement, however, disability rights was an abstraction compared with the basic existential issues raised by the independent living movement. While historical accounts generally treat the independent living movement as almost synonymous with the disability rights movement, some participants see the two as distinct. Independent living leaders had always been concerned about discrimination against people with disabilities, but in the early 1970s their efforts were focused on the practicalities of running the independent living centers. Only with the arrival of section 504 did rights come to the forefront of the disability movement.[22]

Section 504 was a "stealth" provision. It was written into the Rehabilitation Act of 1973 by congressional liberals and received little scrutiny, even when President Nixon twice vetoed the bill because of its other provisions.[23] When Congress overrode the second veto it became law. Section 504 was deceptively simple. It held that "no otherwise qualified individual in the United States . . . shall, solely by reason of his handicap, be excluded from participation in, be denied the benefits of, or be subjected to discrimination under any program or activity receiving Federal assistance."[24] Was this merely an expression of an aspiration? A blueprint for governmentwide antidiscrimination rules? An invitation to disabled people to sue government-funded agencies that discriminated against them? The regulations based on the bill leaned heavily toward making section 504 a disability rights law comparable to title VI of the Civil Rights Act of 1964. But in one significant respect the regulations went beyond traditional rights laws. As developed by the Office for Civil Rights of the Department of Health, Education and Welfare (HEW), the regulations included a requirement that employers provide "reasonable accommodation" to disabled workers.[25] To comply with the law, federally funded agencies would have to do more than simply prove they had not discriminated against disabled people. Where necessary, they might have to make arrangements to ensure that people with disabilities could perform the job. Thus physical barriers and unequal access to facilities were for the first time made a civil rights violation.

In the spring of 1975 the Office for Civil Rights completed a draft of the section 504 regulations, but the HEW secretary, David Matthews, stalled them. There the matter stood until 1977, when the Carter administration took over, and Joseph Califano became the new department secretary. When Califano also seemed to delay, disability activists held a wheelchair parade in front of his home and later sat in at his office overnight.[26] The center of protest, however, was California, where the West Coast wing of the disability movement conducted a sit-in at a San Francisco federal building. With more than a hundred disabled people camped, many in wheelchairs and some on a hunger strike, Califano relented.

It is an exaggeration to say that the controversy over the section 504 regulations created the disability rights movement, but as Richard Scotch has argued, the controversy did greatly strengthen the movement. As part of the effort to implement the regulations, many disability groups received government funding, some of which was used to train people with disabilities to assert their newfound rights.[27] But more important than the funding was the example of the San Francisco protest, which for the first time brought together people of different disabilities—deafness, blindness, cerebral palsy, spinal cord injury, mental retardation, mental illness, and others.[28] Until the 1970s, groups representing these disabilities, when active politically at all, had worked on their own, and the staggering differences among them seemed larger than their common interests.[29] In a fight over disability rights, however, they became united.[30] Thus the protests over section 504 attained for the disability movement the same kind of significance that the Montgomery bus boycott had for the civil rights movement or the Stonewall riot had for the gay rights movement.

The Rights Model

In the aftermath of the section 504 controversy, a "rights model," or, as some called it, a "minority model," of the situation of disabled people emerged in the writings of disability activists and their academic sympathizers. These writings echoed the themes of the independent living movement but moved beyond its focus on the critique of traditional rehabilitation programs. The theorists of the rights model were influenced most by the civil rights movement. Some of the leaders of the disability movement had begun their activities in politics through their involvement in civil rights efforts; others had simply grown up watching the movement on television. The proponents of the rights model drew strong parallels between disabled people and racial minorities. The rights model would become the philosophical cornerstone of the ADA.

The essence of the rights model is the contention that disabled people are oppressed by society more than by their disabilities. "The general public does not associate the word 'discrimination' with the segregation and exclusion of disabled people," wrote Robert Funk, the first director of the Disability Rights Education and Defense Fund (DREDF). "Historically the inferior economic and social status of disabled people has been viewed as the inevitable consequence of the physical and mental differences imposed by disability."[31] According to the rights model, however, every building with narrow hallways, every sidewalk curb without a "cut," every subway without an elevator, and every elevator without Braille buttons is an act of discrimination against disabled people. Separate transportation, separate housing and separate educational programs are acts of segregation comparable to Jim Crow laws. Frank Bowe, the first executive director of the American Coalition of Citizens with Disabilities (ACCD), compared the historical oppression of blacks to the legacy of oppression of disabled people:

> The tragedy is that for two hundred years disabled people have not been asked about their needs and desires. Buildings went up

before their inaccessibility was "discovered"—and then it was too late. During America's periods of greatest growth, when subways were constructed, television and motion pictures produced, telephone lines laid, school programs designed, and jobs manufactured, disabled people were hidden away in attics, "special" programs, and institutions, unseen and their voices unheard. Day by day, year by year, America became ever more oppressive to its hidden minority.[32]

Society allows physical and social barriers to exist because of pervasive prejudice against disabled people, just as Jim Crow laws were allowed to exist because of white racism. Of course, whereas racism is often overtly hostile to blacks, prejudice against disabled people is often more subtle. It usually takes the form of pity. But pity, according to the disability rights theorists, can be even more damaging than hatred. Many see disabled people as "childlike, helpless, hopeless, nonfunctioning and noncontributing members of society," who are not expected to lead normal lives.[33]

This attitude, according to the rights model, is reflected in the way government chooses to aid disabled people. Instead of spending money on services to help them become more independent, government devotes nearly all its disability budget to welfare payments: "It looks as though the federal government prefers to keep disabled people down [rather] than help them up."[34]

Paternalism toward disabled people is also reflected, according to the rights theory, in private charity efforts, particularly telethons. Thus proponents of the theory condemned an effort many thought the hallmark of goodwill, the Jerry Lewis Muscular Dystrophy Association Telethon. Evan Kemp Jr., a disability rights leader who himself had muscular dystrophy, argued that the telethon depicted disabled people as poor, suffering children whose lives were hopeless in the absence of a cure. In the effort to arouse pity, Kemp wrote, Lewis had reinforced "stereotypes that offend our self-respect, harm our efforts to live independent lives and segregate us from the mainstream of society." Kemp, whose own parents had helped to create the telethon, called on Lewis to "show disabled people working, raising families and generally sharing in community life."[35] Similar criticism moved the National Easter Seal Society and United Cerebral Palsy Associations telethons to drop the pity approach.[36]

If, as proponents of the rights model asserted, the fundamental problem for disabled people was discrimination caused by prejudice, the solution was for people with disabilities to claim their rights. The arrangement of society to suit only the nondisabled violated basic norms of freedom and equality. Thus people with disabilities should treat barrier removal and other modifications not as a privilege conceded to them, but as a right that had been denied, an injustice to be rectified. The act of demanding rights would also undermine the paternalistic view society took of a person with a disability: "How can we keep alive our vision of him as the helpless victim of a handicapping condition when he is putting together a political organization and agitating for change?"[37]

The rights model, then, entailed political action based on a radical reconceptualization of the disabled person's role in society. On its face it hardly seemed the stuff of Republican politics. Yet in the 1980s many elements of the rights model came to be accepted by Reagan and Bush administration officials. This acquiescence paved the way for the ADA.

How Conservatives Embraced the Rights Model

After the exhilaration of the victory on section 504, the disability movement faced a backlash in the late 1970s and early 1980s. The transportation industry, for example, fought section 504 rules that mandated full accessibility of buses and trains, winning a U.S. Court of Appeals decision that struck down the rules as beyond the scope of section 504 regulation.[38] The victory of Ronald Reagan, with his call for getting government off the backs of the American people, seemed to presage further setbacks. As part of his crusade against regulation, Reagan appointed Vice President George Bush to head a task force for regulatory relief. Two of the task force's early targets were section 504 and the Education for All Handicapped Children Act.[39]

The perceived threat posed by the task force mobilized the disability rights movement. In January 1982, DREDF expanded beyond its Berkeley base to create a Washington office staffed by Robert Funk and Pat Wright, who devoted their efforts to fighting the proposed revisions.[40] They were joined by Evan Kemp Jr., who was director of the Disability Rights Center backed by Ralph Nader. Their first move was to orchestrate a write-in campaign against revisions in the disability laws. The administration was deluged with letters, demonstrating the muscle of the disability movement.[41]

The disability rights advocates also began meeting with C. Boyden Gray, Bush's legal counsel. Kemp had become friends with Gray years before, and he set to work to "educate" Gray, who had known little about disability policy before he came to the task force.[42] What Kemp, along with Wright and Funk, taught Gray was an understanding of the rights model of disability congenial to the worldview of a conservative Republican. Kemp told Gray that disabled people did not want the paternalistic, heavy hand of government doling out welfare to them. The disability regulations were not handouts, Kemp argued. They were accommodations made so that people with disabilities could become independent and support themselves with jobs. Kemp contended that the costs of the accommodations in section 504 were minimal compared with the heavy costs of welfare spending on disabled people. The disability rights advocates reinforced this message about paternalism and independence by inviting Gray and Bush to visit independent living centers and meet with disabled people.[43]

These efforts paid off. On March 21, 1983, Vice President Bush announced in a letter sent to leaders of disability groups that the administration would not try to change section 504.[44] The administration also dropped plans to alter the education regulations. Although these moves did not end the conflicts between the Reagan administration and disability advocates, the long-term effects of the episode turned out to be powerful. Disability rights leaders found in Gray "the strongest advocate we have ever had in any administration," as one commented.[45] Gray would demonstrate his newfound commitment to disability rights during the development of the ADA. Kemp, meanwhile, formed a relationship with Bush that continued long after the controversy over section 504. During the balance of the Reagan administration, the vice president asked Kemp for his help in drafting speeches on disability issues. In 1987 he recommended Kemp for a seat on the Equal Employment Opportunity Commission and in 1989 named him chairman. Perhaps most important, Bush and Gray came to accept key elements of the rights model. For Gray the fight over section 504 was a turning point in the Bush administration's support of ADA: "It all germinated back in that time."[46]

The National Council on the Handicapped

Meanwhile, in a far more obscure corner of the Reagan administration, another group of conservative Republicans also came to embrace the rights model. The National Council on the Handicapped, created during the Carter administration, had kept a very low profile during its first few years. But in 1984 the council was asked to produce a report "analyzing Federal programs and presenting legislative recommendations to enhance the productivity and quality of life of Americans with disabilities."[47] That report, created by a council dominated by conservative Reaganites, became a blueprint for the ADA.

Reagan had replaced nearly all of the Carter appointees on the council with his supporters, mainly conservative Republicans. Several were fundraisers in the 1980 Reagan presidential campaign. The leaders of the disability movement doubted anything valuable could come from such a cast, but they may have overlooked the unique qualities of some of its more forceful members. Among them was Justin Dart Jr. The son of a rich and very conservative businessman, Dart had been struck with polio at the age of eighteen. His work on disability policy in his home state of Texas convinced him that the disability movement needed to make civil rights its priority. Rehabilitation programs, education, and residential institutions had been substantially improved, Dart believed. Significant, though limited, civil rights laws had been enacted. But public knowledge of these changes, and full implementation of the laws, had lagged. Laws such as section 504 left vast gaps because it and the other provisions of the 1973 Rehabilitation Act covered only government agencies or businesses and institutions receiving federal funds. [48]

Perhaps more important, Dart thought, *attitudes* had not changed, even though disabled people had proved their capabilities time and again. "The basic assumption of inequality remained intact," Dart concluded. "The great majority of people with severe disabilities remained isolated, unemployed, impoverished and dependent."[49] The main problem for disabled people, Dart believed, was that "we were considered subhuman." [50]

Dart had been deeply impressed with the impact of the 1964 Civil Rights Act. He had attended college in the segregated South and had even started a college civil rights group—which attracted all of five members. "I would have bet every penny I had that I would never see the day when integration was accepted."[51] Civil rights laws, he believed, were a powerful way to change American attitudes. "To Americans, total equality is a sacred concept of transcending power and majesty. 'We hold these truths . . .' and 'I have a dream . . .' are far easier to communicate than partial rights and particular services."[52] Thus Dart decided to devote his life to passing a comprehensive civil rights law for disabled people.

When Dart was appointed to the National Council on the Handicapped in 1981, he was able to put his views into action.[53] Realizing that he had to create a constituency for a comprehensive civil rights bill, he used his own money to travel from state to state, meeting disability leaders and building support for the civil rights approach. In these meetings he developed a statement on disability policy that stressed the need to promote independence and maximize productivity among disabled people. The statement included a recommendation that "Congress and the executive branch should act forthwith to include persons with disabilities in the Civil Rights Act of 1964, the Equal Opportunity Act of 1972 and other civil rights legislation and regulation." In 1983 Dart got the council to endorse and publish this statement as a "National Policy for Persons with Disabilities."[54]

Together with Sandra Parrino, the chairperson of the council, Dart worked to make a rights law a part of the council's agenda. They hired Lex Frieden, a leader in the independent living movement, and Robert Burgdorf Jr., a prominent disability rights lawyer, as staff for the council. When the council began to discuss civil rights, it soon became clear that the idea resonated even with the council's very conservative members. All of them had had close experience with disabled people and so could relate to cases in which a disabled person had been discriminated against unfairly. Moreover, Dart's message of independence for disabled people was one the Reaganites on the council appreciated. Burgdorf pointed out that most of the $60 billion spent annually on disabled people by the federal government was going to welfare programs; only about $3 billion was used to help disabled people become productive and independent. The council members, Burgdorf says, considered civil rights "simply a way to get from a society that takes care of people with disabilities to a society that tries to help people become productive and mainstream."[55] Civil rights ended up at the top of the council's agenda.

The council agreed with Dart that a comprehensive civil rights bill for disabled people should be created, one that would go beyond section 504's narrow coverage of federal governmental institutions and groups receiving federal funds. Burgdorf recommended a stand-alone bill rather than an amendment to the 1964 Civil Rights Act, and this was accepted by the council.

In 1986 the council produced its report, *Toward Independence*. The tone of the report can best be summarized by its epigraph, a quotation from Theodore Roosevelt: "Our country calls not for the life of ease, but for the life of strenuous endeavor."[56] The report adopted many of the precepts of the rights model of disability, but refracted them through the prism of Reaganite conservatism. For instance, the report emphasized the costs to the government of federal disability welfare programs, which "are premised upon the dependency of the people who receive benefits."[57] The introduction to *Toward Independence* quoted approvingly a UN report that concluded, "More people are forced into limited lives and made to suffer by . . . man-made obstacles than by any specific physical or mental disability."[58] The report then warned that unless structural and attitudinal barriers to people with disabilities were reduced, the costs of services and care for disabled people would mushroom with the aging of the baby boom generation.[59] Thus concern about the personal costs of discrimination was mixed with a call for fiscal prudence.

Unlike the theorists who developed the rights model of disability, the writers of *Toward Independence* did not put the situation of disabled people into the context of earlier struggles of blacks and women. The historical precedent of the civil rights movement was never mentioned. Indeed, except in referring to the titles of particular laws, the report avoided the use of the term "civil rights" altogether. Instead it stressed "equality of opportunity," "dignity," and, most of all, "independence." ("Independence" was used twenty-one times in the first fourteen pages.) "Equality and independence," the report argued, "have been fundamental elements of the American form of government since its inception."[60] *Toward Independence* also quoted from a Ronald Reagan speech on disability policy: "By returning to our traditional values of self-reliance, human dignity, and independence, we can find the solution together. We can help replace chaos with order in Federal programs, and we can promote opportunity and offer the promise of sharing the joys and responsibilities of community life."[61]

The title of the report was taken from a speech in which Reagan declared that "we must encourage the provision of rehabilitation and other comprehensive services oriented *toward independence* within the context of family and community."[62] Thus the report embraced the rights theorists' belief that traditional disability policy induced dependency, but left behind their emphasis on society's oppression of disabled people.

Although its analysis of disability was conservative, the recommendations of *Toward Independence* were sweeping. Foremost was its endorsement of a comprehensive equal opportunity law for people with disabilities. The law's coverage would be even wider than that of traditional civil rights laws. Duties under the law, the report concluded, should include removal of architectural, transportation, and communication barriers. The law should be administratively enforced but should include a private right of action in federal court and fines for violators.[63]

To help build the case for an antidiscrimination law, the council had commissioned a survey of disabled people to document their living conditions and attitudes. Among the findings reported in *Toward Independence* was that only one-third held jobs, but two-thirds of all unemployed disabled people wanted to work. The study also concluded that disabled people were more socially isolated, less educated, and less happy with their lives than other Americans.[64] These conclusions would be cited constantly in the debate over the ADA.

Frustrated with congressional inaction on their proposal, the council voted in 1987 to draft a disability rights bill based on the outline in *Toward Independence*. Council leaders shopped the bill around to sympathetic members of Congress, particularly Lowell Weicker in the Senate and Tony Coelho in the House, both key advocates of disability legislation. In January 1988 the council published its follow-up to *Toward Independence*, titled *On the Threshold of Independence*. The new report included the first version of the Americans with Disabilities Act.[65] Later that spring, after negotiations with disability groups, Weicker, followed by Coelho, introduced the first version of the ADA.[66]

The Enactment of the ADA

Weicker and Coelho submitted the bill mainly for symbolic reasons. There were hearings late in the fall, but no serious action was ever contemplated. Yet the draft did have an important effect: during the 1988 presidential campaign, George Bush endorsed the bill in concept. In his presidential nomination acceptance speech at the Republican national convention, he pledged that he would "do whatever it takes to make sure the disabled are included in the mainstream." Since his experience with Reagan's Task Force for Regulatory Relief, Bush had become a disability rights believer. And he had been influenced by another group of Reagan appointees, the members of the Commission on the Human Immunodeficiency Virus Epidemic. He said he was "very much persuaded" by the commission's conclusion that discrimination against AIDS carriers should be made illegal and its endorsement of the ADA as a vehicle for this.[67] Bush's stance was reinforced after the 1988 election. A pollster for Louis Harris and Associates estimated in a letter to the president that up to half his 4 million vote margin in the election had come from disabled voters who had switched from the Democratic party to the Republican candidate.[68] This estimate was circulated in the White House and became a point of pride for C. Boyden Gray, who had urged that disability rights be a priority in the Bush administration.[69]

Bush's endorsement of the ADA before the election set the tone for the legislative struggle that ensued. When he took office, he was committed to passing the bill, and there was little or no public opposition within the White House. "Shut up and get on with it was the attitude," according to one top administration official.[70]

ADA in the Senate

Tom Harkin, the chair of the Subcommittee on the Handicapped (later renamed the Subcommittee on Disability Policy), and Ted Kennedy, the chairman of the Labor and Human Resources Committee, became the prime movers of the ADA in the Senate. They determined early on that the first version of the ADA, based largely on the proposal from the National Council on the Handicapped, would have to be extensively revised.[71] The Reagan-appointed conservatives on the council had approved a surprisingly radical measure. Dubbed by skeptics "the make the world flat bill," the first version of the ADA would have required all buildings to be made accessible within five years unless doing so would fundamentally alter the nature of a program or threaten a company's existence. This "bankruptcy" provision, among others, would have to be modified, the senators decided, if the bill was to stand a chance in Congress.[72]

In January 1989 a core group of disability activists and Senate staff members began revising the bill.[73] The group adopted a strategy that would become a primary emphasis in the debate over the ADA. The first version of the ADA had often used language from the regulations and case law that had been developed in section 504 enforcement. In employment cases, for example, employers were required to provide "reasonable accommodation," the same phrase used in section 504 employment cases. But in many respects, such as the infamous "bankruptcy" provision, the first draft deviated significantly from section 504. Robert Silverstein, chief counsel of the Senate Subcommittee on Disability Policy, argued that the ADA should as much as possible draw language and concepts from the enforcement of section 504.[74] As a result, the group changed the bankruptcy provision so that a company would only have to prove that a modification entailed an "undue hardship"—the same defense businesses used in section 504 cases. Instead of mandating what some called flat earth modifications to existing buildings, changes would be required only if "readily achievable," again language from case law from section 504 rulings. The use of this language was meant to reassure anxious members of Congress that the ADA was simply an extension of section 504, and that years of experience with the language of the act would guarantee smooth implementation of the ADA. As one participant said, "Every time we departed from 504, we had to have a damn good reason to do so, and also one that was politically viable."[75]

The strategy worked. Although business groups criticized aspects of the second draft, there was little outright opposition. Over some provisions, principally those affecting public transportation and food service, major controversies erupted.[76] But on the general subject of discrimination against those with disabilities, most business groups adopted the premises of the ADA and supported the bill from the beginning. The National Association of Manufacturers, the Chamber of Commerce, the Labor Policy Association, and the American Society of Personnel Administrators—the big business groups most involved in the ADA—worked to smooth the bill's edges rather than oppose it fundamentally. Among national general business groups, only the National Federation of Independent Business and National Small Business United, both representing small business owners, opposed the ADA outright, and only the NFIB developed any kind of a critique of the rights model of disability.[77] As an NFIB official said, there was an "awfully meager alliance" of business groups against the ADA.[78]

One reason for business support of the ADA was that many larger corporations had learned to live with disability rights requirements because they were federal contractors and subject to section 504 provisions. Many companies were also probably concerned about the bad publicity that would result from opposing a bill to help disabled people. Finally, many business spokesmen seemed to accept the premise of the ADA that disabled people were a minority group deserving civil rights protections.[79]

The approach of the business community was also tactical. As the Senate was revising the ADA, the Bush administration let it be known that it was committed to passing the bill. Although the administration would work with business groups to address their concerns, it would not support direct attempts to block the ADA.[80] The administration's position meant that efforts to defeat the bill faced long odds. Consequently most groups labored to modify, rather than defeat, the legislation. In a memo to other business lobbyists, a Chamber of Commerce official concluded that bipartisan support for the ADA, together with President Bush's endorsement "adds up to almost certain passage in one form or another." The memo invited the lobbyists to join a working group "whose goal would be to help fashion the legislation so that it is acceptable to the business community while addressing the needs of the disabled."[81] This was the posture of most business groups throughout congressional consideration of the ADA.

The top priority for the business lobbyists was to limit the awards that ADA plaintiffs could win in court. Under the Civil Rights Act of 1964, plaintiffs in employment discrimination cases were eligible to win an injunction giving them back their jobs, back pay, and attorneys' fees. Racial minorities, however, were not limited to the remedies in the Civil Rights Act of 1964. They could also sue under the 1866 Civil Rights Act, often called section 1981, a law that had collected dust on the books until it was revitalized during the modern civil rights movement.[82] Section 1981 allowed injunctive relief, back pay, and reimbursement of legal fees, but it also gave plaintiffs the right to collect "pain and suffering" damages and punitive damages. These extra provisions created the possibility of very large verdicts—and made it easier for prospective plaintiffs to find lawyers willing to represent them. Women and religious minorities, not covered under section 1981, were limited to the rewards of the Civil Rights Act of 1964.

The revised version of the bill gave disabled plaintiffs in employment cases the same remedies as those available in section 1981. In cases involving discrimination in public accommodations, the remedies were tied to the 1988 Fair Housing Amendments Act, which also made plaintiffs eligible for a full range of damages. For business groups this was anathema; they feared a litigation explosion. The business community was particularly apprehensive because under section 1981 juries could decide discrimination cases, and it was expected that disabled people would make extremely sympathetic plaintiffs in jury trials. The threat of punitive damages in such cases loomed large. Business lobbyists also complained that language in the legislation—"reasonable accommodation," "undue hardship," and "readily achievable"—was so vague as to make compliance with the law a guessing game and the jury trials a lottery.

The Bush administration took up the demands of the business interests in negotiations with Senate leaders. Attorney General Richard Thornburgh outlined the executive branch's view in testimony before the Senate Subcommittee on the Handicapped on June 22, 1989, a month after introduction of the revised bill. Thornburgh pledged the president's support for a comprehensive civil rights measure, but he urged that remedies and enforcement mechanisms in the ADA bill ought to parallel those in the 1964 Civil Rights Act. Because "we are a litigious society," Thornburgh said, the administration was "merely making a plea for the tried and true remedies." The changes Thornburgh advocated eliminated the use of juries and the possibility of punitive or pain and suffering damages in ADA lawsuits. In addition, Thornburgh urged that the language of the bill parallel section 504 as much as possible, and that compromises be made to protect small businesses and transit systems.[83]

Soon after Thornburgh's testimony, Harkin and Kennedy made a deal with the White House. The deal focused on remedies. The senators agreed to cut back the scope of the remedies in exchange for a broader range of coverage than in previous civil rights laws. Remedies and enforcement procedures for employment discrimination in the ADA were tied to those in the Civil Rights Act, as the administration wanted. The only remedy available to those bringing public accommodations lawsuits was an injunction. This would make accommodations lawsuits less attractive to lawyers for plaintiffs, who would not be able to collect a contingency fee based on monetary damages. But the compromise did include a provision authorizing the attorney general to seek monetary damages on behalf of individuals harmed as a result of a "pattern or practice" of discrimination, and to mete out fines of $50,000 for a first violation and $100,000 for additional violations.[84]

In exchange the senators got broader coverage of businesses than under the Civil Rights Act. The 1964 act reached only restaurants, stores, gas stations, hotels, motels, theaters, and other places of entertainment. The revised bill covered a long list of businesses and institutions. Pharmacies, a major interest for disabled people, were included along with such venues as lawyers' offices, zoos, homeless shelters, and golf courses.[85]

Bolstered by the Bush administration's endorsement, the ADA reached the Senate floor three months later, on September 7, 1989. Harkin introduced the bill as a "landmark statement of basic human rights" that would also enhance "international competitiveness."[86] These two themes, of rights and of economic productivity, dominated the debate. Concerns about the cost to business were expressed by a few Democrats, but the only outspoken opposition to the bill came from a handful of conservative Republicans. The Americans with Disabilities Act swept the Senate on a vote of 76-8.

The Question of Remedies on the House Side

Steny Hoyer, a Maryland Democrat, was assigned by the House leadership to refine the details of the ADA with Steve Bartlett, a Texas Republican. Bartlett, an ADA supporter, attempted to find a way to rectify the many complaints of businesses. Their lobbyists were particularly critical of what they considered vague language in the bill. Bartlett was sympathetic to this concern but also frustrated by the inability of some business groups to offer acceptable alternatives.[87]

Some of the proposals offered by the National Federation of Independent Business were deemed politically infeasible. For instance, NFIB suggested that a "reasonable accommodation" in employment should cost no more than a certain percentage of an employee's wages. A ceiling on the cost of accommodations, however, was opposed by Bartlett because it could become a floor—employers, he reckoned, would spend up to the ceiling to put their fears of litigation to rest. Anyway, House Democrats and disability groups saw ceilings as a copout.[88] Similarly, NFIB's suggestion that businesses with fewer than fifteen employees be exempted from the public accommodations section of the ADA was rejected out of hand.

After several months of negotiations, Bartlett and Hoyer produced a draft that made several concessions to businesses, including a longer phase-in for small employers, deference to employers' job descriptions in defining the "essential functions" of a job, and coordination of complaints filed under the ADA and section 504. The compromise also included language requiring courts to consider "site-specific factors" in determining whether an accommodation would create an "undue hardship" for an employer, or whether an accommodation was "readily achievable."[89] This meant that a court would decide whether an accommodation in a chain restaurant was an undue burden based on the financial condition of the particular location rather than the chain as a whole. Though slowed, the big bill seemed to be moving ahead.

Then an old issue resurfaced: remedies. In February of 1990 Senator Edward Kennedy and Representative Augustus Hawkins introduced a bill amending the Civil Rights Act of 1964. The Kennedy-Hawkins bill was supposed to reverse a string of adverse Supreme Court decisions, but it also included a provision expanding the remedies available to plaintiffs in civil rights cases. In addition, it enabled plaintiffs to demand jury trials.[90]

As part of their deal with the White House, Kennedy and Harkins had tied to the ADA the same remedies and procedures as in the Civil Rights Act. So if the Kennedy-Hawkins amendments were adopted, disabled plaintiffs would also be eligible for expanded remedies and jury trials. For the Bush administration, this arrangement would signify very different rules of the game. The limitations on remedies the administration thought it had negotiated earlier would be stripped away by the Kennedy-Hawkins measure. Accordingly, Thornburgh sought to delete from the ADA the reference to the Civil Rights Act of 1964, pleading that only limited remedies were in his original deal.[91]

Not surprisingly, those who had worked on the Senate side of the deal saw things differently. The point of the deal, according to them, was that ADA plaintiffs should be governed by the same remedies accorded other minority groups. If Congress chose to grant expanded remedies to women, religious minorities, and racial minorities, logic dictated that disabled people should get them too.[92] Democrats in Congress, along with disability and civil rights groups, insisted on retaining the reference to the Civil Rights Act.

When the ADA reached the House floor, one of the last remaining issues was an amendment to restrict its remedies. In introducing the amendment, Wisconsin Republican F. James Sensenbrenner urged his colleagues to respect the spirit of the original compromise, arguing that because the ADA was a new type of legislation, it should be treated differently from the Civil Rights Act. Most businesses had little experience with disability discrimination laws, Sensenbrenner observed, so the possibility of compensatory and punitive damages awards and jury trials "raises the stakes much higher without any corresponding increasing benefit to the disabled." Moreover, expanded remedies should be provided only after a thorough examination of the effects; Congress had not considered expanded remedies during the bill's committee process and was not likely to give them much careful reflection during debate on the Kennedy-Hawkins bill.[93]

Democrats who opposed the Sensenbrenner amendment had a simple riposte: disabled people should be treated the same as other oppressed groups. California Democrat Don Edwards charged that the amendment "provides for a two-tier system, where women and minorities get a better break than persons with disabilities." Colorado Democrat Pat Schroeder summed up the logic of this view when she contended that "there are no rights without remedies," thus "you have lesser rights if you have lesser remedies."[94]

Kansas Democrat Dan Glickman, in contrast, deemphasized the importance of remedies, arguing that "rights and remedies are not the same thing," and that "a court of law should be the place of last resort, not first resort, to enforce civil rights." Glickman had added an amendment to the ADA urging that parties use arbitration instead of litigation to settle disability rights claims. Yet Glickman also argued that disabled people should not be locked into a lesser set of remedies. The argument over remedies, Glickman said, should be dealt with later, during consideration of Kennedy-Hawkins.[95]

Glickman's view prevailed; the Sensenbrenner amendment was defeated 192–227. The vote split mostly along party and ideological lines, with Republicans supporting the amendment 146–24 and Democrats opposing it 46–203. Conservative Southern Democrats provided 36 of the 46 Democratic votes in favor. Aside from these Southerners, the White House was unable to attract enough Democratic defectors to limit remedies.[96]

The final passage was not nearly so close; the ADA romped 403–20. With Evan Kemp and Justin Dart at his side, President Bush proudly signed the bill into law on July 26, 1990.[97]

Remedies and the Civil Rights Act of 1991

Enactment of the ADA still left the question of remedies unresolved. Democrats in Congress had beaten back attempts to detach disabled people from remedies available to other alleged victims of discrimination. The pending Kennedy-Hawkins scheme proposed to expand those remedies to allow plaintiffs in discrimination lawsuits to collect both pain and suffering and punitive damages. Remedies, however, became a secondary issue in the debate on that bill. Republicans, led by George Bush, focused on a provision that would have reversed a Supreme Court decision and reimposed a requirement that defendants in civil rights cases prove that employment practices resulting in "disparate impacts" were a "business necessity." Bush and the Republicans contended that businesses would sidestep this requirement by developing quotas so as to ward off discrimination suits. Calling Kennedy-Hawkins a "quota bill," Bush vetoed the 1990 Civil Rights Act. An effort to override the veto failed in the Senate by one vote.

The following year congressional Democrats reintroduced the bill. After complex negotiations and much softening in the GOP, Bush signed a compromise measure. The Civil Rights Act of 1991 for the first time allowed both pain and suffering and punitive damages, but capped them in proportion to the size of the business involved. For employers with 14 to 101 workers these damages could not exceed $50,000. The upper limit for employers with more than 500 employees was $300,000. A special provision in the bill barred damages in "reasonable accommodation" cases under the ADA or the 1973 Rehabilitation Act if the defendant demonstrated a good-faith effort to comply.[98]

Nonetheless, passage of the bill meant that plaintiffs in ADA employment cases were eligible for both a jury trial and an expanded range of remedies, just what many business groups and supporters of the Sensenbrenner amendment had dreaded. The only major attempt to curb the litigious design of the ADA had largely failed.

Explaining the ADA

Why did so many disparate players, from President Bush to civil rights leaders, disability activists, and even some captains of industry, get behind the disabilities act? Why did a Republican administration sign on to a new source of litigation, even while resisting some changes in other civil rights laws on account of their litigation-creating potential? Why did U.S. business not unite to stop a burdensome new mandate?

One answer to these questions is that, paradoxically, disabled people are a uniquely powerful force—or at least a group uniquely difficult to challenge. Disabled people are diffused throughout society, among Democrats and Republicans, rich and poor. Every politician who worked on the ADA, from George Bush down, could point to a close friend or relative with a disability. Probably every person in America can make a similar claim. Moreover, while the paternalism and pity many feel toward disabled persons may be unwelcome, those sentiments also confer political advantages. The great majority of Americans believe that disabled people are blameless victims and deserve help, whether through public or private charity. This basic fact about disability politics helps explain why the ADA sailed through Congress drawing few vocal opponents. It is not good public relations to fight with disabled people. All those involved in the ADA debate, including the business representatives, had a strong incentive to keep their reservations to themselves.

But these unique aspects of disability politics do not suffice to explain the ADA's allure. If politicians want to be seen as doing good for the disabled, the question still remains: why did they do this particular good thing rather than another? Policymakers, for example, might have increased funding for rehabilitation or raised the monthly welfare payments that many handicapped persons receive.

Moreover, politicians have often said no to advocates for the disabled. Indeed, at the federal level many of the disability movement's demands—fuller funding for independent living centers, changes in social security benefit laws, medical insurance reform, even funding for personal assistants—have gone largely unheeded. The greatest victories of advocates have come through rights-oriented measures, particularly the ADA, section 504, and the Education for All Handicapped Children Act but also the Fair Housing Amendments Act of 1988 and the Civil Rights Restoration Act of 1988. Thus it is the success of disability rights laws in particular, not the disability movement in general, that must be explained.

One might argue that rights laws have a strong appeal simply because the analogy between the disability rights movement and the civil rights movement is compelling. Indeed, much of the discrimination faced by disabled people is easily analogized to that faced by African Americans, as congressional testimony vividly illustrated. A woman with cerebral palsy told of being refused entrance to a movie theater. A mother of a baby who had died of AIDS told of undertakers who refused to embalm the infant.[99] Tony Coelho, the congressman who first introduced the disabilities bill in the House, told of nearly being driven to suicide by the discrimination he faced after he was diagnosed with epilepsy.[100] These stories sounded very much like those that helped galvanize the civil rights movement. The force of the analogy to civil rights was clearly demonstrated in the debate over remedies. To restrict remedies, Bush officials and their business constituents had to argue that disabled individuals did not deserve the same protections afforded other minority groups. Yet in promoting the ADA, the administration had also embraced the rights model, with its implicit analogy between racial minorities and persons with disabilities. Before the key House vote the Democrats stressed emphatically that the two groups should be protected similarly, and when most of the Democrats stuck together they prevailed. Thus the rights model became the central rationale for expanded remedies.

But as the story of Lori Vande Zande suggests, the situation of disabled people is in many respects very different from that of racial minorities—and disability rights laws constitute a major departure from other kinds of civil rights legislation. With the exception of affirmative action programs, neutrality has been a presumed principle of civil rights laws: people should not treat members of one group differently from those of another. In the ADA, however, the requirement is often the opposite; as the Vande Zande case indicates, employers can be charged with discrimination when they do *not* take account of differences. The concept of reasonable accommodation was lifted from civil rights law governing religious minorities, but in disability law it has been considerably broadened. Indeed while the ADA is called an antidiscrimination law, it is in many respects a prodiscrimination law. Employers and managers of public facilities must be prepared to spend money—sometimes a lot of money—to accommodate each disabled person based on his or her particular disability.

Further, because everyone agrees there are some rational bases for discriminating against disabled people, the ADA inevitably permits some kinds of discrimination.[101] Blind men cannot be cab drivers, mentally retarded people cannot be college professors, paraplegics cannot be football players. The standard of the ADA is whether, with a "reasonable accommodation," the disabled person can perform the "essential functions" of a job. If, as with Vande Zande's desktop computer, the accommodation demanded is deemed unreasonable, then the employer has the right to discriminate against anyone who cannot perform the essential functions of a job without it. Also, much to the displeasure of activists, the ADA leaves many physical barriers intact. Businesses need only remove structural barriers if removal is "readily achievable." Office buildings need not be accessible until they are renovated. And although subways are required to have at least one accessible car in each train, only "key stations" are required to be accessible. Thus the ADA is far from a blanket prohibition against discrimination and structural barriers. Instead, it draws a faint line between types of discrimination and barriers that are socially acceptable or too expensive to remedy and those that are not.[102] Those who drafted the ADA gave judges the job of brightening that line.

Thus the problem of disability is fundamentally different from the problem of race, and the solutions contained in the ADA are far from identical to those in traditional civil rights law. Yet few challenged the concept that the ADA was the analogue of civil rights law. What was it, then, about the rights analogy that so many policymakers found persuasive?

The Rights Model and American Values

Part of the answer lies in the distrust of public programs that is widespread among Americans. The appeal of the rhetoric of rights stems in part from its rejection of the welfare state, a maneuver that fits the ideological preferences of both disability groups and conservatives. In the case of disability policy, a disadvantaged group did not seem to be requesting social assistance, only affirming a legal right to participate as equally as possible in the mainstream of society.

It is not too much to say that for the Bush administration the ADA became a kind of welfare reform. Its view was that on-budget "programs" reduce people to dependency. The disability activists agreed.[103] Their frustrating experiences with rehabilitation professionals and with disability bureaucracies led them to take a dim view of paternalistic agencies. In addition, the essence of the activists' campaign was to show that the disabled are not needy, pitiable creatures. Demonstrations of need are the typical way groups justify sharing governmental resources. For the activists, demonstrations of need were part of the problem, not the solution. That is why they despised the well-intentioned ministrations of Jerry Lewis, the muscular dystrophy telethon leader. The rights path enabled the disability lobby to reallocate resources without emphasizing neediness. It exploited the magical element of rights: a *need*, something one begs to have fulfilled, can be turned into a just *claim*, something that is owed. Expressing a need seems to infantilize the needer; claiming a right seems adult and dignified.

American activists have attempted, with some success, to export the rights agenda to other nations. But nowhere has the disability rights idea gone farther than in the United States. Maybe this is because most other industrialized societies have larger public sectors and deeper safety nets and attach less stigma to dependency. Perhaps where neediness is deemed less shameful, and self-help less essential (or virtuous), the politics of rights making loses energy. For better or worse, Americans may be exchanging a somewhat lower level of social spending for a higher pitch of rights activism. [104]

Litigation and the Decentralized State

The American emphasis on rights laws may also have something to do with aspects of the U.S. political structure. The appeal of such rights laws as the ADA is that they allow politicians to claim credit for helping disabled people while taking the costs off budget. Politicians, in other words, have a strong incentive to issue mandates such as the ADA, particularly at a time when alternatives are limited by fiscal constraints. Activists, recognizing this, couch their demands in the form of rights. But why choose to mandate through the courts rather than by direct administration? Bureaucratic programs are subject to the changing priorities of each administration and Congress.[105] The judiciary is less susceptible to political and budgetary vicissitudes of the moment. Funding and staffing of the EEOC or the Justice Department can change, but regardless of what happens to such agencies in the future, disability activists can always have their day in court, so to speak. And in the decentralized, relatively nonhierarchical American court system, there is always a good chance of finding a judge sympathetic to their claims.

Courts also allow activists to force state and local governments to meet national standards. Even federal bureaucracies sympathetic to the goals of activists have no easy way to control independent local authorities, except perhaps by withdrawing federal grants. Litigation offers another method by which to enforce unfunded mandates against lower levels of government. And if the federal government chooses to look the other way when state and local governments fail to comply, the private advocates can force the public miscreants into court. Thus it should be no surprise that U.S. advocates for the disabled have not pressed for the creation of a special administrative body.[106] Incentives associated with the structure of American government have encouraged judicially based enforcement.

Costs of the System

Implementation through the courts entails considerable costs. The shortcomings of the ADA's adversarial legalism—uncertainty, delay, high transaction costs, high penalties, distrust, and scattershot enforcement—have become increasingly apparent in the seven years since the law's enactment.

Uncertainty

ADA enforcement is beset by uncertainty. Key terms in the legislation are vague. The authors of the act and the regulations written afterward tried to define terms such as "reasonable accommodation," "undue hardship," and "qualified individual with a disability." Indeed, the ADA is the most detailed civil rights statute ever written.

But because the drafters found themselves needing flexibility to deal with a wide range of unique cases, they chose to keep much of the language of the law open-ended.

For example, neither the law nor the regulations spell out exactly what conditions are to be considered a disability.[107] Thus this basic question turns out to be a matter of considerable controversy. Through 1995, in sixty lawsuits in which the definition of disability arose as an issue, courts found for the plaintiff in only twelve cases. Often reflecting the narrow constructions of Republican appointees, courts have ruled that people with carpal tunnel syndrome, chemical imbalance, sleep disorders, loss of a lung, cancer, and even multiple sclerosis are not disabled under the ADA.[108] As a result, plaintiffs in employment cases face a dilemma: on one hand, they must prove that they are impaired enough to be disabled, but on the other, they must show they are not so impaired as to be unqualified for a job. Thus verdicts for plaintiffs are relatively few and summary judgment rulings for employers frequent. Of course, what this means for employers is far from clear. Their win rate may reflect settlement practices: the defendants may be settling claims they think they cannot beat in court and contesting those, like the one involving Vande Zande, that they think can be beaten in summary judgment. In any event, in the hands of the judiciary the ADA so far appears to be something of a disappointment for its proponents.

At the same time, in a decentralized court system there are plenty of exceptions to the general pattern, and these cases add a big element of unpredictability. For example, although obesity has generally been determined not to be a disability, a store manager won more than $1 million under the ADA after being fired when he sought medical treatment for his weight problems.[109] The Rhode Island Federal District Court awarded an obese woman $100,000 in compensatory damages in a section 504 employment discrimination claim. The district court concluded that obesity was a disability if it was "caused by systemic or metabolic factors and constitutes an immutable condition," though the First Circuit Court which reviewed the case found that the claim would be valid even if the woman's obesity was deemed mutable.[110]

Uncertainty greatly complicates the decisions of managers and employers under the ADA. For example, there is the especially difficult matter of accommodating people with addictions or mental disorders. A reasonable accommodation might include time off for treatment, flexible schedules, and a restructured job. But how to draw the line between illnesses that need to be accommodated—mood swings, phobias, problems dealing with others—and those that do not is anybody's guess. Uncertain, some employers capitulate to employee demands that others might deem unreasonable. The school superintendent of Hamden, Connecticut, was arrested and pleaded guilty to drunken driving, then disappeared for ten days. When the man was fired from his job, he filed a complaint alleging that the school had discriminated against him on the basis of a disability—alcoholism. In exchange for dropping the charges, the school board agreed to give the superintendent a partial salary and lifetime medical and life insurance benefits.[111] Better, the board reasoned, to pay this price than risk a lawsuit.

One selling point of the ADA was that some of its key concepts, "reasonable accommodation" and "undue hardship," were lifted from section 504 and had already been tested in the courts. This, it was argued, would make the ADA relatively easy to enforce, because many employers already had experience with the law. The assumption behind this argument was that over time legal concepts become more stable and less ambiguous as judges flesh them out. But the supposition is less solid than it seems in a system in which a decentralized, policymaking judiciary is often wrestling with challenges and revisions to legal language. Indeed, as the federal judiciary gradually changes hands, putting more Democrat-appointed judges on the bench, more expansive readings of the ADA are likely. It is not too farfetched to imagine that the ADA will one day be invoked to bar discrimination against unattractive people or unusually short or tall people because it can be argued that they are "regarded as being impaired." In any case, stability in the law is improbable. The decentralization of American courts, the use of jurors as decisionmakers, and the endless reinterpretation of statutory language ensure that the ADA will remain a floating legal crapshoot for plaintiffs and defendants alike.

Delay

Actually, the ADA was not supposed to be enforced just by the courts. Under the law, aggrieved individuals can first file their complaints with appropriate federal agencies that are supposed to examine and possibly mediate disputes before they can be litigated. But, of course, having opened the flood gates for claims of employment discrimination, ADA mandates (along with other civil rights mandates) soon overloaded these bureaus. The volume of discrimination claims taken by the Equal Employment Opportunity Commission jumped from 62,000 in 1990 to 91,000 by 1994. The U.S. Department of Justice, which handles access discrimination cases, has also been swamped. As of mid-1995, the EEOC was staggering under a backlog of 100,000 civil rights cases of all kinds, including 18,000 unprocessed ADA claims, and was taking nearly a year to process what cases it could.[112] More than one-third of the 2,649 ADA public accommodations cases that had been filed with the Justice Department remained unopened as of mid-1994.[113]

Unable to keep up with, much less resolve, so much of the caseload, the EEOC and the Justice Department have all but encouraged complainants to take their troubles directly to the courts (the Justice Department has decided to concentrate chiefly on joining lawsuits it thinks will set major precedents).[114] But the federal courts are backlogged too. In 1995 the median time required to dispose of civil cases that went to trial in district courts was nineteen months.[115]

The upshot has been a method of redressing grievances that often satisfies no one. Many plaintiffs, like Lori Vande Zande, move on to other jobs before their cases finally get settled. Meanwhile, employers have to nurse ADA-induced legal headaches over many months or even years.

Transaction Costs

Disputes in an adversarial and legalistic system involve heavy transaction costs. Lawyering is required in such a system, and lawyers are expensive. The EEOC complaint process is supposed to provide a route to resolving discrimination claims that is less costly than litigation. Unfortunately, because the agency succeeds in mediating only a small number of nonfrivolous cases, the transaction costs still turn out to be steep when considered as a percentage of awards. By September 1996, 72,687 claims of disability discrimination had been submitted to the EEOC, with total awards reaching $117 million. But in only about 15 percent of the cases had the complainant re-

TABLE 6-1. *Employment Discrimination Cases Filed in Federal Court, 1989–95*[a]

Year	Cases	Year	Cases
1989	9,000	1993	12,221
1990	8,413	1994[c]	15,256
1991	8,144	1995	18,225
1992[b]	10,275		

Source: Administrative Office of U.S. Courts, table CIV 14.

a. Cases filed in twelve-month period ending June 30.

b. ADA regulations for employers of more than twenty-five people effective July 1992. Civil Rights Act of 1991, which expanded the range of remedies in discrimination litigation, effective November 1991.

c. ADA regulations for employers of between fifteen and twenty-four people effective July 1994.

ceived a benefit; the other 85 percent had either been closed for lack of reasonable cause or had become "administrative closures," an omnibus category that indicates that for one of several reasons the case was not fully processed.[116] Thus the vast majority of EEOC claims are either unresolved or are found to be baseless. Nonetheless, each claim that is investigated requires employers to conduct their own investigations, respond to EEOC questions, and prepare a defense based on the evidence.

The costs associated with an EEOC complaint look like a bargain next to the costs of fighting cases out in court, where some of the EEOC's "no reasonable cause" and "administrative closure" cases finally wind up.[117] It is unclear how many cases move from the EEOC into the courts because, incredibly, there are no reliable data on ADA filings. Overall employment discrimination filings under various federal laws have grown from around 8,000 in the years before the disabilities act went into effect to nearly 19,000 in 1995 (see table 6-1). How much of this increase is attributable to the ADA is unclear; a 1995 study by the Justice Department located a total of only 650 privately filed ADA cases.[118]

Cases that go to court doubtless run up many times the expense of an EEOC proceeding. Research on personal injury litigation has found that successful plaintiffs collect on average about half of the total outlay of litigation, with most of the rest going to the lawyers.[119]

Discrimination lawsuits may well involve even higher transaction costs, and ADA lawsuits higher still because of the ambiguous and unsettled nature of the law. When a California arbitrator awarded $1.1 million to one successful ADA plaintiff, his attorney got $800,000 of it.[120] Transaction costs like this can both discourage potential plaintiffs from pursing worthy cases *and* encourage defendants to settle unworthy ones.

Penalties

Opportunities for plaintiffs ballooned when Congress granted them the right to receive awards for pain and suffering and punitive damages. Although such damages in employment cases were capped at $300,000, the threat of even this limited sum transforms the rules of the game. Without such awards, lawyers working on a contingency fee basis would have little chance of collecting a sizable payoff, thus little incentive to take ADA cases. The threat of a large verdict is a hook for obtaining a lawyer and a device for inducing defendants to settle. The device, however, is not always benign; defendants may well settle questionable cases rather than gamble with a jury verdict.

Big wins by plaintiffs make more news than vindicated defendants and so get more attention than their numbers warrant. The first case brought under the ADA by the EEOC resulted in "a defense lawyer's nightmare," a more than $500,000 verdict against an employer who fired a man with brain cancer.[121] (The award was later reduced to $200,000 by a federal circuit court.) Another well-publicized case involved a Coca Cola executive who was fired while being treated for alcoholism. He hit pay dirt: a $7.1 million verdict, though likely to be much less in the end because of the caps.[122] A truck driver won a $5.5 million award when his company failed to transfer him to a new job after he suffered a seizure.[123] In most cases the amounts are not that large, but pain and suffering awards or punitive damages can be a large component of the total, sometimes dwarfing any other compensation.

If damages were awarded in a predictable pattern, their effects might be less unsettling. But given the uncertainties of ADA litigation, the vagaries of U.S. courts, and the use of juries in disability discrimination complaints, large verdicts are guaranteed to strike like lightning, hitting some defendants and missing others.

Distrust and Defensiveness

A vague and costly law can create counterproductive responses from those it seeks to regulate. Defensive employers spend their time and money trying to figure out how to avoid litigation rather than how to promote the ADA's goals. Firms may begin to fear disabled employees, who in turn may fear that if they raise issues of accommodation they will be branded troublemakers. The specter of litigation pits managers and workers against one another.

The ADA has spawned a cottage industry of consultants who advise organizations on how to avoid lawsuits. One article proposes an elaborate formula in which the value of each "essential function" of a job and the importance of various qualifications for the job are rated by evaluators, then used to determine the relative cost of an accommodation. The article suggests capping accommodation costs at somewhere between 10 percent and 15 percent of an employee's annual salary. The percentage is necessarily arbitrary because Congress refused to create a ceiling on ADA accommodation costs. But management is promised that the result "will be an empirically derived, defensible and fair" policy.[124]

The ultimate defensive play among employers is to avoid hiring disabled job applicants. Discrimination in hiring is difficult to prove, so the risk of being sued is low. Perversely, when employers act in the spirit of the ADA and hire disabled people, the threat of litigation rises sharply. Only 10 percent of ADA complaints with the EEOC involve hiring; the rest were brought by current or terminated employees (table 6-2).

Laying off a disabled person who has not performed well can be expensive and treacherous. More than half of all ADA Title I (employment) lawsuits involve terminations, and this is where some of the most outrageous plaintiff claims can be found. The *Wall Street Journal* gathered in one article the stories of a government clerk who claimed she was manic depressive and was fired for repeatedly making rude outbursts; a bus driver with severe diabetes who contested his dismissal even though he was at serious risk of losing consciousness; and a philosophy professor who claimed a mental handicap after he was fired for sexual assault.[125] Plaintiffs in such ludicrous lawsuits almost invariably lose. Often employers obtain summary judgments. But defending against even a ridiculous lawsuit can be time consuming and costly.

TABLE 6-2. *ADA Employment Claims, by Type of Violation Most Often Cited, July 1992–September 1996*

Violation	Number	Percent
Discharge	37,760	51.9
No reasonable accommodation	20,447	28.1
Harassment	8,718	12.0
Hiring	7,095	9.8
Discipline	5,676	7.8
Layoff	3,407	4.7
Promotion	2,827	3.9
Benefits	2,807	3.9
Wages	2,501	3.4
Rehire	2,457	3.4
Suspension	1,608	2.2

Source: Equal Employment Opportunity Commission, cumulative ADA charge data for July 26, 1992 to September 30, 1996.

Mistargeted Enforcement

A prerequisite for any complaint-based system of enforcement is that citizens know something about the law. From 1990 to 1994 the federal government spent $44 million trying to educate employers, disabled workers, and the public about the ADA.[126] Yet a 1994 survey found only 40 percent of people with disabilities were even aware of the law's existence.[127] Among clients of vocational rehabilitation programs surveyed in 1994, 58 percent were aware of the ADA, but only 8 percent said they knew how to file a complaint.[128] Needless to say, even among those familiar with the law, many lack the resources or ability to put it to use.[129]

A complaint-based system of enforcement favors the claims of the better off. As it happens, 90 percent of those who use the ADA *are already employed*. And the modal ADA case does not involve wheelchair users like Vande Zande but instead people citing bad backs, perhaps, or mental disorders (table 6-3). The law's principal clients, in other words, are people with the common afflictions of middle-aged workers. If the point of the ADA was to bring people with graver impairments like blindness, deafness, or partial paralysis into the work force, the pattern of enforcement seems hardly to comport with that goal.

TABLE 6-3. *ADA Employment Claims, by Type of Impairment Most Often Cited, July 1992–September 1996*

Impairment	Number	Percent
Back impairment	13,243	18.2
Emotional-psychiatric	9,216	12.7
Neurological impairment	8,201	11.3
Extremities	6,562	9.0
Heart impairment	3,003	4.1
Diabetes	2,605	3.6
Substance abuse	2,437	3.3
Hearing impairment	2,094	2.8
Vision impairment	1,911	2.6
Blood disorders	1,883	2.6
HIV (subcategory)	1,276	1.8
Cancer	1,706	2.3
Asthma	1,266	1.7

Source: See table 6-2. List is incomplete; percentages do not add to 100.

Rights Do Not Create Jobs

The ADA was written on the premise that disabled people were oppressed more by society than by their disabilities. During debate over the ADA, proponents found plenty of evidence, anecdotal and statistical, of prejudice against disabled people. Advocates also were able to document higher levels of poverty, unemployment, and social isolation among the disabled. Missing from the debate, however, was any careful study of the actual determinants of employment among disabled people. ADA proponents too easily assumed that discrimination was the main cause of joblessness among disabled individuals.

If prejudice and structural barriers were in fact the main cause of unemployment among the disabled, the ADA might operate as advertised by its enthusiasts. The weight of the evidence, however, suggests that discrimination, while a factor, is only one source of the employment problem, and the effects of antidiscrimination rules are easily swamped by larger forces, such as changes in the structure of labor markets. Moreover, the problems faced by disabled persons who seek employment are diverse. The vast majority of working-age people with a disability are older adults who have acquired medical conditions such as arthritis, coronary disease, or backaches. Prejudi-

cial discrimination, the evil on which the backers of the ADA concentrated, does not appear to be much of an issue for this group, which
constitutes about 80 percent of the working-age disabled population,
though antidiscrimination laws can perhaps encourage employers to
retain and accommodate these workers as their health deteriorates.[130]

In studies comparing disabled and nondisabled workers, researchers have found that after controlling for health, education, and
experience, a wage differential of between 15 percent and 35
percent—which they impute to discrimination—remains. It is not
clear, however, what role rights laws would have in narrowing this
gap. When Marjorie Baldwin and William Johnson compared salaries
in 1972, before federal and state disability laws were enacted, with
salaries in 1984, they found the wage gap at best unchanged.[131]

Discrimination is but one difficulty facing seriously disabled
people seeking to join the labor force. For example, the loss of public
welfare and health benefits is a strong disincentive to employment.
Because disabled people tend to have more health problems than the
nondisabled, they are often unable to take jobs that offer inadequate
health care packages. Moreover, as economist Walter Oi puts it, "Disability steals time." Disabled people on average need more sick days,
more time for sleep, more time for getting around, and more time for
obtaining medical care. Because of this, many severely disabled
persons prefer part-time or flexible jobs, or no job at all, leaving them
with lower incomes.[132]

A 1994 Harris survey reflected these concerns. When asked why
they were not working, or not working full time, 80 percent of
working-age disabled cited low-paying jobs, 58 percent cited the need
for medical treatment or therapy, 35 percent cited a lack of work in
the field, and 31 percent cited the danger of losing benefits, all
matters the ADA does not address. Of the kinds of concerns the ADA
does attempt to address, employer attitudes were cited by 40 percent,
lack of access to transportation by 24 percent, and accommodations
by 16 percent.[133] Thirty percent also reported encountering job discrimination, but clearly this was just one among many obstacles.[134]

Add these facts to the inherent limitations of a court-based enforcement process, and it is not surprising that research generally
fails to demonstrate any clear employment bonus from antidiscrimination laws.[135] In a survey of very highly educated disabled people (a
population presumably most likely to benefit from the ADA), 39

percent said the law had made no difference *or made it harder* to obtain a job; only 28 percent said it had improved employment prospects, although the respondents did report improvements in other aspects of employment such as accommodation and barrier removal.[136] Meanwhile the ADA does not appear to have brought disabled people from welfare to work, as its proponents had envisioned. Enrollment in the two major disability welfare programs, SSI and SSDI, ballooned in the first several years after passage of the act.[137]

Of course the ADA is still a fairly new law, and it may yet prove beneficial to some groups of disabled people in the labor market, especially those already employed. Experts think the law, supplemented by other changes in disability policy, could help encourage employers to accommodate newly disabled workers. These experts doubt, however, that the law will help those on welfare find employment.[138] Thus it seems very unlikely now, five years after the employment provisions of the ADA went into operation, that the law will have the broad effects optimists had proclaimed. The effects of civil rights laws on the employment of African Americans has also been much debated, but studies demonstrate that the gap between black and white incomes narrowed in the early years of statutes, and even critics have had to acknowledge large employment gains during these years.[139] Nothing comparable can be seen so far in the case of the Americans with Disabilities Act.

One likely indication of the effect of ADA on employment of disabled people is the experience with earlier state and federal disability laws. The regulations for section 504, which governs disability discrimination in federally funded programs and in federal employment, went into effect in 1973. Between 1970 and 1982, when the government work force as a whole grew by a third, the proportion of disabled government workers rose from 9.9 percent to 10.2 percent. But from 1982 to 1987—years in which section 504 was in force—the proportion of government workers with disabilities decreased from 10.2 percent to 9.4 percent, and the absolute number of workers with disabilities dropped by 18 percent. Thus section 504 did not prevent workers with disabilities from bearing more than their share of government downsizing, although people with disabilities in government did fare better than those in other economic sectors undergoing retrenchment.[140]

State disability rights laws proliferated in the wake of section 504. By the time the ADA was enacted, forty-six states had similar laws, many of them granting extensive antidiscrimination rights and remedies comparable to the ADA.[141] Was this period of rights activism at the state level also a period of employment growth? The answer depends in part on whether one focuses on the whole disabled population or on just those looking for work. Baldwin and Johnson found big gains in employment for disabled men in the labor force between 1972 and 1984. But Edward Yelin found that between 1970 and 1992 the labor force participation rate for disabled people declined 2 percent; for the population as a whole during this same period it increased 12 percent.[142]

Yelin's research concludes that people with disabilities are a contingent labor force, laid off first when industries are in decline but also likely to benefit disproportionately when the economy improves, as they did during the expansionary 1980s. Yelin along with Baldwin and Johnson argue that ADA enforcement needs to be more carefully targeted if it is to have an effect on employment. They urge more careful research on employment levels in various industries and on costs and benefits of accommodations across disabilities and occupations.[143]

Costs of Accommodation

To some, the fact that disability rights laws may not gain employment for more disabled people is irrelevant. The rights of disabled people should not be abridged, whether or not nondiscrimination laws lead "toward independence," as the report by the National Council on the Handicapped prophesied. The argument is powerful if applied to simple prejudice, the kind that stopped Tony Coelho from getting a job simply because he had epilepsy or that prevented Lisa Carl from attending a movie because of her cerebral palsy. But can the argument be stretched to include "structural discrimination" (like the idea that stairs and other physical obstacles or even forty-hour work weeks discriminate against disabled people)? Some disability activists may believe that stairs and other obstacles to people with disabilities are objects of prejudice comparable to Jim Crow signs, but few in Congress who voted for the ADA would agree. The drafters of the ADA recognized as much when they subjected rights of accommodation to rudimentary cost-benefit standards, namely "reasonable accommodation" and "undue hardship."

In the absence of any law, disabled people themselves bear the burden of special accommodations. Given the fact that disabled people are on average poorer than the rest of society, this is an injustice. But it is not at all clear that shifting the cost of accommodation to another party is necessarily more just.[144] Of course, if one accepts the rights model's thesis that lack of accommodation is a kind of discrimination, the cost of rectifying structural barriers should fall on whoever has discriminated. But if accommodation is a good thing for society—a positive externality—then society as a whole should pay for it explicitly. The rights rhetoric that suffuses the ADA has served as a convenient way of disguising what is, at bottom, a selective off-budget mandate.[145]

Current law provides only a minimal subsidy for accommodation expenses. Small businesses get a 50 percent tax credit of up to $5,000 to defray ADA compliance costs. Businesses of any size can deduct up to $15,000 each year for some types of ADA costs.[146] These provisions would be sufficient if the cost of accommodations were minimal. Studies suggest that the costs of simple physical accommodation under title I, the employment section of the law, *average* $500 or less.[147] The estimated costs of accommodations, however, need to take account of much more than removing physical barriers. Changing working hours, eliminating nonessential functions from a job, allowing employees long absences during illness, and so on, ought to be factored in too. Broadly construed, the economic cost of accommodation is not likely to be trivial.

The costs of title III, the section governing public accommodations, will undoubtedly soar. The immediate mandate of title III is that public facilities be made accessible wherever "readily achievable."[148] As with "reasonable accommodation," this phrase will receive a variety of exegeses from the courts, but in the short term the judiciary is not likely to take an expansive interpretation. Much more expensive will be title III mandates for full accessibility in new construction and alteration of existing facilities. All workplaces will be required to meet these standards unless they are deemed "structurally impracticable," a very high hurdle.[149] One business consultant has estimated the total cost of accessibility standards for office buildings alone at $45 billion. The American Hospital Association estimates its costs at $20 billion.[150] No research has been performed on the aggregate costs of the ADA accessibility requirements, but as these figures indicate, they are potentially huge. Moreover, the costs will fall unevenly and will be largely unfunded. In some cases, they may well deter businesses and nonprofit agencies from renovating or building new facilities.

Title II of the ADA also hits state and local governments with a big bill. In the medium-sized city of Aurora, Colorado, just installing curb cuts will cost $30 million. The U.S. Conference of Mayors estimates that cities will spend $2.2 billion to comply with the ADA from 1994 to 1998; the National Association of Counties has estimated that county governments will spend $2.8 billion over the same period.[151] Costs to states are probably larger.[152] The Federal Transit Administration estimates that in the 1990s transit agencies will spend $65 million annually to make buses and rail cars accessible, $130 million to make stations accessible, and $700 million to provide additional paratransit services.[153]

If government agencies balk at these costs, they will be hauled into court, where judges will decide what exactly is an "undue burden." That task in itself will pose difficulties. But at least the costs of title II accommodations will be widely shared and not pushed onto individual businesses, unlike those under titles I and III.

Rights Can Be Messy

Under the rights model, costs and benefits are not to be weighed; discrimination is simply considered immoral and intolerable, whatever the price. That was the logic behind the first draft of the ADA, the "flat earth" version. But if one does not accept the rights model, costs and benefits matter a lot, and laws that mandate great infrastructure costs for a minimal social return are troubling. The ADA departs significantly from a pure rights model by providing defenses such as "undue burden," implying that costs are an issue. Thus the law looks like certain environmental statutes, which combine strong regulatory standards with various statutory hedges. Enforcement of the ADA may well end up looking like enforcement of the Clean Air Act: courts that are sympathetic to the regulations will focus on the standards, while courts that are sympathetic to the regulated will focus on how to hedge. Thus a kind of ad hoc, piecemeal, cost-benefit calculus will be conducted by the federal judiciary.[154]

This poses at least two basic problems. First, because the courts never speak with one voice, the law will receive multiple interpretations. Second, judicial deliberation about costs and benefits will sometimes become bizarre because courts lack the capacity for systematic policy evaluation.

Alternative Policies

The ultimate goal of the framers of the ADA was to bring disabled people into the mainstream of American life. To advance this public purpose, however, the act emphasizes various rights to be enforced through costly and unpredictable litigation. Is there an alternative to this litigious scheme? A brief comparison with the disability policies of some other Western nations is useful here.

Some Foreign Contrasts

The U.S. approach to disability policy has remained unusual. Many nations have embraced the U.S. disability movement's goal of freedom and independence for disabled people, but few have sought to reach that objective through antidiscrimination laws, and none has provided the ADA's extensive right to litigate claims. The dominant approach in western Europe has been the use of quotas (table 6-4). Employers are required to hire a certain percentage of disabled workers, usually drawn from a registry. The quotas are often underenforced and the targets rarely achieved, yet disability groups abroad typically favor retaining them.[155]

The German quota program is generally viewed as the most successful. Begun after the First World War, it currently sets a 6 percent target for employers with sixteen or more employees to employ severely handicapped people who are able to work only 50 percent of the time or less. Those employers who fail to reach the target must pay a special "compensation contribution" of DM 200 each month for every unfilled place in the quota, a levy that is used, in turn, to promote the employment of disabled people. Most employers pay the levy rather than fulfill the quota, but the larger employers often meet it. In 1982 employment of the handicapped reached 5.9 percent, but by 1992 it had slipped to 4.3 percent.[156] Research suggests that the German system is effective in retaining workers who have become disabled during their working lives, but less effective in recruiting disabled persons not already in the labor market.[157]

A second approach, increasingly common in western Europe, is to

TABLE 6-4. *Disability Employment Policies in Sixteen Nations, 1993*

Country	Quotas	Permanent employer subsidies	Antidiscrimination laws	Accommodation subsidies
Australia	. . .	. . .	X	X
Belgium	*a*	X	. . .	X
Britain	. . .		X	
Canada	*b*	. . .	X	X
Denmark	. . .	X	. . .	X
France	X	X	*c*	X
Germany	X	X	. . .	X
Greece	X	. . .	. . .	X
Ireland	X*d*	X	. . .	X
Italy	X	X*e*	. . .	X*e*
Luxembourg	X	X	. . .	X
Netherlands	X	. . .	. . .	. . .
Portugal	. . .	. . .	. . .	X
Spain	X	. . .	. . .	X
Sweden	. . .	X	. . .	X
United States	. . .	. . .	X	X

Source: Neil Lunt and Patricia Thornton, *Employment Policies for Disabled People* (British Employment Department, 1993).

a. Quota law on books is not enforced.

b. Employers of more than one hundred people are required to file an annual report detailing representation of four groups, including disabled people, and may be investigated if they are below employment targets.

c. Criminal penalties for discrimination on the basis of disability; civil action for quota violations.

d. Quotes in government employment only.

e. Some regions provide subsidies; no national program.

subsidize employers for hiring disabled people or to subsidize the disabled self-employed people themselves. In some nations this subsidy comes in a lump sum or is time limited; in others it is based on an assessment of lost productivity and continues indefinitely. Many nations also give grants for changes in the work environment, some of them far more extensive than the U.S. tax credits. Denmark's program, which reimburses employers for the costs of personal assistants, such as sign language interpreters, is especially generous.[158]

Besides quotas and direct subsidies, most economically advanced nations still rely predominantly on rehabilitation programs and welfare payments to improve the lives of the disabled. Disability discrimination laws have found a place mainly in Anglo-Saxon nations: Australia, Canada, New Zealand, Great Britain, and, most aggressively, the United States. Australia and Canada have national and provincial disability laws that resemble the Americans with Disabilities Act. Their laws require employers and managers of facilities and programs to provide "reasonable accommodation," although this appears to be a much more limited requirement than it is in the United States.[159]

But the Australian and Canadian laws differ from the ADA in a key respect: they are enforced by investigative boards and tribunals rather than courts.[160] In Ontario, for example, a commission investigates and attempts to settle complaints. If conciliation is unsuccessful, a board of inquiry is instated. The board hears the complaint in an informal proceeding and has broad power to issue injunctions to force compliance with the law. In addition, the board may issue monetary awards, including lost wages and benefits. However, "general damages" for mental anguish are capped at $10,000. The board's decision may be appealed to the courts, but for the most part grievances are redressed without litigation.[161]

The latest to adopt a disability rights law is Britain. The Disability Discrimination Act outlaws discrimination in employment and access to facilities. The British law does not appear to sweep as broadly as the ADA. The law allows complainants in employment cases to bring their claims to an industrial tribunal; public accessibility cases can be brought to court. Pain and suffering damages are allowed.[162] The struggle over disability rights in Britain offers a fascinating contrast to that in the United States. British disability activists were dissatisfied with the Disability Discrimination Act because it lacked a bureaucratic agency with the power and resources to enforce the law. Some British business interests also argued for a "one-stop shop," a disability commission that would coordinate implementation.[163] In the United States, neither disability activists nor business groups considered the creation of such an agency. The British story suggests that even where disability rights laws have come closest to the U.S. model, activists have preferred administrative remedies to legal wrangling.

The Agency Alternative

For better or worse, it is highly unlikely that the United States would adopt either the quotas or the more extensive subsidy schemes of western Europe, whatever their merits.[164] These programs are part of a form of government intervention in the labor market resisted in the United States. Nor is the United States likely to abandon the basic commitment to accommodating disabled people through the ADA and other disability rights laws. Nonetheless, international comparisons may suggest ways the United States might better implement the laws it has. Compared with other nations, even those with rights laws, the U.S. policy appears to be less flexible in accommodating mandates, less willing to distribute transparently the costs of such mandates, and, above all, much more willing to take quarrels to court. Reducing adversarial legalism in disability policy requires stepping away from judicial enforcement and toward administrative implementation.

The elements of such a shift might include:

1. *Creation of a New Disability Agency.* The agency would administer all the national disability rights laws, thus bringing together the scattered enforcement programs of various federal agencies. This consolidation would reflect the fact that disability discrimination laws pose a unique set of issues and hence should not be treated as just another brand of civil rights law.

2. *Elimination of Private Rights of Action.* The agency should be in charge of all enforcement; no private litigation would be allowed. Nor would the agency be obligated to act on any complaint whatsoever. The large volume of frivolous or opportunistic cases would be screened out. To do this, the agency ought to be funded more generously than the operations it would replace. The goal of the agency in enforcing disability laws should be to achieve integration flexibly and at the lowest cost to society. The agency, for example, would be explicitly charged with conducting research to target particular industries or types of facilities where discrimination is particularly egregious or where employment and accessibility gains can be achieved at least cost.[165]

3. *Strict Limits on Judicial Review of Agency Decisions.* The agency should be permitted to develop industry-specific regulations fleshing out phrases such as "reasonable accommodation" and "undue

burden" in close consultation with disability groups and businesses. Again, in developing regulations the objective should be to provide accessibility at least cost. Judicial review of agency rule making and enforcement priorities should be limited so that only actions that clearly exceed the bounds of the agency's statutory authority could be overturned.

4. *On-Budget Subsidies for Mandated Accommodations.* A partial or full tax credit for the costs of all mandated accommodations could prove extremely expensive, especially if the credit is extended to construction and renovation expenses under title III. But budgeting such costs explicitly might improve compliance and make the mandates more equitable, or at least force taxpayers to decide how much disability remediation is worth buying.

Politically, to be sure, these proposals seem farfetched, since they would undoubtedly antagonize not only disability activists and conservative supporters of the ADA, but also the law's harshest critics. All of these groups have reasons to oppose a bureaucracy of such scope. In fact, the reasons Americans are so attracted to court-based enforcement, and thus so prone to adversarial legalism, are all the more clear once this administrative option is imagined. Conservatives supported the ADA in part because they wanted to avoid creating a new bureaucracy or new budgetary commitments. Their argument was that the ADA would not enlarge the welfare state; if anything, the law would move people *off* welfare. It seems implausible that these visionaries would now favor the creation of a powerful, centralized regulatory bureaucracy or the added expenditure of subsidizing accommodations.

Nor would advocates for the disabled be charmed by the idea of an agency. Their bad experiences with administrative enforcement of section 504, together with their commitment to independence from bureaucrats and various paternalistic helpers, would incline them to be skeptical. Moreover, unlike their counterparts in the British disability movement, U.S. activists might conclude that an enforcement agency would be easily intimidated and vulnerable to budget cuts. Indeed, the underfunding of the EEOC and the other agencies charged with enforcing the ADA seems to vindicate this view. Better, it would seem, to put enforcement in the hands of hundreds of courts and thousands of litigants, safe from the clutches of unsympathetic and budget-conscious politicians.

Finally, many of the ADA's critics are not likely to be impressed with the agency alternative either. If one objects to the large infrastructure expenses and accommodation rights imposed by the ADA on the grounds of pure economic efficiency, a scheme that simply shifts enforcement from courts to a new bureaucracy and costs from business to the government solves nothing.

Despite all the complaints about adversarial legalism in American public policy, and despite all the costs it imposes, there is not much of a constituency for limiting the phenomenon. As familiar as all sides are with the dangers and difficulties of litigation, Americans are even more concerned about the dangers of big-time bureaucratic regulation.

Conclusion

Disability activists seek to enable disabled people to participate fully and equally in all aspects of day-to-day life. In the United States the disability movement has adopted rights and litigation, what I have called the tools of adversarial legalism, as the primary means to this end. This choice has been influenced by the individualistic and antistatist cast of American political culture and by the fragmented structure of U.S. government, both of which have led U.S. reformers of every kind to look to the courts for intervention.

But litigation is a clumsy and expensive tool, often abused. Thus rights-based disability policies like the ADA are frequently unfair, intrusive, uncertain, and inefficient. The cost of adversarial legalism can be seen in many areas of U.S. public policy. Environmental policy is notoriously beset by it, as regulators and regulatees get buffeted by litigation.[166] Pitched court battles between industry and government engulf occupational health and safety rules.[167] Personal injury litigation delivers uneven, unpredictable compensation to victims at often inordinate cost. It is hard to put a price tag on these problems, unlike the more obvious costs of the manifold welfare and labor regulations of western Europe. All the same, America's adversarialism limits the effectiveness of some U.S. domestic social policies.

The Americans with Disabilities Act exemplifies the limitation. This ambitious social experiment was trumpeted as a means of bolstering the competitiveness of the U.S. economy by facilitating job opportunities and accommodations for handicapped citizens. The principal economic consequence of this project, however, has been to stimulate additional lawsuits in an already litigious U.S. labor market, while adding few disabled employees to the work force. The ADA's message of freedom and independence for people with disabilities is morally uplifting.[168] In the end, this may be all that matters. But for now, as a substantive solution to the needs of disabled people, much less to the exigencies of many U.S. businesses, the law disappoints.

COMMENT BY WALTER Y. OI

The Americans with Disabilities Act is a piece of legislation that has the right intentions but fails to provide the programs necessary to achieve those intentions. Discrimination in the labor market and the failure of society to acknowledge its responsibility to ensure rights to access for people with disabilities were presumed to be the principal reasons for their status as second-class citizens. I opposed the ADA in 1990 because it held forth the promise of the American dream without supplying a program for attaining that dream. Thomas Burke provides us in the first section of his chapter with a description of the developments leading to the passage of the ADA. At the conference, Burke amplified on the reason for the "rights" track by pointing to the diversity of disabling conditions, a point that was articulated in the interpretative guidelines issued by the Equal Employment Opportunities Commission with respect to the impossibility of defining a bright line separating disabled from nondisabled individuals. "This case by case approach is essential if qualified individuals with varying disabilities are to receive equal opportunities to compete for an infinitely diverse range of jobs. For this reason, neither the ADA nor this regulation can supply the correct answer in advance for each employment decision concerning an individual with a disability."

Thus a "rights" approach enforced by litigation is allegedly the only way to ensure compliance with a nondiscriminatory employment policy. Like Burke, I am not persuaded by this argument. Burke's comparison of U.S. disability policies with those in other countries and his evaluation of the effectiveness of the ADA in achieving its announced goals of equality, dignity, and independence are less satisfactory.

On the Rights Track   293

A Policy for a Disadvantaged Class

The shape of a policy to improve the well-being of a disadvantaged class depends on the reason for the disadvantage. Societies have always supported those in poverty. Churches and local governments in the Middle Ages assumed the responsibility of supplying food and shelter. Questions were never raised about caring for the deserving poor who for reasons of health, age, and capacities were unable to work and earn a livelihood. However, the citizens were skeptical about some beggars who became physically threatening when they did not receive enough alms. The English Poor Laws adopted a doctrine of pauperism—namely, if one gave the poor a dole, they would never leave poverty. Some reformists embraced a policy of work for the impoverished who would be housed in poorhouses. Nearly all these poorhouses went bankrupt.[169]

We are still struggling to find the proper policy to combat poverty. A Civil Rights Act was passed in 1964 to improve the status of African Americans. Policies have been adopted to assist those disadvantaged by a disabling condition. These efforts began with state workmen's compensation laws, which supplied income and some medical care to persons injured at a workplace covered by the laws. Congress enacted legislation to provide income benefits to the blind and permanently disabled. That coverage was extended to other disabling conditions under the Supplemental Security Income program. The Social Security Administration introduced a broader disability insurance program in 1956.

In spite of these policies, however, people with disabilities are still in a weak economic position. Only 27.8 percent of working-age men with a work disability were gainfully employed in March 1988 compared with 74.4 percent of nondisabled men.[170] Additionally, disabled persons were denied access to many public and quasi-public places by architectural and transport barriers. Fifty years ago, the responsibility for improving the lives of this disadvantaged class would have been left to families, friends, and private charities. But by the late 1970s, people with disabilities had observed that other disadvantaged classes turned to the state for transfers of cash and in-kind incomes as well as for the creation and protection of civil rights. Indeed, recipients of checks from social service agencies talked about their "welfare rights," which almost became an entitlement. In the late 1970s and the 1980s Congress enacted amendments to section 504 of the Rehabilitation Act of 1973, passed the Education for All Handicapped Children, and worked on an omnibus policy. On July 26, 1990, President Bush signed the Americans with Disabilities Act.

The Rights Model and Its Employment Aim

Section 504 of the Rehabilitation Act of 1973 set the stage for the ADA in its language: "No otherwise qualified individual in the United States . . . shall by reason of handicap be excluded from participation in, or be denied the benefits of, or be subjected to discrimination under any program or activity receiving federal assistance." One can almost catch the congressional staff members plagiarizing the language from earlier legislation by substituting "handicap" for "race." According to Burke, the essence of the disability rights movement (at least among activists) is the belief that disabled people are oppressed more by society than by their disabilities. There are surely similarities in the way the disabled are segregated and subject to discrimination in personal affairs and in the labor market. Burke observes that people with disabilities should treat the removal of barriers and other modifications not as a privilege conceded to them, but as a right that had been denied, an injustice to be rectified. He describes those who pushed through the legislation, identifying Justin Dart and Evan Kemp as the leading proponents. But there is unlikely to be much agreement on the two or three persons who are most responsible for a policy change. I would have singled out Lex Frieden and tried to identify some of the key people on the pertinent congressional staffs who drafted the legislation.

In addition to rights to access to public places and services, title I created equal employment rights which can be summed up as follows: "A covered entity is prohibited from discriminating against a qualified individual with a disability in regard to job application, hiring, discharge, compensation, training, or other terms, conditions, or privileges of employment. Employers are required to make reasonable accommodations to the known physical or mental limitations of an otherwise qualified individual unless to do so would impose an undue hardship." No clearly defined line separates a person with a disability from the rest. Who decides when an applicant is qualified? A reasonable accommodation is to be determined by the need for it and whether it imposes an undue hardship. Operational definitions and the resolution of disputes are important in enforcing the act to ensure the attainment of the employment goal.

An Elastic Supply of Disabled Workers

Ethicon, a division of Johnson & Johnson that manufactures surgical needles, was named as an employer of the year by the President's Committee on Employment of People with Disabilities for employing nearly 200 developmentally disabled workers at its plant in San Angelo, Texas. I inquired about the training, turnover, and performance of these workers and expressed my surprise that a community the size of San Angelo had as many as 200 developmentally disabled individuals willing and qualified to work. The representative of Ethicon told me, "We pay them at union scales, and with that kind of money, there are lots of developmentally disabled folks who want to work."

Disability is not like race or gender. The ADA defines a person as disabled if he or she has a physical or mental impairment that substantially limits one or more of the major life activities, has a record of such an impairment, and is regarded as having such an impairment. Martin Geary, an assistant secretary of health and human services in the Bush administration, persuaded me that disability is subjective. The impairment has to be obvious and the person must accept the fact of a serious limitation or must have been told that he or she has such an impairment. As long as a person can cope, he or she is often unwilling to be considered disabled. The impossibility of developing general guidelines is apparent is the Equal Employment Opportunity Commission regulations: "This case-by-case approach is essential if qualified individuals with varying disabilities are to receive equal opportunities to compete for an infinitely diverse range of jobs. For this reason, neither the ADA nor this regulation can supply the correct answer in advance for each employment decision concerning an individual with a disability."

Jane West contends that even this case-by-case determination may be inadequate because a case today, meaning an employment decision involving a particular firm and a named individual, could be different from the apparently "same" case tomorrow: "unlike race and gender, disability is often a dynamic and changing characteristic. . . . Furthermore, some disabilities change in their intensity from day to day or week to week and may require different accommodations at various times."[171] Disabilities are different, and it is important to distinguish among them on the bases of severity, age at onset, and diagnostic group, which serves as a proxy for life expectancy.[172] The incidence of disability is sure to respond to the incentives and penalties for being classified as a person with a disability. The number of disabled persons based on self-assessments has been growing even though health interview surveys indicate a declining incidence of disabling conditions.

Workplace Accommodations

Title I of the ADA mandates that a covered entity is prohibited from practicing employment discrimination against an otherwise qualified person with a disability who can perform the *essential functions* of the job with or without *reasonable accommodations*. An employee may sometimes be asked to drive a car, but driving may not be an essential function if there are enough other employees with licenses who could perform any driving chores. The larger the work force, the fewer the number of essential functions that have to be performed by an otherwise qualified person. It is claimed that the vast majority of workplaces entail little cost to provide reasonable accommodation. A study by Sears revealed an average cost of only $112, while a Louis Harris survey commissioned by the international Center for the Disabled in 1994 found an average cost per accommodation of only $223. Kerwin Charles reported that the most frequently mentioned accommodations involve flexible hours, shorter hours, time-off privileges for physician visits, and reassignments to other positions within the firm.[173] The so-called cost of these accommodations is usually reported to be zero, which may sometimes be a gross understatement. Jobs are not easily described by listing the essential functions. There can be a significant pay gap between part-time and full-time employees on what sometimes appears to be the same job. Evidence of this type ought to be studied in assessing what constitutes pay equity and accommodation costs.

Access to Public Places and Services

Professor Burke directs attention to the three primary concepts in the disability rights movement: equality of opportunity, dignity, and independence. All three are promoted by a policy of open access. The accommodations needed to realize access are often group specific. Should their costs be allocated to those who benefit from them? Consider the example of lift line service as opposed to installation of elevator lifts for all urban buses. The cost per ride using the elevator-equipped buses is substantially higher than the cost per ride on a lift line van. Yet a proponent of disability rights would argue for equipping the buses because the service is, in principle, available to all potential wheel-bound riders. Again, there have to be substantial option values for wide hallways and large bathrooms to justify the access requirements for apartment buildings and motels.

Explanations for and Disappointment with the ADA

In his analysis Burke appeals to a principle of distributive justice to explain the passage of the ADA. But he also comments that Americans believe disabled people are blameless victims and deserve help whether through public or private charities. I suspect that both arguments were advanced in support of the act; is this borne out in the legislative record? The rights track seeks to achieve a just distribution through the establishment of judicial rights enforced through litigation rather than bureaucratic regulation. Sandra Parrino, chairperson of the National Council of the Handicapped, proclaimed, "Current federal expenditures for disability can be significantly redirected from dependency-related approaches to programs that enhance independence and productivity of people with disabilities, thereby engendering future efficiencies in federal spending."[174] At the time she made this statement, $60 billion was being spent annually on benefit payments and medical care while only $3 billion was devoted to training and rehabilitation. I suspect that the allocation of federal and state monies to dependency-related activities versus independence-promoting activities in employment has not changed much. In 1986, some 33 percent of disabled working-age adults were employed, but this rate dropped to 31 percent in 1994. The civil rights approach was clearly inadequate to solve the employment problem. As Nancy Lee Jones has commented, "Seldom do race, sex, or national origin present any obstacle to an individual when performing a job or participating in a program. Disabilities by their very nature, however, may make certain jobs or types of participation impossible."[175] Insufficient attention was paid to the nature of a disabling condition and the wide diversity of disabling conditions. The proponents of the ADA had not thought through the difficult issues involved in raising the earnings capabilities of people with disabilities. Like the utopian writers, the activists behind the rights movement and the framers of the legislation were right with respect to the attributes of an ideal world with well-paying and stimulating work for all disabled persons and a barrier-free environment in which to enjoy the fruits of an upper middle-class income. But like Charles Fourier and Karl Marx, they were not quite so strong in the details of the programs that would get us there.

Finally, Burke comments on the difference between U.S. disability policies and those in Europe. He speculates that the U.S. emphasis on rights stems from America's negative view of welfare programs and of neediness more generally. He lists eight nations—France, Germany, Greece, Ireland, Italy, Luxembourg, The Netherlands, and Spain—that have enacted employment quotas (Japan could be added to that list). Companies with 500 or more employees are required in Germany to set aside 6 percent of all jobs for people with disabilities (I believe that the quota in Japan is 2 or 3 percent). Failure to meet the quota obliges the employer to make an annual contribution to a fund to be used to train and educate disabled persons. Two questions arise. First, how should one go about setting the figure for the quota? Should it be 6 percent, 4 percent, or what? Recall that in the March 1988 Current Population Studies, 8.6 percent of working-age adults reported the presence of a work disability.[176] Second, what is the proper penalty or tax for noncompliance? I suspect that Congress refused to impose an employment quota because of the decision in *Griggs v. Duke Power Co.* (1971). The framers of the Americans with Disabilities Act were hoping to obtain what Richard Burkhauser called "Morality on the Cheap," doing good without the need to ask for a budget appropriation.[177]

COMMENT BY WALTER OLSON

Since leaving office George Bush has repeatedly cited the Americans with Disabilities Act as the most important domestic legislation of his presidency. It is certainly among the most remarkable. The *New*

York Times called it an "unabashed venture into social engineering," yet it sailed through easily with the votes of Newt Gingrich, Phil Gramm, Orrin Hatch and Strom Thurmond. Analysts from the National Association of Manufacturers called it potentially the most costly business mandate in American history, but most organized industry groups, including the NAM itself, did not see fit to oppose it. It was drafted in large part by the Washington office of the American Civil Liberties Union with provisions to maximize the scope for litigation, then was pushed to passage with the ardent support of a chief executive whose most passionate campaign moments had come when he denounced the ACLU in his first White House run and decried excessive litigation in his second. Although it shifted billions of dollars from some people's pockets to those of others, the bill apparently attracted no attention from political action committees and came indeed about as close as legislation ever comes to a pure instance of lawmakers' passing something because they wanted to be well thought of rather than because they expected anything more tangible from it.

The story of the ADA can be depressing for someone who thinks massive new legislation destined to convulse whole sectors of society should be preceded by a battle of intelligently argued think-tank monographs on both sides, with plenty of numbers and the best light of social science being brought to bear. The fact is that most members of Congress showed only the most perfunctory interest in the actual job situation of the disabled or the likely effects of the law. ADA supporters presented a few snippets of data on the supposedly low cost of accommodation and the desire of disabled persons to find work, data that were repeated again and again. These numbers proved almost nothing; Thomas Burke has pointed out some of the weaknesses of the purported costs of accommodation, and others could be pointed out as well. But the numbers were accepted at face value, as was the law's assertion that 43 million Americans were disabled, a number that could just as defensibly have been set at 8 million or at 108 million. A few economists who had studied disability, such as Walter Oi and Richard Burkhauser, offered sound advice, but legislators managed to ignore that advice almost entirely.

Even now, as Burke points out, research data on results are remarkably scanty considering the law's importance. We know some things about employment and about the number of persons collecting government disability benefits. But no one has investigated many of the law's other effects, which I think is in a way rational given that so few minds seemed to change when the bombshell went off about how the share of disabled persons holding jobs had gone down after the law's passage. If that did not change anyone's mind, I see no reason why further new data would. My comments will therefore not conclude with the usual call for more research.

I generally admired Burke's comments, and my differences with him are mostly of emphasis. In particular, I recognize that cautious judges have been giving a narrower scope to required accommodation than many on either side had expected. Even so, I take a more alarmist view than he does of the mischief likely to stem from this law; it is very vague and far-reaching in its dictates, businesses are petrified of being caught up in its provisions, and its doctrines are not easily comprehended without a more widespread will to do so than at present prevails. New York courts are currently debating whether to interpret a thirty-year-old civil rights law to block a subway fare hike on the grounds that it inflicts a greater burden on minorities to give suburban commuter rail lines a heavier subsidy per trip. I do not think it fanciful to expect that twenty or twenty-five years hence someone will be creatively invoking the ADA in some equally unexpected way to override democratic or private decisionmaking. That was certainly the history with section 504, which started out much more modestly.

I would like to touch on three points. First, I want to offer some added background on the job situation of the disabled, because it helps explain the ADA's failure to achieve its employment aims and also why that failure should not have been surprising. Second, I want to add a comment or two about Burke's observations on the road not taken in handicap law, namely a strong-agency model. Finally, I want to offer a caution on our tendency to run together adversarialism and rights as concepts.

The public campaign for the ADA leaned heavily on the proposition that more disabled would be able to find jobs. "Enabling millions of disabled people to work," declared a *Boston Globe* editorial, "will more than repay the cost of making such accommodation." "If the bill helps them find jobs, not only will they pay taxes, they'll give up an annual $60 billion in government disability benefits," ran the *USA Today* account. The *New York Times* editorially found such arguments "crucial." ADA advocate Frank Bowe summed it all up: "Spending money on independence will save much more on dependence. . . . This is a problem we can 'solve by throwing money at it.'"

The interesting thing was that in the preceding twenty years the federal government had in effect already conducted an experiment on this very subject, and the results were available for all to peruse. During that period Congress had passed a raft of very strong laws that should have much improved the job prospects of the disabled. Section 504 had forced local government to spend billions on accessible public transit, put universities through massive renovations, and required government and its contractors not only to offer employment accommodation to the disabled but also to practice affirmative action on their behalf. Lawmakers had also mandated the monumentally expensive special education system, which should have been good for the job prospects of future disabled adults.

Anyone would have expected these laws to lead to a marked improvement in the job status of the disabled. Anyone would have been wrong. Beginning in the early 1970s the labor force participation of the disabled instead began to deteriorate rapidly. For disabled men, it fell from 64 percent in the early 1970s to 54 percent in the mid-1980s. Disabled women likewise lost ground compared with women in general. When they were employed at all, disabled persons retreated from full-time into part-time work; the share of disabled men working full time, for example, fell from 30 to 23 percent from 1981 to 1988. And the earnings shortfall of disabled compared with able-bodied workers widened between 1980 and 1987 from 23 to 30 percent for men and from 30 to 38 percent for women. Confirming these trends, the number of successful placements in vocational rehabilitation programs began to falter, declining from 325,000 in 1975 to 220,000.

Changes in technology made this decline even harder to explain. Computers and other new inventions were being hailed as a triumph over physical limitation and as the perfect workplace leveler. Voice activation, talking screens, telecommuting, and the widespread replacement of physical with keyboard controls were bringing many jobs within reach of disabled persons for the first time.

ADA advocates were accustomed to explain everything bad that happened to the disabled by reference to discrimination and exclusion. Employers "simply do not want to hire or accommodate physically disabled workers," said Sandra Parrino of the National Council on Disability, which is why the disabled are "forced to accept welfare." The scarcity of disabled persons in society's most desirable jobs, according to ADA drafter Robert Burgdorf Jr., "appears to be largely the result of discrimination." Advocates pointed to surveys showing that disabled persons said they wanted to work, yet most were out of the labor force. What more proof could we need that the fault lay with those doing the hiring?

But that explanation made no sense. Almost everyone agreed that these affronts had lessened perceptibly over this long period of consciousness raising. And there was another obvious fact, although it was very little talked of during the ADA campaign: the most important, visible form of discrimination regarding the handicapped was discrimination in their favor. Explicit hire-the-handicapped campaigns had long been common in both government and big companies, where they roused none of the controversy associated with favoritism toward other disadvantaged groups.

In short, the reported decline in disabled people's job participation after the ADA's passage simply continued an unhappy trend that had been going on for years in defiance of legislation aimed at expanding employment of them. The only possible explanation requires a look at the elephant-in-the-living-room issue from which ADA proponents averted their eyes, the system of federal payments to the disabled.

These payments had been liberalized and taken over from the states in the early 1970s, with Congress not only boosting payments substantially but broadening the definition of disability and easing procedural rules for obtaining a disability determination. Outlays began a dizzying rise, and the number of nonelderly persons legally defined as disabled proceeded to triple in sixteen years, as if the country had been through a major war, although public health data revealed not the least decline in the well-being of the relevant population. The problem, of course, is that disability is far from an objective medical matter. Friendly doctors and lawyers could help get a person on the program; some had practices devoted to nothing else.

But the disability program imposed on recipients (including the traditional disabled whose extent of disability was not in question) an even more insidious welfare trap than did Aid to Families with Dependent Children: recipients often gave up even more by choos-

ing to work instead of staying home. Experience with other programs had shown that when recipients were caught in a disincentive trap, survey answers expressing an abstract desire to work were
of little value in predicting whether they would actually take available jobs. Nor had program officials had much success in altering
their decisions by tinkering with existing jobs to make their schedules more convenient, match the client's skills and preferences more
closely, and so forth. Yet the promises for the ADA followed exactly
this format: tailor jobs more closely and welfare dependency will
end.

Let me turn to Burke's discussion of the road not taken: establishing an agency with strong powers to enforce a law like this as
opposed to a general free-for-all pushed forward by anyone who
cares to sue. Without actually favoring such an agency, I find this
omission highly revealing as an indication of how the system in
America now works as opposed to what came before in this country
and what still prevails in most countries. There is some literature on
how and when this cultural shift took place in the civil rights movement, whose agenda set the general tone for the ADA. Until 1972 or
so, according to these accounts, civil rights advocates had pushed to
make the EEOC a strong agency by giving it cease-and-desist
powers. Then abruptly they dropped the idea and began fostering
individual litigation to which they have clung ever since: higher
damages, more generous attorney fee awards, little or no conciliation, and so forth.

There is much more to be said about the adversarial approach that
the ADA so well typifies, but I would close with one caution. It is easy
to confound the prevalence of rights talk in America with the prevalence of adversarialism and litigation. There is a rhetorical overlap in
that litigious persons go around constantly talking about their rights.
Yet the two concepts are in fact distinct; societies with less-than-clear
rights can be at each other's throats, and many applications of
rights—for instance, the routine enforcement of property rights in
land against theft and trespass—are done amid very low levels of litigation even here. The source of our adversarialism may lie not so
much in America's longstanding identification as the land of rights,
but in what kind of rights we have been inventing recently and how
exactly we invite people to vindicate them. But that is a story for
another day.

NOTES

1. *Congressional Record*, daily ed, September 7, 1989, p. S10714.

2. Cary Segall, "Disabled Woman Suing State," *Wisconsin State Journal* (March 9, 1993), p. 1D; and Elizabeth Brixey, "Access Always on Some Minds," *Wisconsin State Journal* (December 10, 1994), p. 1C. To Judge Richard Posner, who wrote an opinion in the case for the Seventh Circuit Court of Appeals, Vande Zande's claim was, if not puzzling, at least unwarranted. In upholding a district court decision, Posner concluded that the accommodations she had asked for were unreasonable and granted the defendant summary judgment in *Vande Zande v. Wisconsin*, U.S. Court of Appeals, Seventh Circuit, January 5, 1995; see *National Disability Law Reporter*, vol. 6 (February 16, 1995), pp. 87–91. Thus the case never reached trial. Vande Zande quit the job and has since been appointed by President Clinton to the Architectural Barriers and Transportation Compliance Board, a federal agency that creates disability accessibility standards.

3. 42 US.C. 12112.

4. 42 US.C. 12131, 12148, 12181, 12182, 12183. In addition, title IV of the ADA mandates that phone companies provide teletype translators so that deaf people can communicate with the hearing.

5. Damages available under Title I are tied to the remedies available to plaintiffs under the *Civil Rights Act of 1964*. 42 U.S.C. 12117.

6. 42 U.S.C. 12131, 12181, 12182, 12183, 12188.

7. Robert A Kagan, "Do Lawyers Cause Adversarial Legalism?" *Law and Social Inquiry*, vol. 19 (Winter 1994), p. 3.

8. *Congressional Record*, daily ed., September 7, 1989, p. S10714.

9. Indeed, in this case the outcome came relatively quickly, since Vande Zande's case never reached trial. If she had won the motion for summary judgment, the case might have dragged on for several more years, with pretrial motions, a jury trial, and possibly an appeal. Segall, "Disabled Woman Suing State," p. 1D.

10. Jane West, *Federal Implementation of the Americans with Disabilities Act, 1991–94* (New York: Milbank Memorial Fund, 1994), p. 11.

11. The figure of 49 million is taken from the 1991–92 Census Bureau Survey of Income and Program Participation cited in Peter David Blanck, "Employment Integration, Economic Opportunity, and the Americans with Disabilities Act: Empirical Study from 1990–93," *Iowa Law Review*, vol. 79 (1994), p. 855, n. 8. A more appropriate measure of disability, according to some researchers, is the number of people who are limited in their abilities to perform everyday activities. This approach generates an estimate of 36 million, including 2 million people in institutionalized settings. See Mitchell P. LaPlante, "The Demographics of Disability," *Milbank Quarterly*, vol. 69, supplement 1/2 (1991), p. 65.

The number of Americans between the ages of sixteen and sixty-four with a "work disability" is estimated (based on 1995 census data) to be 16.9 million, or 10.1 percent of the working-age population. Mitchell P. Laplante and others, "Disability and Employment," *Disability Statistics Abstract*, vol. 11 (1996), p. 1.

12. 42 U.S.C. 12102.

13. For disallowance of history of treatment for mental illness see testimony of John L. Wodatch, Justice Department, U.S. Senate Subcommittee on Disability Policy, July 26, 1995. On insurers and AIDS benefits see "Ruling May Stop Insurers from Limiting AIDS Benefits," *San Francisco Chronicle*, October 19, 1994, p. E3. On blind people and juries see 816 F. Supp. 12 (D.D.C. 1993).

14. Congress banned discrimination against the handicapped in civil service in 1964. Five states adopted similar bans; a few even had nondiscrimination laws in certain job categories, particularly teaching. See Jacobus tenBroek, "The Right to Live in the World: The Disabled in the Law of Torts," *California Law Review*, vol. 54 (1966), p. 846.

Access for mobility-impaired people was raised as an issue in the 1950s by paralyzed veterans who fought for accessible facilities at Veterans Administration hospitals. In 1959 several disability groups met with the American Standards Association to agree on standards for architectural accessibility. These were adopted by many states in the mid-1960s as part of building accessibility laws and eventually by the federal government for its buildings. See Rita Varela, "Changing Social Attitudes and Legislation Regarding Disability," in Nancy M. Crewe, Irving Kenneth Zola and Associates, eds., *Independent Living for Physically Disabled People* (San Francisco: Jossey-Bass, 1983), pp. 28–48.

These early laws were generally enforced by administrative mechanisms. An exception was Wisconsin's accessibility law, which created a private right of action. See tenBroek, "Right to Live in the World," p. 863.

15. Richard K. Scotch, *From Good Will to Civil Rights:Transforming Federal Disability Policy* (Temple University Press, 1984), p. 36.

16. Edward D. Berkowitz, "The American Disability System in Historical Perspective," in Edward D. Berkowitz, ed., *Disability Policies and Government Programs* (Praeger, 1979), pp. 44–45.

17. Gerben DeJong, "The Movement for Independent Living: Origins, Ideology and Implications for Disability Research," Medical Rehabilitation Institute, Tufts–New England Medical Center, March 1979, pp. 32–37.

18. DeJong, "Movement for Independent Living," p. 60.

19. Edward D. Berkowitz, *Disabled Policy: America's Programs for the Handicapped* (Cambridge University Press, 1987), p. 203.

20. Jacobus tenBroek, "The Disabled in the Law of Welfare," *California Law Review*, vol. 54 (1966), p. 809; tenBroek,"The Right to Live in the World," p. 841; and Leonard Kriegel, "Uncle Tom and Tiny Tim: Some Reflections on the Cripple as Negro," *American Scholar*, vol. 38 (1969), pp. 412–30.

21. In *The Pennsylvania Association for Retarded Children et al v. Commonwealth of Pennsylvania et al.*, 343 F. Supp. 279 (1972), a federal court concluded that the plaintiffs had a "colorable" claim under both the equal protection clause and the due process clause in approving a settlement reached between

the parties, but the decision did not reach the issue of suspect or semisuspect status. In *Mills et al.* v. *Board of Education of the District of Columbia et al.*, 348 F. Supp. 866 (1972), the court found a violation of the due process clause because the District was excluding mentally retarded children from schooling, but the decision also rested on local statutes. These cases paved the way for the 1975 passage of the Education of All Handicapped Children Act, which guarantees all children with disabilities a "free, appropriate education."

The clearest discussion of the place of disabled people in constitutional law came much later in *Cleburne* v. *Cleburne Living Center, Inc.*, 473 U.S. 432 (1984). Here the Supreme Court ruled that the mentally retarded were not a suspect class deserving of special protection under the Fourteenth Amendment.

22. Interviews with Evan Kemp Jr. and Bob Funk, December 16, 1993, Washington D.C., and Lex Frieden, April 21, 1994, Washington, D.C. Funk contends that the civil rights model might not have come to prominence if not for section 504 because the proponents of independent living were interested mainly in creating a more effective model of service delivery. But David Pfeiffer, a Massachusetts-based disability activist, contends disability rights was an important focus of the disability movement even before section 504 (personal communication, May 6, 1996).

Frieden notes that in Berkeley one could easily see the distinction between the two parts of the disability movement: "CIL (the Center for Independent Living) was on one side of Telegraph Avenue and DREDF (the Disability Rights and Education Defense Fund) was on the other side of the street. And a lot of times that street was pretty wide. There were differences of opinion even on Telegraph Avenue on where the movement should go, and there still are." In contrast, Arlene Mayerson, a top DREDF attorney, sees little distinction between the independent living movement and the civil rights movement. Interview with Mayerson, June 2, 1994, Berkeley, California.

23. Robert A. Katzmann, *Institutional Disability: The Saga of Transportation Policy for the Disabled* (Brookings, 1986).

24. 87 Stat. 355.

25. Katzmann, *Institutional Disability*, pp. 50–54; and Robert L. Burgdorf Jr., *Disability Discrimination in Employment Law* (District of Columbia School of Law, 1995), p. 275.

26. Katzmann, *Institutional Disability*, pp. 56–57.

27. Scotch, *From Good Will to Civil Rights*, pp. 150–51.

28. Edward V. Roberts, "Into the Mainstream: The Civil Rights of People with Disabilities," *Civil Rights Digest*, vol. 11 (Winter 1979), pp. 23–24.

29. Susan Olson has noted that for blind and deaf people there are inherent communication problems for working together. "Perhaps because of this and because they organized earliest and separately, deaf and blind persons have been among the slowest to acknowledge a need for cross-disability cooperation." She commented that the bylaws of the National Federation of the Blind went so far as to prohibit coalitions with other disability groups. Susan M. Olson, *Clients and Lawyers: Securing the Rights of Disabled Persons* (Westport, Conn.: Greenwood Press, 1984), p. 48.

30. Robert Katzmann concludes that "it is questionable whether the [American Coalition for Citizens with Disabilities] could have been born without the rights premise. If government defined federal policy toward the disabled as a matter of claims involving the allocation of finite resources, then presumably each of the many groups within the ACCD would have competed with the others to secure funds for its own constituency." Katzmann, *Institutional Disability*, p. 111.

31. Robert Funk, "Disability Rights: From Caste to Class in the Context of Civil Rights," in Alan Gartner and Tom Joe, eds., *Images of the Disabled, Disabling Images* (Praeger, 1987), p. 7.

32. Frank Bowe, *Handicapping America: Barriers to Disabled People* (Harper and Row, 1978), p. 224. See also Harlan Hahn, "Introduction: Disability Policy and the Problem of Discrimination," *American Behavioral Scientist*, vol. 28 (January-February 1985), pp. 293–318.

33. Evan Kemp Jr., "Aiding the Disabled: No Pity, Please," *New York Times*, September 3, 1981, p. A19. Harlan Hahn, an academic who has written extensively on disability issues, sees a sinister side to paternalism because it "enables the dominant elements of a society to express profound and sincere sympathy for the members of a minority group while, at the same time, keeping them in a position of social and economic subordination." See "Disability and Rehabilitation Policy: Is Paternalistic Neglect Really Benign?" *Public Administration Review*, vol. 42 (July-August 1982), pp. 385–89.

34. Frank Bowe, *Rehabilitating America: Toward Independence for Disabled and Elderly People* (Harper and Row, 1980), p. xi; and Bowe, *Handicapping America*, p. 171.

35. Kemp, "Aiding the Disabled," p. A19.

36. Joseph P. Shapiro, *No Pity: People with Disabilities Forging a New Civil Rights Movement* (Times Books, 1993), pp. 23–24.

37. John Gliedman and William Roth, *The Unexpected Minority: Handicapped Children in America* (Harcourt Brace Jovanovich, 1980), p. 34. Renee Anspach sees in disability activism a kind of identity politics; "From Stigma to Identity Politics: Political Activism among the Physically Disabled and Former Mental Patients," *Social Science and Medicine*, vol. 13A (1979), pp. 765–73.

38. *APTA v. Lewis*, 655 F.2d 1272 (D.C. Cir. 1981).

39. Shapiro, *No Pity*.

40. Felicity Barringer, "How Handicapped Won Access Rule Fight," *Washington Post*, April 12, 1983, p. A10.

41. Interview with C. Boyden Gray, December 13, 1993, Washington, D.C.; and Shapiro, *No Pity*, p. 120.

42. Interview with Bob Funk and Evan Kemp Jr., December 16, 1993, Washington, D.C.

43. Interviews with Funk, Gray, and Kemp.

44. Katzmann, *Institutional Disability*, p. 125. David Pfeiffer, a disability activist and historian of the disability movement, argues that the Reagan administration's turn on section 504 arose from its interest in the two "Baby

Doe" cases, which involved controversy over whether to provide lifesaving medical treatments to disabled babies. The administration found section 504 useful in arguing that treatment should be provided (personal communication, May 6, 1996).

45. Interview with Pat Wright, executive director, DREDF, February 3, 1994, Washington, D.C.

46. Interviews with Funk, Gray, and Kemp.

47. National Council on the Handicapped, *Toward Independence* (February 1986), p. iv.

48. Shapiro, *No Pity*, p. 108.

49. Justin W. Dart Jr., "The ADA: A Promise to Be Kept," in Lawrence O. Gostin and Henry A. Beyer, *Americans with Disabilities Act: Rights and Responsibilities of All Americans* (Baltimore: Paul H. Brookes, 1993), p. xxi.

50. Interview with Justin Dart Jr., June 18, 1994, Washington, D.C.

51. Ibid.

52. Dart, "The ADA: A Promise to Be Kept," p. xxii.

53. Interview with Dart.

54. National Council on the Handicapped, *National Policy for Persons with Disabilities* (1983), p. 7.

55. Interview with Robert Burgdorf Jr., February 23, 1994, Washington, D.C.

56. *Toward Independence*, p. 1.

57. Ibid., p. 12.

58. Ibid., p. 1.

59. Ibid., p. 2. In her transmittal letter to President Reagan, Parrino argued that if the recommendations of the council were implemented, "current Federal expenditures for disability can be significantly redirected from dependency-related approaches to programs that enhance independence and productivity of people with disabilities, thereby engendering future efficiencies in Federal spending." Ibid., p. ii.

60. Ibid., p. 8.

61. Ibid., p. 8.

62. Ibid., p. 8.

63. Ibid., pp. 20–21.

64. Louis Harris and Associates, *The International Center for the Disabled Survey of Disabled Americans: Bringing Disabled Americans into the Mainstream* (March 1986), pp. 23–51.

65. National Council on the Handicapped, *On the Threshold of Independence: Progress on Legislative Recommendations from* Toward Independence (January 1988), pp. 25–39.

66. S2345, *Congressional Record*, April 28, 1988, p. S5089; and HR4498, *Congressional Record*, April 29, 1988, p. H2757.

67. Julie Kosterlitz, "Joining Forces," *National Journal* (January 28, 1989), p. 194; and United States Presidential Commission on the Human Immunodeficiency Virus Epidemic (1988), p. 123, reproduced in House Committee on Education and Labor, *Legislative History of The Americans with Disabilities Act*, vol. 2 (December 1990), p. 981.

68. Shapiro, *No Pity*, p. 125.

69. Phil McCombs, "The Distant Drum of C. Boyden Gray," *Washington Post*, March 31, 1989, pp. D1, D8; and interview with Gray, December 13, 1993.

70. Interview with Bill Roper, former deputy assistant to the president for domestic policy, June 9, 1994, Atlanta, Georgia. Roger Clegg, a deputy assistant attorney general in the civil rights division, remembers that he "expressed fundamental misgivings" but recalls only limited public discussion in the White House over the merits of the ADA. "The point was made early on that the president had made a promise during the campaign that he supported the ADA, and so once you know that . . . there's not much point in continuing to oppose it." Interview with Roger Clegg, May 17, 1994, Washington, D.C.

71. Interview with Robert Silverstein, chief counsel, Subcommittee on Disability Policy, December 16, 1993.

72. Paula Yost, "Tedious Meetings, Testy Exchanges Produced Disability Rights Bill," *Washington Post*, August 7, 1989, p. A4.

73. Interview with Chai Feldblum, March 21, 1994, Washington, D.C.; and interview with Pat Wright, February 3, 1994.

74. Sara D. Watson, "A Study in Legislative Strategy: The Passage of the ADA," in Jane West, ed., *The Americans with Disabilities Act: From Policy to Practice*, p. 29.

75. Interview with Arlene Mayerson, Disability Rights Education and Defense Fund, June 2, 1994, Berkeley, California.

76. Lobbying on the ADA's transportation section was intense. Controversy over the transportation sections represented yet another round in a long debate among mass transit system officials, bus and train companies, and disability activists over how disabled people should be accommodated. Robert Katzmann traces this debate in his book *Institutional Disability* (Brookings, 1986) and updates it through to the Americans with Disabilities Act in Katzmann, "Transportation Policy," *Milbank Quarterly*, vol. 69, supplement 1/2 (1991), pp. 214–37.

77. NFIB never disagreed that disabled people should have "the same protections currently contained in other federal civil rights laws prohibiting discrimination on the basis of race, sex, national origin, and religion," as one representative put it. But NFIB argued that the ADA was in fundamental respects different from other civil rights laws because it covered a broader scope of private businesses, required affirmative and possibly costly actions on the part of business, had stiffer remedies, and was more adversarial and legalistic in tone. Thus, far more compromise was necessary, NFIB argued, to make the bill workable and fair. See statement of Sally Douglas, National Federation of Independent Business, Senate Subcommittee on the Handicapped, Hearings on the Americans with Disabilities Act of 1989, May 10, 1989.

78. Interview with John Motley, director of federal government relations, National Federation of Independent Business, June 9, 1994, Washington, D.C.

79. Sara D. Watson makes this point in "Study in Legislative Strategy," pp. 25–34.

80. Interviews with John Tysse, lobbyist, Labor Policy Association, May 27, 1994, Washington, D.C.; Wendy Lechner, legislative representative, National Federation of Independent Business, July 29, 1994; Lawrence Lorber, lobbyist, National Association of Manufacturers and ASPA, May 19 and May 26, 1994, Washington, D.C.; and Bill Roper, June 9, 1994.

81. Quoted by Senator Tom Harkin in *Americans with Disabilities Act of 1989*, Hearings before the Senate Subcommittee on the Handicapped and Committee on Labor and Human Resources, 101 Cong 1 sess. (Government Printing Office, 1989), p. 23.

82. Information on section 1981 is from "Compromise Civil Rights Bill Passed," *1991 Congressional Quarterly Almanac* (Congressional Quarterly, 1991), pp. 251–52, and "1991 Civil Rights Law Provisions," *1991 Congressional Quarterly Almanac*, pp. 258–61.

83. Testimony of Richard L. Thornburgh, attorney general of the United States, before the Senate Subcommittee on the Handicapped, Committee on Labor and Human Resources, *Americans With Disabilities Act of 1989*, June 22, 1989.

84. 42 U.S.C. 12188.

85. Letter from Attorney General Richard Thornburgh, March 12, 1990, quoted in *Congressional Record*, daily ed., May 29, 1990, p. H2613.

86. *Congressional Record*, daily ed., September 7, 1989, p. S10714.

87. At a hearing in which one NFIB member attacked several provisions in the bill, Bartlett was critical: "It becomes at this point extremely essential, extremely helpful and necessary for the NFIB or your business or others who have objections to give us your objections in the form of objections. That is to say, 'Here is what the Senate-passed bill says, here is why we don't like these words, and here is a suggestion to alter those words.' I am not suggesting you didn't give us good testimony, you did, but your testimony doesn't lead us anywhere." House Subcommittees on Employment Opportunities and Select Education, Committee on Education and Labor, *Americans with Disabilities Act of 1989*, September 13, 1989.

88. *Congressional Record*, daily ed., May 17, 1990, p. H2472. A ceiling on reasonable accommodations amounting to 10 percent of an employee's annual wages was defeated on the House floor (p. H2475).

89. *The Americans with Disabilities Act: A Practical and Legal Guide to Impact, Enforcement, and Compliance* (Washington: Bureau of National Affairs, 1990), p. 44; and "Landmark Disability Bill Closer to Enactment," *1989 CQ Almanac* (Congressional Quarterly, 1989), p. 252.

90. "Bush Vetoes Job Bias Bill; Override Fails," *1990 CQ Almanac*, pp. 462–73.

91. Letter from Thornburgh in *Congressional Record*, daily ed., May 22, 1990, p. H2613.

92. Interviews with Feldblum and Silverstein.

93. *Congressional Record*, daily ed., May 22, 1990, pp. H2612, H2613.

94. Ibid., p. H2615.

95. Ibid., p. H2616.

96. "House Votes," *Congressional Quarterly Daily Edition*, May 26, 1990, p. 1688.

97. "Remarks on Signing the Americans with Disabilities Act of 1990," *Personal Papers of the Presidents*, vol. 7, July 26, 1990, pp. 1067–68.

98. "1991 Civil Rights Law Provisions," p. 258.

99. Testimony of Lisa Carl, Betty Corey, and Emory Corey, *Americans with Disabilities Act of 1989*, Hearings, pp. 101–05.

100. Testimony of Tony Coelho, Senate Subcommittee on the Handicapped and House Subcommittee on Select Education, *Americans with Disabilities Act of 1988*, September 27, 1988.

101. In the Harris survey commissioned by the National Council on the Handicapped, disabled people were asked which was the greater obstacle to getting a better job, employer reactions to their disability or the disability itself. Seventy-one percent said that the disability was the greater barrier; only 18 percent thought employer reactions were more important. Thus the respondents disagreed with a central tenet of the rights model, that socially imposed barriers limit disabled people more than their physical impairments. Louis Harris and Associates, *ICD Survey of Disabled Americans*, March 1986, p. 79.

102. Some of these divergences are discussed in Commission on Civil Rights, *Accommodating the Spectrum of Individual Abilities*, Clearing House publication 81 (September 1983), pp. 141–58; and West, "Evolution of Disability Rights," pp. 3–15.

103. Interview with C. Boyden Gray; and Dart, "ADA," p. xxv.

104. Arnold Heidenheimer and colleagues, summarizing the literature on comparative public policy among developed nations, suggest that the feudal legacies of continental Europe and Japan have made these nations more statist than the United States and Britain, where "national bureaucracies . . . were forced to accommodate themselves to preexisting forms of popular political participation." Arnold J. Heidenheimer, Hugh Heclo, and Carolyn Teich Adams, *Comparative Public Policy: The Politics of Social Choice in America, Europe and Japan*, 3d ed. (St. Martin's Press, 1990), p. 22. The welfare state in the United States is both smaller and different in kind from those in most other economically advanced nations because it relies more on individually earned benefits and on means-tested benefits that stigmatize the receiver. Gosta Esping-Anderson groups the United States with Britain as a "social-assistance" welfare state whose practices "strengthen the market since all but those who fail in the market will be encouraged to contract private-sector welfare." *The Three Worlds of Welfare Capitalism* (Princeton University Press, 1992), p. 22. See also Heidenheimer, Heclo, and Adams, *Comparative Public Policy*, p. 249. From 1960 to 1986 the United States spent less on social security as a percentage of GNP than Austria, Norway, Sweden, Belgium, Britain, Denmark, France, Italy, the Netherlands, Switzerland, or West Germany, and roughly equaled only Canada and Japan. Heidenheimer, Heclo, and Adams, *Comparative Public Policy*, p. 226. A 1974 survey found Americans less likely than citizens of Britain, the Netherlands, or West Germany to believe the government was responsible for education, health care, housing, old age security, and unemployment. Heidenheimer, Heclo,

and Adams, *Comparative Public Policy*, p. 354. Sven Steinmo argues that the institutional fragmentation of political authority in the United States explains the "meager social welfare policies" because fragmantation has led to more limited taxation. Tax revenue as a percentage of GNP in the United States is significantly lower than in Europe or Japan. See "Why Is Government So Small in America?" *Governance: An International Journal of Policy and Administration*, vol. 8 (July 1995), pp. 303, 306, 327.

105.   Robert A. Kagan, "Adversarial Legalism and American Government," *Journal of Policy Analysis and Management*, vol. 10, no. 3 (1991), pp. 369–406.

106.   When asked why no one considered a purely bureaucratic mechanism for enforcing the ADA, participants in the bill's creation did not offer a clear answer. Several of the disability activists mentioned the deficiencies of previous administrative mechanisms in disability policy. The Architectural Barriers and Transportation Compliance Board, for example, was widely criticized by disability advocates as underfunded and ineffective. Bureaucratic enforcement of section 504 was similarly considered, as one review put it, "at best lethargic and at worst ineffectual." Bonnie P. Tucker, "Section 504 of the Rehabilitation Act after Ten Years of Enforcement: The Past and the Future," *University of Illinois Law Review*, no. 4 (1989), p. 877.

It is hard to tell whether these experiences with bureaucratic regulation shaped the creation of the ADA, in large part because the debate over the ADA never included any discussion of the merits of bureaucratic versus judicial enforcement. This issue simply did not seem to be on the minds of disability activists.

107.   The Justice Department's regulations provide a list of examples of what it considers to be an impairment. The phrase "physical or mental impairment" includes, but is not limited to, such contagious and noncontagious diseases and conditions as orthopedic, visual, speech, and hearing impairments, cerebral palsy, epilepsy, muscular dystrophy, multiple sclerosis, cancer, heart disease, diabetes, mental retardation, emotional illness, specific learning disabilities, HIV disease (whether symptomatic or asymptomatic), tuberculosis, drug addiction, and alcoholism.

This is as close to a list as the definition of disability gets. Simply having an impairment, however, does not mean a plaintiff is disabled under the law; a court must also find that the impairment "substantially limits major life activities." The regulations provide a suggestive but not definitive list of "major life activities." Thus those covered by the ADA confront a series of ambiguities in the law. 28 C.F.R. 36 (1991), p. 35548.

108.   Testimony of Melinda Maloney, LRP Publications, before the Senate Subcommittee on Disability Policy, July 26, 1995.

109.   This case was, however, tried under the California state disability rights law, which allows larger damage verdicts. Barbara Steuart, "Vague and Vaguer," *Recorder* (October 9, 1995), p. 3.

110.   Robert L. Burgdorf Jr., *Disability Discrimination in Employment Law* (Washington: Bureau of National Affairs, 1995), pp. 132–33.

111. Lucinda Harper, "Head Games: Mental Health Law Protects Many People But Vexes Employers," *Wall Street Journal*, July 19, 1994, p. A1.

112. Statement of Gilbert Casellas, EEOC chairman, before the Senate Labor and Human Resources Committee, May 23, 1995; and West, *Federal Implementation*, p. 19.

113. West, *Federal Implementation*, pp. 20–21.

114. Ibid., p. 21.

115. Administrative Office of the United States Courts, *Statistical Tables for the Federal Judiciary* (June 30, 1995), table C5.

116. Equal Employment Opportunity Commission, *Americans with Disabilities Act of 1990—Statistics, FY 1992–FY 1996* (chart).

117. Under EEOC rules, complainants can demand a "right to sue" letter 180 days after filing. Kristi Bleyer, "The Americans with Disabilities Act: Enforcement Mechanisms," *Mental and Physical Disability Law Reporter* (May-June 1992), pp. 347–48.

118. Administrative Office of the U.S. Courts, *Judicial Business of the United States Courts* (1996), table C2A; "U.S. District Courts Civil Cases Commenced by Nature of Suit," table CIV 14; and Janet Reno and Richard Thornburgh, "ADA—Not a Disabling Mandate," *Wall Street Journal*, July 26, 1995, p. A12.

119. Institute for Civil Justice, *1992–93 Annual Report* (Santa Monica, Calif.: RAND, 1993), p. 22.

120. Steuart, "Vague and Vaguer," p. 3.

121. Lisa J. Stansky, "Opening Doors," *ABA Journal* (March 1996), pp. 66–67.

122. Robert Frank and Alex Markels, "Coca-Cola Loses ADA Alcoholism Case," *Wall Street Journal*, July 3, 1995, p. B3.

123. "Federal Jury Hands Victory to the EEOC in Disabilities Case," *Wall Street Journal*, January 7, 1997, p. B11.

124. John Hollwitz, Deborah F. Goodman, and Dean Bolte, "Complying with the Americans with Disabilities Act: Assessing the Costs of Reasonable Accommodation," *Public Personnel Management*, vol. 24 (Summer 1995).

125. James Bovard, "The Disabilities Act's Parade of Absurdities," *Wall Street Journal*, June 27, 1995, p. A18.

126. West, *Federal Implementation*, p. 8.

127. *National Organization on Disability/Harris Survey of Americans with Disabilities* (New York: Louis Harris and Associates, 1994), p. 124.

128. The study also surveyed those on a mailing list of the World Institute on Disability and found 98 percent of respondents knew of the ADA, but this sample was highly educated and far more likely to be knowledgeable of disability policy than the total population of disabled people. In the sample, 74.9 percent reported having a college degree or more education, whereas only 14 percent of respondents had a college degree in the Harris Poll's 1994 survey of disabled people. See Martha J. McGaughey, Susan M. Foley, and Catherine F. Ard, "Implementation of the Americans with Disabilities Act: Perceptions and Experiences of Individuals with Disabilities," Starr Center on Mental Retardation, Brandeis University, March 1996, pp. 8, 14, 18.

129. Sociolegal research suggests that victims of discrimination tend to swallow their grievances more readily than, for example, persons who have been injured in an accident. See, for instance, Richard E. Miller and Austin Sarat, "Grievances, Claims and Disputes: Assessing the Adversary Culture," in Sheldon Goldman and Austin Sarat, eds., *American Court Systems: Readings in Judicial Process and Behavior*, 2d ed. (Longman, 1989), p. 57; and Kristin Bumiller, *The Civil Rights Society: The Social Construction of Victims* (Johns Hopkins University Press, 1988), p. 109. Then, too, disability rights organizations, which help arrange legal counsel for complainants, are swamped and underfunded and thus unable to help all potential litigants. See Lisa J. Stansky, "Opening Doors," *ABA Journal* (March 1996), p. 67.

130. Marjorie Baldwin and William G. Johnson, "Labor Market Discrimination against Men with Disabilities," *Journal of Human Resources*, vol. 29 (Winter 1994), pp. 1–19.

131. Ibid., p. 12; see also Marjorie L. Baldwin, "Can the ADA Achieve Its Employment Goals?" *Annals of the American Academy of Political and Social Sciences*, vol. 596 (1997), p. 43, citing Baldwin and Johnson, "Labor Market Discrimination against Men with Disabilities in the Year of the ADA"; and William G. Johnson and James Lambrinos, "Wage Discrimination against Handicapped Men and Women," *Journal of Human Resources*, vol. 20 (Spring 1985), pp. 264–77.

132. Walter Y. Oi, "Work for Americans with Disabilities," in Richard D. Lambert and Alan W. Heston, eds., *Annals of the American Academy of Political and Social Science*, vol. 523 (London: Sage Publications, 1992), pp. 159–74.

133. *National Organization on Disability/Harris Survey of Americans with Disabilities*, pp. 60, 68.

134. Ibid., p. 72. In her survey of vocational rehabilitation clients, McGaughey found 33 percent reported job discrimination after the ADA had been passed. A survey of those on the mailing list of the World Institute on Disability found 28 percent reporting discrimination. In addition, 10 percent of the vocational rehabilitation clients and 54 percent of the WID mailing list sample reported discrimination in receiving public accommodations. McGaughey, Foley, and Ard, "Implementation of the Americans with Disabilities Act," p. 14.

135. The gap in participation in the labor force between disabled people and the nondisabled does not appear to be shrinking; see Laura Trupin and others, "Trends in Labor Force Participation among Persons with Disabilities, 1983–1994" (forthcoming), table I; and Edward Yelin, "The Labor Market and Persons with and without Disabilities," report to NIDRR and the Social Security Administration Office of Disability, table 3. But see also Census Bureau, "Employment Rate of Persons with Disabilities," table 1, which shows a small narrowing in the employment rate for some definitions of disability. Peter David Blanck's small-scale study of mentally retarded adults in Oklahoma found significant increases in employment and income during a period that coincided with the passage and implementation of the ADA. See "Empirical Study of the Americans with Disability Act: Employment Issues from 1990 to 1994," *Behavioral Sciences and the Law*, vol. 14 (1996), pp. 5–27.

In one survey the percentage of disabled people working actually fell from 33 percent in 1986 before the ADA was enacted to 31 percent in 1994. The survey also measured changes in the social and recreational activities of disabled, finding no significant changes in levels of socializing with friends, patronizing supermarkets and restaurants, or attending religious services, music performances, movies, and sports events. These findings, however, may have been affected by the fact that the 1994 sample was slightly more severely disabled than the 1986 sample. See *The National Organization on Disability/Harris Survey of Americans with Disabilities*, pp. 37, 26, 101–04.

136. McGaughey, Foley, and Ard, "Implementation of the Americans with Disabilities Act," pp. 7, 20. A plurality, however, said that the ADA had improved interview and test accommodations and that it had aided in job accommodations and barrier removal.

137. Between 1990 and 1994 there was a 44 percent increase in the ratio of disability welfare recipients to workers. Richard V. Burkhauser, "Post-ADA: Are People with Disabilities Expected to Work?" *Annals of the American Academy of Political and Social Science*, vol. 549 (1997), table 1. Both SSDI and SSI expanded at "disturbing rates," according to Edward Berkowitz, who concludes that "nothing in the performance SSDI or SSI suggested that ADA had begun to change the nation's approach to disability." See "Implications for Income Maintenance Policy," in Jane West, ed., *Implementing the Americans with Disabilities Act* (Blackwell, 1996), p. 201.

138. Richard Burkhauser concludes that "it is unlikely that any of the 3.97 million workers receiving SSDI benefits or the 3.29 million blind or disabled adults under the age of 65 who were receiving SSI benefits in December 1994 will return to work." See "Are People with Disabilities Expected to Work?" p. 79. See also Baldwin, "Can the ADA Achieve Its Employment Goals?"; Berkowitz, "Implications for Income Maintenance Policy"; and William G. Johnson, "The Future of Disability Policy: Benefit Payments or Civil Rights?" *Annals of the American Academy of Political and Social Sciences*, vol. 596 (1997), pp. 160–72.

139. Paul Burstein and Mark Evan Edwards have written that "black men's earnings rose significantly compared to white men's during the late 19602 and early 1970s, and even those who say EEO legislation has had little long-term impact attribute gains during this period to federal EEO efforts." See "The Impact of Employment Discrimination Litigation on Racial Disparity in Earnings: Evidence and Unresolved Issues," *Law and Society Review*, vol. 28, no. 1 (1994), p. 88. See also Richard B. Freeman, "Black Economic Progress after 1964: Who Has Gained and Why?" in Sherwin Rosen, ed., *Studies in Labor Markets* (University of Chicago Press, 1981), pp. 247–94.

140. Edward H. Yelin, "The Recent History and Immediate Future of Employment among Persons with Disabilities," *Milbank Quarterly*, vol. 69, supplements 1/2 (1991), pp. 136–37.

141. Stephen L. Percy, "ADA, Disability Rights, and Evolving Regulatory Federalism," *Publius*, vol. 23 (Fall 1993), p. 96.

142. Baldwin and Johnson, "Labor Market Discrimination"; and Edward

H. Yelin, "The Employment of People with and without Disabilities in an Age of Insecurity," *Annals of the American Academy of Political and Social Science*, vol. 597 (1997), tables 1 and 2.

143. Edward H. Yelin and Patricia P. Katz, "Making Work More Central to Disability Policy," *Milbank Quarterly*, vol. 72 (Winter 1994), p. 615; and Baldwin and Johnson, "Labor Market Discrimination," p. 14.

144. Some businesses will be in a position to pass on their costs to customers, but this will vary from industry to industry and company to company. Furthermore, the ADA also covers nonprofit organizations, many of whom will be in a poor position to pass costs on.

145. As Richard Burkhauser has said, the ADA represents "morality on the cheap" because it employs the rhetoric of rights to mandate structural changes without paying for them. "Morality on the Cheap: The Americans with Disability Act," *Regulation*, vol. 13 (Summer 1990), pp. 47–56.

146. Robert L. Burgdorf Jr., *Disability Discrimination in Employment Law* (Bureau of National Affairs, 1995), pp. 326, 327.

147. Peter David Blanck, *Communicating the Americans with Disability Act: Transcending Compliance: A Case Report on Sears, Roebuck and Co.*, report to the Annenberg Washington Program, Northwestern University, 1994, p. 12; *National Organization on Disability/Harris Survey on Employment of People with Disabilities*, p. 34; and Job Accommodation Network survey, cited in West, *Federal Implementation*, p. 30.

148. 42 U.S.C. 12181.

149. 42 U.S.C. 12183.

150. Robert Genetski, "The True Cost of Government," *Wall Street Journal*, February 19, 1992, p. A14.

151. André Henderson, "The Looming Disabilities Deadline," *Governing*, December 1994, pp. 22–23.

152. There has been no nationwide survey of state costs, but estimates made by some states are revealing. Illinois, for example, has said it will spend $100 million to comply with the ADA, while Missouri has estimated $38 million. Fred W. Lindecke, "Leading the Way: Cooperation Can Open Doors for Americans with Disabilities Act," *St. Louis Post-Dispatch*, March 27, 1995, p. 1A.

153. General Accounting Office, *Americans with Disabilities Act: Challenges Faced by Transit Agencies in Complying with the Act's Requirements*, GAO/RCED-94-58 (1994), pp. 7, 13.

154. In the case of the Clean Air Act the main source of this dualism was that enforcement cases went to one set of courts while rule-making cases went to another. See generally R. Shep Melnick, *Regulation and the Courts: The Case of the Clean Air Act* (Brookings, 1983).

155. In Great Britain a 3 percent quota in hiring was not achieved after 1961, and by 1993 the actual rate of hiring was 0.07 percent. Brian Doyle, *Disability, Discrimination and Equal Opportunities: A Comparative Study of the Employment Rights of Disabled Persons* (London: Mansell, 1995), p. 260.

156. Lisa Waddington, *Disability, Employment and the European Community* (Antwerp: Metro, 1995), pp. 230–32.

157. Neil Lunt and Patricia Thornton, *Employment Policies for Disabled People: A Review of Legislation and Services in Fifteen Countries*, Research Series 16 (York, U.K.: Employment Department Group, 1993), p. 160.

158. Lunt and Thornton, *Employment Policies*, p. 41.

159. Doyle, *Disability, Discrimination and Equal Opportunities*, pp. 228–32.

160. Canada does have a constitutional provision in the 1982 Charter of Rights and Freedoms specifically outlawing discrimination based on "mental or physical disability." This provision, however, only applies to actions taken by the federal and provincial governments. A few cases have been brought under this provision, including one that struck down municipal regulations restricting group care homes for disabled people. Cliona Kimber, "Disability Discrimination Law in Canada," in Gerard Quinn, Maeve McDonagh, and Cliona Kimber, *Disability Discrimination Law in the United States, Australia and Canada* (Dublin: Oak Tree Press, 1993), p. 192.

161. Judith Keene, *Human Rights in Ontario*, 2d ed. (Scarborough, Ontario: Carswell, 1992), pp. 263, 335, 372–75.

162. For an analysis of the British law, see Brian J. Doyle, *Disability Discrimination: The New Law* (Bristol: Jordans, 1996).

163. The Tory government had turned back a stronger disability rights law because it opposed the creation of a "centralized, bureaucratic, monitoring and policing body." Mark Suzman, "Financial Times Guide to the UK's Disability Discrimination Act," *Financial Times*, November 6, 1995, p. 12.

164. The United States does have two small employer-subsidy programs, the Job Training Partnership Act (JTPA) and the Targeted Jobs Tax Credit (TJTC). The JTPA contributes 50 percent of the first six months of wages for those considered economically disadvantaged, which can include people with disabilities. In 1989 about 37,000 adults with disabilities and 43,000 youths between the ages of sixteen and twenty-one with disabilities were enrolled in the program. The TJTC pays 40 percent of the wage costs of a new employee for one year, with a maximum credit of $6,000. Disabled people who register with a vocational rehabilitation office are one of ten groups eligible for the credit; in 1987 about 40,000 were certified. Lunt and Thornton, *Employment Policies*, pp. 166, 171.

165. Edward Yelin argues that "the passive strategy of waiting for aggrieved individuals to file claims will not suffice," and urges a program of statistical research to highlight problem industries. "Recent History," p. 146.

166. Melnick, *Regulation and the Courts*. For a particularly poignant example, see Robert A. Kagan, "Adversarial Legalism and American Government," *Journal of Policy Analysis and Management*, vol. 10, no. 3 (1991), pp. 369–406.

167. See for example Joseph L. Badaracco Jr., *Loading the Dice: A Five-Country Study of Vinyl Chloride Regulation* (Harvard Business School Press, 1985).

168. David M. Engel and Frank W. Munger make this point in "Rights, Remembrance and the Reconciliation of Difference," *Law and Society Review*, vol. 30, no. 1 (1996), pp. 7–53.

169. J. A. Garraty, *Unemployment in History: Economic Thought and Public Policy* (Harper and Row, 1978), pp. 46–47.

170. Walter Y. Oi, "Employment and Benefits for People with Diverse Disabilities," in Jerry Mashaw and others, eds., *Disability, Work, and Cash Benefits* (Kalamazoo: W. E. Upjohn Institute for Employment Research, 1996), p. 107.

171. Jane West, "The Social and Policy Context of the Act," in *The Americans with Disabilities Act: From Policy to Practice* (New York: Milbank Memorial Fund, 1991), pp. 3–24.

172. Oi, "Employment and Benefits," pp. 103–27.

173. Kerwin Charles, "An Inquiry into the Labor Market Consequences of Disabling Illness," Ph.D. dissertation, Cornell University, 1996.

174. National Council on the Handicapped, *Toward Independence*, p. 1.

175. Nancy Lee Jones, "Essential Requirements of the Act: A Short History and Overview," in *Americans with Disabilities Act*, pp. 25–54.

176. Oi, "Employment and Benefits," p. 105.

177. Burkhauser, "Morality on the Cheap," pp. 47–56.

Chapter 7

Internationalizing Regulatory Reform

Roger G. Noll

A N UNUSUAL FEATURE of this book is its focus on international aspects of regulatory policy. While U.S. regulatory policy has been politically controversial since its inception, until the late 1970s the debate focused on whether government legitimately could control various aspects of private production and transactions and whether specific regulations and the net effect of all regulation generated positive social benefits. As the United States and its major trading partners eased into the current regime of relatively free trade, the regulatory policy debate was internationalized in three important ways. First, opponents of regulation—especially companies that opposed environmental, health, and safety regulation—argued that excessive regulation eroded the "competitiveness" of U.S. industry and contributed to persistent trade deficits. Second, everyone concerned with regulation began to look abroad for new ideas about how to reduce the burdens of regulation. Third, as direct trade barriers fell, and in many cases became negligible, countries began to incorporate regulatory policy into trade negotiations as a means of reducing indirect trade barriers.

The chapters of this book explore all of these issues and in so doing contribute new information to the ongoing debate about regulatory reform. The purpose of this chapter is to provide a general overview of the regulatory reform debate, its international ramifications, and

The author gratefully acknowledges useful comments from Scott Jacobs, Akira Kawamoto, and Bernard Phillips and financial support for much of the work of preparing this chapter from the Markle Foundation and the Organization for Economic Cooperation and Development.

the experiences of other countries with regulation and regulatory reform proposals. In addition, I examine how international trade negotiations can play a significant role in regulatory reform.

The Evolution of Regulatory Reform

In most advanced industrialized democracies, regulatory reform has been a salient political issue for two decades or more. The concept of regulatory reform is broad and somewhat vague and sometimes has been advanced by ideological proponents of either harsh or lax changes that, in reality, would be wildly inefficient. Notwithstanding these proposals, the core idea of regulatory reform—at least among scholars of business policy—is to improve the efficiency of policies that intervene in decisions about market entry, production methods, product attributes, and transactions arrangements between suppliers and customers. Reform can mean deregulation, privatization combined with the creation of a regulatory authority, or more targeted and focused regulation—sometimes of products that thus far have escaped regulation—that makes greater use of economic incentives, economic policy analysis, and policy coordination among agencies.

The debate about regulatory reform is neither empty nor sterile. Most nations have significantly changed some major regulatory policies and are considering further reforms. Regulatory reform is politically salient for two main reasons. First, regulatory policies impose significant costs, and reform can reduce these costs without sacrificing regulatory objectives. Second, as direct trade barriers—tariffs and quotas on imports—have fallen, regulation has become an increasingly important source of distortions in international trade and a more frequent cause of trade conflicts.

As a result of the growing importance of the international effects of domestic regulation, regulatory policy has become an issue in international negotiations about trade and investment policies. International agreements have initiated multilateral coordination of regulatory reform. For example, the European Union has adopted several procedures, some incorporated into the Treaty of Rome, to harmonize some environmental, health, and safety regulations and has promulgated plans to liberalize airlines and telecommunications regulation by 1998. Likewise, both the North American Free Trade Agreement (NAFTA) and the most recent extensions of the General Agreement on Tariffs and Trade (GATT) establish dispute resolution institutions to adjudicate claims that a trading partner is attempting to gain an unfair trade advantage by using regulation as an indirect trade barrier or by applying lax regulation to businesses that produce exported products.

The elevation of regulatory policy to an issue of international economic policy is controversial. Some charge that internationalizing regulatory reform is an attempt by zealots to impose stringent regulation on nations that neither need nor want it. Others contend that emphasizing the trade consequences of regulation amounts to advocacy of a regulatory "race to the bottom," whereby the nations that have done the most to pursue socially desirable regulatory policies are being forced to abandon them because these regulations affect trade.

The primary objective of this chapter is to examine the relationship between regulatory reform and international economic integration. This chapter has two main messages. First, internationalization of regulatory reform is inevitable, and not just because the social and economic problems that give rise to regulation cross borders, as is emphasized by advocates of international environmental regulation.[1] Even without these cross-border problems, regulation inevitably is an international issue because, when other forms of trade barriers are low, regulations can significantly affect the allocation of sales of regulated products among nations. Second, the internationalization of regulatory reform is not likely to produce either of two disaster scenarios: widespread overregulation or massive underregulation. Instead, internationalization of regulatory reform is a healthy development that is likely to improve the efficiency of regulation while removing trade distortions that arise from inefficient regulation.

Market Access: The Parable of the Teleshopper

Ultimately, regulatory reform is worth pursuing only if it is a means for improving the quality of life. The international significance of regulatory reform for ordinary citizens is made apparent by considering the problems of a consumer who attempts to buy products across an international boundary by using the telephone to place an order from a catalog or to shop using the World Wide Web (or, from outside France, Minitel).[2] This example is especially relevant for thinking about the future of international cooperation in regulation because of the extraordinarily rapid growth of electronic communication and its potential for completely restructuring transactions arrangements.

Step one: connecting buyer and seller. Teleshopping requires a telephone connection, either to call in an order orally or by fax, or to place an order while surfing the Web. Regulation can interfere with teleshopping by setting excessive prices for calls or thwarting Internet connections. Regulatory pricing policy in most nations sets much higher prices for international calling than for domestic calls over a similar distance. In the United States and some other countries, off-peak long distance calls are pennies per minute, whereas international calls over the same distance can be one hundred times that amount and far greater than the cost of service. Among OECD countries, the prices charged to Internet access providers vary widely, with annual costs from as low as $10,000 to as high as $30,000.[3] Internet usage also is more costly in countries that charge for local calls and where residential lines support only very slow data transmission rates, so that connections of an hour or more are necessary to engage in catalog shopping on the World Wide Web. In other nations, residential users have access to high-speed digital connections that can transmit the same information in a few minutes.[4] A policy to supply slow access lines at a high usage price creates high transaction costs that effectively bar market access for most international teleshopping.

Step two: making the transaction. For teleshoppers to be able to buy products, they must have access to an easy means of cross-currency transactions through credit cards or electronic fund transfers. Here regulation of financial institutions can intervene to make such transactions difficult, slow, and costly. Some countries make transactions in other currencies difficult and expensive. Likewise, in some countries international banking transactions are subject to distorting fees and taxes.

Step three: shipping the order. In some countries, parcel delivery is unregulated and competitive, while in others it is heavily regulated, largely to prevent competition with the delivery of packages by the postal system. In the latter cases, parcel delivery is slower and much more costly. The price for express parcel delivery (within a day or two) for a given distance differs among OECD nations by a factor of twenty, depending on the countries of origin and destination. For example, a seven-pound parcel can be shipped on two-day delivery for $15 from New York to Los Angeles, $66 from New York to Paris, $94 from Paris to New York, or $61 over the much shorter distance from Paris to Frankfurt.[5] Obviously, for all but the most expensive goods, shipping charges to and from France make teleshopping prohibitive.

Step four: getting the order over the border. When a product crosses the border, a customs agent may impound it because it has not been certified to satisfy environmental, health, and safety standards in the destination country. Even when both sending and receiving countries have equivalent standards, they may not have a mutual recognition agreement, so that the same product may have to pass exactly the same test separately in every country in which it is sold.[6] Or, the product may be subject to disposal regulations that require involvement of the manufacturer or seller, so that foreign products are effectively banned, even though other disposal arrangements are easy to arrange. Environmental, health, and safety standards are a common, continuing source of trade barriers that lead to conflicts among trading partners. Cases that illustrate this problem are *Cassis de Dijon* and *German Bottles* in the European Union, *Canadian Red Raspberries* in the Canadian-American Free Trade Agreement, *CAFE Standards* in the General Agreement on Trade and Tariffs, and *Venezuelan Gasoline*, the first case decided by the World Trade Organization (WTO).[7] The cases involving automobile fuel efficiency and reformulated gasoline, as described by David Vogel in chapter 3, are especially instructive, because in both of these cases the U.S. government quite explicitly tried to rig regulatory rules to protect domestic producers from foreign competition.

The parable of the teleshopper illustrates how regulations can distort trade, even though in most cases (but not the ones cited above) the regulations probably were not designed to be indirect trade barriers. In the parable, trade distortions are created by a full array of regulatory policies: traditional utility regulation, prudential regulation of financial institutions, transportation regulation, product quality regulation, and environmental regulation. This example is especially pertinent, for teleshopping is a rapidly growing part of retail trade in countries where regulation does not add high additional costs per transaction. One objective of regulatory reform is to make certain that no unnecessary costs are imposed in achieving legitimate regulatory policy objectives.

Rationalizing Regulatory Objectives and Methods

The parable of the teleshopper is based on the premise that some of the observed variation in the cost of regulation reflects inefficiency, rather than valid policy objectives. All regulation carries the danger that it will reduce efficiency by increasing production costs without generating significant social benefits. In addition, all forms of regulation may further reduce economic efficiency by thwarting competition, especially the entry of firms into markets that are not competitive or that are served by inefficient incumbents.

All of the preceding chapters of this book argue that in several important areas, U.S. regulation has imposed unnecessary costs. The nature of the problem varies from case to case. Excesses in the tort liability system imposed severe damage on small airplane manufacturers (chapter 2). Pork barrel politics converted the quest for clean-burning automotive fuel to a massive subsidy of midwestern farmers (chapter 3). Unnecessarily complex and adversarial processes cause the system for setting standards and resolving conflicts to impose over $100 billion per year in legal costs (chapter 4). Excessively detailed laws have prevented regulators from adopting cost-effective approaches to curtailing pollution from oil refineries because the underlying statute is excessively detailed and formalistic (chapter 5). By adopting a legal-rights, antidiscrimination approach to dealing with disabled citizens, the Americans with Disabilities Act imposes enormous costs but fails to achieve some readily available, not very expensive, reasonable policy objectives (chapter 6). Of course, these chapters also contain examples of excessively costly regulations and legal rules elsewhere. Indeed, considering all aspects of regulation (including liability law), the United States probably does not have the least efficient or least effective system; however, in most areas, one can find some instructive examples of how regulatory objectives roughly comparable to those in this country are achieved at lower cost somewhere else.

If a regulation imposes costs but serves no valid social purpose, or more generally if regulatory methods serve a valid purpose but are grossly inefficient, the consequence is an inefficient domestic economy. Because an industry's inefficiency is the result of government policies, a poorly performing industry frequently receives a sympathetic response when it seeks protection against foreign competitors that face more efficient regulation and hence lower regulatory compliance costs. Consequently, as a political matter, domestic regulatory reform can be complementary with liberalizing trade and foreign investment policies.

Alternatively, some differences in the cost of regulation may reflect valid differences in policy arising from differences in circumstances among countries. For example, the amount of damaging pollution that is caused by a given amount of polluting emissions varies according to physical, ecological, and climatological differences among locations. In addition, avoiding the aesthetic effects of environmental pollution is likely to be valued more highly in a wealthy nation than in a poor one. Both factors are a legitimate source of comparative advantage in international trade; however, an industry facing especially stringent regulations for either reason also is likely to complain about unlevel playing fields and to be viewed sympathetically by its national government.

The economic importance of regulation-induced trade barriers is frequently mischaracterized as a "competitiveness" issue that involves the overall trade performance of a nation, as measured by balance of trade or domestic unemployment in export industries. The economics of regulation-induced trade distortions is more subtle and complex than this account. Stringent regulation causes a particular product to be more expensive and thereby shifts the composition of national economic activity into other, less regulated activities. If the pattern of regulations, both stringent and lax, reflects an efficient response to a real problem, this shift in the composition of production is desirable: on balance, it improves the economic welfare of a nation. But if some regulations are too stringent, or others are too lax, the pattern of regulation is harmful to national economic welfare because it penalizes products that are more valuable than the products it favors.

If stringent regulation arises in traded goods under a liberal trade regime, the shift in the industrial composition of domestic output is even larger because exports displace domestic production for intensely regulated products, while domestic production displaces imports for less regulated products. Again, if regulatory rules are efficient, the change in the pattern of trade is desirable, and the effect of the shift in the composition of exports and imports improves the productivity of the domestic economy. If regulatory rules are inefficient, the result is a trade distortion: some lost exports could be produced most cheaply at home, and some imports are being driven out by less efficient domestic production. The effect is to reduce productivity and economic welfare not only at home but also among trading partners.

To construct efficient regulatory and international economic policies, public officials need to be able to distinguish between inefficient regulation and valid differences in circumstances as causes of international differences in the cost of regulatory policies. Moreover, in the latter case, the appropriate conceptual model for guiding policy is that the social issues that give rise to regulation may cause efficient differences among nations in the stringency and cost of regulation. The latter cost differences should be viewed as valid sources of comparative advantage among nations. In these cases, the focus of policy should not be to level the regulatory playing field but to let trade reallocate activity to low-cost sources of supply, perhaps facilitated politically by adjustment assistance. A nation that has especially valuable environmental resources, or that places an especially high value on avoiding work-related injuries, is better off if it adjusts the composition of its economy away from activities that lead to either problem.

Economic Analysis of Regulation

To distinguish between valid and excessively stringent or lax regulation requires a coherent, comprehensive analytical method for assessing the basis for differences among nations in the costs of regulatory compliance. The movement toward free trade opens new possibilities for competition, through international trade or foreign investment, and hence new opportunities to improve the performance of markets that have formerly been protected by regulation. But regulation may provide significant net social benefits that might be sacrificed if it is simply relaxed or eliminated.

Economic efficiency analysis provides a means for identifying whether regulation as practiced comes reasonably close to meeting this standard. In cases where regulation is warranted, economic efficiency analysis identifies cost-effective methods of regulation and therefore is a useful tool to assist nations in harmonizing regulations so that they do not distort trade and are compatible with liberalization of trade and foreign investment. International agreements about regulation are a means for pursuing cost-effective regulatory methods while reaching mutual agreement not to engage in a race to the bottom.

The economic analysis of regulation focuses on market failure, which occurs when private transactions do not reflect the social costs and benefits of an activity. Markets are an efficient method for organizing production and distribution when the number of buyers and sellers is large, when buyers and producers are reasonably informed about the consequences of making and producing a product, and when all of the benefits and costs of producing and consuming a product are experienced only by producers and consumers. Market failures arise when a market departs significantly from any of these characteristics. The three types of market failure are imperfect information, externalities, and monopoly. (A fourth market failure, ruinous competition, has been alleged but has been found to be an empty vessel.) Ruinous competition and monopoly are the primary basis for economic regulation, or the regulation of prices, profits, and entry. Externalities and imperfect information form the primary basis for social regulation, such as controlling pollution, improving the safety and healthfulness of products and workplaces, and requiring full disclosure of the characteristics of products.

Economic Regulation

Ruinous competition is a condition in which a competitive industry engages in price wars that bankrupt the participants or cause wild, unpredictable price swings that prevent buyers from being able to rely on price predictability. Much regulation that was enacted during the Great Depression, such as regulation of trucking, airlines, and hydrocarbon fuels, was based on the belief that the Great Depression was caused by excessive price cutting. Economic deregulation in several countries has generated considerable evidence that in these areas competition is efficient, regulation is unnecessary, and the ruinous competition argument is simply wrong. In the United States, economic regulation has been either removed or substantially relaxed in industries accounting for approximately 10 percent of gross domestic product. Recent assessments of the magnitude of the annual economic benefits of these changes (primarily in the form of lower prices to consumers) are at least $13.7 billion for airlines and $10.6 billion for trucking.[8] In Australia, deregulation reduced prices for air travel by 21 percent.[9]

Regulating industries that could be structurally competitive is certainly costly to the domestic economy, but it can also distort trade. To the extent that these regulations apply to services used by export industries, they raise costs and distort both exports and imports. An especially good example is international transportation, which has not been deregulated as rapidly as domestic regulation and, as a result, reduces trade by raising its price.

Monopoly occurs when a single seller can restrict supply and force buyers to pay a price that substantially exceeds production cost. If monopoly arises from mergers, unfair trading practices, or regulatory entry barriers, the cure may be simply to promote competition. Economic regulation can make sense only if the monopoly is natural, that is, the technology underpinning the industry is such that only one firm can serve a market at minimum cost.

Natural monopoly is the rationale for much economic regulation, especially in utility industries such as communications, electricity, and water distribution. If regulation or nationalization is justified for a natural monopoly, it must not cause even greater inefficiency than an unfettered market. In the 1980s, two types of research findings called into question both assumptions. First, studies found little or no evidence of scale economies in many segments of supposedly natural monopolies.[10] Second, countries that allowed competitive entry and engaged in less restrictive regulation had lower prices and more productive industries. For example, relaxation of regulation in railroads and telecommunication produced economic benefits of approximately $11 billion and $1 billion, respectively.[11]

International comparisons find that productivity in the utility sector is substantially higher in countries with more liberal policies.[12] In particular, when combined with policies to facilitate transactions among retail electric utilities, free entry and almost complete deregulation in electrical generation are feasible and offer considerable cost savings. In the 1990s, over half of new generation facilities are expected to be constructed, owned, and operated by independent power producers.[13]

If economic regulation is retained because an incumbent's market power is likely to be durable, the agenda for regulatory reform contains two items. The first is to adopt regulations that give firms sharper incentives for reducing costs. The second is to require that practices in monopolized markets do not impede competition and reduce efficiency in other markets.

In the first category of reforms are price-cap regulation and earnings-sharing regulation, both of which allow regulated firms to keep some of the profits from improved efficiency.[14] The alternatives to incentive regulation are either cost-based price regulation or prices that are set by elected political officials, such as by inclusion in a statute, with no necessary connection to costs or market conditions. The difficulty with the first approach is that it rewards inefficiency by increasing allowed prices in proportion to costs. The problem with the second is that extreme politicization of prices inevitably leads to massive financial losses, which are then matched by subsidies. Price-cap and earnings-sharing regulation begin with a set of prices that allow the firm roughly to break even but to keep part of the profits it derives from cost reductions. Price-cap regulation also gives the firm flexibility to change prices as long as, according to an averaging formula, they generally do not increase.

Telecommunications in the United States provides a useful laboratory for assessing the effects of incentive regulation. Before reform, the U.S. telecommunications industry was a monopoly that was regulated on the basis of cost-based pricing and generally regarded as among the most efficient in the world. Nevertheless, in an attempt to improve efficiency, parts of the industry were opened to competition. The parts that were regarded as insufficiently competitive to allow deregulation were regulated by many different regulatory jurisdictions, both federal and state, and these regulatory authorities have adopted several different forms of price regulation. The results of recent research indicate that price-cap regulation has substantially increased the rate of productivity advance and has led to lower prices and more rapid diffusion of new technology, such as digital switches, advanced signalling, and particularly fiber optic cable.[15]

The second category of regulatory reform attempts to minimize the extent to which regulated monopolies leverage their market power by gaining an undeserved advantage in markets that are related to the monopoly but can be competitive. Examples are equipment sales to regulated monopolists and products for which the monopoly service is an important input. Here policy reforms include proactive intervention by agencies charged with making competition policy to scrutinize regulations for anticompetitive effects; equal access, equal interconnection, and open bidding requirements so that affiliates of the monopolist are not treated differently than their independent competitors; and separation requirements for unregulated activities of regulated firms.

One success story apparently is in Norway, which created a separate state-owned power pool, Statnett Marked, to manage bulk power sales across the territorial boundaries of regional electric utilities. This reform, though too recent to have been systematically evaluated, appears to have substantially increased transactions and narrowed price differences for electricity among regions.[16] A similar experiment began in California in December 1995, when alternative suppliers of electrical energy were given access to utility distribution systems to begin marketing electricity directly to consumers.

Regulatory reform has faced difficulty in preventing regulated monopolies from dominating vertically related, potentially competitive markets. In the United States, policies to protect against vertical leveraging have given rise to persistent conflicts before regulatory agencies and antitrust courts for nearly a century.[17] The United Kingdom did not adopt separation remedies, and one recent study concludes that competitive entry has been less extensive than was desirable.[18]

Several countries have privatized formerly public enterprises, providing experience about the comparative efficiency of the two organizational forms. A recent study of generation facilities that account for over 40 percent of the world's capacity finds that private utilities produce electricity at about 5 percent lower cost than public enterprise utilities.[19] A study of privatization in Britain finds efficiency gains of 12 percent for British Telecom, 4.3 percent for National Freight, and 1.6 percent for British Airways.[20] A study of British Gas concludes that privatization increased productivity by 2.3 percent; however, inconsistent results for a productivity effect were found for the regional electric utilities.[21] A study of privatization in Chile and Mexico found an increase in economywide economic benefits of 50 percent for Telmex, 155 percent for Chile Telecom, 49 percent for Aeromexico, and lesser but positive benefits for other cases.[22]

The lessons from reform of economic regulation in many nations are as follows. First, substantial gains in efficiency can be captured from improving the institutional environment of regulated infrastructural industries, such as by privatizing nationalized companies and adopting incentive regulation. These reforms provide direct domestic benefits in the form of lower prices for consumers, but they also remove a trade distortion by lowering the costs of export industries that make intensive use of the services of infrastructural monopolies. Second, because the case for natural monopoly is problematic, eliminating entry restrictions can introduce still greater efficiency. Because in many infrastructural industries only one firm has been allowed to offer service, the most plausible entrant is frequently the entrenched incumbent in another nation. Hence trading partners' mutual relaxation of foreign investment restrictions is a promising mechanism for speeding the evolution to competition after formal monopoly franchises have been removed.

Social Regulation

Environmental protection is an example of regulation to deal with externalities, that is, the consequences of production or consumption that affect the welfare of parties other than the producer or the consumer. In this case, regulatory reform means not deregulation, but the use of more flexible methods of regulation. In almost all countries, the standard method of regulating pollution is to set technical standards for each source.[23] As Marc Landy and Loren Case point out in chapter 5, these standards frequently are more rigorous for new production facilities than for established enterprises, and so they distort market entry. The stringency and cost of standards also vary among industries, further distorting the pattern of economic activity to favor the less rigorously regulated sectors. For example, a study of sulfur oxides emissions in Los Angeles found that the marginal cost of abatement for the most heavily controlled sources (electric utilities) was $20,000 per ton, whereas other controlled sources (glass bottle manufacturing) faced marginal costs of abatement of around $200 and still other sources (dry cleaners) remained completely uncontrolled.[24]

Because progress in environmental protection has been slow, some nations have begun to experiment with the use of economic incentives rather than technical standards. The two primary methods for achieving greater efficiency by introducing economic incentives into environmental regulation are emissions trading and effluent fees. The advantage of both is that they are competitively neutral among industries and firms.

The first experiments with emissions trading began in the United States in the late 1970s, with controlled trading options for six air pollutants; two or more sources could propose regulations that reallo-

cated pollution among them, subject to many procedural requirements and technical constraints. Despite a burdensome process, this
program definitely saved hundreds of millions, possibly billions, of
dollars in compliance costs without reducing environmental quality.[25]

Singapore and the United States have used emissions markets to
meet national commitments for reductions in emissions of chlorofluorocarbons under the Montreal protocol. In the U.S. case, emissions allowances were allocated according to historical production, but emitters were permitted to buy and sell allowances.[26] In Singapore,
emissions allocations were sold through an auction.[27]

Another example is the use of offsets in Germany and the United
States, whereby new sources of pollution in a heavily polluted area
are not permitted unless they reduce emissions from other facilities
by more than the amount of emissions created by the new facility.[28]

Effluent fees are a tax on the emission of harmful pollutants. The
textbook model of effluent fees is to set the tax high enough to reflect
the damage created by pollution so that polluters have a financial incentive to abate if pollution abatement is less costly than the harm it
creates. Although many countries set effluent fees, these fees are
almost never high enough to create a significant financial incentive to
abate. Sometimes fees are selectively imposed because too few resources are allocated to enforcement or because politics enters into
decisions about how much tax to levy on each source of pollution.[29]

In a few cases, effluent fees are reasonably effective. One example
is water effluent fees in the Netherlands.[30] Effluent fees in the Netherlands are much higher than such charges elsewhere and so induce
much more abatement at the source, thereby more closely approxi-
mating the least-cost division of responsibility between source controls and sewage treatment. In Japan, effluent fees for sulfur dioxide
emissions provide a fund for compensating victims of unhealthful air
pollution.[31] Whether these fees are adequate is debatable, but the
principle that the polluter pays for its damage motivates the fees.

The international consequence of incentive-based environmental
regulatory reforms is to reallocate production among nations in a
manner that reduces total social costs. These reforms reduce compliance costs for industries that need to control harmful pollutants. As a
result, the relative price of the products of these industries falls, and
if their products are traded these industries gain a larger share of the
world market. In some cases, the principal effect is to substitute do-

mestic production for exports that appeared attractive only because they were produced in a less costly regulatory environment, and in other cases it is to increase exports of the industries that experience lower regulatory compliance costs. In all cases, all prices and exchange rates will adjust so that some other industries experience some compensating adjustment in net imports, and total trade can either rise or fall. But in all cases, the net effect is an increase in world productivity and income as production moves to areas where the true social costs are lowest.

Another international implication of incentive-based environmental regulation is that it aids location decisions of international firms. The relative anonymity of incentive-based environmental reforms eliminates the possibility that environmental standards will be applied in a discriminatory fashion against foreign investors. Because entry requires only that the new facility buy permits or pay emissions taxes, rather than receive an emissions standard and a permit to operate, incentive-based environmental regulation eliminates a source of regulatory barriers to entry.

So-called cultural externalities sometimes are used to justify regulation of competitive markets. Examples are preserving democracy, a nation's cultural identity, small business (such as retail shops and family farms), social cohesion between rural and urban communities (through cross-subsidies for infrastructural services), or excess capacity in infrastructure in case of natural disaster or war. These rationales are difficult to assess, for they are tautological: they define the national interest as the present market structure. In many cases, these rationales seem to be a relatively transparent excuse for protection and cartelization.

Economic regulation of competitive markets is extremely costly. For example, retail trade is often regulated by controlling entry, setting a maximum store size, and limiting shop hours, either through local zoning or national law. These regulations undermine competition by encouraging cartelization and reduce productivity by causing shops to be too small and underutilized. In the nations with the strictest regulations, Italy and Japan, the number of retail outlets is roughly double the number that would be expected on the basis of other market characteristics.[32]

Regardless of the validity of social externalities as market failures, these objectives usually can be attained more effectively by direct subsidy or procurement by competitive bidding than by regulations that attempt to achieve them by elevating some prices and preventing competition. For example, one means to ensure transportation or communications services to remote communities is to introduce competitive bidding for providing service, where the franchise specifies price and service quality, and to require serving all customers who seek service at the price, subject to penalties for noncompliance. Many public objectives can be accomplished more cheaply, with less distortion, by resorting to the procurement model rather than regulation.

If the procurement model is adopted, these types of regulatory objectives need not cause trade distortions. Foreign suppliers can submit the low bid to supply subsidized service, and if they are still denied the contract, the trade-distorting purpose of the regulation is exposed and can become an issue for international dispute resolution and negotiation.

Protective standards are regulations that deal with informational market failures. This broad and heterogeneous category of regulation includes product safety, drug efficacy, workplace safety, prudence in financial services, and protection against fraudulent advertising and product labeling. At the heart of such regulations are two basic concerns. One is that one side of a market—consumers or workers—has access to less information about the quality of the product or workplace than the other side and so might be victimized. The other concern is that neither side of the market will have an adequate incentive to acquire valuable information that would be useful for evaluating products and workplaces, which, if known, might change producer behavior.

As with environmental regulation, the issue in protective regulation is not whether such regulation is ever justified, but how best to achieve regulatory objectives more efficiently. Protective standards can cause several economic problems. First, they can retard beneficial technological change by introducing inflexibility in designing products and workplaces. Second, they can prevent informed decisions that reflect individual differences in attitudes about or susceptibilities to risk. Third, they create a process that can be used by producers to create barriers to competition, especially international market access.

In this area of regulation, reform has taken many forms, depending on the nature of the problem. One direction of reform is to require full disclosure, backed by documentation of claims, so that both sides of a market have the same information, and then to let the market determine the appropriate degree of risk. Another direction of reform is the internationalization of standards processes so that a consumer product or workplace equipment need prove its acceptability only once, rather than separately in each country. Still another approach is to focus on performance standards, rather than design standards, in order to allow greater variety in technical approaches to solving the same problem in order to encourage cost minimization and technological progress. Finally, another approach is to subsidize product testing by independent authorities (governmental or private) and to publicize the results.

A recent OECD survey indicates that most firms in four industries (toys, lawn mowers, microwave ovens, and bicycle helmets) regard the present standards system as excessively cumbersome and costly, and about one-third responded that some national standards processes prevented them from entering markets, even though they had satisfied equivalent standards elsewhere.[33] The purpose of reform is to avoid these effects when they have nothing to do with the protective purposes of regulation.

Priorities for Reform

The preceding analysis, like most of this book, focuses on specific types of regulations and institutional reforms and by implication constitutes a long list of areas in which literally every nation can find useful examples from other countries about how to make regulation more cost effective. I now take a somewhat different approach by focusing on three general regulatory reform priorities: competition policy, procedural requirements such as mandatory benefit-cost analysis, and internationalization of reform.

An effective policy of regulatory reform should be regarded as a process as well as a series of distinct policy actions. Whereas reform frequently is initiated by a discrete policy action, the objectives of reform generally apply to all aspects of regulation, and to achieve them requires proactive, continuing supportive policies. The primary mechanisms that have been developed for institutionalizing the reform process are competition advocacy, mandatory economic policy analysis, and international entities for enforcing trade agreements.

All of these policies are closely related to the efficiency concepts that are discussed in this chapter. In the absence of any of the market failures discussed here, an unregulated competitive market is efficient. If many of the hypothesized market failures that underpin regulatory policy are illusory or unimportant, regulatory reform means abandoning regulation and undertaking a vigorous policy to promote competition.

The presence of a significant market failure provides a rationale for continued government intervention but does not require sacrificing either competitive markets or economic efficiency. In these cases, regulatory interventions will be most effective if, first, they focus narrowly on curing the market failure while minimizing the extent to which they disrupt competition, and, second, if these interventions are designed to achieve their policy objectives efficiently. Hence, even when regulation is present, there is usually a heightened role for competition policy, and, to help identify the most cost-effective ways to attack market failures, regulations should be developed with the aid of a comprehensive economic impact analysis.

Finally, internationalization of regulatory reform facilitates the reform process and provides additional insurance against backsliding. The arena of international trade negotiations provides an opportunity for expanding the benefits of domestic reform by pairing them with foreign reforms that grant domestic firms greater access to external markets. And, once the agreement is reached, international trade enforcement institutions, such as the World Trade Organization and the Court of Europe, provide additional protection against subsequent regulatory actions that distort trade.

Competition Policy

Policies to promote competition are always in some tension with regulation, and effective regulatory reform usually requires rethinking how this tension should be resolved. The essence of the tension is that regulatory policy promulgates common rules of behavior for firms within a market and sometimes encourages monopoly, whereas competition policy seeks to eliminate monopoly and to force firms to operate independently. Obviously, fixing a price or adopting a common production technology through a regulatory process is far different conceptually than insisting that each firm make price and production decisions separately and letting the competitive process determine the ultimate performance of the industry.

The anticompetitive danger from regulatory policy arises from the fact that it asks a regulatory authority to make decisions that normally would be made by firms that are engaged in competition. Consequently, the power to regulate has the potential for abuse by a group of participants in a market if they can make use of the regulatory process to reduce competition among them, at the expense of other groups in the market. For example, a regulatory standard may reduce pollution, improve product quality, or make the workplace safer, but it may also do none of these and instead simply require that consumers buy one type of product rather than another, benefiting the producer of that product at the expense of competitors and consumers.

One way that regulation can serve anticompetitive purposes is to favor domestic products over imported ones, thereby creating an indirect trade barrier, as was the case in the U.S. standards for automobile fuel efficiency and reformulated gasoline, discussed in chapter 3. As direct trade barriers have declined, the distorting effects of regulation on trade, whether intentional or inadvertent, have become more visible and controversial. In all areas of regulation, trade is affected by regulatory rules and policies; however, if regulation is genuinely aimed at a market failure, the effects do not distort trade and are not anticompetitive. The controversiality of the trade effects arises from uncertainties about whether some regulations are an efficient means of correcting a market failure or are a devious, distorting trade barrier.

Evidence that the latter case occurs is the presence of parallel distortions in the politics of trade policy. Domestic producers are advantaged over foreign producers because they are likely to be more effective participants in the domestic political process and thus constitute a more likely source of important political support for or opposition to a government. Even if a statute or an international treaty expresses the objective of avoiding anticompetitive regulations, an anticompetitive outcome is difficult to avoid because the development of regulations inevitably leads to product-specific or industry-specific debates. These specific regulations require detailed analyses of the nature of the problem that has given rise to regulation and its possible solutions. The process of undertaking such an analysis advantages domestic industries: politically, because they can apply direct political pressure to regulators; and procedurally, because they possess much of the information that is necessary to assess the benefits and costs of regulation.

The anticompetitive use of regulation, whether against domestic or foreign competitors, is sufficiently common that it has been given a name: "regulatory capture." This term invokes an unfortunate connotation of corruption, whereby regulators are consciously acting on behalf of one economic interest at the expense of others and to the detriment of the economy. Although in some cases regulation has served as little more than a means for creating a monopoly or a cartel where competition would otherwise reign free, more subtle forms of capture are probably more important. Regulators must adopt regulations on the basis of the information that is available and the proposals that are made to them. All too frequently a particular regulatory issue does not capture the attention of anyone other than a few companies that are affected by it. If these companies propose a regulation that will reduce competition and increase their profits, the regulator may not recognize the fact, or may not have enough information to identify a regulation that is less anticompetitive.

An important role for competition policy is to review regulatory policy for unnecessary anticompetitive effects. For example, an agency responsible for competition policy can systematically review important pending regulatory proceedings and provide its views about the effects of alternative regulations on competition. The agency can also review major regulatory areas and proposals for new regulatory legislation in order to assess the competitive effects of the fundamental approach to regulation that is being taken and, where relevant, to propose equally effective but less anticompetitive alternatives. Of course, when regulation involves privatization, partial deregulation, or reliance on information and incentives, rather than regulatory rules, a competition policy agency has the responsibility to ensure that centralized decisions by a regulator are not replaced by monopolization or cartelization instead of competition. Finally, the agency can bring actions against companies that make use of the regulatory process for anticompetitive purposes. Several examples illustrate the positive role that competition policy agencies can play in the regulatory reform process.

Regarding economic regulation, the introduction of competition into formerly monopolized infrastructural industries has raised important questions about interconnections between established firms and competitive entrants. For example, effective entry into telecommunications requires competitively neutral arrangements for allowing customers of one company to connect with customers of another and for granting competitors in some services equal access to monopoly services so that the incumbent carrier can not leverage a safe monopoly into market power in vertically related markets.

In part, questions of interconnection arrangements can be a regulatory problem, such as setting efficient prices for some monopolized service elements that have competitive implications in other markets or setting technical standards for interconnection. Regulatory reform has meant in part granting firms more flexibility in making these decisions themselves. However, when regulation prevents a monopolist from exercising full monopoly power in regulated markets, a strong incentive is created to leverage the regulated monopoly into competitive areas. The means that incumbent monopolists have used to accomplish this objective are to deny competitors access to monopoly services that are essential parts of competitive services and to engage in abusive conduct, such as price discrimination, predatory pricing, or degradation of service, to undercut the success of a competitor.[34]

For example, the U.S. antitrust complaint against AT&T that led to a more competitive, less regulated American telephone industry alleged that AT&T had unfairly discriminated against competitors in several ways.[35] First, in long distance, it had offered competitors technically inferior connections to their customers through its local telephone systems. Second, with respect to telephone equipment owned by customers, AT&T had unnecessarily required interface devices at wall connections on the spurious ground that equipment manufactured by competitors was unreliable and could damage the network.

Later, during the period of airline deregulation, the largest airline carriers, which controlled most computerized airline reservation and ticketing systems, discriminated against smaller airlines, especially new entrants that sought to compete with them.[36] One method was "screen bias," whereby the flights of unfavored carriers were not shown on the computer screen until the travel agent had rejected numerous other flights on favored carriers. Another method was to refuse to list airlines that were vigorous competitors or to charge higher fees to sell their tickets than those charged to more cooperative carriers. In both telecommunications and airlines, the objective and effect of these activities was to use a relatively secure monopoly in one market (local telephone service, computerized reservations) to thwart competition in another market (long distance and customer equipment, airline service).

In the environmental, health, and safety area, regulatory standards can create entry barriers and facilitate the formation of cartels. For example, collaborative recycling arrangements sometimes are attractive for capturing economies of scale and coordination among manufacturers, but they can also give firms opportunities for coordinating pricing and production behavior.[37] Likewise, product standards that differ very slightly among countries can serve solely to protect a domestic market for a single supplier, as the European Commission concluded in reviewing a herbicide regulation in Germany.[38]

Three approaches to dealing with these problems have been adopted: private litigation by entrants against incumbent monopolists; mandates to regulatory authorities to consider competition effects in making regulatory rules; and a formal role for competition policy agencies in regulatory decision processes.[39] One of the most difficult problems in liberalizing formerly monopolized markets has been creating conditions in which comparative efficiency in dealing with customers is allowed to determine the relative success of competitors. Without some institutional solution to the problem of protecting against both anticompetitive actions by incumbent monopolists and regulations that have a valid purpose but, perhaps inadvertently, unnecessarily harm competition, the full benefits of liberalization in these areas can not be captured.

Although opinion has not yet crystallized on a single best method for introducing competition policy into regulatory decisionmaking, certainly the necessary components of an effective plan are as follows. First, monopolies should not be exempted from competition laws and policies. Second, regulators should be given a formal mandate not to interfere with competition policy to any greater extent than is necessary to achieve regulatory policy objectives. Third, competition agencies should have the authority and formal responsibility to review the competitive consequences of regulations.

Procedural Reform

Procedural reform refers to a variety of proposals for improving the quality of regulation by improving its structure and procedures. Examples of such reforms are changes in rights of standing before regulatory authorities, the burden of proof, the standard of proof, the nature of judicial review, and the place of the regulatory authority in the hierarchy of government agencies. The structure and process of regulation are important determinants of the three major aspects of regulatory outcomes: stringency (how tough is the regulatory requirement?); equity (how are the burdens and benefits of regulation allocated across industries, geography, and demographic categories?); and efficiency (does the regulation achieve its purposes at lowest possible cost?).

Here the primary concern is efficiency. The structure and process of regulation are important because they affect the flow of information both in the regulatory process and to citizens about the basis for a regulatory rule. In essence, structure and process determine the relative weights given to different interests and types of information in making regulatory policy.[40] An important purpose of structural reform is to improve the efficiency of regulation by making the process more open and transparent.[41]

MANDATORY BENEFIT-COST ANALYSIS.   A prominent example of procedural reform is to require some form of economic policy analysis, which refers to a range of analytic methods for evaluating policies. The most common form is benefit-cost analysis. Related methods include comparative risk analysis and cost-effectiveness analysis. The issue at stake in regulatory policy is the extent to which economic policy analysis should play a role in the process of developing new regulations and regulatory policies.

The purpose of economic policy analysis of regulatory proposals is to provide a systematic framework for organizing relevant information for informing decisions and to offer insight about the extent to which regulation is consistent and coherent across different areas of regulatory policy. A major criticism of regulation is that lessons from one domain of regulation are slow to spill over into others and that different regulations that deal with similar issues but were adopted at different times by different regulators take vastly different approaches.

One study of 185 U.S. regulatory proposals for improving health discovered no correlation between the cost effectiveness of the proposals for saving lives and whether they were implemented.[42] For example, this study points out that the existing standard for regulating the flammability of children's clothing has a cost of $1.5 million per life saved, but another proposal to require smoke alarms in homes with children present, which would have cost only $200,000 per life saved, was rejected. The authors found that the best estimate of total life-years saved from all of the adopted regulations was 592,000 a year at a cost of approximately $21.4 billion. Had this sum been spent in the most effective way, the total annual number of life-years saved would have been 1,230,000, or more than double the number currently being saved.

Another recent study compiled the results of ninety-one benefit-cost analyses undertaken for major regulations adopted or pending in the United States between 1990 and 1995. The good news is that the study finds that the fifty-four final regulations that were adopted, taken together, generated net benefits of nearly $300 billion in discounted present value. The bad news is that thirty-one of these regulations have negative net benefits, and three had negative net benefits exceeding $10 billion.[43]

The primary controversial issues concerning economic policy analysis are how it should be undertaken and the status that it should have in the regulatory process. Proposals about the formal role of economic analysis include establishing an agency for undertaking such analyses, allowing the agency to select its targets and to have standing in regulatory proceedings, and requiring that all regulations pass a benefit-cost test before they are adopted. OECD member countries illustrate almost the full range of possibilities.[44] Although no nation yet requires that all regulations pass a benefit-cost test, legislation to that effect has been proposed in the United States and a similar proposal was made by a panel of expert advisers to the European Commission.

Making economic policy analysis mandatory is controversial, and indeed the commission rejected the proposal of its expert panel, referring to standard arguments against mandatory policy analysis:

> The Commission supports the thrust of this proposal. But the practicability of cost-benefit analysis has to be examined on a case by case basis. In the particular field of the environment, there is a question of what constitutes a "reasonable" balance between costs and benefits. The benefits for environment and society are mostly qualitative and often impossible to express in monetary values unlike, for example, the costs to business. The Treaty (130r(3)) also requires that the costs and benefits of *non-action* also be examined.[45]

The commission's decision to reject a requirement that a regulation generates positive net benefits is reasonable, but the reasons given contain important misperceptions.

To begin, a competent benefit-cost analysis does not ignore the costs and benefits of inaction. Benefits and costs are measured as incremental changes from the status quo, so that the net benefits of a policy change are identically equal to the net cost of inaction. Indeed, a competent benefit-cost analysis goes beyond this to estimate the incremental benefits and costs of all relevant alternatives to both the status quo and the proposed regulation.

A more important misperception is the common belief that costs are easier to quantify than benefits, causing benefit-cost analysis to be biased in favor of inaction. This belief is incorrect for two basic reasons: uncertainties and unquantifiable effects complicate the cost side, too; and the presence of imprecision is a matter to be identified and explicitly taken into account, not to be ignored by sweeping analysis under the rug.

On the cost side, allocating resources to regulatory compliance instead of other activities also poses risks to life and the environment that are difficult to quantify. For example, there is a strong, statistically significant correlation between disposable family income and rates of morbidity and mortality. One study estimates that if a regulatory action imposes a cost of $50 million, one additional death will occur because of the reduction in purchasing power that must occur to pay for the cost of the regulation.[46] And, of course, if a regulation causes a reallocation of economic activity to other products, this reallocation inevitably will lead to increases in exposures to some other hazards and some environmental damage, in part offsetting the benefits of the regulation.

Although the appropriate cost for the value of a life saved is surely subject to considerable uncertainty, the preceding observations provide an important insight: most likely, no regulation that imposes a cost exceeding $50 million per life saved should be adopted, not because $50 million is a good estimate of the value of a life, but because a regulation that costs that much will cause at least as much indirect damage as it is intended to cure.

Of course, the precise relation between personal income and health is subject to uncertainty (the confidence interval for the $50 million estimate is wide). But scientific estimates of the health effects of pollutants or unsafe products, and engineering estimates of the effects of standards to reduce these risks, are also subject to uncertainty. Likewise, compliance costs, too, can be difficult to quantify, especially if they impose performance requirements that are likely to lead to the development of new abatement technology, with its own environmental and health consequences that can not be known until the technology is developed and applied. Just as there is no reason to refuse to consider science and engineering studies because they are not precise, there is also no good reason to ignore economic analysis because it is subject to uncertainty. Instead, the appropriate response to uncertainty is to identify its sources, to perform sensitivity analyses to ascertain the importance of these uncertainties with respect to the desirability of a policy action, and to monitor the effects of regulatory actions in order to measure uncertain effects so as to reduce uncertainties associated with future regulatory actions.

Nevertheless, the proposal to insist that every regulation pass a benefit-cost test goes too far, for it, too, is based on a misperception. The role of economic policy analysis is not to replace democratic political processes for making collective decisions. In the end, public officials are responsible for policy. The purpose of economic analysis is to assist them in making informed decisions and to assist citizens in evaluating the regulations that are imposed on them.

Recently, a group of U.S. economists proposed a new role for benefit-cost analysis in environmental, health, and safety regulation.[47] They set out the purposes of analysis: to encourage greater consistency and transparency in regulatory policy, as well as to improve the efficiency of regulation. To this end, they proposed that all major regulations be subject to mandatory benefit-cost analysis before a final regulation is adopted. In addition, they proposed that all benefit-cost analysis should have three features: first, the analysis should be based upon a common set of assumptions about common parameters, such as the social discount rate and the value of reductions in morbidity and mortality; second, it should examine the sensitivity of the magnitude of net benefits with respect to the value of key parameters of the analysis; and third, it should be subject to a system of peer review. Finally, the group proposed that agencies be required to provide a justification for rejecting a regulation that is expected to yield positive net benefits and for adopting a regulation that has negative net expected benefits or that achieves positive net benefits only when it uses nonstandard assumptions about key parameters.

These recommendations do not require that agencies base decision on benefit-cost analysis, but they do introduce transparency about not only the consequences of an agency's actions but also the reasons an agency has for its decisions. Moreover, by basing analyses on common sets of assumptions, political leaders would have improved information for allocating resources for writing and enforcing regulations among agencies and programs.

OTHER PROCESS REFORMS.   In addition to mandatory economic policy analysis, other reforms of the regulatory process have also received considerable attention.[48] One example is broader participation in the regulatory process. In many cases, only a firm that is subject to a regulation is given a role in developing regulations. Not only are other public agencies and affected parties excluded, but the information upon which the regulation is based remains confidential. Consequently, organizations such as citizen groups, trade associations of businesses that transact with regulated entities, and competition agencies have no role in developing regulations and no access to information for evaluating the outcomes. The proposed reform is to make processes less formal and more open in order to make regulation more broadly responsive and transparent.

Another process reform, derived from observations about the litigiousness of the American system, as described by Robert Kagan and Lee Axelrad in chapter 4, is to grant regulators far more flexibility and authority in how they develop, enforce, and amend regulations. Specific actions include giving agencies more resources for developing regulations, reducing the rights of private parties to appeal regulatory decisions, and replacing the tort liability system with some form of social insurance.

Internationalization

Until recently, the regulatory reform debate has been regarded primarily as a question of domestic economic policy. However, as implied by the parable of the teleshopper, a narrow, nationalistic view of regulatory reform is not valid. The increasing integration of the world economy has made regulation an important factor distorting international economic integration. As a result, recent trade negotiations and agreements inevitably have included provisions relating to regulatory issues. For example, the Uruguay round of GATT led to an agreement that internal political constraints could not override principles of open access and created the World Trade Organization Committee on the Environment.[49]

Conceptually, regulatory distortions take two distinct forms: domestic and international. Domestic distortions are the undesirable direct economic effects of regulation within a nation's borders: unnecessary costs, supercompetitive prices, inflexibility in adjusting to changing technology and demand, and unjust redistribution of wealth. International distortions are the effects on the patterns of trade and investment that arise because of regulation. The latter arise from circumstances in which regulation discriminates against foreign firms and products, thus constituting an indirect trade barrier that benefits a domestic interest at the expense of international interests and, indirectly, domestic economic efficiency.

This conceptual division implies a prioritization scheme: to focus international coordination and cooperation on regulatory issues that cause international distortions. The inefficiencies of regulation that are purely domestic can be significant, but they do not imply an international priority for reform. In essence, these effects are unfortunate, but the costs are confined to the country that causes them. If inefficient regulation has significant international repercussions, coordination and cooperation among nations in regulatory reform have the same status as multinational arrangements for reducing direct trade barriers. Mutuality in reform creates economic benefits that are broadly shared among domestic consumers and trading partners.

Whether an international effect is a distortion is frequently a matter of controversy. Nations frequently pursue different regulatory policies because their citizens place different values on the same market failures. Trade policy has attempted to make distinctions between differences in the stringency of regulation of purely domestic activities and other differences that seem to impose one nation's values on activities within another or that have a distributional purpose—in particular, that of redistributing income in favor of trade-vulnerable sectors. Although distinguishing among these cases is frequently quite difficult, the concern here is with regulations that are inefficient because they either ignore the values of citizens of other countries with respect to their own regulatory policies or sacrifice cost minimization for the purpose of domestic income redistribution.

As a practical matter, very little distorting regulation has purely domestic effects. International boundaries rarely define natural market barriers that can not be crossed, and in most cases the most efficient organization of an industry is international. For example, infrastructural industries (energy utilities, communications, transportation, finance) all operate more efficiently if their networks are organized according to the pattern of transactions, and in a relatively open world economy, these patterns do not respect national borders. Even many segments of retail trade are more efficient if international chains of outlets are permitted.

An additional advantage of pursuing mutuality in regulatory reform is that it elevates the domestic political debate about regulation to a matter of international cooperation. From a political perspective, making regulatory reform an international issue is highly desirable. A common political barrier to domestic regulatory reform is that if it is perceived as a domestic issue and is debated one issue at a time, well-organized special interests are more likely to have the political power to block it. For most specific regulatory issues, the beneficiaries of reform are numerous, but their per capita benefits are frequently too low or indirect to generate significant political pressure for reform. If the reform debate is elevated to a matter of international policy that encompasses numerous reform issues, broader attention and participation from all interests are more likely, thereby reducing the ability of a single interest to block reform.

A useful analogy is to the process of setting tariffs.[50] When each nation independently sets each tariff separately, the outcome is likely to be tariffs that are higher than those that would be negotiated bilaterally as part of a comprehensive trade agreement. The reason is that debating tariffs one product at a time maximizes the influence of organized interests with a direct stake in a policy. If a tariff on a specific product is under review, the domestic industry that makes the product is likely to be intensely interested and to exercise whatever political influence it has to obtain a favorable policy decision. However, because the final price of the product is less important to each buyer than to each producer, buyers are less likely to participate in the debate. Consequently, each important domestic industry may receive and preserve a tariff or a favorable regulation when policy is debated in a purely domestic context one industry at a time, but receive neither protective tariffs nor protective regulations when policy is developed multinationally and covers many industries.

As with tariffs, when each regulation is considered separately as a matter of domestic policy, the government is likely to be under less pressure to adopt an efficient policy. If a regulation imposes unnecessary costs uniformly on firms in a domestic industry, sales of the industry's product may be suppressed somewhat by higher prices, but the individual firms are unlikely to suffer very much because none is being disadvantaged relative to a competitor. If international trade threatens the industry, however, the industry will energetically seek relief. The politically expedient move may be to inhibit trade competition, either by using regulation as an indirect trade barrier or by banning trade while invoking a rhetorical attack on the lax standards of a trading partner. This approach placates the overly regulated industry and the other interests that place high value on the regulatory policy. The harmed interests, foreign producers, are more easily ignored because these groups do not vote domestically.

Just as simultaneous negotiations over tariffs on all products facilitate reaching agreements that provide freer trade, so, too, do simultaneous negotiations of numerous areas of regulation facilitate eliminating regulatory indirect trade barriers. As with tariffs, the inclusion of multiple regulatory policies within the same negotiation creates more opportunities for mutually beneficial bargains to reduce distortions simultaneously on all fronts. Recent experience with multilateral negotiations bears out this belief. On both the trade and regulatory fronts, with the sole exception of the Agreement on Trade in Civil Aircraft, no single-issue negotiation under the GATT and few outside of it have produced a significant commitment to openness, and many have included new, onerous regulatory requirements. Examples of failures are the International Dairy Agreement, which establishes minimum world prices for dairy products; the Multi-Fibre Agreement, which countenanced import quotas; and the Montreal protocols, which set world limits on emissions of ozone-depleting chlorofluorocarbons (CFCs) but prohibited reallocations among nations of either production or consumption of CFC-related products through trade or international investment.

The lesson from these examples is that incorporation of regulation into trade agreements should follow the same principles that have been generally followed (with some disastrous exceptions) with respect to tariffs and quotas. Specifically, when regulation is part of international negotiation, it must extend, not contract, the feasible range of liberalizing agreements. Introducing regulatory rules into single-product negotiations can lead to an increase in trade distortions (by using regulation to inhibit trade), and negotiating a single regulatory issue can lead to agreements that adopt common, coordinated regulatory distortions. In particular, negotiations about a single product or area of regulation run the risk of creating an alliance between protectionists and the most ardent advocates of a particular regulatory policy who seek regulations that go far beyond those that maximize net social benefits.

The same argument applies to the enforcement of agreements not to adopt anticompetitive regulations. If enforcement powers reside solely in domestic agencies, a particular case in which a regulation disadvantages foreign producers involves an unbalanced underlying politics. Domestic producers are likely to be more effectively represented than foreigners in the process of the agency and in the background political system in which the agency must operate. Consequently, actions to eliminate the anticompetitive international effects of regulation are likely to face more political resistance than support. By contrast, international institutions for resolving regulatory trade disputes operate in a more balanced political environment. These institutions are a means whereby nations mutually can commit to maintain procompetitive regulatory reforms. The GATT and WTO disputes about automobile fuel efficiency and reformulated gasoline illustrate how domestic regulatory agencies, but not international institutions, are willing to sacrifice competition as well as some of the effectiveness of regulatory policies in order to advantage domestic producers.

For these reasons, internationalization of regulatory reform succeeds only if it enfranchises foreign producers in domestic regulatory policy across a spectrum of industries. In the context of a particular dispute about the trade effects of a particular regulation, intervention by an international organization frequently brings accusations that foreigners are meddling with domestic policy. In reality, all international agreements entail some loss of the ability to act independently in order to achieve something else of value, which in this case is a worldwide regulatory system that is more efficient and free of trade distortions. Such an institution generates net economic benefits to each country, even if specific cases create some domestic losers. The creation of institutions for enforcing agreements to eliminate indirect trade barriers is a means to balance the political influence of these domestic losers. Each nation contains its own victims of trade barriers arising from inefficient regulation, and these groups can work through their governments to seek mutual agreements about relaxing regulatory trade barriers in other countries.

Conclusion

The growing movement for regulatory reform throughout the world has increased the potential significance of explicitly internationalizing the reform process. If some nations are operating a relatively efficient regulatory system while others are not, international cost differences arising from regulation are likely to surface as political issues in high-cost countries. Perhaps the result will be reform, but an equally plausible scenario is protection against "unfair" competition. Initiating multisectoral international negotiations over phased reform now offers the opportunity to seize the initiative, casting the agenda in terms of improved efficiency rather than retaliation against unfair trade. A trade agreement that, in each country, enfranchised competition policy agencies and required benefit-cost analysis in international disputes about regulatory policy decisions also would facilitate both free trade and regulatory reform.

If regulatory reform is considered internationally, several issues must be addressed. An obvious step is harmonization of environmental, health, and safety regulations and technical standards, which has received considerable attention for several years. Another important step is to eliminate regulatory barriers to entry. The political danger here is that eliminating entry barriers can be disruptive if regulation is imposing significant inefficiencies on domestic firms. Hence, coordination of regulatory reform is more likely to succeed if it proceeds in phases that include parallel actions to privatize nationalized industries and to introduce less distorting methods of regulation (emissions fees and taxes, price caps, and competitive bidding for subsidized services).

The implications of this analysis are that regulatory reform should not be discussed solely in a domestic context and should not be addressed by considering each area of regulation separately. Extensive fragmentation of regulatory reform into specific issues involving particular products and industries diminishes prospects for reform in any area and works against continuing international economic liberalization. When the focus is on one area of regulation, the arguments are easily structured in the rhetoric of creating level playing fields for domestic producers, which too frequently means creating new distortions to protect existing inefficiencies. The most effective way for defining areas of coordination of regulatory reform is likely to be broad, cross-cutting issues, such as relaxing entry barriers and actively insinuating competition policy into the regulatory process. This approach more naturally focuses discussion on facilitating market entry and eliminating distortions to trade.

Nations that decide to impose costs on themselves by pursuing inefficient regulatory policies probably will remain free to do so. But international economic integration causes these actions to export some of the costs to others in the form of distortions of trade and investment. If international economic agreements do a better job of forcing nations to bear the costs of their own inefficient policies, regulatory reform is more likely. Hence the movement to make regulatory issues part of international economic agreements ought to be viewed as a welcome change.

NOTES

1. See, for example, Philip Shabecoff, *A New Name for Peace: International Environmentalism, Sustainable Development, and Democracy* (University Press of New England, 1996).

2. The "parable of the teleshopper" originally was suggested by Bernard J. Phillips. See OECD, "A Global Marketplace for Consumers" (1995).

3. OECD, "Information Infrastructure Convergence and Pricing: The Internet," working paper, Working Party on Telecommunications and Information Services, January 30-31, 1996, p. 32. Internet access prices tend to be much lower in countries, such as the United States, that permit competition in long distance access and information services.

4. Ibid., p. 26.

5. All prices are in U.S. dollars. OECD, "Parcel Delivery in the Global Marketplace," Committee on Consumer Policy, 1995, p. 12.

6. OECD, "Consumer Product Safety Standards and Conformity Assessment: Their Effect on International Trade," Committee on Consumer Policy, 1996, p. 28.

7. In each of these cases, a standard was found to be an unfair indirect trade barrier. The issues involved were: *Cassis de Dijon*, alcohol content and labeling requirements for liqueurs (1979 ECR 649); *German Bottles*, requirements for beverage container return systems (Infringement 1104/88 EC doc. IP [90]337); *Canadian Red Raspberries*, standards for color and size for consumer goods (55 Fed. Reg. 14848 [1990]); *CAFE Standards*, the use by the United States of separate formulas for domestic and foreign production of automobiles for enforcing compliance with fleet average fuel economy regulations; and *Venezuelan Gasoline*, requirements for improved gasoline formulations to reduce automobile emissions.

8. Clifford Winston, "Economic Deregulation: Days of Reckoning for Microeconomists," *Journal of Economic Literature*, vol. 31 (September 1993), p. 1284.

9. OECD, "Regulatory Reform: A Country Study of Australia," PUMA/REG(96)1, Public Management Service, 1996, p. 50.

10. See Randy A. Nelson and Walter J. Primeaux, "The Effects of Competition on Transmission and Distribution Costs in the Municipal Electric Industry," *Land Economics*, vol. 64 (November 1988), pp. 338–46, which finds that scale economies are sufficiently small that they are offset by the efficiency advantages of competition in about forty U.S. cities that have competing utilities. Jeffrey I. Bernstein, "Dynamic Factor Demands and Adjustment Costs: An Analysis of Bell Canada's Technology," *Information Economics and Policy*, vol. 3 (1988), pp. 5–24, finds no significant scale economies in telephone service. See also the references in these articles.

11. Winston, "Economic Deregulation."

12. Martin Neil Bailey, "Competition, Regulation, and Efficiency in Service Industries," *Brookings Papers on Economic Activity: Microeconomics*, 2:1993, pp. 71–130.

13. Utility Data Institute, *State Directory of New Electric Power Plants* (Washington, 1994).

14. For an excellent review of incentive regulation, see David Baron, "The Design of Regulatory Mechanisms and Institutions," in Richard Schmalensee and Robert Willig, eds., *The Handbook of Industrial Organization* (New York: North Holland, 1989), vol. 2, pp. 1349–1447.

15. Sumit K. Majumdar, "Regulation and Productive Efficiency: Evidence from the U.S. Telecommunications Industry," working paper (University of Michigan, July 1995); Robert W. Crandall and Leonard Waverman, *Talk Is Cheap: The Promise of Regulatory Reform in North American Telecommunications* (Brookings, 1996), pp. 213–15; and Shane Greenstein, Susan McMaster, and Pablo T. Spiller, "The Effect of Incentive Regulation on Infrastructure Modernization: Local Exchange Companies' Deployment of Digital Infrastructure," *Journal of Economics and Management Strategy*, vol. 4 (Summer 1995), pp. 187–236.

16. David M. Newberry, "'Regulatory Policies and Reform in the Electric Supply Industry," in Claudio R. Frischtak, ed., *Regulatory Policies and Reform: A Comparative Perspective* (Washington: World Bank, Private Sector Development Department, 1995), pp. 288–89, 296.

17. Roger G. Noll, "The Role of Antitrust in Telecommunications," *Antitrust Bulletin* (Fall 1995), pp. 501–28.

18. Mark Armstrong, Simon Cowan, and John Vickers, *Regulatory Reform: Economic Analysis and British Experience* (MIT Press, 1994), especially pp. 355–58.

19. Newberry, "Regulatory Policies and Reform in the Electric Supply Industry," p. 296.

20. Mary Shirley and Ahmed Galal, *Bureaucrats in Business: The Economics and Politics of Government Ownership* (Oxford University Press for World Bank, 1995), p. 39.

21. Kenneth Button and Thomas Weyman-Jones, "Impacts of Privatization Policy in Europe," *Contemporary Economic Policy*, vol. 12 (October 1994), pp. 23–33.

22. Shirley and Galal, *Bureaucrats in Business*, p. 39.

23. For an excellent review of the status of environmental regulation worldwide, see Raymond S. Hartman and David Wheeler, "Incentive Regulation: Market-Based Pollution Control for the Real World," in Frischtak, ed., *Regulatory Policies and Reform*, pp. 210–235.

24. Robert W. Hahn and Roger G. Noll, "Designing a Market for Tradable Emissions Permits," in Wesley Magat, ed., *Reform of Environmental Regulation* (Lexington, Mass.: Lexington Books, 1982), pp. 119–46.

25. Robert W. Hahn, "Economic Prescriptions for Environmental Problems: How the Patient Followed the Doctor's Orders," *Journal of Economic Perspectives*, vol. 3 (Spring 1989), p. 100.

26. Ibid.

27. D. O'Connor, "Policy and Entrepreneurial Response to the Montreal Protocol: Some Evidence from the Dynamic Asian Economies," Technical Paper 51, OECD, Development Center, 1993.

28. Hartman and Wheeler, "Incentive Regulation."

29. For example, Poland's effluent fee system appears not to have worked for these reasons. Piotr Wilczynski "Environmental Management in Centrally Planned Non-Market Economies of Eastern Europe," working paper 35 (Washington: World Bank, Environment Department, 1990).

30. Mikael Skou Anderson, "Economic Instruments and Clean Water: Why Institutions and Policy Design Matter," PUMA/REG(94)5, OECD, April 1994; and Hahn, "Economic Prescriptions."

31. D. O'Connor, "Managing the Environment with Rapid Industrialization," Development Center, OECD, Paris, 1993.

32. OECD, "Structure and Change in Distribution Systems: An Analysis of Seven OECD Member Countries," ECO/CPE/WP1(92)7, Economics Department, 1992. Since the time of this study, Japan has begun liberalizing retail trade. See also Bailey, "Competition, Regulation, and Efficiency," who finds that labor productivity in retail trade is twice as high in the United States as in Japan.

33. OECD, "Consumer Product Safety Standards."

34. OECD, "Mini-Roundtable on the Role and Enforcement of Competition Policy in Regulated Sectors," DAFFE/CLP/M(94)2/ANN4, Directorate for Financial, Fiscal and Enterprise Affairs, Paris, 1994, p. 3.

Roger G. Noll

35. Roger G. Noll and Bruce M. Owen, "The Anticompetitive Uses of Regulation: United States v. AT&T (1982)," in John E. Kwoka Jr. and Lawrence J. White, eds., *The Antitrust Revolution: The Role of Economics*, 2d ed. (Harper-Collins College, 1994), pp. 328–75.

36. Margaret E. Guerin-Calvert and Roger G. Noll, "Computer Reservations Systems and Their Network Linkages to the Airline Industry," in Margaret E. Guerin-Calvert and Steven S. Wildman, eds., *Electronic Services Networks: A Business and Public Policy Challenge* (Praeger, 1991), pp. 145–87.

37. OECD, "Role and Enforcement of Competition Policy in Regulated Sectors: Note by the Netherlands Delegation," DAFFE/CLP(94)14, Directorate for Financial, Fiscal and Enterprise Affairs, Paris, 1994, p. 5.

38. OECD, "Competition Policy and the Agro-Food Sector," COM/AGR/APM/TD/WP(95)73/REV1, Directorate for Food, Agriculture and Fisheries, Paris, 1995, pp. 10–11.

39. OECD, "Role and Enforcement of Competition Policy in Regulated Sectors: Note by the Australian Delegation," DAFFE/CLP(94)13, Directorate for Financial, Fiscal and Enterprise Affairs, Paris, 1994, pp. 5–7.

40. Mathew D. McCubbins, Roger G. Noll, and Barry R. Weingast, "Administrative Procedures as Instruments of Political Control," *Journal of Law, Economics and Organization*, vol. 3 (1987), pp. 243–77; and "Structure and Process, Politics and Policy: Administrative Arrangements and the Political Control of Agencies," *Virginia Law Review*, vol. 75 (March 1989), pp. 431–82.

41. OECD, "Recommendation of the Council of the OECD on Improving the Quality of Government Regulation," OECD/GD(95)95, Paris, 1995, pp. 7–8.

42. Tammy O. Tengs and John D. Graham, "The Opportunity Costs of Haphazard Social Investments in Life-Saving," in Robert W. Hahn, ed., *Risks, Costs, and Lives Saved: Getting Better Results from Regulation* (Oxford University Press, 1996), pp. 169, 172–73.

43. Robert W. Hahn, "Regulatory Reform: What Do the Government's Numbers Tell Us?" in ibid., pp. 212–13, 218–19, 224. The good news is not without qualification, for this finding rests on the accuracy of the assessment of the risks that gave rise to the regulation, but as Hahn points out, in many cases these risks are substantially overstated by regulatory agencies.

44. OECD, "Control and Management of Government Regulation," PUMA(95)9, Public Management Service, Paris, 1995, pp. 18–22.

45. Commission of the European Communities, "Comments of the Commission on the Report of the Independent Experts Group on Legislative and Administrative Simplification," SEC(95) 2121 final, 1995, pp. 26–27.

46. W. Kip Viscusi, "The Dangers of Unbounded Commitments to Regulate Risk," in Hahn, ed., *Risks, Costs and Lives Saved*, p. 162.

47. Kenneth J. Arrow and others, "Is There a Role for Benefit-Cost Analysis in Environmental, Health, and Safety Regulation?" *Science*, vol. 272 (April 12, 1996), pp. 221–22; and *Benefit-Cost Analysis in Environmental, Health and Safety Regulation: A Statement of Principles* (Washington: American Enterprise Institute, 1996).

48. For a broader discussion of some of these reforms, see OECD, "Control and Management"; and "Public Consultation in Regulatory Devel-

opment: Practices and Experiences in Ten OECD Countries," PUMA/REG(94)15, Paris, 1994.

49. For a discussion of the incorporation of environmental issues into trade agreements and enforcement organizations, see Frieder Roessler, "Diverging Domestic Policies and Multilateral Trade Integration," in Jagdish Baghwati and Robert Hudec, eds., *Fair Trade and Harmonization: Prerequisites for Free Trade*, vol. 2: *Legal Analysis* (MIT Press, 1996), pp. 21–55.

50. See Judith Goldstein, "International Institutions and Domestic Politics: GATT, WTO, and Liberalization of International Trade," Stanford University, Center for Economic Policy Research, September 1996.

Bibliography of Cross-National Socio-Legal Studies

THIS BIBLIOGRAPHY was compiled by Robert A. Kagan and Lee Axelrad. For information on the coverage of the entries, see table 4-1 on p. 151.

Badaracco, Joseph L. Jr. *Loading the Dice: A Five-Country Study of Vinyl Chloride Regulation.* Harvard Business School Press, 1985.

Bayley, David. *Forces of Order: Police Behavior in Japan and the United States.* University of California Press, 1976.

Bok, Derek C. "Reflections on the Distinctive Character of American Labor Laws." *Harvard Law Review,* vol. 84 (1971), pp. 1394–1463.

Braithwaite, John. *To Punish or Persuade: Enforcement of Coal Mine Safety.* State University of New York, 1985.

_____. "The Nursing Home Industry," in Michael Tonry and Albert J. Reiss, eds., *Beyond the Law: Crime in Complex Organizations,* vol. 18: *Crime and Justice.* University of Chicago Press, 1993, pp. 11–54.

Brickman, Ronald, Sheila Jasanoff, and Thomas Ilgen. *Controlling Chemicals: The Politics of Regulation in Europe and the United States.* Cornell University Press, 1985.

Charkham, Jonathan P. *Keeping Good Company: A Study of Corporate Governance in Five Countries.* Oxford University Press, 1994.

Day, Patricia, and Rudolf Klein. "The Regulation of Nursing Homes: A Comparative Perspective." *Milbank Quarterly,* vol. 65, no.3 (1987), pp. 303–47.

Flanagan, Robert J. *Labor Relations and the Litigation Explosion.* Brookings, 1987.

358   Bibliography

Glendon, Mary Ann. *Abortion and Divorce in Western Law.* Harvard University Press, 1987.

Jasanoff, Sheila. *Risk Management and Political Culture: A Comparative Study of Science in the Policy Context.* New York: Russell Sage Foundation, 1986.

Kelman, Steven. *Regulating America, Regulating Sweden: A Comparative Study of Occupational Safety and Health Policy.* MIT Press, 1981.

David L. Kirp, *Doing Good by Doing Little: Race and Schooling in Britain.* University of California Press, 1979.

Kirp, David L. "Professionalization as a Policy Choice: British Special Education in Comparative Perspective." *World Politics,* vol. 3 (1982), pp. 137–74.

Langbein, John H. "The German Advantage in Civil Procedure." *University of Chicago Law Review,* vol. 52 (1985), p. 823.

Litt, David G., and others. "Politics, Bureaucracies, and Financial Markets: Bank Entry into Commercial Paper Underwriting in the United States and Japan." *University of Pennsylvania Law Review,* vol. 139 (December 1990), pp. 369–453.

Lohof, Andrew. *The Cleanup of Inactive Hazardous Waste Sites in Selected Industrialized Countries,* discussion paper 69. Washington: American Petroleum Institute, August 1991.

Lundqvist, Lennart J. *The Hare and The Tortoise: Clean Air Policies in the United States and Sweden.* University of Michigan Press, 1980.

Quam, Lois, Robert Dingwall, and Paul Fenn. "Medical Malpractice in Perspective I: The American Experience." *British Medical Journal,* vol. 294 (June 13, 1987), pp. 1529–32.

Quam, Lois, Paul Fenn, and Robert Dingwall. "Medical Malpractice in Perspective II: The Implications for Britain." *British Medical Journal,* vol. 294 (June 20, 1987), pp. 1597–1600.

Reich, Robert B. "Bailout: A Comparative Study in Law and Industrial Structure." *Yale Journal on Regulation,* vol. 2, no. 2 (1985), p. 163.

Schwartz, Gary T. "Product Liability and Medical Malpractice in Comparative Context." In Peter W. Huber and Robert E. Litan, eds., *The Liability Maze: The Impact of Liability Law on Safety and Innovation.* Brookings, 1991, pp. 28–80.

Tanase, Takao. "The Management of Disputes: Automobile Accident Compensation in Japan." *Law and Society Review,* vol. 24, no. 3 (1990), pp. 651–89.

Teff, Harvey. "Drug Approval in England and the United States." *American Journal of Comparative Law*, vol. 33 (1985), pp. 567–610.

Vogel, David. *National Styles of Regulation: Environmental Policy in Great Britain and the United States*. Cornell University Press, 1986.

Wokutch, Richard E. *Worker Protection, Japanese Style: Occupational Safety and Health in the Auto Industry*. Ithaca, N.Y.: ILR Press, 1992.

Index